TOEIC

PRACTICE EXAMS

with audio CDs

Lin Lougheed
Ed.D., Teachers College
Columbia University

BARRON'S

Photo Credits
All photos are courtesy of Shutterstock.com

All inquiries should be addressed to:
Barron's Educational Series, Inc.
250 Wireless Boulevard
Hauppauge, New York 11788
www.barronseduc.com

Library of Congress Catalog Card Number: 2010000483

ISBN-13: 978-0-7641-9784-0
ISBN-10: 0-7641-9784-3

Library of Congress Cataloging-in-Publication Data
Lougheed, Lin, 1946–
    TOEIC practice exams : book with audio cds / Lin Lougheed.
      p. cm.
  Includes bibliographical references and index.
  ISBN-13: 978-0-7641-9784-0 (alk. paper)
  ISBN-10: 0-7641-9784-3 (alk. paper)
  1. Test of English for International Communication—Study guides. 2. English
language—Textbooks for foreign speakers. 3. English language—Examinations—
Study guides. I. Barron's Educational Series, Inc. II. Title. III. Title: Test of English
for International Communication practice exams.
    PE1128.L657 2010
    428.2'4—dc22   2010000483

PRINTED IN THE UNITED STATES OF AMERICA
9 8 7 6 5 4 3 2 1

FSC
Mixed Sources
Product group from well-managed
forests and other controlled sources

Cert no. SW-COC-002507
www.fsc.org
© 1996 Forest Stewardship Council

Contents

Introduction

WHAT IS THE TOEIC LISTENING AND READING TEST?

The **TOEIC** (Test of English for International Communication) **Listening and Reading** measures your ability to understand spoken and written English in a variety of real-world situations. The listening comprehension section is divided into four parts with a total of 100 questions, and the reading comprehension section is divided into three parts, also with a total of 100 questions.

HOW TO USE THIS BOOK

This book has six complete practice tests for **TOEIC Listening and Reading**. You can use this book to familiarize yourself with the Listening and Reading sections of the TOEIC test. You can use it for extra practice when taking a TOEIC preparation course or when studying on your own. You can use this book to supplement the activities in other Barron's TOEIC preparation materials.

Start by taking the first test. Try to simulate a real test experience. Set aside two hours without interruptions. When you are finished, compare your answers with those in the appendix. Determine the areas where you need to improve the most. Do you need to improve your language skills, test-taking skills, or vocabulary?

You can improve your language skills and test-taking skills by studying *Barron's TOEIC.* You can improve your vocabulary by studying Barron's *600 Essential Words for the TOEIC.*

 TIP

Audioscripts for Parts 1–4 of each test can be found on pages 333–411. If you do not have access to an audio CD player, please refer to the audioscripts when prompted to listen to an audio passage.

As you continue to study, take another test every month (or week, or two weeks) to see how much you have learned and where you still need to improve.

In addition to studying specifically for the test, you can improve your performance on the TOEIC by working to develop your English language skills in general. You need to make some time available every day to study English. You need to sign a TOEIC Study Contract.

TOEIC LISTENING AND READING STUDY CONTRACT

You must make a commitment to study English. Sign a contract with yourself. A contract is a legal document that establishes procedures. You should not break a contract—especially a contract with yourself.

- Print your name below on the first line.
- Write how much time you will spend each week studying English on the following lines. Think about how much time you have to study every day and every week. Make your schedule realistic.
- Sign your name and date the contract on the last line.
- At the end of each week, add up your hours. Did you meet the requirements of your contract?

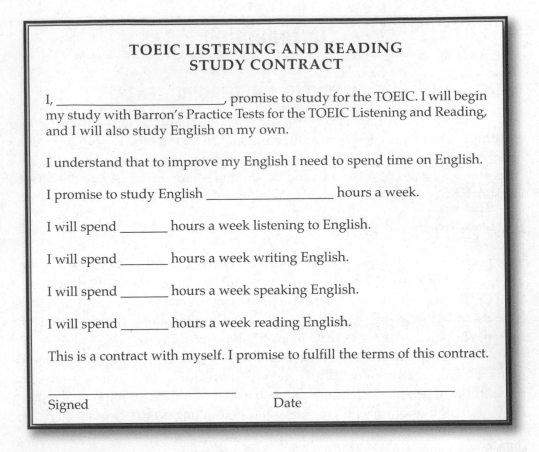

> ## TOEIC LISTENING AND READING
> ## STUDY CONTRACT
>
> I, _____, promise to study for the TOEIC. I will begin my study with Barron's Practice Tests for the TOEIC Listening and Reading, and I will also study English on my own.
>
> I understand that to improve my English I need to spend time on English.
>
> I promise to study English _____ hours a week.
>
> I will spend _____ hours a week listening to English.
>
> I will spend _____ hours a week writing English.
>
> I will spend _____ hours a week speaking English.
>
> I will spend _____ hours a week reading English.
>
> This is a contract with myself. I promise to fulfill the terms of this contract.
>
> _____   _____
> Signed   Date

SELF-STUDY ACTIVITIES

Here are some ways you can study English on your own. Check the ones you plan to try. Add some of your own ideas.

Internet-Based Self-Study Activities

LISTENING
___ Podcasts on the Internet
___ News websites: CNN, BBC, NBC, ABC, CBS
___ Movies in English
___ YouTube
___ _____
___ _____

SPEAKING
___ Use Skype to talk to English speakers
___ _____
___ _____

WRITING
___ Write e-mails to website contacts
___ Write a blog
___ Leave comments on blogs
___ Post messages in a chat room
___ Use Facebook and MySpace

___ _____

___ _____

READING
___ Read news and magazine articles online
___ Do web research on topics that interest you
___ Follow blogs that interest you

___ _____

___ _____

Other Self-Study Activities

LISTENING
___ Listen to CNN and BBC on the radio
___ Watch movies and TV in English
___ Listen to music in English

___ _____

___ _____

SPEAKING
___ Describe what you see and do out loud
___ Practice speaking with a conversation buddy

___ _____

___ _____

WRITING
___ Write a daily journal
___ Write a letter to an English speaker
___ Make lists of the things you see every day
___ Write descriptions of your family and friends

___ _____

___ _____

READING
___ Read newspapers and magazines in English
___ Read books in English

___ _____

___ _____

Examples of Self-Study Activities

You can use websites, books, newspapers, movies, and TV programs to practice reading, writing, speaking, and listening in English.

- Read about it.
- Paraphrase and write about it.
- Give a talk or presentation about it.
- Record or make a video of your presentation
- Listen to or watch what you recorded. Write down your presentation.
- Correct your mistakes.
- Do it all again.

Plan a Trip

Go to *www.concierge.com.*

Choose a city, choose a hotel, go to that hotel's website and choose a room, and then choose some sites to visit (*reading*). Write a report about the city. Tell why you want to go there. Describe the hotel and the room you will reserve. Tell what sites you plan to visit and when. Where will you eat? How will you get around?

Now write a letter to someone recommending this place (*writing*). Pretend you have to give a lecture on your planned trip (*speaking*). Make a video of yourself talking about this place. Then watch the video and write down what you said. Correct any mistakes you made and record the presentation again. Then choose another city and do all of this again.

Shop for an Electronic Product

Go to *www.cnet.com.*

Choose an electronic product and read about it (*reading*). Write a report about the product. Tell why you want to buy one. Describe its features.

Now write a letter to someone recommending this product (*writing*). Pretend you have to give a talk about this product (*speaking*). Make a video of yourself talking about this product. Then watch the video and write down what you said. Correct any mistakes you made and record the presentation again. Then choose another product and do all of this again.

Discuss a Book or a CD

Go to *www.amazon.com.*

Choose a book, CD, or another product. Read the product description and reviews (*reading*). Write a report about the product. Tell why you want to buy one or why it is interesting to you. Describe its features.

Now write a letter to someone recommending this product (*writing*). Pretend you have to give a talk about this product (*speaking*). Make a video of yourself talking about this product. Then watch the video and write down what you said. Correct any mistakes you made and record the presentation again. Then choose another product and do all of this again.

Discuss Any Subject

Go to *http://simple.wikipedia.org/wiki/Main_Page.*

This website is written in simple English. Pick any subject and read the entry (*reading*). Write a short essay about the topic (*writing*). Give a presentation about it (*speaking*). Record the presentation. Then watch the video and write down what you said. Correct any mistakes you made and record the presentation again. Choose another topic and do all of this again.

Discuss Any Event

Go to *http://news.google.com.*

Google News has a variety of links. Pick one event and read the articles about it (*reading*). Write a short essay about the event (*writing*). Give a presentation about it (*speaking*). Record the presentation. Then watch the video and write down what you said. Correct any mistakes you made and record the presentation again. Then choose another event and do all of this again.

Report the News

Listen to an English language news report on the radio or watch a news program on TV (*listening*). Take notes as you listen. Write a summary of what you heard (*writing*).

Pretend you are a news reporter. Use the information from your notes to report the news (*speaking*). Record the presentation. Then watch the video and write down what you said. Correct any mistakes you made and record the presentation again. Then listen to another news program and do all of this again.

Express an Opinion

Read a letter to the editor in the newspaper (*reading*). Write a letter in response in which you say whether or not you agree with the opinion expressed in the first letter. Explain why (*writing*). Pretend you have to give a talk explaining your opinion (*speaking*). Record yourself giving the talk. Then watch the video and write down what you said. Correct any mistakes you made and record the presentation again. Then read another letter to the editor and do all of this again.

Review a Book or Movie

Read a book (*reading*). Think about your opinion of the book. What did you like about it? What didn't you like about it? Who would you recommend it to and why? Pretend you are a book reviewer for a newspaper. Write a review of the book with your opinion and recommendations (*writing*).

Give an oral presentation about the book. Explain what the book is about and what your opinion is (*speaking*). Record yourself giving the presentation. Then watch the video and write down what you said. Correct any mistakes you made and record the presentation again. Then read another book and do all of this again.

You can do this same activity after watching a movie (*listening*).

Summarize a TV Show

Watch a TV show in English (*listening*). Take notes as you listen. After watching, write a summary of the show (*writing*).

Use your notes to give an oral summary of the show. Explain the characters, setting, and plot (*speaking*). Record yourself speaking. Then watch the video and write down what you said. Correct any mistakes you made and record the presentation again. Then watch another TV show and do all of this again.

Answer Sheet
TOEIC PRACTICE TEST 1

Listening Comprehension

Part 1: Photographs

1. Ⓐ Ⓑ Ⓒ Ⓓ
2. Ⓐ Ⓑ Ⓒ Ⓓ
3. Ⓐ Ⓑ Ⓒ Ⓓ
4. Ⓐ Ⓑ Ⓒ Ⓓ
5. Ⓐ Ⓑ Ⓒ Ⓓ
6. Ⓐ Ⓑ Ⓒ Ⓓ
7. Ⓐ Ⓑ Ⓒ Ⓓ
8. Ⓐ Ⓑ Ⓒ Ⓓ
9. Ⓐ Ⓑ Ⓒ Ⓓ
10. Ⓐ Ⓑ Ⓒ Ⓓ

Part 2: Question-Response

11. Ⓐ Ⓑ Ⓒ
12. Ⓐ Ⓑ Ⓒ
13. Ⓐ Ⓑ Ⓒ
14. Ⓐ Ⓑ Ⓒ
15. Ⓐ Ⓑ Ⓒ
16. Ⓐ Ⓑ Ⓒ
17. Ⓐ Ⓑ Ⓒ
18. Ⓐ Ⓑ Ⓒ
19. Ⓐ Ⓑ Ⓒ
20. Ⓐ Ⓑ Ⓒ
21. Ⓐ Ⓑ Ⓒ
22. Ⓐ Ⓑ Ⓒ
23. Ⓐ Ⓑ Ⓒ
24. Ⓐ Ⓑ Ⓒ
25. Ⓐ Ⓑ Ⓒ
26. Ⓐ Ⓑ Ⓒ
27. Ⓐ Ⓑ Ⓒ
28. Ⓐ Ⓑ Ⓒ
29. Ⓐ Ⓑ Ⓒ
30. Ⓐ Ⓑ Ⓒ
31. Ⓐ Ⓑ Ⓒ
32. Ⓐ Ⓑ Ⓒ
33. Ⓐ Ⓑ Ⓒ
34. Ⓐ Ⓑ Ⓒ
35. Ⓐ Ⓑ Ⓒ
36. Ⓐ Ⓑ Ⓒ
37. Ⓐ Ⓑ Ⓒ
38. Ⓐ Ⓑ Ⓒ
39. Ⓐ Ⓑ Ⓒ
40. Ⓐ Ⓑ Ⓒ

Part 3: Conversations

41. Ⓐ Ⓑ Ⓒ Ⓓ
42. Ⓐ Ⓑ Ⓒ Ⓓ
43. Ⓐ Ⓑ Ⓒ Ⓓ
44. Ⓐ Ⓑ Ⓒ Ⓓ
45. Ⓐ Ⓑ Ⓒ Ⓓ
46. Ⓐ Ⓑ Ⓒ Ⓓ
47. Ⓐ Ⓑ Ⓒ Ⓓ
48. Ⓐ Ⓑ Ⓒ Ⓓ
49. Ⓐ Ⓑ Ⓒ Ⓓ
50. Ⓐ Ⓑ Ⓒ Ⓓ
51. Ⓐ Ⓑ Ⓒ Ⓓ
52. Ⓐ Ⓑ Ⓒ Ⓓ
53. Ⓐ Ⓑ Ⓒ Ⓓ
54. Ⓐ Ⓑ Ⓒ Ⓓ
55. Ⓐ Ⓑ Ⓒ Ⓓ
56. Ⓐ Ⓑ Ⓒ Ⓓ
57. Ⓐ Ⓑ Ⓒ Ⓓ
58. Ⓐ Ⓑ Ⓒ Ⓓ
59. Ⓐ Ⓑ Ⓒ Ⓓ
60. Ⓐ Ⓑ Ⓒ Ⓓ
61. Ⓐ Ⓑ Ⓒ Ⓓ
62. Ⓐ Ⓑ Ⓒ Ⓓ
63. Ⓐ Ⓑ Ⓒ Ⓓ
64. Ⓐ Ⓑ Ⓒ Ⓓ
65. Ⓐ Ⓑ Ⓒ Ⓓ
66. Ⓐ Ⓑ Ⓒ Ⓓ
67. Ⓐ Ⓑ Ⓒ Ⓓ
68. Ⓐ Ⓑ Ⓒ Ⓓ
69. Ⓐ Ⓑ Ⓒ Ⓓ
70. Ⓐ Ⓑ Ⓒ Ⓓ

Part 4: Talks

71. Ⓐ Ⓑ Ⓒ Ⓓ
72. Ⓐ Ⓑ Ⓒ Ⓓ
73. Ⓐ Ⓑ Ⓒ Ⓓ
74. Ⓐ Ⓑ Ⓒ Ⓓ
75. Ⓐ Ⓑ Ⓒ Ⓓ
76. Ⓐ Ⓑ Ⓒ Ⓓ
77. Ⓐ Ⓑ Ⓒ Ⓓ
78. Ⓐ Ⓑ Ⓒ Ⓓ
79. Ⓐ Ⓑ Ⓒ Ⓓ
80. Ⓐ Ⓑ Ⓒ Ⓓ
81. Ⓐ Ⓑ Ⓒ Ⓓ
82. Ⓐ Ⓑ Ⓒ Ⓓ
83. Ⓐ Ⓑ Ⓒ Ⓓ
84. Ⓐ Ⓑ Ⓒ Ⓓ
85. Ⓐ Ⓑ Ⓒ Ⓓ
86. Ⓐ Ⓑ Ⓒ Ⓓ
87. Ⓐ Ⓑ Ⓒ Ⓓ
88. Ⓐ Ⓑ Ⓒ Ⓓ
89. Ⓐ Ⓑ Ⓒ Ⓓ
90. Ⓐ Ⓑ Ⓒ Ⓓ
91. Ⓐ Ⓑ Ⓒ Ⓓ
92. Ⓐ Ⓑ Ⓒ Ⓓ
93. Ⓐ Ⓑ Ⓒ Ⓓ
94. Ⓐ Ⓑ Ⓒ Ⓓ
95. Ⓐ Ⓑ Ⓒ Ⓓ
96. Ⓐ Ⓑ Ⓒ Ⓓ
97. Ⓐ Ⓑ Ⓒ Ⓓ
98. Ⓐ Ⓑ Ⓒ Ⓓ
99. Ⓐ Ⓑ Ⓒ Ⓓ
100. Ⓐ Ⓑ Ⓒ Ⓓ

Answer Sheet
TOEIC PRACTICE TEST 1

Reading

Part 5: Incomplete Sentences

101. Ⓐ Ⓑ Ⓒ Ⓓ   112. Ⓐ Ⓑ Ⓒ Ⓓ   122. Ⓐ Ⓑ Ⓒ Ⓓ   132. Ⓐ Ⓑ Ⓒ Ⓓ
102. Ⓐ Ⓑ Ⓒ Ⓓ   113. Ⓐ Ⓑ Ⓒ Ⓓ   123. Ⓐ Ⓑ Ⓒ Ⓓ   133. Ⓐ Ⓑ Ⓒ Ⓓ
103. Ⓐ Ⓑ Ⓒ Ⓓ   114. Ⓐ Ⓑ Ⓒ Ⓓ   124. Ⓐ Ⓑ Ⓒ Ⓓ   134. Ⓐ Ⓑ Ⓒ Ⓓ
104 Ⓐ Ⓑ Ⓒ Ⓓ   115. Ⓐ Ⓑ Ⓒ Ⓓ   125. Ⓐ Ⓑ Ⓒ Ⓓ   135. Ⓐ Ⓑ Ⓒ Ⓓ
106. Ⓐ Ⓑ Ⓒ Ⓓ   116. Ⓐ Ⓑ Ⓒ Ⓓ   126. Ⓐ Ⓑ Ⓒ Ⓓ   136. Ⓐ Ⓑ Ⓒ Ⓓ
107. Ⓐ Ⓑ Ⓒ Ⓓ   117. Ⓐ Ⓑ Ⓒ Ⓓ   127. Ⓐ Ⓑ Ⓒ Ⓓ   137. Ⓐ Ⓑ Ⓒ Ⓓ
108. Ⓐ Ⓑ Ⓒ Ⓓ   118. Ⓐ Ⓑ Ⓒ Ⓓ   128. Ⓐ Ⓑ Ⓒ Ⓓ   138. Ⓐ Ⓑ Ⓒ Ⓓ
109. Ⓐ Ⓑ Ⓒ Ⓓ   119. Ⓐ Ⓑ Ⓒ Ⓓ   129. Ⓐ Ⓑ Ⓒ Ⓓ   139. Ⓐ Ⓑ Ⓒ Ⓓ
110. Ⓐ Ⓑ Ⓒ Ⓓ   120. Ⓐ Ⓑ Ⓒ Ⓓ   130. Ⓐ Ⓑ Ⓒ Ⓓ   140. Ⓐ Ⓑ Ⓒ Ⓓ
111. Ⓐ Ⓑ Ⓒ Ⓓ   121. Ⓐ Ⓑ Ⓒ Ⓓ   131. Ⓐ Ⓑ Ⓒ Ⓓ

Part 6: Text Completion

141. Ⓐ Ⓑ Ⓒ Ⓓ   144. Ⓐ Ⓑ Ⓒ Ⓓ   147. Ⓐ Ⓑ Ⓒ Ⓓ   150. Ⓐ Ⓑ Ⓒ Ⓓ
142. Ⓐ Ⓑ Ⓒ Ⓓ   145. Ⓐ Ⓑ Ⓒ Ⓓ   148. Ⓐ Ⓑ Ⓒ Ⓓ   151. Ⓐ Ⓑ Ⓒ Ⓓ
143. Ⓐ Ⓑ Ⓒ Ⓓ   146. Ⓐ Ⓑ Ⓒ Ⓓ   149. Ⓐ Ⓑ Ⓒ Ⓓ   152. Ⓐ Ⓑ Ⓒ Ⓓ

Part 7: Reading Comprehension

153. Ⓐ Ⓑ Ⓒ Ⓓ   166. Ⓐ Ⓑ Ⓒ Ⓓ   179. Ⓐ Ⓑ Ⓒ Ⓓ   192. Ⓐ Ⓑ Ⓒ Ⓓ
154. Ⓐ Ⓑ Ⓒ Ⓓ   167. Ⓐ Ⓑ Ⓒ Ⓓ   180. Ⓐ Ⓑ Ⓒ Ⓓ   193. Ⓐ Ⓑ Ⓒ Ⓓ
155. Ⓐ Ⓑ Ⓒ Ⓓ   168. Ⓐ Ⓑ Ⓒ Ⓓ   181. Ⓐ Ⓑ Ⓒ Ⓓ   194. Ⓐ Ⓑ Ⓒ Ⓓ
156. Ⓐ Ⓑ Ⓒ Ⓓ   169. Ⓐ Ⓑ Ⓒ Ⓓ   182. Ⓐ Ⓑ Ⓒ Ⓓ   195. Ⓐ Ⓑ Ⓒ Ⓓ
157. Ⓐ Ⓑ Ⓒ Ⓓ   170. Ⓐ Ⓑ Ⓒ Ⓓ   183. Ⓐ Ⓑ Ⓒ Ⓓ   196. Ⓐ Ⓑ Ⓒ Ⓓ
158. Ⓐ Ⓑ Ⓒ Ⓓ   171. Ⓐ Ⓑ Ⓒ Ⓓ   184. Ⓐ Ⓑ Ⓒ Ⓓ   197. Ⓐ Ⓑ Ⓒ Ⓓ
159. Ⓐ Ⓑ Ⓒ Ⓓ   172. Ⓐ Ⓑ Ⓒ Ⓓ   185. Ⓐ Ⓑ Ⓒ Ⓓ   198. Ⓐ Ⓑ Ⓒ Ⓓ
160. Ⓐ Ⓑ Ⓒ Ⓓ   173. Ⓐ Ⓑ Ⓒ Ⓓ   186. Ⓐ Ⓑ Ⓒ Ⓓ   199. Ⓐ Ⓑ Ⓒ Ⓓ
161. Ⓐ Ⓑ Ⓒ Ⓓ   174. Ⓐ Ⓑ Ⓒ Ⓓ   187. Ⓐ Ⓑ Ⓒ Ⓓ   200. Ⓐ Ⓑ Ⓒ Ⓓ
162. Ⓐ Ⓑ Ⓒ Ⓓ   175. Ⓐ Ⓑ Ⓒ Ⓓ   188. Ⓐ Ⓑ Ⓒ Ⓓ
163. Ⓐ Ⓑ Ⓒ Ⓓ   176. Ⓐ Ⓑ Ⓒ Ⓓ   189. Ⓐ Ⓑ Ⓒ Ⓓ
164. Ⓐ Ⓑ Ⓒ Ⓓ   177. Ⓐ Ⓑ Ⓒ Ⓓ   190. Ⓐ Ⓑ Ⓒ Ⓓ
165. Ⓐ Ⓑ Ⓒ Ⓓ   178. Ⓐ Ⓑ Ⓒ Ⓓ   191. Ⓐ Ⓑ Ⓒ Ⓓ

TOEIC Practice Test 1

LISTENING COMPREHENSION

In this section of the test, you will have the chance to show how well you understand spoken English. There are four parts to this section, with special directions for each part. You will find the Answer Sheet for Practice Test 1 on page 7. Detach it from the book and use it to record your answers. Check your answers using the Answer Key on page 40 and see the Answers Explained on page 42.

TIP

If you do not have access to an audio CD player, please refer to the audioscripts starting on page 333 when prompted to listen to an audio passage.

CD 1
TRACK 2

Part 1: Photographs

Directions: You will see a photograph. You will hear four statements about the photograph. Choose the statement that most closely matches the photograph and fill in the corresponding oval on your answer sheet.

Example

Now listen to the four statements.

Sample Answer

Ⓐ Ⓑ Ⓒ Ⓓ

Statement (B), "She's reading a magazine," best describes what you see in the picture. Therefore, you should choose answer (B).

1.

4.

2.

5.

3.

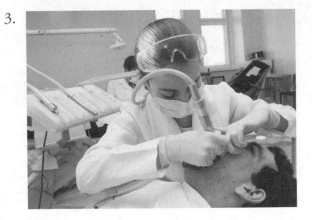

6.

7.

8.

9.

10.

Part 2: Question-Response

Directions: You will hear a question and three possible responses. Choose the response that most closely answers the question and fill in the corresponding oval on your answer sheet.

Example

Now listen to the sample question.

You will hear:

How is the weather?

You will also hear:

(A) It's raining.
(B) He's fine, thanks.
(C) He's my boss.

The best response to the question *How is the weather?* is choice (A), *It's raining.* Therefore, you should choose answer (A).

11. Mark your answer on your answer sheet.

12. Mark your answer on your answer sheet.

13. Mark your answer on your answer sheet.

14. Mark your answer on your answer sheet.

15. Mark your answer on your answer sheet.

16. Mark your answer on your answer sheet.

17. Mark your answer on your answer sheet.

18. Mark your answer on your answer sheet.

19. Mark your answer on your answer sheet.

20. Mark your answer on your answer sheet.

21. Mark your answer on your answer sheet.

22. Mark your answer on your answer sheet.

23. Mark your answer on your answer sheet.

24. Mark your answer on your answer sheet.

25. Mark your answer on your answer sheet.

26. Mark your answer on your answer sheet.

27. Mark your answer on your answer sheet.

28. Mark your answer on your answer sheet.

29. Mark your answer on your answer sheet.

30. Mark your answer on your answer sheet.

31. Mark your answer on your answer sheet.

32. Mark your answer on your answer sheet.

33. Mark your answer on your answer sheet.

34. Mark your answer on your answer sheet.

35. Mark your answer on your answer sheet.

36. Mark your answer on your answer sheet.

37. Mark your answer on your answer sheet.

38. Mark your answer on your answer sheet.

39. Mark your answer on your answer sheet.

40. Mark your answer on your answer sheet.

Part 3: Conversations

Directions: You will hear a conversation between two people. You will see three questions on each conversation and four possible answers. Choose the best answer to each question and fill in the corresponding oval on your answer sheet.

41. What time will they leave for the airport?
    (A) 2:00
    (B) 2:05
    (C) 3:00
    (D) 4:30

42. How will they get to the airport?
    (A) Bus
    (B) Car
    (C) Taxi
    (D) Subway

43. Where will the speakers meet?
    (A) The airport
    (B) The woman's office
    (C) The man's office
    (D) The subway station

44. Where does this conversation take place?
    (A) A store
    (B) An office
    (C) A post office
    (D) A bank

45. What is the man looking for?
    (A) Envelopes
    (B) Printers
    (C) Paper
    (D) Money

46. What does the woman offer to do?
    (A) Take something off the shelf
    (B) Suggest a new style
    (C) Place an order
    (D) Count the man's money

47. What will the man be doing at 11:00 tomorrow morning?
    (A) Talking with Mr. Lee
    (B) Meeting with the accountants
    (C) Writing a letter
    (D) Eating lunch

48. What does Mr. Lee want to discuss?
    (A) A phone call
    (B) A marketing plan
    (C) The meeting agenda
    (D) The accounts

49. What time does the man want to see Mr. Lee?
    (A) 2:00
    (B) 7:00
    (C) 9:00
    (D) 10:00

50. When will the copies be ready?
    (A) Before lunch
    (B) This afternoon
    (C) Tonight
    (D) Tomorrow morning

51. How many copies will the woman make?
    (A) 10
    (B) 70
    (C) 75
    (D) 85

52. What does the woman ask the man for?
    (A) Lunch
    (B) A file
    (C) Some addresses
    (D) Labels

53. How many nights does the woman want to stay at the hotel?
    (A) 1
    (B) 2
    (C) 3
    (D) 4

54. What does the woman ask the man to do?
    (A) Read a book
    (B) Call the hotel
    (C) Go sightseeing
    (D) Type some reports

55. When will the man do what the woman asks?
    (A) Right now
    (B) This morning
    (C) After lunch
    (D) Tonight

56. What's the weather like?
    (A) Foggy
    (B) Snowy
    (C) Rainy
    (D) Clear

57. Why will Jack be late?
    (A) He's sick
    (B) There's a traffic problem
    (C) The train was delayed
    (D) He's at a meeting

58. How late will he be?
    (A) One minute
    (B) Eleven minutes
    (C) One hour
    (D) Two hours

59. Where does the man want to go?
    (A) Her office
    (B) The post office
    (C) The library
    (D) A park

60. Where is it?
    (A) Two blocks from the parking lot
    (B) Across the street from the bank
    (C) Straight ahead
    (D) On a corner

61. How many blocks away is it?
    (A) 2
    (B) 3
    (C) 5
    (D) 7

62. Why is the man excited?
    (A) He found a lost item.
    (B) He's going to a banquet.
    (C) He's employee of the year.
    (D) The woman is speaking with him.

63. When is the banquet?
    (A) September
    (B) October
    (C) November
    (D) December

64. What does the woman offer to do?
    (A) Help the man write a speech
    (B) Serve at the banquet
    (C) Give the man a party
    (D) Go to the bank

65. What does the woman want to do?
    (A) Get something to eat
    (B) Buy clothes
    (C) Make a phone call
    (D) Drink coffee

66. How will the man pay?
    (A) Check
    (B) Money order
    (C) Credit card
    (D) Cash

67. What time is it now?
    (A) 2:00
    (B) 8:00
    (C) 9:00
    (D) 10:00

---

68. Who is the woman shopping for?
    (A) Herself
    (B) Her husband
    (C) Her brother
    (D) Her boss

69. What color suit does the woman want?
    (A) White
    (B) Beige
    (C) Blue
    (D) Black

70. How much does the suit cost?
    (A) $200
    (B) $400
    (C) $500
    (D) $900

Part 4: Talks

Directions: You will hear a talk given by a single speaker. You will see three questions on each talk, each with four possible answers. Choose the best answer to each question and fill in the corresponding oval on your answer sheet.

71. What will happen in five minutes?
    (A) Passengers will get on the train.
    (B) The train will leave for New York.
    (C) Tickets will go on sale.
    (D) The store will open.

72. What gate will the train leave from?
    (A) Gate 7
    (B) Gate 11
    (C) Gate 16
    (D) Gate 60

73. What should passengers do with their luggage?
    (A) Check it
    (B) Show it to the gate agent
    (C) Put it on the overhead rack
    (D) Leave it beside the track

74. What kind of a business is Prescott?
    (A) Accountants
    (B) Party-planning service
    (C) Bank
    (D) Credit card company

75. What should a caller press to speak to a customer service representative?
    (A) 3
    (B) 4
    (C) 5
    (D) 6

76. What can a caller do by pressing 0?
    (A) Open an account
    (B) Transfer funds
    (C) Place an order
    (D) Hear the menu again

77. When do people often lack energy?
    (A) In the morning
    (B) During lunch
    (C) In the afternoon
    (D) At the end of the day

78. What does the speaker recommend to maintain energy?
    (A) Have lunch
    (B) Drink coffee
    (C) Eat sugar
    (D) Take a walk

79. How often should this be done?
    (A) Once an hour
    (B) Every five minutes
    (C) Every 45 minutes
    (D) Two times a day

80. What is sold at Magruders?
    (A) Clothes
    (B) Furniture
    (C) Computers
    (D) Cars

81. How big a discount is offered?
    (A) 50%
    (B) 55%
    (C) 60%
    (D) 65%

82. When does the sale begin?
    (A) Next week
    (B) On the weekend
    (C) At the end of the month
    (D) Next month

83. What is being offered?
    (A) Computer repair service
    (B) Computer technician training course
    (C) Computer-based employment service
    (D) Computers and related equipment

84. How much does it cost?
    (A) $200
    (B) $600
    (C) $2,000
    (D) $6,000

85. How can one take advantage of the offer?
    (A) Go online
    (B) Visit the office
    (C) Call on the phone
    (D) Send a letter

86. How is the weather today?
    (A) Snowing
    (B) Raining
    (C) Clear
    (D) Windy

87. What does the speaker suggest listeners do?
    (A) Put on shorts and sandals
    (B) Report accidents
    (C) Take the train
    (D) Stay home

88. When will the weather change?
    (A) This afternoon
    (B) This evening
    (C) Tonight
    (D) Tomorrow morning

89. What will happen on the first floor?
    (A) Workshops will be held.
    (B) Lunch will be served.
    (C) The guest speaker will speak.
    (D) Computers will be made available.

90. What time will the demonstration be held?
    (A) 12:00
    (B) 1:30
    (C) 2:00
    (D) 5:00

91. Where will refreshments be served?
    (A) In the conference room
    (B) At the restaurant
    (C) In the garden
    (D) On the patio

92. What is the problem?
    (A) A train station is closed.
    (B) Buses can't run.
    (C) Parking is not available.
    (D) The curb is broken.

93. What is the cause of the problem?
    (A) Rain
    (B) Construction
    (C) Crowds
    (D) Traffic

94. How long will the problem last?
    (A) 2 weeks
    (B) 3 weeks
    (C) 4 weeks
    (D) 5 weeks

95. How many countries will the president visit on his tour?
    (A) 2
    (B) 4
    (C) 5
    (D) 10

96. What will the president talk about with national leaders?
    (A) Economics
    (B) Leadership
    (C) War
    (D) Science

97. What will the president do when his trip is over?
(A) Attend a banquet
(B) Receive an award
(C) Eat at a restaurant
(D) Go to the beach

98. What opportunity is offered?
(A) A meeting
(B) A workshop
(C) A train ride
(D) A shopping trip

99. When will it happen?
(A) Next Monday
(B) At the end of the week
(C) In September
(D) Next month

100. What should people bring?
(A) A computer
(B) A camera
(C) Some lunch
(D) The list

READING

In this section of the test, you will have the chance to show how well you understand written English. There are three parts to this section, with special directions for each part.

**YOU WILL HAVE ONE HOUR AND FIFTEEN MINUTES
TO COMPLETE PARTS 5, 6, AND 7 OF THE TEST.**

Part 5: Incomplete Sentences

Directions: You will see a sentence with a missing word. Four possible answers follow the sentence. Choose the best answer to the question and fill in the corresponding oval on your answer sheet.

101. The document that you requested _____ on your desk.
   (A) is
   (B) am
   (C) are
   (D) were

102. The _____ businessperson always dresses appropriately.
   (A) success
   (B) succeed
   (C) successful
   (D) succession

103. You will find all the pencils you need _____ that drawer.
   (A) through
   (B) under
   (C) on
   (D) in

104. Several important pieces of information were _____ from the report.
   (A) omit
   (B) omitted
   (C) omitting
   (D) omission

105. If the weather is bad, we _____ the trip.
   (A) will cancel
   (B) have canceled
   (C) canceled
   (D) are canceling

106. You can always count on Ms. Cho, as she is one of our most _____ employees.
   (A) depend
   (B) depending
   (C) dependable
   (D) dependence

107. Mr. Jones finally _____ a promotion, and he was very happy to get it.
   (A) deceived
   (B) conceived
   (C) perceived
   (D) received

108. The office was in excellent condition when we moved in because the former _____ was very tidy.
   (A) occupy
   (B) occupied
   (C) occupant
   (D) occupancy

109. No one can go home _____ the work is finished.
    (A) if
    (B) until
    (C) since
    (D) because

110. Just walk _____ that door and you will see the copy machine on the other side.
    (A) under
    (B) around
    (C) between
    (D) through

111. There were several qualified candidates for the job, but we could _____ only one.
    (A) chose
    (B) chosen
    (C) choose
    (D) choice

112. In order to be _____ to the building, you must show proper identification.
    (A) admitted
    (B) emitted
    (C) remitted
    (D) submitted

113. There's a phone on the table _____ my desk.
    (A) inside
    (B) outside
    (C) beside
    (D) reside

114. It is a bit scary riding this elevator because it _____ at such a rapid rate.
    (A) decreases
    (B) descends
    (C) devalues
    (D) diminishes

115. _____ your time card whenever you enter or leave the building.
    (A) Punch
    (B) Punches
    (C) Punched
    (D) Punching

116. When payday _____, all employees will receive their checks in the mail.
    (A) arrived
    (B) arrives
    (C) arriving
    (D) will arrive

117. Ms. Wilson was fired _____ she always arrived late and never finished her work on time.
    (A) unless
    (B) though
    (C) because
    (D) however

118. Our boss is very organized and tidy and _____ that we keep the office neat.
    (A) consists
    (B) persists
    (C) resists
    (D) insists

119. _____ Mr. Lee works very hard and always meets his deadlines, he still hasn't been given a promotion.
    (A) Since
    (B) Even
    (C) Despite
    (D) Although

120. He _____ an employee of this company ever since he first started working.
    (A) is
    (B) was
    (C) has been
    (D) will be

121. The walls are in bad shape and will require _____ before we can begin painting them.
(A) preparation
(B) preparatory
(C) preparer
(D) prepare

122. If we _____ all night, we might have finished the report on time.
(A) worked
(B) had worked
(C) have worked
(D) would have worked

123. It is necessary to have at least one advanced degree in order to _____ in today's job market.
(A) compete
(B) competent
(C) competitive
(D) competition

124. Because so few people showed _____ for the meeting, we decided to postpone it to a later date.
(A) through
(B) down
(C) off
(D) up

125. The office is right _____ the street from the subway station.
(A) next
(B) across
(C) under
(D) between

126. If you wish to speak with the director, you should _____ an appointment first.
(A) will make
(B) making
(C) make
(D) made

127. The_____ of our products is well known throughout the world.
(A) quality
(B) quantity
(C) quantify
(D) qualify

128. All employees are expected _____ at the office on time every day.
(A) arrive
(B) arrived
(C) arriving
(D) to arrive

129. All expenses must be approved _____ the department head at the beginning of each month.
(A) by
(B) to
(C) for
(D) from

130. The meeting will take place tomorrow from 10:00 _____ 11:00.
(A) at
(B) to
(C) on
(D) in

131. We _____ finish this work soon because the deadline is approaching.
(A) have
(B) had to
(C) have to
(D) will have

132. This _____ is very important, so think it over carefully.
(A) decidedly
(B) decisive
(C) decision
(D) decide

133. _____ off the lights before you leave the office.
    (A) Turn
    (B) Turned
    (C) Turning
    (D) Will turn

134. The new rug looks very nice _____ that table.
    (A) bottom
    (B) floor
    (C) down
    (D) under

135. The books that he recommended _____ not very interesting.
    (A) was
    (B) were
    (C) is
    (D) did

136. Mr. Kim is not a particularly interesting speaker, and several people fell asleep _____ his lecture.
    (A) although
    (B) while
    (C) because
    (D) during

137. Our business is rapidly _____ and we are hiring many new people.
    (A) expand
    (B) expands
    (C) expanding
    (D) has expanded

138. The building _____ during the heavy thunderstorm last night.
    (A) damage
    (B) damaged
    (C) was damaged
    (D) was damaging

139. People who have no _____ are seldom disappointed.
    (A) expectations
    (B) expectancy
    (C) expects
    (D) expect

140. Please don't ask for personal information about our employees, as we keep that information _____.
    (A) consequential
    (B) confidential
    (C) conservative
    (D) considerate

Part 6: Text Completion

Directions: You will see four passages, each with three blanks. Under each blank are four answer options. Choose the word or phrase that best completes the statement.

Questions 141–143 refer to the following newspaper article.

The Evergreen Department Store has been hit hard by the current recession. Sales have been _____ at a rapid rate. "Fewer and fewer customers are

    141. (A) decreasing
         (B) increasing
         (C) maintaining
         (D) advertising

coming into the store," says Violet Dupree, floor manager at Evergreen. Ms. Dupree explained that earnings during the past fiscal year were the worst the store had ever seen since it opened for business 25 years ago. She went on to say, "The worst part of it is that we have had to _____ a number

    142. (A) train
         (B) lay off
         (C) take on
         (D) interview

of fine employees." Job loss is becoming a more widespread problem as the recession deepens, and applications for unemployment _____ are on

    143. (A) beneficiaries
         (B) benefactors
         (C) beneficial
         (D) benefits

the rise. Evergreen is just one more in a long list of local businesses that have been falling victim to the current economic crisis.

Questions 144–146 refer to the following letter.

April 21, 20--

Martha Dinsmore
Pet Supply Company
3774 State Street
Westminister, VA

Dear Ms. Dinsmore,

This is to serve as a letter of recommendation for Andrew Richardson, a former employee of my company, PT, Inc. Mr. Richardson _____ for my company

144. (A) works
     (B) worked
     (C) has worked
     (D) had worked

for three years, from June of 20-- until he left to continue his university studies two years ago. Mr. Richardson was a great asset to my company. He always fulfilled his responsibilities in a careful and thorough manner. He was also extremely _____. We could always count on him to do what he promised

145. (A) punctual
     (B) prepared
     (C) reliable
     (D) organized

to do. He was eager to pursue professional development opportunities and attended a number of training workshops while employed by PT. His upbeat personality was also a great addition to our workplace. I think everyone on the PT staff would agree that it was indeed a pleasure to work with _____.

146. (A) he
     (B) us
     (C) her
     (D) him

I highly recommend Mr. Richardson for the position he has applied for at your company. If you have any questions, please don't hesitate to contact me.

Sincerely,

Patricia Thompson
President

Questions 147–149 refer to the following notice.

STORE POLICY REGARDING RETURNED MERCHANDISE

Customer satisfaction is our top priority. If you are dissatisfied with your purchase for any reason, you may return it to the store for a full _____ ,

147. (A) refund
(B) refusal
(C) referral
(D) restoration

no questions asked, providing the following conditions are met:

- The item is returned with its original packaging intact.
- The item is accompanied by the store receipt.
- The item is returned within 30 days of purchase.

Customers returning items after 30 days but within 90 days of purchase or without _____ original packaging will receive store credit. We are

148. (A) its
(B) his
(C) their
(D) your

sorry but we cannot accept returns on items after 90 days of the purchase date or without a store receipt. Any questions about the return policy should _____ to the Management Office.

149. (A) direct
(B) directs
(C) directed
(D) be directed

Questions 150–152 refer to the following advertisement.

Misty View Office Complex has several office spaces for rent. Misty View is _____ located near several bus lines and is just a short,

150. (A) convenient
    (B) convenience
    (C) conveniently
    (D) conventionally

five-block walk from the subway station. Your clients who drive will never have to worry about finding a place to park. Misty View has _____

151. (A) scarce
    (B) ample
    (C) covered
    (D) underground

visitor parking. Tenant parking is also available for an additional monthly fee. Rents start at $2 per square foot, all utilities included. Six-month, one-year, and five-year leases are available. _____ this opportunity to locate

152. (A) Miss
    (B) Missing
    (C) Don't miss
    (D) Shouldn't miss

your business in the city's prime office building. Call our leasing office today to make an appointment to visit Misty View and find out why it has become the city's most desirable business location.

Part 7: Reading Comprehension

Directions: You will see single and double reading passages followed by several questions. Each question has four answer choices. Choose the best answer to the question and fill in the corresponding oval on your answer sheet.

Questions 153–156 refer to the following article.

Park and Smith, a financial planning company based in Lakeview, has opened a branch office in downtown Salem in the building owned by the Salem Office Properties real estate company. Park and Smith is taking over office space formerly occupied by the law offices of James Robertson. The space had been vacant for a year and a half. The new Park and Smith office was open for business as of yesterday. Greta Park, president of Park and Smith, says that her company chose the Salem location because of a rising demand for financial planning services in the area. "Salem is a growing community," she explained, "and the town's citizens are becoming more affluent. It is just the type of community where services such as ours are needed." Park and Smith closed its branch offices in Johnstown and Freeburg at the end of last year. These communities are close enough to Lakeview to be served by the main office there, Ms. Park explained, but having an office in Salem will facilitate expanding services to the entire eastern part of the state. The branch's opening comes just a few months after the opening of the PD Miller stock brokerage firm at the Salem Center office complex.

153. What kind of a business is Smith and Park?
   (A) Financial planning
   (B) Law office
   (C) Real estate
   (D) Stock brokerage

154. When did Park and Smith open its branch office in Salem?
   (A) Yesterday
   (B) A few months ago
   (C) At the end of last year
   (D) A year and a half ago

155. Why did Smith and Park open a branch office in Salem?
   (A) They closed their other branch offices.
   (B) It's close to the main office.
   (C) There is a need for their services there.
   (D) The rent is reasonable.

156. The word *facilitate* in line 24 is closest in meaning to
   (A) fund.
   (B) assist.
   (C) impede.
   (D) upgrade.

Questions 157–159 refer to the following article.

Boris Lutz of Greenfield recently won the Good Citizen Prize for service to the local community. The prize is given annually at the Greenfield Bank to a bank employee who has demonstrated good citizenship by contributing to community projects in some way. The purpose is to promote community goodwill and acknowledge bank employees' contributions to the greater Greenfield community. Lutz, a teller at the Simsbury Village branch of the bank, received the honor from his bank coworkers. "Boris has always given generously of his time to community groups," explained his supervisor, Doris Wilson. "We thought it was about time his contributions were acknowledged. We at the bank are all so pleased that he is this year's winner." This is the second year the prize has been given. Last year the honor went to Maria Pendleton, assistant to the bank's president.

157. What did Boris Lutz get?
(A) A bank account
(B) A promotion
(C) An assistant
(D) An award

158. Who gave it to him?
(A) His supervisor
(B) His colleagues
(C) The bank's president
(D) A community leader

159. How do people at the bank feel about it?
(A) Happy
(B) Displeased
(C) Honored
(D) Angry

Questions 160–163 refer to the following letter.

To the Editor:

I read with great concern the report in your newspaper this morning about the plans of the Holbrook Manufacturing Company to build a factory in this city. The project has received strong support from the city council, based on their belief that Holbrook will bring a significant number of jobs to our area and boost the local economy. Apparently, they are blind to the reality. Holbrook is well known for its innovative manufacturing methods, which are largely automated. Because of this, very little manual labor is required. Holbrook's system generally requires highly skilled technicians, who would likely come here from other places to work at the factory. There will be few, if any, jobs for local citizens. What do we get in return for this? A large, unsightly building that will require the destruction of natural areas and throw pollution into our air and water. The city council must approve Holbrook's project before they begin construction of the factory. Holbrook's board of directors, eager to break ground on the project as early as next month, have urged the city council to move forward with their vote, and it will take place tomorrow night rather than two weeks from now, as originally planned. This gives even less time for council members to develop an informed opinion. I strongly urge them not to bow to the pressure of Holbrook and to vote against the proposed project.

Sincerely,

Henry Judson

160. Why did Henry Judson write this letter?
(A) To protest a new factory
(B) To analyze the economy
(C) To explain sources of pollution
(D) To get elected to the city council

161. What kind of people generally work at Holbrook?
(A) Manual laborers
(B) Blind people
(C) Trained specialists
(D) Economists

162. When will the city council vote on the Holbrook project?
(A) This morning
(B) Tomorrow night
(C) Two weeks from now
(D) Early next month

163. The word *unsightly* in line 10 is closest in meaning to
(A) attractive.
(B) enormous.
(C) costly.
(D) ugly.

Questions 164–165 refer to the following advertisement.

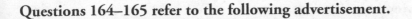

Mary's Lunch, Inc.

You work hard, and you deserve good food. Mary's Lunch, Inc. provides everything from snacks to four-course dinners for your conference, meeting, office party, or any other business occasion. We deliver to most downtown locations.

Menu choices can be viewed on our website: www.maryslunch.com. Our planning consultants can help you plan your next event and will explain our pricing system. Simply call 987-3722 or stop by our office during normal business hours.

---

164. What kind of business is advertised?
    (A) Kitchen supply
    (B) Grocery store
    (C) Catering
    (D) Restaurant

165. What is available on the website?
    (A) Office hours
    (B) Consultants
    (C) Menus
    (D) Prices

Questions 166–168 refer to the following advertisement.

ATTENTION!

Babcock is now hiring for positions in a variety of locations. We have fantastic opportunities available for writers, editors, and proofreaders. See below for a partial list of currently available positions.

Visit the Careers page on our website to find out more and to apply for any of these positions. To access a particular job posting, copy and paste the job number into the search field on the Careers page. Or, browse through the list of available positions. When you find a position for which you are qualified, complete the online job application. You may also attach your resume. Letters of recommendation are not required at this point. Please do not call the office. All job application information is included on the website.

Now hiring:
Proofreader. Job #4882
Requires two years' experience OR proof of relevant training.

Assistant Editor. Job #6874
No previous experience required. Must have a degree in English, journalism, or a related field.

Editorial Intern. Job #5822
No previous experience required. Current college student preferred.

Staff Writer. Job #5773
Requires minimum of three years' experience in a similar position.

---

166. What kind of business is Babcock probably engaged in?
   (A) Training
   (B) Publishing
   (C) Career counseling
   (D) Internet services

167. How can someone apply for a job at Babcock?
   (A) Visit the website
   (B) Call the office
   (C) Mail a resume
   (D) Write a letter

168. Which of the advertised jobs requires previous experience?
   (A) Proofreader
   (B) Assistant Editor
   (C) Editorial Intern
   (D) Staff Writer

Questions 169–170 refer to the following invoice.

WTF Office Renovators
P.O. Box 17
Newforth, MA 01253

December 16, 20--
Invoice #004

Client name:
Williams and Drivers Law Offices
34 Highland Ave., Suite 5
Newforth, MA 01253

Painting, 2 rooms:	$500
Carpentry repair work:	$750
Total due:	$1,250

Previous account balance: $600
Paid in full. Thank you!

The work described herein covers work completed during the month of
November. Please pay the entire amount by the end of next month.

Thank you for your business.

---

169. How much is due?
    (A) $500
    (B) $750
    (C) $1,250
    (D) $1,850

170. When is it due?
    (A) November 30
    (B) December 16
    (C) December 31
    (D) January 31

Questions 171–174 refer to the following instructions.

SAFETY INSTRUCTIONS

To avoid personal injury or property damage, follow these safety instructions when using this product:

- Keep product away from radiators and other heat sources and in a place where air can circulate freely around it.
- Do not make or receive calls while standing in or near water, such as a sink, bathtub, or swimming pool.
- Do not place furniture or other items on top of the power cord.
- Do not apply excess force when dialing. This could result in permanent damage to the buttons.
- Disconnect product from electrical outlet before cleaning. Do not use liquid cleaners and do not immerse product in water. Instead, wipe thoroughly and gently with a damp cloth.
- Avoid using product during an electrical storm.
- If repair work is required, contact the manufacturer at the phone number listed on the front cover of this manual.

---

171. What kind of product are these instructions for?
     (A) Power cord
     (B) Telephone
     (C) Bathtub
     (D) Radiator

172. What should the customer do if repairs are needed?
     (A) Call the manufacturer
     (B) Clean the product thoroughly
     (C) Return the product to the store
     (D) Look for instructions in the manual

173. When should the product not be used?
     (A) During a thunderstorm
     (B) Before unplugging it
     (C) When air is not circulating
     (D) After an electrical power loss

174. What do the instructions say about cleaning the product?
     (A) Use liquid soap.
     (B) Scrub it hard.
     (C) Unplug it first.
     (D) Dip it in water.

Questions 175–178 refer to the following article.

Andrew Peterson, president of the Mount Auburn Bank, announced yesterday afternoon that Jolene Simmons has been appointed as the bank's new director of human resources. Ms. Simmons has more than 20 years' experience in the banking industry. After completing her undergraduate degree, she worked for Halt and Levin, a local accounting firm. She left the firm after several years and started her banking career as a teller at the Windsor Bank. She eventually worked her way up to a position as branch manager at the Riverside branch of that institution. Two years ago, she left that job to pursue a master's degree in human resource management at State University, which she completed last month. "She comes to us highly recommended both by her previous employers and by her instructors at the university," says Mr. Peterson. Ms. Simmons will begin her new job at the beginning of next year.

175. What was Ms. Simmons's most recent job?
 (A) Human resources assistant
 (B) Accountant
 (C) Branch manager
 (D) University instructor

176. Where did Ms. Simmons work as a teller?
 (A) Mount Auburn Bank
 (B) Halt and Levin Bank
 (C) Windsor Bank
 (D) Riverside Bank

177. When did Ms. Simmons complete her university degree?
 (A) Twenty years ago
 (B) Two years ago
 (C) A year ago
 (D) A month ago

178. The word *previous* in line 8 is closest in meaning to
 (A) former.
 (B) preferred.
 (C) future.
 (D) professional.

Questions 179–180 refer to the following notice.

BECAUSE OF THE HOLIDAY, WEEKEND PARKING REGULATIONS WILL BE IN EFFECT THROUGHOUT THE CITY ALL DAY TOMORROW. THERE WILL BE NO CHARGE FOR PARKING IN METERED PARKING PLACES; HOWEVER, DOWNTOWN PUBLIC PARKING GARAGES WILL BE CLOSED. SUBWAYS AND BUSES WILL FOLLOW THE SUNDAY SCHEDULE, AND WEEKEND FARES AND SENIOR CITIZEN DISCOUNTS WILL BE IN EFFECT ALL DAY. CONSTRUCTION ON THE GREEN RIVER BRIDGE WILL BE SUSPENDED, BUT THE BRIDGE WILL REMAIN CLOSED.

179. What will be free tomorrow?
 (A) Metered parking
 (B) Garage parking
 (C) Subway fares
 (D) Bridge use

180. Why will this be free?
 (A) It's the weekend.
 (B) It's a holiday.
 (C) There is construction.
 (D) The bridge is closed.

Questions 181–185 refer to the following schedule and e-mail.

Business Association Conference
Friday, May 15 • San Francisco, CA
Schedule of Presentations and Workshops

Time	Place	Event	Presenter
8:30–9:00	Auditorium	Opening Remarks	Raymond Larkins
9:15–10:15	Conference Rooms	Room A: Business Law	Myra Johnson
		Room B: Hiring Practices	Joe Rizzoli
10:30–11:30	Conference Rooms	Room A: The Future of Business	Sam Choi
		Room B: Effective Management	Mary Kim
11:30–12:30	Exhibit Hall	Exhibits	Various
12:30–1:45	Lunch	Dining Room	n/a
2:00–4:00	Conference Rooms	Room A: Contract Negotiation	Raymond Larkins
		Room B: Local business tour*	Ellen Peters

*Tour participants will gather in Room B, then proceed together to the hotel parking lot, where the tour bus will be waiting.

To: Raymond Larkins
From: Myra Johnson
Subject: Meeting at conference

Hi, Raymond,

I will be flying to San Francisco to attend the Business Association Conference next Friday, and I understand you will be there, too. I was hoping we could have a chance to meet sometime during the day Friday for about 30 minutes. I think we should take the opportunity to go over the project in person. Let me know when would be a good time for you. I will be giving a workshop on business law, but other than that my schedule is flexible. Anytime before 6:00 would work for me. I can't stay later than that since I'm driving to Sacramento in the evening and don't want to arrive there too late. A colleague will be signing his book at a store there, and I want to attend. I'm looking forward to your presentation on contracts. I wouldn't miss that for anything. Perhaps we could have our meeting immediately afterward. Let me know what works best for you.
Myra

181. How will Myra get to San Francisco?
(A) Bus
(B) Plane
(C) Train
(D) Car

182. What does Myra want to discuss with Raymond?
(A) A workshop
(B) A contract
(C) A project
(D) A law

183. What time is Myra NOT available to meet with Raymond?
(A) 9:15
(B) 10:30
(C) 11:30
(D) 2:00

184. Where will Myra probably be at 2:30?
(A) In the auditorium
(B) In Room A
(C) In Room B
(D) In the hotel parking lot

185. What will Myra do on Friday night?
(A) Meet with Raymond
(B) Sign a contract
(C) Give a workshop
(D) Attend a book signing

Questions 186–190 refer to the following two letters.

July 30, 20--

David Mendez
Director of Marketing
The Grover Company
1809 Lyme Road
Newland, IL

Dear Mr. Mendez,

I have heard that there is an opening for a researcher in the Marketing Department, and my supervisor, Marla Petrowski, suggested that I contact you about applying for it. I have worked at Grover for three years now as an office assistant in the Accounting Department. I previously worked for a year at a small marketing firm called R-J Associates. That is the only marketing job experience I have, but I have a degree in marketing, which I completed last month. Now I would like to get a position in my field. Through my years working at Grover, I have become quite familiar with the way this company works, and I feel that I would have a great deal to offer Grover's Marketing Department.

I am enclosing my resume and could also provide you with letters of reference from my university professors. Thank you for your attention. I look forward to hearing from you.

Sincerely,

Sylvia Krim

August 8, 20--

Sylvia Krim
Accounting Department
The Grover Company
1809 Lyme Road
Newland, IL

Dear Ms. Krim,

Thank you for your letter expressing interest in applying for the position in the Marketing Department. I have spoken with Ms. Petrowski, who highly recommends you for the job. I have also shown your credentials to our head researcher, and we both agree that you would be a good asset to our department. Unfortunately, the position you are interested in is not an entry-level job. We generally require at least twice the amount of marketing job experience that you have, as a minimum, for that type of position. Although you appear to have a good reference from your former employer, we feel that you are not yet qualified for the job. However, I anticipate that we will have an opening for a marketing assistant, possibly as soon as September. I will let you know when that position becomes available in case you might be interested in applying for it. I hope you will. In the meantime, please accept my best wishes for your continued success.

Sincerely,

David Mendez
Director of Marketing

186. What job is Ms. Krim interested in applying for?
(A) Marketing assistant
(B) Researcher
(C) Office assistant
(D) Accountant

187. When did Ms. Krim finish her degree in marketing?
(A) June
(B) July
(C) August
(D) September

188. Who recommends Ms. Krim for the job?
(A) The director of marketing
(B) A university professor
(C) The head researcher
(D) Her supervisor

189. How many years of experience are required for the job she wants?
(A) One
(B) Two
(C) Three
(D) Four

190. What will Mr. Mendez do?
(A) Hire Ms. Krim right away
(B) Check Ms. Krim's credentials
(C) Speak with Ms. Krim's former employer
(D) Notify Ms. Krim when a position is available

Questions 191–195 refer to the following memo and e-mail.

MEMO

To: All personnel
From: Marvin McLean, Office Manager
Re: Workplace safety workshop
Date: November 17

On December 7, a workshop on workplace safety will be offered by Elvira Walters of the National Workplace Safety Commission. The workshop will take place in Conference Room 2 from 9:30 to 11:30. This workshop is required for all department heads and recommended for all staff members. Please let me know before November 22 if you plan to attend. Also, please let me know if you cannot attend at this time but are still interested. If there is enough interest, we will offer the workshop again at a later date. Finally, because the end of the year is fast approaching, let me take this opportunity to remind everyone that attendance at a minimum of three staff development workshops per year is required of all personnel. A schedule of upcoming workshops is posted outside my office.

To: marvin_mclean@zipsys.com
From: sandy_bayliss@zipsys.com
Subject: safety workshop

Hi, Marvin,
I would like to attend next month's workshop on workplace safety that was mentioned in the memo you sent out yesterday. Please put me on the list. After this workshop, I will have fulfilled my attendance requirement for this year. Also, I would like to apologize in advance because I will probably arrive about 15 minutes late. I have to be downtown early that morning for a breakfast meeting, but it shouldn't last much past 9:00, and then I can catch the subway to the office. I hope a slightly late arrival won't be a problem.
Thanks.
Sandy

---

191. Who has to attend the workshop?
(A) All staff members
(B) The security officer
(C) Department heads
(D) The office manager

192. When did Sandy Bayliss write her e-mail message?
(A) November 17
(B) November 18
(C) November 22
(D) December 7

193. What time will Sandy Bayliss probably arrive at the workshop?
(A) 9:00
(B) 9:15
(C) 9:30
(D) 9:45

194. How many workshops has Sandy Bayliss already attended this year?
(A) One
(B) Two
(C) Three
(D) Four

195. Where will Sandy's breakfast meeting take place?
(A) At Marvin McLean's office
(B) At her office
(C) Downtown
(D) In Conference Room 2

Questions 196–200 refer to the following warranty notice and letter.

NOTICE OF WARRANTY
Paper Eater 2000 Deluxe Office Paper Shredder

Paper Eater, Inc. warrants to the original purchaser of this product that it is free from defects for one year from the date of purchase. We will repair any manufacturing defects, or if we deem repair to be impracticable, we will replace the entire product with a new one. Repair or replacement are guaranteed only when the product has not been mishandled and has been used according to our instructions. Products that have been dropped or thrown or to which any item other than paper, such as staples, paper clips, or pieces of plastic, have been introduced are not covered by the terms of this warranty.

When returning a product for repair, please enclose it in its original packaging and include a purchase receipt and the model number. Customers will be charged for any repairs outside the limits of this warranty.

April 1, 20--

Customer Service Department
Paper Eater, Inc.
17 Main Street
Harlowe's Junction, OH

Dear Customer Service,

I was excited about my recent purchase of a Paper Eater 2000 Deluxe Office Paper Shredder. Many sensitive financial reports come through my office, so a reliable and durable paper shredder is a necessity for me. I chose the Paper Eater 2000 Deluxe because I read many good reviews of it online and in consumer magazines. At first it lived up to its reputation, shredding large volumes of paper without a glitch. At one point, I even spilled a box of paper clips into it, but that didn't appear to slow it down. Then last week it completely stopped, and I have not been able to get it going again. I have to say I am not pleased about this at all. I have owned this machine only since the beginning of February. I would expect that a machine with such a good reputation would last a good deal longer. I am returning the machine herewith, wrapped up in a brand new box. The receipt, including place and date of purchase and the machine's model number, are enclosed. Please send me my refund as soon as possible. Thank you.

Sincerely,

Arnold Ahern

196. When did the customer buy his paper shredder?
    (A) A week ago
    (B) A month ago
    (C) Two months ago
    (D) One year ago

197. What does the customer shred in his paper shredder?
    (A) Financial reports
    (B) Magazines
    (C) Receipts
    (D) Product instructions

198. How does the customer feel about the paper shredder now?
    (A) Excited
    (B) Displeased
    (C) Good
    (D) Sensitive

199. What did the customer neglect to include when returning the shredder?
    (A) The receipt
    (B) The model number
    (C) The refund form
    (D) The original packaging

200. How will the customer service department probably respond?
    (A) They will issue a refund.
    (B) They will replace the product.
    (C) They will charge for the repair.
    (D) They will sell the customer a new product.

Answer Key
PRACTICE TEST 1

Listening Comprehension

Part 1: Photographs

1. C	4. A	7. C	9. A
2. B	5. A	8. B	10. D
3. D	6. D		

Part 2: Question-Response

11. A	19. B	27. A	35. B
12. B	20. A	28. A	36. B
13. C	21. C	29. C	37. C
14. B	22. A	30. B	38. A
15. C	23. B	31. A	39. C
16. A	24. C	32. A	40. B
17. A	25. B	33. C	
18. C	26. B	34. A	

Part 3: Conversations

41. C	49. A	57. B	65. A
42. D	50. D	58. C	66. D
43. B	51. D	59. B	67. D
44. A	52. C	60. D	68. B
45. A	53. C	61. D	69. D
46. C	54. B	62. C	70. C
47. B	55. C	63. B	
48. B	56. A	64. A	

Part 4: Talks

71. A	79. A	87. D	95. C
72. B	80. B	88. D	96. A
73. C	81. D	89. A	97. D
74. C	82. A	90. C	98. B
75. D	83. B	91. D	99. D
76. D	84. C	92. A	100. A
77. C	85. A	93. B	
78. D	86. A	94. B	

Answer Key

PRACTICE TEST 1

Reading

Part 5: Incomplete Sentences

101. **A**	111. **C**	121. **A**	131. **C**
102. **C**	112. **A**	122. **B**	132. **C**
103. **D**	113. **C**	123. **A**	133. **A**
104. **B**	114. **B**	124. **D**	134. **D**
105. **A**	115. **A**	125. **B**	135. **B**
106. **C**	116. **B**	126. **C**	136. **D**
107. **D**	117. **C**	127. **A**	137. **C**
108. **C**	118. **D**	128. **D**	138. **C**
109. **B**	119. **D**	129. **A**	139. **A**
110. **D**	120. **C**	130. **B**	140. **B**

Part 6: Text Completion

141. **A**	144. **B**	147. **A**	150. **C**
142. **B**	145. **C**	148. **C**	151. **B**
143. **D**	146. **D**	149. **D**	152. **C**

Part 7: Reading Comprehension

153. **A**	165. **C**	177. **D**	189. **B**
154. **A**	166. **B**	178. **A**	190. **D**
155. **C**	167. **A**	179. **A**	191. **C**
156. **B**	168. **D**	180. **B**	192. **B**
157. **D**	169. **C**	181. **B**	193. **D**
158. **B**	170. **D**	182. **C**	194. **B**
159. **A**	171. **B**	183. **A**	195. **C**
160. **A**	172. **A**	184. **B**	196. **C**
161. **C**	173. **A**	185. **D**	197. **A**
162. **B**	174. **C**	186. **B**	198. **B**
163. **D**	175. **C**	187. **A**	199. **D**
164. **C**	176. **C**	188. **D**	200. **C**

TOEIC PRACTICE TEST 1—ANSWERS EXPLAINED

Listening Comprehension

PART 1: PHOTOGRAPHS

1. **(C)** A group of businesspeople at a conference table are clapping their hands; they have probably just finished listening to a presentation. Choice (A) misidentifies the action they are doing with their hands. Choice (B) identifies the glasses that are on the table, but no one is filling them. Choice (D) refers to the movement of their hands, but they are *applauding* not *waving*.

2. **(B)** People are carrying umbrellas and the street looks wet, so it's a rainy day. Choice (A) confuses similar-sounding words *rain* and *train*. Choice (C) correctly identifies the umbrellas but not their location. Choice (D) correctly identifies the action of the people but not their location.

3. **(D)** A dentist is working on or examining a patient's teeth. Choice (A) confuses the dentist's drill in the photo with a carpenter's drill. Choice (B) misidentifies the position of the patient. Choice (C) correctly identifies the gloves, but misidentifies the person wearing them.

4. **(A)** A man and a woman are looking at a house under construction and the woman is pointing to it, so they must be talking about it. Choice (B) identifies the incomplete window in the house, but there is no glass in it yet, so it can't be closed. Choice (C) refers to the plans in their hands, but they are referring to the plans, not printing them. Choice (D) confuses similar-sounding words *house* and *mouse*.

5. **(A)** The plane is at the airport, not up in the air, so it has already landed. Choice (B) uses the associated word *passengers*, but there are none in the photo. Choice (C) confuses similar-sounding words *plane* and *train*. Choice (D) uses the associated word *pilot*, but there isn't one in the photo.

6. **(D)** A couple is looking at clothes in a store window. Choice (A) correctly identifies the hats in the photo, but they are on the people's heads, not in their hands. Choice (B) mentions the window, but it is not broken. Choice (C) mentions the people's bags, but the bags are in their hands, not in the car.

7. **(C)** A man in business attire is standing and talking to a group of people also dressed in business attire—his colleagues. Choice (A) confuses similar-sounding words *talking* and *walking*. Choice (B) confuses *business suit* with *bathing suit*. Choice (D) misidentifies the man's action; he is *gesturing* with his hands, not *looking out* a window.

8. **(B)** This is a sidewalk café and chairs and tables are placed outside on the sidewalk. Choice (A) correctly identifies the people as customers, but they are *outside*, not *inside*. Choice (C) uses the associated word *waiter*. Choice (D) misidentifies the location of the tables.

9. **(A)** A woman is holding a newspaper and looking at it. Choice (B) confuses similar-sounding words *reading* and *eating*. Choice (C) correctly identifies the

action, *looking*, but confuses *newspaper* with *new shoes*. Choice (D) associates reporting the *news* with *newspaper*.

10. **(D)** Cars on a highway are moving under a highway bridge. Choice (A) uses the associated word *truck*, but no trucks are visible. Choice (B) is incorrect because the bridge crosses a highway, not a river. Choice (C) is incorrect because there is a lot of traffic on the highway.

PART 2: QUESTION-RESPONSE

11. **(A)** This answers the question *What time?* Choice (B) confuses the meaning of the word *program*. Choice (C) repeats the word *begin*.

12. **(B)** This answers the question about possession. Choice (A) confuses the meaning of the word *coat*. Choice (C) confuses similar-sounding words *coat* and *note*.

13. **(C)** The mention of rain prompts the second speaker to offer an umbrella. Choice (A) confuses similar-sounding words *rain* and *again*. Choice (B) confuses similar-sounding words *rain* and *train*.

14. **(B)** *On your desk* answers the question *Where?* Choice (A) confuses *new* and *newspaper*. Choice (C) associates *newspaper* with *read*.

15. **(C)** This answers the question *How many?* Choice (A) confuses the meaning of the word *meeting*. Choice (B) confuses *showed up* with *showed*.

16. **(A)** *My boss* answers the question *Who?* Choice (B) confuses *assignment* with the similar-sounding phrase *signed it*. Choice (C) answers the question *When?*

17. **(A)** This answers the question *How long?* Choice (B) repeats the word *long*. Choice (C) confuses similar-sounding words *last* and *fast*.

18. **(C)** The complaint about the warm room prompts the speaker to offer to open a window. Choice (A) repeats the phrase *in here*. Choice (B) confuses *warm* with the similar-sounding word *warned*.

19. **(B)** *No* answers the tag question *isn't it?* Choice (A) repeats the word *desk*. Choice (C) repeats the phrase *by the door*.

20. **(A)** *In an hour* answers the question *When?* Choice (B) confuses *arrive* with the similar-sounding word *drive*. Choice (C) answers the question *How?*

21. **(C)** *Mr. Kim* answers the question *Who?* Choice (A) associates *phone* with *call*. Choice (B) repeats the word *phone*.

22. **(A)** *Black and silver* answers the question about color. Choice (B) repeats the word *car*. Choice (C) associates *car* with *drive*.

23. **(B)** This answers the question *Where?* Choice (A) repeats the words *copy machine*. Choice (C) repeats the word *find*.

24. **(C)** The mention of being hungry prompts the second speaker to suggest a lunch break. Choice (A) confuses similar-sounding words *hungry* and *hurry*. Choice (B) confuses similar-sounding words *hungry* and *angry*.

25. **(B)** This explains the reason for the lateness. Choice (A) confuses similar-sounding words *late* and *eight*. Choice (C) confuses similar-sounding words *late* and *plate*.

26. **(B)** This answers the question about a place to eat. Choice (A) associates *eat* with *food*. Choice (C) confuses similar-sounding words *eat* and *seat*.

27. **(A)** This is a logical response to a remark about how long the trip will take. Choice (B) repeats the word *airport*. Choice (C) associates *airport* with *fly*.

28. **(A)** *Not much* answers the question *How much?* Choice (B) confuses *cost* with the similar-sounding word *lost*. Choice (C) repeats the word *computer*.

29. **(C)** *Friday* answers the question *What day?* Choice (A) confuses the meaning of the word *meeting*. Choice (B) confuses similar-sounding words *meeting* and *seating*.

30. **(B)** This answers the question *Who?* Choice (A) confuses similar-sounding words *dinner* and *thinner*. Choice (C) associates *dinner* with *ate*.

31. **(A)** This answers the yes-no question about the building. Choice (B) repeats the word *building*. Choice (C) repeats the word *work*.

32. **(A)** This answers the question about possession. Choices (B) and (C) repeat parts of the word *briefcase*.

33. **(C)** This answers the yes-no question about the letters. Choice (A) confuses similar-sounding words *letters* and *later*. Choice (B) associates *letters* with *envelopes*.

34. **(A)** Feeling sick is the reason for not being at the office. Choice (B) repeats the word *office*. Choice (C) confuses *yesterday* with similar-sounding words *day* and *today*.

35. **(B)** This is a logical response to the comment about the hotel. Choice (A) confuses similar-sounding words *hotel* and *tell*. Choice (C) associates *hotel* with *reservation*.

36. **(B)** *The subway* answers the question about how to get *downtown*. Choice (A) repeats part of the word *downtown*. Choice (C) repeats the entire word *downtown*.

37. **(C)** *Tomorrow* answers the question *When?* Choice (A) associates *call* with *phone*. Choice (B) confuses the meaning of the word *call*.

38. **(A)** This explains Tom's problem. Choice (B) confuses *matter* with the similar-sounding word *chatter*. Choice (C) confuses *matter* with the similar-sounding word *flatter*.

39. **(C)** *Hot tea* answers the question about a drink. Choice (A) associates *drink* with *glass*. Choice (B) confuses similar-sounding words *drink* and *think*.

40. **(B)** *Across the street* answers the question *Where?* Choice (A) confuses similar-sounding words *car* and *card*. Choice (C) associates *car* with *drive*.

PART 3: CONVERSATIONS

41. **(C)** The man suggests that they leave at 3:00 and the woman agrees. Choices (A) and (B) confuse the similar-sounding words *due* and *two*. Choice (D) is the time the plane will arrive.

42. **(D)** The woman suggests going by subway and the man agrees. Choice (A) confuses the similar-sounding words *bus* and *but*. Choice (B) confuses the similar-sounding words *car* and *far*. Choice (C) is what the woman says they shouldn't do.

43. **(B)** The man says he will meet the woman at her office. Choice (A) is where they will go together. Choice (C) repeats the word *office*. Choice (D) is also where they will go together.

44. **(A)** The envelopes are on aisle 6 and they are on sale, both situations that suggest this is a store. Choice (B) associates *envelopes*, *printers*, and *ink* with an office. Choice (C) associates *envelope* with a post office. Choice (D) associates *save money* with a bank.

45. **(A)** The man asks where the envelopes are. Choices (B) and (C) are confused with the printer paper that is on the shelf near the envelopes. Choice (D) repeats the word *money*.

46. **(C)** The woman says she will order more envelopes if the man can't find the style he wants on the shelf. Choice (A) repeats the word *shelf*. Choice (B) repeats the word *style*. Choice (D) confuses *count* with the similar-sounding word *discount* and repeats the word *money*.

47. **(B)** This is what the man says he will be doing at that time. Choice (A) is what Mr. Lee wants. Choice (C) confuses *later* with the similar-sounding word *letter*. Choice (D) is what the man will do after his meeting with the accountants.

48. **(B)** The woman says that Mr. Lee wants to go over the marketing plan. Choice (A) is confused with the phone call between Mr. Lee and the woman about making the appointment. Choice (C) is confused with the meeting that the man will be at. Choice (D) is confused with the accountants who will be at the meeting.

49. **(A)** This is the time the man suggests. Choice (B) confuses 11 with the similar-sounding number 7. Choice (C) confuses 9 with the similar-sounding word *find*. Choice (D) confuses 10 with the similar-sounding word *then*.

50. **(D)** This is when the woman says the copies will be ready. Choice (A) is when the woman got the originals. Choice (B) is when the man wants them. Choice (C) confuses *right* with the similar-sounding word *night*.

51. **(D)** This is the total number of copies the woman mentions. Choice (A) is the number of extra copies she will make. Choice (B) confuses 75 with 70. Choice (C) is the number of copies the man asked for.

52. **(C)** This is what the woman asks for. Choice (A) repeats the word *lunch*, which is related to when the woman got the originals. Choices (B) and (D) repeat things the woman mentioned, but she didn't ask the man for them.

53. **(C)** The man has reserved two nights at the hotel and the woman asks him to add one more. Choice (A) is not mentioned. Choice (B) is the number of nights the man has reserved. Choice (D) confuses the number 4 with the word *for*.

54. **(B)** The woman asks the man to call the hotel back and add one more night to her reservation. Choice (A) confuses the meaning of the word *book*. Choice (C) is what the woman wants to do while she is at the hotel. Choice (D) is what the man is doing now.

55. **(C)** This is when the man says he will do it. Choice (A) is when the man is typing reports. Choice (B) is when the man called the hotel. Choice (D) confuses *tonight* with *night*.

56. **(A)** The woman mentions the *thick fog*. Choice (B) confuses similar-sounding words *know* and *snow*. Choice (C) confuses similar-sounding words *train* and *rain*. Choice (D) is how the man hopes the weather will be soon.

57. **(B)** The man explains that Jack will be late because *the traffic is so heavy*. Choice (A) confuses similar-sounding words *thick* and *sick*. Choice (C) is what the woman says didn't happen to her. Choice (D) is where the man will go later on.

58. **(C)** This is what the man tells the woman. Choice (A) repeats the woman's words *I wasn't delayed even one minute*. Choice (B) confuses similar-sounding words *even* and *eleven*. Choice (D) is confused with the time the man has to be at a meeting.

59. **(B)** The man asks for directions to the post office. Choice (A) repeats the word *office*. Choice (C) is near the post office. Choice (D) confuses *parking lot* with *park*.

60. **(D)** The woman says *you'll see it on the corner*. Choice (A) repeats *two blocks* and *parking lot*. Choice (B) is incorrect because it is *next to* not *across the street from* the bank. Choice (C) repeats the first part of the directions.

61. **(D)** The woman says to go straight ahead for five blocks and then turn and go two more blocks. Choice (A) repeats the number *two*. Choice (B) confuses similar-sounding words *free* and *three*. Choice (C) repeats the number *five*.

62. **(C)** This is the news the man is telling the woman about. Choice (A) confuses *found out* with *found*. Choice (B) is true but it is not the reason for the man's excitement. Choice (D) confuses *speech* with *speaking*.

63. **(B)** The woman says that it is September now and the banquet is next month. Choice (A) is the current month. Choices (C) and (D) sound similar to *September*.

64. **(A)** This is what the woman says she will do. Choice (B) confuses similar-sounding words *deserve* and *serve*. Choice (C) confuses similar-sounding words *part* and *party*. Choice (D) confuses similar-sounding words *banquet* and *bank*.

65. **(A)** The woman is hungry and looking for a place to eat. Choice (B) confuses similar-sounding words *closed* and *clothes*. Choice (C) is what the man says he will do. Choice (D) associates *café* with *coffee*.

66. **(D)** The man says he has cash and will pay. Choice (A) confuses the meaning of the word *check*. Choice (B) confuses the meaning of the word *order*. Choice (C) is mentioned by the woman, but the man says he doesn't have this.

67. **(D)** This is what the man says. Choice (A) confuses similar-sounding words *do* and *two*. Choice (B) confuses similar-sounding words *late* and *eight*. Choice (C) confuses similar-sounding words *mind* and *nine*.

68. **(B)** The woman says she is looking for a business suit for her husband. Choice (A) is who the woman says she isn't shopping for. Choice (C) confuses *another* with the similar-sounding word *brother*. Choice (D) is mentioned, but not as the recipient of the suit.

69. **(D)** This is the color suit the woman says she wants. Choices (A), (B), and (C) are the colors of the summer suits that the woman rejects.

70. **(C)** This is the price the man gives. Choice (A) confuses the word *too* with the number *two*. Choice (B) confuses the word *for* with the number *four*. Choice (D) confuses similar-sounding words *fine* and *nine*.

PART 4: TALKS

71. **(A)** The speaker says that the train *will begin boarding* in five minutes. Choice (B) is mentioned but is not what will happen in five minutes. Choice (C) repeats the word *tickets*. Choice (D) confuses the meaning of the word *store*.

72. **(B)** This is the gate number the speaker gives. Choice (A) is confused with the time the train will depart. Choice (C) is the train number. Choice (D) sounds similar to the train number.

73. **(C)** This is the instruction the speaker gives. Choice (A) is confused with *check your ticket*. Choice (B) is what should be done with tickets. Choice (D) confuses similar-sounding words *rack* and *track*.

74. **(C)** At Prescott, a customer can open an account, transfer funds, order checks, and apply for a loan, so it is a bank. Choice (A) confuses *account* with *accountants*. Choice (B) confuses the meaning of the word *party*. Choice (D) repeats the word *credit card*.

75. **(D)** The recording says to press 6 to speak with a customer service representative. Choice (A) is the number to press to ask questions about an existing account. Choice (B) is the number to press to order new checks. Choice (C) is the number to press to apply for a loan.

76. **(D)** The recording says to press zero in order to hear the menu again. Choice (A) is what the caller can do by pressing one. Choice (B) is what the caller can do by pressing two. Choice (C) is what the caller can do by pressing four.

77. **(C)** The speaker says that this is often a problem *after lunch*, that is, in the afternoon. Choice (A) is when people feel energetic. Choice (B) repeats the word *lunch*. Choice (D) is confused with *until the workday ends*.

78. **(D)** The speaker says to *take a brisk walk*. Choice (A) repeats the word *lunch*. Choices (B) and (C) are things the speaker says not to do.

79. **(A)** The speaker says to do this every hour. Choice (B) is how long it should be done. Choice (C) sounds similar to *for five minutes*. Choice (D) is not mentioned.

80. **(B)** The speaker mentions such items as desks, chairs, and bookshelves, so it is a furniture store. Choice (A) confuses similar-sounding words *closing* and *clothes*. Choice (C) confuses *computer stands* with *computers*. Choice (D) confuses similar-sounding words *far* and *car*.

81. **(D)** This is the discount the speaker mentions. Choices (A), (B), and (C) sound similar to the correct answer.

82. **(A)** This is the time the speaker mentions. Choice (B) is confused with both *week* and *end*. Choice (C) is when the sale ends. Choice (D) repeats the word *month*.

83. **(B)** The ad is for the Computer Training Institute, where people are trained as computer technicians. Choice (A) is what you can learn to do in the training course. Choice (C) is confused with the employment service offered to graduates of the training course. Choice (D) is what students in the training course learn to repair.

84. **(C)** The ad mentions this as the cost of the six-month course. Choice (A) sounds similar to the correct answer. Choices (B) and (D) sound similar to the length of the course—six months.

85. **(A)** Listeners are told to visit a website to sign up for the course. Choice (B) repeats the word *office*. Choice (C) confuses similar-sounding words *all* and *call*. Choice (D) is not mentioned.

86. **(A)** The speaker says that snow is falling. Choice (B) confuses similar-sounding words *train* and *rain*. Choices (C) and (D) are how the weather will be tomorrow.

87. **(D)** The speaker says *don't go out*. Choice (A) is what the speaker says not to do. Choice (B) is confused with *accidents have been reported*. Choice (C) is confused with *commuter trains are experiencing delays*.

88. **(D)** The weather will be clear tomorrow. Choices (A), (B), and (C) are all times when the snow will continue to fall.

89. **(A)** The speaker says that workshops will be held in the conference rooms on the first floor. Choices (B) and (C) are what will happen in the restaurant on the ground floor. Choice (D) is confused with the demonstration of computer software that will take place in the auditorium.

90. **(C)** The demonstration of computer software will take place at 2:00. Choice (A) is when lunch will be served. Choice (B) is when afternoon workshops will begin. Choice (D) is when refreshments will be served.

91. **(D)** The speakers says that refreshments will be enjoyed outside on the patio. Choice (A) is where workshops will take place. Choice (B) is where lunch will be served. Choice (C) is confused with the name of the place where lunch will be served, the *Garden Restaurant*.

92. **(A)** The speaker says *Park Street Station is closed*. Choice (B) is incorrect because the speaker says that bus service is available. Choice (C) confuses the meaning of the word *park* and repeats the word *available*. Choice (D) repeats the word *curb*.

93. **(B)** This is the problem the speaker mentions. Choice (A) confuses similar-sounding words *train* and *rain*. Choice (C) repeats the word *crowd*. Choice (D) repeats the word *traffic*.

94. **(B)** The speaker says that the station will reopen in three weeks. Choice (A) confuses similar-sounding words *due* and *two*. Choice (C) confuses the word *for* with the number *four*. Choice (D) is not mentioned.

95. **(C)** The president will take a *five-nation tour*. Choice (A) confuses the word *to* with the number *two*. Choice (B) confuses the word *for* with the number *four*. Choice (D) is the number of days his trip will last.

96. **(A)** The president will *discuss the current economic situation*. Choice (B) confuses *leaders* with *leadership*. Choice (C) confuses similar-sounding words *where* and *war*. Choice (D) is confused with the scientists who will be at the banquet.

97. **(D)** The president will take a few days of rest at his beach house. Choice (A) is something he will do during his trip. Choice (B) is confused with the awards he will give at the banquet. Choice (C) confuses similar-sounding words *rest* and *restaurant*.

98. **(B)** The speaker is offering the opportunity to attend a management training workshop. Choice (A) is where the opportunity is announced. Choice (C) confuses the meaning of the word *train*. Choice (D) confuses *workshop* with *shop*.

99. **(D)** This is when the speaker says the workshop is offered. Choice (A) confuses similar-sounding words *month* and *Monday*. Choice (B) is when the speaker wants to hear from all those wishing to attend. Choice (C) confuses *December*, when the workshop will take place, with the similar-sounding word *September*.

100. **(A)** This is what the speaker says people will need to bring. Choice (B) is mentioned but not as something to bring. Choice (C) will be provided. Choice (D) refers to the list of attendees the speaker will make.

READING

PART 5: INCOMPLETE SENTENCES

101. **(A)** *Document* is a singular noun and takes the third person singular form of the verb to be: *is*. Choice (B) is the first person singular form. Choices (C) and (D) are plural forms.

102. **(C)** This is the adjective form, used to describe the noun *businessperson*. Choices (A) and (D) are nouns. Choice (B) is a verb.

103. **(D)** The pencils are inside, or in, the drawer. Choice (A) describes movement from one side to another. Choices (B) and (C) are extremely unlikely places to find a pencil relative to a drawer.

104. **(B)** This is a passive voice sentence and uses the past participle form of the verb. Choice (A) is the simple present or base form. Choice (C) is the present participle. Choice (D) is the noun form.

105. **(A)** A future real conditional sentence uses future tense in the main clause. Choice (B) is present perfect. Choice (C) is simple past. Choice (D) is present progressive.

106. **(C)** This is the adjective form, used to describe the noun *employees*. Choice (A) is a present tense or base form verb. Choice (B) is a present participle verb. Choice (D) is a noun.

107. **(D)** *Received* means *got*. Choices (A), (B), and (C) all look similar to the correct answer but have very different meanings.

108. **(C)** This is the noun form referring to a person in the position of subject of the clause. Choice (A) is a verb. Choice (B) is a past tense verb. Choice (D) is a noun but refers to a situation, not a person.

109. **(B)** *Until* introduces the time clause, which tells us when the action in the main clause, *go home*, will occur. Choice (A) introduces a condition, which would not make sense with the negative idea of the main clause. Choices (C)

and (D) introduce a reason that, again, would not make sense with the negative idea of the main clause.

110. **(D)** *Through* means to move from one side to the other. Choices (A), (B), and (C) are not logical for the context of a door.

111. **(C)** The base form of the verb follows the modal *could*. Choice (A) is past tense. Choice (B) is past participle. Choice (D) is a noun.

112. **(A)** *Admitted* means to *be let in*. Choices (B), (C), and (D) all look similar to the correct answer but have very different meanings.

113. **(C)** *Beside* means *next to*. Choices (A), (B), and (D) look similar to the correct answer but do not fit the context of the sentence.

114. **(B)** *Descends* means *goes down*. Choices (A), (C), and (D) all have the meaning of *goes down* but are not used to describe the motion of an elevator.

115. **(A)** This is an imperative verb, telling the listener what to do. Choice (B) is simple present tense. Choice (C) is simple past tense. Choice (D) is present participle.

116. **(B)** A future time clause uses a present tense verb. Choice (A) is past tense. Choice (C) is the present participle form. Choice (D) is future tense.

117. **(C)** *Because* indicates a cause-and-effect relationship between the two events. Choice (A) introduces a condition. Choices (B) and (D) imply contrast.

118. **(D)** *Insists* in this context means *requires*. Choices (A), (B), and (C) look similar to the correct answer but have very different meanings.

119. **(D)** *Although* implies a contrast between the two clauses; one would expect hardworking Mr. Lee to get a promotion, but he hasn't gotten one. Choice (A) indicates a cause-and-effect relationship. Choice (B) could be used with *though* but cannot stand alone in this sentence. Choice (C) needs to be followed by a gerund, not a clause.

120. **(C)** This is a present perfect verb used to describe an action that started in the past and continues into the present. Choice (A) is simple present tense. Choice (B) is past tense. Choice (D) is future tense.

121. **(A)** A noun form is needed as the object of the verb *require*. Choice (B) is an adjective. Choice (C) is a noun but refers to a person, so it does not fit the context. Choice (D) is a verb.

122. **(B)** This is a past unreal conditional *if* clause, so it uses the past perfect form of the verb. Choice (A) is simple past. Choice (C) is present perfect. Choice (D) is past conditional and is used for a main clause.

123. **(A)** The base form of a verb is needed to complete the infinitive verb in the sentence. Choices (B) and (C) are adjectives. Choice (D) is a noun.

124. **(D)** *Show up* means *appear* or *arrive*. (A), (B), and (C) cannot be logically used in this sentence.

125. **(B)** *Across the street from* means *on the other side of the street*. Choices (A), (C), and (D) are not followed by *from*.

126. **(C)** The modal *should* is followed by a base form verb. Choice (A) is future tense. Choice (B) is present participle. Choice (D) is past tense.

127. **(A)** *Quality* is a noun meaning *excellence* or *high value*. Choices (B) and (C) look similar to the correct answer but have different meanings. Choice (D) is a verb, not a noun.

128. **(D)** *Expect* is followed by the infinitive form of the verb. Choice (A) is base form or present tense. Choice (B) is past tense. Choice (C) is present participle or a gerund.

129. **(A)** In a passive-voice sentence, *by* introduces the performer of the action. Choices (B), (C), and (D) are not used in this position in a passive-voice sentence.

130. **(B)** Time expressions with *from . . . to* tell when an event begins and ends. Choices (A), (C), and (D) are not used in expressions with *from*.

131. **(C)** *Have to* plus the base form of a verb indicates necessity. Choices (A) and (D) lack the word *to*. Choice (B) is past tense so cannot be used in this sentence about the present.

132. **(C)** A noun is required to act as the subject of the sentence. Choice (A) is an adverb. Choice (B) is an adjective. Choice (D) is a verb.

133. **(A)** This is an imperative verb, telling the listener what to do. Choice (B) is past tense. Choice (C) is present participle or a gerund. Choice (D) is future tense.

134. **(D)** This is a preposition of place describing the position of the rug. Choices (A) and (B) are nouns. Choice (C) is an adverb.

135. **(B)** *Were* agrees with the plural noun *books*. Choices (A) and (C) are singular. Choice (D) is an auxiliary verb and cannot be used without a main verb.

136. **(D)** *During* is a preposition, placed before a noun, describing when the people fell asleep. Choices (A), (B), and (C) are used to introduce a clause.

137. **(C)** The present participle form is needed to complete the present continuous verb *is expanding*. Choices (A) and (B) are simple present tense. Choice (D) is present perfect.

138. **(C)** The subject of the sentence, *the building*, received the action, so a passive-voice verb is required. Choices (A), (B), and (D) are all active-voice forms.

139. **(A)** A noun is needed to act as the object of the verb *have*. Choice (B) is a noun but has a meaning that doesn't fit the context of the sentence. Choices (C) and (D) are verbs.

140. **(B)** *Confidential* means *private* or *secret*. Choices (A), (C), and (D) look similar to the correct answer but don't fit the context of the sentence.

PART 6: TEXT COMPLETION

141. **(A)** We know that sales are *decreasing*, or going down, because fewer customers are coming into the store. Choice (B) is the opposite meaning. Choice (C) means *staying the same*. Choice (D) is related to sales but doesn't fit the context.

142. **(B)** The store has had to *lay off*, or fire, employees because business has been so bad. Choices (A) and (D) are things they might do with new employees. Choice (C) means *hire*, the opposite of the correct answer.

143. **(D)** Unemployed people might seek *benefits*, or assistance, from the government. Choice (A) refers to people who receive benefits. Choice (B) refers to people who help others. Choice (C) is an adjective describing things that are good or helpful.

144. **(B)** This is a simple past tense verb used to describe an action that was completed in the past, two years ago. Choice (A) is simple present. Choice (C) is present perfect. Choice (D) is past perfect.

145. **(C)** We know that Mr. Richardson is reliable because the next sentence says *We could always count on him.* Choices (A), (B), and (D) are also good qualities for an employee but do not fit the context.

146. **(D)** *Him* refers to Mr. Richardson. It is an object pronoun after a preposition. Choice (A) is a subject pronoun. Choice (B) is an object pronoun, but it is first person plural. Choice (C) refers to a woman.

147. **(A)** A *refund* is a return of money, which is what customers hope for when they return purchases. Choices (B), (C), and (D) look similar to the correct answer but don't fit the context.

148. **(C)** *Their* refers to the third person plural noun *items*. Choices (A) and (B) refer to a third person singular noun. Choice (D) is second person.

149. **(D)** The subject of the sentence, *questions*, receives the action (presumably it is the customers who perform it), so passive voice is required. Choices (A), (B), and (C) are all active voice.

150. **(C)** The adverb form is used to modify the adjective *located*. Choice (A) is an adjective. Choice (B) is a noun. Choice (D) is an adverb but belongs to a different word family and has a completely different meaning.

151. **(B)** *Ample* means *plentiful*. Choice (A) is opposite in meaning, so it isn't logical here. Choices (C) and (D) could be used to describe parking but don't fit the context.

152. **(C)** This is an imperative verb form telling readers what to do. Choice (A) could be imperative but is affirmative, so it isn't logical here. Choice (B) is a gerund. Choice (D) isn't imperative, so it requires mention of the subject.

PART 7: READING COMPREHENSION

153. **(A)** The company type is stated in the first sentence. Choice (B) is confused with the previous tenant of the office. Choice (C) is confused with the type of company that owns the office building. Choice (D) is confused with the other company that opened recently nearby.

154. **(A)** The article says *The new Park and Smith office was open for business as of yesterday.* Choice (B) is when the stock brokerage office opened. Choice (C) is when the company closed other branch offices. Choice (D) is confused with how long the office space had been vacant.

155. **(C)** The company president says *It is just the type of community where services such as ours are needed.* Choice (A) is true but not the reason they opened an office in Salem. Choice (B) is confused with the reason why the other branch offices were closed. Choice (D) is associated with renting a new office but not mentioned.

156. **(B)** The word *facilitate* means *to make something happen more easily.* Choices (A), (C), and (D) don't fit the meaning of the sentence.

157. **(D)** Boris Lutz won a prize, or award. Choice (A) is associated with his place of work—a bank. Choice (B) confuses the meaning of *promote* as it is used here—to promote, or encourage, goodwill. Choice (C) is confused with Maria Pendleton's job.

158. **(B)** The article says that Boris Lutz received the honor from his coworkers. Choices (A) and (C) are mentioned but are not the correct answer. Choice (D) repeats the word *community*.

159. **(A)** Boris's supervisor says that people at the bank are *pleased*, or happy. Choice (B) is confused with *pleased*. Choice (C) is how Boris feels. Choice (D) is not mentioned.

160. **(A)** Henry Judson explains several reasons why he doesn't like the factory and urges the city council members to vote against it. Choices (B), (C), and (D) repeat words used in the letter but are not the correct answer.

161. **(C)** Henry Judson explains that the company usually hires highly skilled technicians. Choice (A) is the type of person who does not usually work at Holbrook. Choice (B) repeats the word *blind* out of context. Choice (D) is related to the word *economy* but is not mentioned.

162. **(B)** This is when Henry Judson says the vote will take place. Choice (A) is when he read the newspaper article. Choice (C) was the original schedule for the vote. Choice (D) is when the company wants to begin construction of the factory.

163. **(D)** *Unsightly* means *ugly*—Henry Judson does not like the looks of the proposed building. Choice (A) is the opposite of the correct meaning. Choices (B) and (C) are words that could be used to describe a building but are not the correct answer.

164. **(C)** This business offers to provide food for conferences, meetings, and office parties, so it is a catering business. Choices (A), (B), and (D) are also businesses involving food but are not the correct answer.

165. **(C)** The advertisement says that the menu can be seen on the website. Choices (A), (B), and (D) are mentioned but are not the correct answer.

166. **(B)** The company wants to hire writers, editors, and proofreaders, so it is probably a publishing company.

167. **(A)** The ad directs job hunters to visit the company's website. Choice (B) is what job hunters are asked not to do. Choice (C) repeats the word *resume,* but the ad does not say to mail a resume, it says to attach one to the online application. Choice (D) repeats the word *letter* as in *letters of recommendation*, which are not required.

168. **(D)** This job requires three years' experience. Choice (A) mentions experience, but training can replace it. Choices (B) and (C) say that previous experience is not required.

169. **(C)** This is the total amount due. Choice (A) is the charge for the painting only. Choice (B) is the charge for the carpentry only. Choice (D) is the total amount due plus the previous balance, but because the previous balance has been paid in full, it is no longer due.

170. **(D)** The bill asks for payment by the end of next month. Because the bill has a December date, January is the next month. Choice (A) is the end of the month when the work was done. Choice (B) is the date on the bill. Choice (C) is the end of the current month.

171. **(B)** The instructions mention making calls and dialing, so the product is a telephone. Choices (A), (C), and (D) are mentioned but are not the correct answer.

172. **(A)** The customer is asked to contact the manufacturer by phone for repair work. Choice (B) is explained but not in connection with repair. Choices (C) and (D) repeat words used in the text.

173. **(A)** According to the instructions, the product should not be used during an electrical, or thunder, storm. Choices (B) and (C) are mentioned but are not related to the question. Choice (D) repeats the word *electrical.*

174. **(C)** The instructions say to disconnect the product from the electrical outlet. Choices (A), (B), and (D) are mentioned as things not to do when cleaning the product.

175. **(C)** She was branch manager at the Riverside branch of the Windsor bank until two years ago, and she has been a student since then. Choice (A) is con-

fused with the new job she will be taking on—human resources director. Choice (B) is confused with her first job, at an accounting firm. Choice (D) is confused with *her instructors at the university*, who recommended her for her new job.

176. **(C)** This is where Ms. Simmons began her banking career. Choice (A) is the location of her new job. Choice (B) is confused with the name of the accounting firm where she used to work. Choice (D) is confused with the name of the branch of the Windsor bank where she was manager.

177. **(D)** According to the article, Ms. Simmons completed her degree last month. Choice (A) is when she began her banking career. Choice (B) is when she began working on her master's degree. Choice (C) is not mentioned.

178. **(A)** *Previous* means *former*, and this sentence refers to Ms. Simmons's employers from before. Choices (B), (C), and (D) don't fit the meaning of the sentence.

179. **(A)** *There will be no charge* for metered parking means *it will be free*. Choice (B) is incorrect because parking garages will be closed. Choice (C) is incorrect because there will be fares for subway rides—weekend fares. Choice (D) is incorrect because the bridge will be closed.

180. **(B)** The free parking is *because of the holiday*. Choice (A) describes the type of parking regulations and fares that will be in effect during the holiday. Choices (C) and (D) are mentioned but are not the reason for free parking.

181. **(B)** Myra writes that she will be flying to San Francisco, so she plans to go by plane. Choice (A) is confused with the bus that will be available for the tour. Choice (C) is not mentioned. Choice (D) is confused with Myra's plan to drive to Sacramento after the conference.

182. **(C)** Myra wants to *go over the project* with Raymond. Choice (A) is confused with the workshops at the conference. Choice (B) is related to the topic of Raymond's workshop. Choice (D) is related to the topic of Myra's workshop.

183. **(A)** Myra will not be available to meet with Raymond while she is giving her workshop on business law, which will take place at 9:15. Choices (B) and (C) are the beginning and ending times of the following workshop session. Choice (D) is the beginning time of the afternoon workshop session.

184. **(B)** According to her e-mail, Myra plans to attend the workshop given by Raymond, which takes place from 2:00 to 4:00. Choices (A), (C), and (D) are places where other conference events will take place.

185. **(D)** Myra will drive to Sacramento to attend a colleague's book signing. Choice (A) is what she wants to do during the day on Friday. Choice (B) repeats the words *sign* and *contract* out of context. Choice (C) is what she will do Friday morning.

186. **(B)** There is an opening for a researcher in the Marketing Department, and this is the position Ms. Krim wants to apply for. Choice (A) is the position Mr.

Mendez suggests she apply for. Choice (C) is her current position. Choice (D) is related to the department she currently works in.

187. **(A)** Ms. Krim says that she finished her degree *last month*. Her letter is dated July, so last month would be June. Choice (B) is the date of her letter. Choice (C) is the date of Mr. Mendez's letter. Choice (D) is when the marketing assistant job may be open.

188. **(D)** Ms. Petrowski, who is Ms. Krim's supervisor, recommends her for the job. Choices (A), (B), and (C) are other people mentioned in the letters.

189. **(B)** Ms. Krim has one year of experience in marketing and Mr. Mendez says that twice that amount is required. Choice (A) is the amount of experience Ms. Krim has. Choice (C) is the number of years she has worked in the accounting department. Choice (D) is not mentioned.

190. **(D)** Mr. Mendez writes that he anticipates that a new position will become available and that he will let Ms. Krim know about it. Choice (A) is what Ms. Krim wants him to do. Choices (B) and (C) are things he has already done.

191. **(C)** The workshop is required for department heads. Choice (A) is the people for whom it is recommended, but not required. Choice (B) is related to the topic—safety—of the workshop. Choice (D) is the person who wrote the memo.

192. **(B)** Sandy Bayliss refers to the memo of *yesterday*, which is dated November 17. Choice (A) is the date the memo was written. Choice (C) is the deadline for signing up for the workshop. Choice (D) is the date of the workshop.

193. **(D)** The workshop begins at 9:30 and she will arrive fifteen minutes late. Choice (A) is when her breakfast meeting will end. Choice (B) is fifteen minutes after the breakfast meeting. Choice (C) is the time the meeting will begin.

194. **(B)** Three workshops are required and this workshop will complete her requirement, so she has already attended two.

195. **(C)** She says that she has to be downtown for a breakfast meeting. Choice (A) refers to the office manager, who wrote the memo. Choice (B) repeats the word *office*. Choice (D) is where the workshop will take place.

196. **(C)** He bought it at the beginning of February and wrote the letter at the beginning of April. Choice (A) is when the shredder stopped working. Choice (B) is not mentioned. Choice (D) is confused with the length of the warranty.

197. **(A)** The customer says that he needs a paper shredder because of the sensitive financial reports that come to his office. Choice (B) is where he read reviews of the product. Choices (C) and (D) are items mentioned in the warranty notice.

198. **(B)** The customer says that he is *not pleased* about it. Choice (A) is how he felt when he bought it. Choice (C) repeats the word *pleased*. Choice (D) is the word used to describe the financial reports.

199. **(D)** The customer wrapped up the shredder in a *brand new box*, instead of in its original packaging as requested in the warranty notice. Choices (A) and (B) are things that he did include. Choice (C) is related to his request for a refund, but a refund form is not requested by the company.

200. **(C)** The warranty notice says, *Customers will be charged for any repairs outside the limits of this warranty.* The repair is outside the limits of the warranty because the customer spilled a box of paper clips into the product. Choice (A) is what the customer requests. Choice (B) is what is done in cases of manufacturing defects. Choice (D) is not mentioned.

Answer Sheet

TOEIC PRACTICE TEST 2

Listening Comprehension

Part 1: Photographs

1. Ⓐ Ⓑ Ⓒ Ⓓ
2. Ⓐ Ⓑ Ⓒ Ⓓ
3. Ⓐ Ⓑ Ⓒ Ⓓ
4. Ⓐ Ⓑ Ⓒ Ⓓ
5. Ⓐ Ⓑ Ⓒ Ⓓ
6. Ⓐ Ⓑ Ⓒ Ⓓ
7. Ⓐ Ⓑ Ⓒ Ⓓ
8. Ⓐ Ⓑ Ⓒ Ⓓ
9. Ⓐ Ⓑ Ⓒ Ⓓ
10. Ⓐ Ⓑ Ⓒ Ⓓ

Part 2: Question-Response

11. Ⓐ Ⓑ Ⓒ
12. Ⓐ Ⓑ Ⓒ
13. Ⓐ Ⓑ Ⓒ
14. Ⓐ Ⓑ Ⓒ
15. Ⓐ Ⓑ Ⓒ
16. Ⓐ Ⓑ Ⓒ
17. Ⓐ Ⓑ Ⓒ
18. Ⓐ Ⓑ Ⓒ
19. Ⓐ Ⓑ Ⓒ
20. Ⓐ Ⓑ Ⓒ
21. Ⓐ Ⓑ Ⓒ
22. Ⓐ Ⓑ Ⓒ
23. Ⓐ Ⓑ Ⓒ
24. Ⓐ Ⓑ Ⓒ
25. Ⓐ Ⓑ Ⓒ
26. Ⓐ Ⓑ Ⓒ
27. Ⓐ Ⓑ Ⓒ
28. Ⓐ Ⓑ Ⓒ
29. Ⓐ Ⓑ Ⓒ
30. Ⓐ Ⓑ Ⓒ
31. Ⓐ Ⓑ Ⓒ
32. Ⓐ Ⓑ Ⓒ
33. Ⓐ Ⓑ Ⓒ
34. Ⓐ Ⓑ Ⓒ
35. Ⓐ Ⓑ Ⓒ
36. Ⓐ Ⓑ Ⓒ
37. Ⓐ Ⓑ Ⓒ
38. Ⓐ Ⓑ Ⓒ
39. Ⓐ Ⓑ Ⓒ
40. Ⓐ Ⓑ Ⓒ

Part 3: Conversations

41. Ⓐ Ⓑ Ⓒ Ⓓ
42. Ⓐ Ⓑ Ⓒ Ⓓ
43. Ⓐ Ⓑ Ⓒ Ⓓ
44. Ⓐ Ⓑ Ⓒ Ⓓ
45. Ⓐ Ⓑ Ⓒ Ⓓ
46. Ⓐ Ⓑ Ⓒ Ⓓ
47. Ⓐ Ⓑ Ⓒ Ⓓ
48. Ⓐ Ⓑ Ⓒ Ⓓ
49. Ⓐ Ⓑ Ⓒ Ⓓ
50. Ⓐ Ⓑ Ⓒ Ⓓ
51. Ⓐ Ⓑ Ⓒ Ⓓ
52. Ⓐ Ⓑ Ⓒ Ⓓ
53. Ⓐ Ⓑ Ⓒ Ⓓ
54. Ⓐ Ⓑ Ⓒ Ⓓ
55. Ⓐ Ⓑ Ⓒ Ⓓ
56. Ⓐ Ⓑ Ⓒ Ⓓ
57. Ⓐ Ⓑ Ⓒ Ⓓ
58. Ⓐ Ⓑ Ⓒ Ⓓ
59. Ⓐ Ⓑ Ⓒ Ⓓ
60. Ⓐ Ⓑ Ⓒ Ⓓ
61. Ⓐ Ⓑ Ⓒ Ⓓ
62. Ⓐ Ⓑ Ⓒ Ⓓ
63. Ⓐ Ⓑ Ⓒ Ⓓ
64. Ⓐ Ⓑ Ⓒ Ⓓ
65. Ⓐ Ⓑ Ⓒ Ⓓ
66. Ⓐ Ⓑ Ⓒ Ⓓ
67. Ⓐ Ⓑ Ⓒ Ⓓ
68. Ⓐ Ⓑ Ⓒ Ⓓ
69. Ⓐ Ⓑ Ⓒ Ⓓ
70. Ⓐ Ⓑ Ⓒ Ⓓ

Part 4: Talks

71. Ⓐ Ⓑ Ⓒ Ⓓ
72. Ⓐ Ⓑ Ⓒ Ⓓ
73. Ⓐ Ⓑ Ⓒ Ⓓ
74. Ⓐ Ⓑ Ⓒ Ⓓ
75. Ⓐ Ⓑ Ⓒ Ⓓ
76. Ⓐ Ⓑ Ⓒ Ⓓ
77. Ⓐ Ⓑ Ⓒ Ⓓ
78. Ⓐ Ⓑ Ⓒ Ⓓ
79. Ⓐ Ⓑ Ⓒ Ⓓ
80. Ⓐ Ⓑ Ⓒ Ⓓ
81. Ⓐ Ⓑ Ⓒ Ⓓ
82. Ⓐ Ⓑ Ⓒ Ⓓ
83. Ⓐ Ⓑ Ⓒ Ⓓ
84. Ⓐ Ⓑ Ⓒ Ⓓ
85. Ⓐ Ⓑ Ⓒ Ⓓ
86. Ⓐ Ⓑ Ⓒ Ⓓ
87. Ⓐ Ⓑ Ⓒ Ⓓ
88. Ⓐ Ⓑ Ⓒ Ⓓ
89. Ⓐ Ⓑ Ⓒ Ⓓ
90. Ⓐ Ⓑ Ⓒ Ⓓ
91. Ⓐ Ⓑ Ⓒ Ⓓ
92. Ⓐ Ⓑ Ⓒ Ⓓ
93. Ⓐ Ⓑ Ⓒ Ⓓ
94. Ⓐ Ⓑ Ⓒ Ⓓ
95. Ⓐ Ⓑ Ⓒ Ⓓ
96. Ⓐ Ⓑ Ⓒ Ⓓ
97. Ⓐ Ⓑ Ⓒ Ⓓ
98. Ⓐ Ⓑ Ⓒ Ⓓ
99. Ⓐ Ⓑ Ⓒ Ⓓ
100. Ⓐ Ⓑ Ⓒ Ⓓ

Answer Sheet
TOEIC PRACTICE TEST 2

Reading

Part 5: Incomplete Sentences

101. Ⓐ Ⓑ Ⓒ Ⓓ
102. Ⓐ Ⓑ Ⓒ Ⓓ
103. Ⓐ Ⓑ Ⓒ Ⓓ
104. Ⓐ Ⓑ Ⓒ Ⓓ
106. Ⓐ Ⓑ Ⓒ Ⓓ
107. Ⓐ Ⓑ Ⓒ Ⓓ
108. Ⓐ Ⓑ Ⓒ Ⓓ
109. Ⓐ Ⓑ Ⓒ Ⓓ
110. Ⓐ Ⓑ Ⓒ Ⓓ
111. Ⓐ Ⓑ Ⓒ Ⓓ

112. Ⓐ Ⓑ Ⓒ Ⓓ
113. Ⓐ Ⓑ Ⓒ Ⓓ
114. Ⓐ Ⓑ Ⓒ Ⓓ
115. Ⓐ Ⓑ Ⓒ Ⓓ
116. Ⓐ Ⓑ Ⓒ Ⓓ
117. Ⓐ Ⓑ Ⓒ Ⓓ
118. Ⓐ Ⓑ Ⓒ Ⓓ
119. Ⓐ Ⓑ Ⓒ Ⓓ
120. Ⓐ Ⓑ Ⓒ Ⓓ
121. Ⓐ Ⓑ Ⓒ Ⓓ

122. Ⓐ Ⓑ Ⓒ Ⓓ
123. Ⓐ Ⓑ Ⓒ Ⓓ
124. Ⓐ Ⓑ Ⓒ Ⓓ
125. Ⓐ Ⓑ Ⓒ Ⓓ
126. Ⓐ Ⓑ Ⓒ Ⓓ
127. Ⓐ Ⓑ Ⓒ Ⓓ
128. Ⓐ Ⓑ Ⓒ Ⓓ
129. Ⓐ Ⓑ Ⓒ Ⓓ
130. Ⓐ Ⓑ Ⓒ Ⓓ
131. Ⓐ Ⓑ Ⓒ Ⓓ

132. Ⓐ Ⓑ Ⓒ Ⓓ
133. Ⓐ Ⓑ Ⓒ Ⓓ
134. Ⓐ Ⓑ Ⓒ Ⓓ
135. Ⓐ Ⓑ Ⓒ Ⓓ
136. Ⓐ Ⓑ Ⓒ Ⓓ
137. Ⓐ Ⓑ Ⓒ Ⓓ
138. Ⓐ Ⓑ Ⓒ Ⓓ
139. Ⓐ Ⓑ Ⓒ Ⓓ
140. Ⓐ Ⓑ Ⓒ Ⓓ

Part 6: Text Completion

141. Ⓐ Ⓑ Ⓒ Ⓓ
142. Ⓐ Ⓑ Ⓒ Ⓓ
143. Ⓐ Ⓑ Ⓒ Ⓓ

144. Ⓐ Ⓑ Ⓒ Ⓓ
145. Ⓐ Ⓑ Ⓒ Ⓓ
146. Ⓐ Ⓑ Ⓒ Ⓓ

147. Ⓐ Ⓑ Ⓒ Ⓓ
148. Ⓐ Ⓑ Ⓒ Ⓓ
149. Ⓐ Ⓑ Ⓒ Ⓓ

150. Ⓐ Ⓑ Ⓒ Ⓓ
151. Ⓐ Ⓑ Ⓒ Ⓓ
152. Ⓐ Ⓑ Ⓒ Ⓓ

Part 7: Reading Comprehension

153. Ⓐ Ⓑ Ⓒ Ⓓ
154. Ⓐ Ⓑ Ⓒ Ⓓ
155. Ⓐ Ⓑ Ⓒ Ⓓ
156. Ⓐ Ⓑ Ⓒ Ⓓ
157. Ⓐ Ⓑ Ⓒ Ⓓ
158. Ⓐ Ⓑ Ⓒ Ⓓ
159. Ⓐ Ⓑ Ⓒ Ⓓ
160. Ⓐ Ⓑ Ⓒ Ⓓ
161. Ⓐ Ⓑ Ⓒ Ⓓ
162. Ⓐ Ⓑ Ⓒ Ⓓ
163. Ⓐ Ⓑ Ⓒ Ⓓ
164. Ⓐ Ⓑ Ⓒ Ⓓ
165. Ⓐ Ⓑ Ⓒ Ⓓ

166. Ⓐ Ⓑ Ⓒ Ⓓ
167. Ⓐ Ⓑ Ⓒ Ⓓ
168. Ⓐ Ⓑ Ⓒ Ⓓ
169. Ⓐ Ⓑ Ⓒ Ⓓ
170. Ⓐ Ⓑ Ⓒ Ⓓ
171. Ⓐ Ⓑ Ⓒ Ⓓ
172. Ⓐ Ⓑ Ⓒ Ⓓ
173. Ⓐ Ⓑ Ⓒ Ⓓ
174. Ⓐ Ⓑ Ⓒ Ⓓ
175. Ⓐ Ⓑ Ⓒ Ⓓ
176. Ⓐ Ⓑ Ⓒ Ⓓ
177. Ⓐ Ⓑ Ⓒ Ⓓ
178. Ⓐ Ⓑ Ⓒ Ⓓ

179. Ⓐ Ⓑ Ⓒ Ⓓ
180. Ⓐ Ⓑ Ⓒ Ⓓ
181. Ⓐ Ⓑ Ⓒ Ⓓ
182. Ⓐ Ⓑ Ⓒ Ⓓ
183. Ⓐ Ⓑ Ⓒ Ⓓ
184. Ⓐ Ⓑ Ⓒ Ⓓ
185. Ⓐ Ⓑ Ⓒ Ⓓ
186. Ⓐ Ⓑ Ⓒ Ⓓ
187. Ⓐ Ⓑ Ⓒ Ⓓ
188. Ⓐ Ⓑ Ⓒ Ⓓ
189. Ⓐ Ⓑ Ⓒ Ⓓ
190. Ⓐ Ⓑ Ⓒ Ⓓ
191. Ⓐ Ⓑ Ⓒ Ⓓ

192. Ⓐ Ⓑ Ⓒ Ⓓ
193. Ⓐ Ⓑ Ⓒ Ⓓ
194. Ⓐ Ⓑ Ⓒ Ⓓ
195. Ⓐ Ⓑ Ⓒ Ⓓ
196. Ⓐ Ⓑ Ⓒ Ⓓ
197. Ⓐ Ⓑ Ⓒ Ⓓ
198. Ⓐ Ⓑ Ⓒ Ⓓ
199. Ⓐ Ⓑ Ⓒ Ⓓ
200. Ⓐ Ⓑ Ⓒ Ⓓ

TOEIC Practice Test 2

LISTENING COMPREHENSION

In this section of the test, you will have the chance to show how well you understand spoken English. There are four parts to this section, with special directions for each part. You will find the Answer Sheet for Practice Test 2 on page 59. Detach it from the book and use it to record your answers. Check your answers using the Answer Key on page 96 and see the Answers Explained on page 98.

TIP

If you do not have access to an audio CD player, please refer to the audio-scripts starting on page 333 when prompted to listen to an audio passage.

CD 1
TRACK
6

Part 1: Photographs

Directions: You will see a photograph. You will hear four statements about the photograph. Choose the statement that most closely matches the photograph and fill in the corresponding oval on your answer sheet.

Example

Now listen to the four statements.

Sample Answer

Ⓐ Ⓑ Ⓒ Ⓓ

Statement (B), "She's reading a magazine," best describes what you see in the picture. Therefore, you should choose answer (B).

TOEIC Practice Test 2

1.

4.

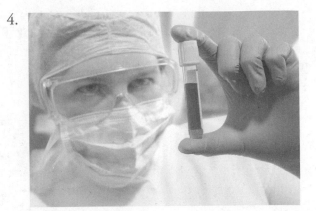

2.

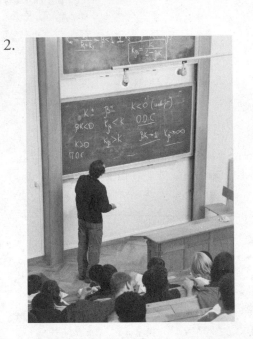

5.

6.

3.

7.

9.

10.
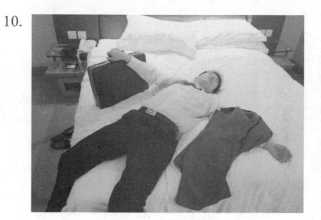

8.

Part 2: Question-Response

Directions: You will hear a question and three possible responses. Choose the response that most closely answers the question and fill in the corresponding oval on your answer sheet.

Example

Now listen to the sample question.

You will hear:

How is the weather?

You will also hear:

(A) It's raining.
(B) He's fine, thanks.
(C) He's my boss.

The best response to the question *How is the weather?* is choice (A), *It's raining*. Therefore, you should choose answer (A).

11. Mark your answer on your answer sheet.
12. Mark your answer on your answer sheet.
13. Mark your answer on your answer sheet.
14. Mark your answer on your answer sheet.
15. Mark your answer on your answer sheet.
16. Mark your answer on your answer sheet.
17. Mark your answer on your answer sheet.
18. Mark your answer on your answer sheet.
19. Mark your answer on your answer sheet.
20. Mark your answer on your answer sheet.
21. Mark your answer on your answer sheet.
22. Mark your answer on your answer sheet.
23. Mark your answer on your answer sheet.
24. Mark your answer on your answer sheet.
25. Mark your answer on your answer sheet.

26. Mark your answer on your answer sheet.
27. Mark your answer on your answer sheet.
28. Mark your answer on your answer sheet.
29. Mark your answer on your answer sheet.
30. Mark your answer on your answer sheet.
31. Mark your answer on your answer sheet.
32. Mark your answer on your answer sheet.
33. Mark your answer on your answer sheet.
34. Mark your answer on your answer sheet.
35. Mark your answer on your answer sheet.
36. Mark your answer on your answer sheet.
37. Mark your answer on your answer sheet.
38. Mark your answer on your answer sheet.
39. Mark your answer on your answer sheet.
40. Mark your answer on your answer sheet.

TOEIC Practice Test 2

Part 3: Conversations

CD 2
TRACK
1

Directions: You will hear a conversation between two people. You will see three questions on each conversation and four possible answers. Choose the best answer to each question and fill in the corresponding oval on your answer sheet.

41. What time will the man probably get to the meeting?
    (A) 9:00
    (B) 9:15
    (C) 10:00
    (D) 10:15

42. Why is the woman calling a meeting?
    (A) To check the accounts
    (B) To explain the late paychecks
    (C) To announce a pay raise
    (D) To discuss next week's work

43. How does the man feel about the situation?
    (A) Happy
    (B) Sad
    (C) Annoyed
    (D) Bored

44. Where does this conversation take place?
    (A) At a restaurant
    (B) On an airplane
    (C) In a movie theater
    (D) On a train

45. What's the weather like?
    (A) Clear
    (B) Cloudy
    (C) Windy
    (D) Snowy

46. When will food be served?
    (A) In 10 minutes
    (B) In 30 minutes
    (C) In an hour
    (D) In two hours

47. What does the woman want to do?
    (A) Move a desk
    (B) Clean the window
    (C) Find a broom
    (D) Fix a table

48. Why can't the man help her do it?
    (A) He's at a workshop.
    (B) He's late for an appointment.
    (C) He's busy with work.
    (D) He hurt his back.

49. When will she do it?
    (A) At 10:00
    (B) This afternoon
    (C) Tomorrow
    (D) On Tuesday

50. What will the man buy?
    (A) Gloves
    (B) Hats
    (C) Scarves
    (D) Bags

51. What color will he take?
    (A) Red
    (B) White
    (C) Brown
    (D) Black

52. How much will he pay?
    (A) $15.00
    (B) $15.50
    (C) $16.50
    (D) $50.00

53. How many copies of the report does the man need?
    (A) 25
    (B) 205
    (C) 220
    (D) 225

54. When does he need them?
    (A) By noon
    (B) This morning
    (C) Tomorrow
    (D) On Tuesday

55. Why can't the woman make the copies now?
    (A) She's too busy.
    (B) He wants too many.
    (C) It's very late.
    (D) The stapler is broken.

56. What does the woman want to do?
    (A) Buy something
    (B) See Mr. Lee
    (C) Go on a trip
    (D) Make an appointment

57. Where is Mr. Lee?
    (A) Out of town
    (B) Downtown
    (C) At home
    (D) In his office

58. When will he return?
    (A) Later today
    (B) Tomorrow morning
    (C) Next week
    (D) Next year

59. Where does the man have to go?
    (A) To work
    (B) To computer class
    (C) To the train station
    (D) To a doctor's appointment

60. Where is the woman's car?
    (A) In the garage
    (B) Across the street
    (C) In the park
    (D) Downtown

61. What color is the car?
    (A) Tan
    (B) Gray
    (C) Blue
    (D) Gold

62. Why did Ms. Jones leave the office early?
    (A) To catch a train
    (B) To go to a meeting
    (C) To avoid bad traffic
    (D) To work on a report

63. What time did Ms. Jones leave the office?
    (A) 3:00
    (B) 4:00
    (C) 8:00
    (D) 10:00

64. What is the weather like?
    (A) Hot
    (B) Rainy
    (C) Snowy
    (D) Cold

65. What did the woman send the man?
    (A) Books
    (B) Reports
    (C) Photocopies
    (D) Photographs

66. When did she send them?
    (A) Two days ago
    (B) Three days ago
    (C) Five days ago
    (D) Eight days ago

67. What does the woman want to do now?
    (A) Report the package as lost
    (B) Resend the package
    (C) Make more copies
    (D) Wait another day

68. What does the woman invite the man to do?
    (A) Play golf
    (B) Play tennis
    (C) Go dancing
    (D) Have dinner

69. Why doesn't the man want to do it?
    (A) He needs to go to the bank.
    (B) He doesn't have a ticket.
    (C) He has to write a letter.
    (D) He's too tired.

70. Where will the man be tonight?
    (A) At the club
    (B) At the park
    (C) At the hotel
    (D) At the restaurant

Part 4: Talks

Directions: You will hear a talk given by a single speaker. You will see three questions on each talk, each with four possible answers. Choose the best answer to each question and fill in the corresponding oval on your answer sheet.

71. When can a customer speak with a technician?
    (A) Between 4:00 and 7:00
    (B) Between 2:00 and 4:00
    (C) Any time before 7:00
    (D) Any time of day

72. How can a caller make an appointment?
    (A) Call back after 7:00
    (B) Go online
    (C) Press 2
    (D) Visit the office

73. What can a caller do by pressing 3?
    (A) Speak with Tech Support
    (B) Buy a new computer
    (C) Get information about a bill
    (D) Hear the menu again

74. What will Dr. Swanson talk about?
    (A) Small business
    (B) Tourism
    (C) Customer relations
    (D) Book promotion

75. What will happen after the talk?
    (A) Refreshments will be served.
    (B) There will be a book sale.
    (C) Dr. Swanson will sign books.
    (D) Another speaker will talk.

76. When will the next lecture take place?
    (A) Tomorrow evening
    (B) Next Thursday
    (C) In a week
    (D) Next month

77. What product is being advertised?
    (A) Chairs
    (B) Desks
    (C) Phones
    (D) Computers

78. Where would this product be used?
    (A) Home
    (B) Office
    (C) Theater
    (D) Classroom

79. How much is the discount?
    (A) 15%
    (B) 16%
    (C) 20%
    (D) 50%

80. What is the weather like today?
    (A) Dry
    (B) Cold
    (C) Rainy
    (D) Cloudy

81. What will the high temperature be?
    (A) 20
    (B) 65
    (C) 80
    (D) 85

82. When will the weather change?
    (A) This morning
    (B) This afternoon
    (C) Tonight
    (D) On Sunday

83. Who is this talk for?
    (A) Parents
    (B) Tourists
    (C) Business travelers
    (D) Restaurant owners

84. What does the speaker recommend eating?
    (A) Salty or sweet food
    (B) A big breakfast
    (C) Fast food
    (D) Dessert

85. Why is this recommended?
    (A) It's fast.
    (B) It's cheap.
    (C) It's healthful.
    (D) It's convenient.

86. What should a caller do in an emergency?
    (A) Speak with the office staff
    (B) Call another dentist
    (C) Ask for Dr. Elizabeth Pekar
    (D) Visit the office immediately

87. What day is the office closed?
    (A) Sunday
    (B) Monday
    (C) Friday
    (D) Saturday

88. How can a caller make an appointment?
    (A) Leave a message
    (B) Contact Dr. Rogers
    (C) Call during office hours
    (D) Phone 324-9014

89. Who would be most interested in the advertised event?
    (A) Career counselors
    (B) City employees
    (C) Hotel managers
    (D) Job seekers

90. What time will the event begin?
    (A) 7:00
    (B) 7:30
    (C) 11:30
    (D) 4:00

91. What should people bring to the event?
    (A) Tickets
    (B) Resumes
    (C) Newspapers
    (D) Applications

92. Where would this announcement be heard?
    (A) On a plane
    (B) On a train
    (C) On a boat
    (D) On a bus

93. How many hours will the trip last?
    (A) Three
    (B) Four
    (C) Five
    (D) Six

94. What's the weather like?
    (A) Cloudy
    (B) Sunny
    (C) Rainy
    (D) Windy

95. What is the problem?
    (A) Banks are closed.
    (B) Water mains broke.
    (C) Streets are flooded.
    (D) Rush hour traffic is heavy.

96. What are citizens asked to do?
    (A) Avoid driving
    (B) Call the police
    (C) Clear up the area
    (D) Stay away from downtown

97. When will the situation improve?
    (A) Today
    (B) Tonight
    (C) By the weekend
    (D) Next month

98. What can guests do at the Lakeside Resort?
    (A) Ride horses
    (B) Play tennis
    (C) Go biking
    (D) Play golf

99. How much does the special weekend package cost?
    (A) $100
    (B) $700
    (C) $1,100
    (D) $1,500

100. When is the resort closed?
    (A) February–March
    (B) April–May
    (C) September–November
    (D) December–January

READING

In this section of the test, you will have the chance to show how well you understand written English. There are three parts to this section, with special directions for each part.

**YOU WILL HAVE ONE HOUR AND FIFTEEN MINUTES
TO COMPLETE PARTS 5, 6, AND 7 OF THE TEST.**

Part 5: Incomplete Sentences

Directions: You will see a sentence with a missing word. Four possible answers follow the sentence. Choose the best answer to the question and fill in the corresponding oval on your answer sheet.

101. Mr. Jones _____ investing in that company, but he finally decided against it.
(A) considered
(B) considerate
(C) considerable
(D) considerably

102. If we hadn't left the house so late, we _____ the plane.
(A) wouldn't have missed
(B) wouldn't miss
(C) won't have missed
(D) won't miss

103. These reports must be turned _____ before the end of the week.
(A) off
(B) on
(C) up
(D) in

104. Samantha worked very hard and put in a lot of overtime hours because she hoped for an _____ in her salary.
(A) incursion
(B) inquiry
(C) increase
(D) inquest

105. They brought extra chairs into the room _____ they expected a large number of people to attend the meeting.
(A) although
(B) since
(C) however
(D) nevertheless

106. We have been asked not to walk _____ the lobby today because it's being painted.
(A) beside
(B) between
(C) around
(D) through

107. By the time we got to the train station, the train _____.
(A) had already left
(B) had already been left
(C) has already left
(D) will have already left

108. Dr. Smith is a well-respected expert and has _____ experience in her field.
(A) extend
(B) extends
(C) extensive
(D) extension

109. _____ he graduated from the university, he got a job at a good company.
(A) Following
(B) Later
(C) After
(D) Next

110. If you don't want to get stuck in a traffic jam, you should avoid _____ during rush hour.
(A) drive
(B) driving
(C) to drive
(D) driven

111. Once you start using the new software, you will be able to do your work much more _____.
(A) ease
(B) easily
(C) easier
(D) easement

112. This report has to be completed _____ 5:00 today at the latest.
(A) until
(B) after
(C) to
(D) by

113. They made a very _____ offer, so we signed the contract.
(A) attract
(B) attracted
(C) attraction
(D) attractive

114. Currently they _____ lower prices than any of their competitors.
(A) are offering
(B) to offer
(C) did offer
(D) offered

115. The government will_____ new price controls on the industry next year.
(A) impose
(B) compose
(C) repose
(D) suppose

116. They will interview each candidate before they _____ who to hire.
(A) decide
(B) are deciding
(C) will decide
(D) decided

117. These rooms _____ before the conference next week.
(A) paint
(B) will paint
(C) are going to paint
(D) will be painted

118. The new chairs that he bought for the office _____ not very comfortable.
(A) is
(B) are
(C) do
(D) was

119. Everyone is expected to arrive at the meeting _____.
(A) promptness
(B) promote
(C) promptly
(D) prompt

120. We will have to come to an agreement _____ the end of this month.
(A) during
(B) before
(C) when
(D) until

121. _____ we paid the painters a lot of money, they did a terrible job.
  (A) Because
  (B) Since
  (C) Although
  (D) Despite

122. After his contract _____, he will have to look for a new job.
  (A) expires
  (B) expects
  (C) exposes
  (D) expands

123. I _____ eat at expensive restaurants because I don't have a lot of extra money.
  (A) always
  (B) often
  (C) usually
  (D) seldom

124. The storm caused a lot of damage to the building and we had to buy new _____ for many of the windows.
  (A) glass
  (B) glasses
  (C) glassy
  (D) glassine

125. If we_____ more time, we would be able to do a more thorough job.
  (A) would have
  (B) will have
  (C) have
  (D) had

126. You should _____ with your boss before committing yourself to that project.
  (A) will speak
  (B) speak
  (C) speaking
  (D) spoken

127. They expect _____ before noon tomorrow.
  (A) arrive
  (B) to arrive
  (C) arriving
  (D) will arrive

128. This store offers a wide _____ of office equipment.
  (A) select
  (B) selective
  (C) selection
  (D) selecting

129. _____ have changed the face of the modern workplace.
  (A) Computers
  (B) Computer
  (C) The computer
  (D) A computer

130. The train _____ Chicago leaves at 4:00 A.M.
  (A) in
  (B) at
  (C) to
  (D) by

131. This car is _____ cheap nor reliable.
  (A) but
  (B) both
  (C) either
  (D) neither

132. This photocopier is expensive, but it is _____ than the other one.
  (A) most durable
  (B) more durable
  (C) durably
  (D) durable

133. _____ this paper in the closet next to the box of envelopes.
(A) Put
(B) Putting
(C) To put
(D) Will put

134. We decided not to rent that office because it was not very _____.
(A) space
(B) spaced
(C) spacious
(D) spaciousness

135. We realized that nobody had been _____ the checkbook.
(A) balance
(B) balances
(C) balanced
(D) balancing

136. Of all the people who applied for the position, Mr. Sato is the _____.
(A) qualified
(B) more qualified
(C) most qualified
(D) qualification

137. Prices are expected to _____ before the end of the year.
(A) up
(B) rise
(C) raise
(D) growth

138. We hired an accountant to _____ the company's financial records.
(A) audit
(B) audition
(C) auditory
(D) auditorium

139. We will have the building _____ before we sign the lease.
(A) inspect
(B) inspected
(C) inspects
(D) to inspect

140. Ms. Lee _____ with us since last November.
(A) works
(B) worked
(C) is working
(D) has been working

Part 6: Text Completion

Directions: You will see four passages, each with three blanks. Under each blank are four answer options. Choose the word or phrase that best completes the statement.

Questions 141–143 refer to the following passage.

Your Paycheck

Checks _____ on a biweekly basis by department heads. Arrangements can

  141. (A) distribute
       (B) distributed
       (C) are distributed
       (D) are distributing

be made with the Accounting Department to have checks mailed to the employee's home address instead, if desired. Each employee should review the check stub carefully. _____ contains a breakdown of all deductions, including state

  142. (A) It
       (B) He
       (C) She
       (D) They

and local taxes, retirement fund contributions, and insurance payments. Any inaccuracies should be reported to the Accounting Department as soon as possible. Every effort will be made to correct any errors in a timely manner. The Human Resources Department conducts monthly workshops that explain in detail how each paycheck deduction is calculated. Anyone interested in _____

                                 143. (A) assisting
                                       (B) attending
                                       (C) accessing
                                       (D) approving

a workshop should contact the Human Resources Department.

Questions 144–146 refer to the following memo.

To: All office staff
From: Rita Johnson
Re: Employee Appreciation Banquet
Date: June 15, 20--

It's time to start planning for the _____ Employee Appreciation

144. (A) daily
       (B) monthly
       (C) annual
       (D) biannual

Banquet. I know you all look forward to this every spring. As you know, the winner of the Employee of the Year Award is chosen by the staff. Please get your nominations to me before the end of this month. The winner will be announced on the night of the banquet.

I have received your comments and complaints and have been looking into a new _____ for this year's banquet. We are hoping to hold it at

145. (A) location
       (B) program
       (C) decoration
       (D) entertainment

the Hamilton Hotel. The rooms there are large, and the hotel is conveniently accessible by public transportation.

I have also paid attention to your comments about the food and will work with the hotel chef to develop a menu that provides a variety of choices. Please let me know if you have any further _____ regarding

146. (A) suggest
       (B) suggests
       (C) suggesting
       (D) suggestions

this year's banquet.

Questions 147–149 refer to the following letter.

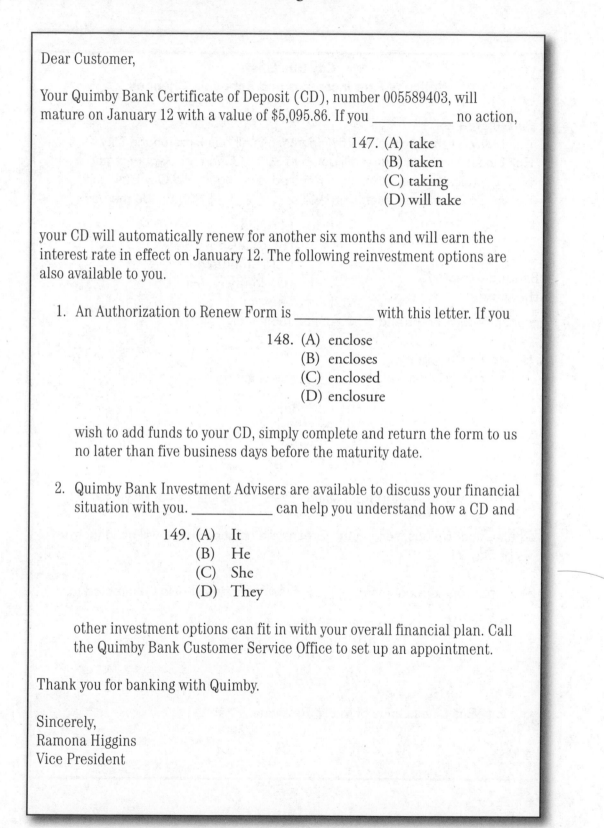

Dear Customer,

Your Quimby Bank Certificate of Deposit (CD), number 005589403, will mature on January 12 with a value of $5,095.86. If you _____ no action,

147. (A) take
(B) taken
(C) taking
(D) will take

your CD will automatically renew for another six months and will earn the interest rate in effect on January 12. The following reinvestment options are also available to you.

1. An Authorization to Renew Form is _____ with this letter. If you

148. (A) enclose
(B) encloses
(C) enclosed
(D) enclosure

wish to add funds to your CD, simply complete and return the form to us no later than five business days before the maturity date.

2. Quimby Bank Investment Advisers are available to discuss your financial situation with you. _____ can help you understand how a CD and

149. (A) It
(B) He
(C) She
(D) They

other investment options can fit in with your overall financial plan. Call the Quimby Bank Customer Service Office to set up an appointment.

Thank you for banking with Quimby.

Sincerely,
Ramona Higgins
Vice President

Questions 150–152 refer to the following notice.

City Bus Lines
Notice of Fare Increases and Schedule Changes

Fare Increases
As of May 31 there will be a 25% increase in all bus fares on the City Bus Lines. The normal fare will go up to $2.50 during regular hours and $3.50 during rush hour. Senior citizens possessing a valid City Bus Line Senior Citizen Identification Card will be _____ $1.25 to ride the bus

150. (A) paid
(B) charged
(C) reimbursed
(D) compensated

during regular hours and $2.00 during rush hour.

Schedule Changes
The number 42 bus, which _____ leaves the train station every

151. (A) promptly
(B) usually
(C) currently
(D) previously

half hour, will leave the train station every 45 minutes as of May 31.

The number 56 bus, serving the Greensville neighborhood, will no longer run as of May 31.

Any questions or concerns _____ these changes should be directed to

152. (A) refusing
(B) regaining
(C) referring
(D) regarding

the City Bus Lines Office of Public Relations.

Part 7: Reading Comprehension

Directions: You will see single and double reading passages followed by several questions. Each question has four answer choices. Choose the best answer to the question and fill in the corresponding oval on your answer sheet.

Questions 153–156 refer to the following article.

The Clear Sound Communications takeover of local telephone service, which was originally welcomed with great optimism, now seems to be heading down the road toward disaster. Ever since Clear Sound bought out the FreeTel Company just under six months ago, it has experienced loss of income, loss of customers, and, perhaps worst of all, the loss of its reputation as a company that delivers on its promises.

When Clear Sound came into the area, it promised that all its telephone customers would have access to high-speed Internet service by the end of the year. Not only has the company failed to deliver on this promise, but customers who are receiving Clear Sound Internet service have expressed great dissatisfaction with it. "The connection goes out all the time. You just can't count on it when you need it," a Clear Sound customer complained at a town meeting last week. Customers have also claimed that repair service is slow and overpriced. Clear Sound, on the other hand, claims that such problems are minor and not widespread. "Every company experiences an adjustment period," explained Richard Whittier, Clear Sound public relations officer. "Before one more year has passed, you can be certain that all operations will be running smoothly and customers will be 100% satisfied," he said.

153. When did Clear Sound take over the FreeTel Company?
(A) Last week
(B) A little less than six months ago
(C) A little more than six months ago
(D) One year ago

154. What kind of company is Clear Sound?
(A) Telephone only
(B) Telephone and Internet
(C) Delivery service
(D) Transportation

155. How do Clear Sound customers currently feel about the company?
(A) Pleased
(B) Optimistic
(C) Unhappy
(D) Bored

156. The word *minor* in paragraph 2, line 12 is closest in meaning to
(A) small.
(B) common.
(C) expected.
(D) important.

Questions 157–158 refer to the following advertisement.

SALE! SALE! SALE!

Grover's Office Supply Store announces its annual winter sale!

All paper items are on sale, with discounts from 15% to 25% off our already low prices.

Sale ends Saturday.

Join our Frequent Buyer's Club and save even more. Stop by the manager's desk for an application. Once we have your contact information in our computer files, you will receive notices of special sales and discounts available to Frequent Buyer's Club members only.

Grover's Office Supply Store.
Supplying your office with all its paper needs.

157. Which of the following items are on sale?
(A) Envelopes
(B) Desks
(C) Filing cabinets
(D) Computers

158. How can a customer become a member of the Frequent Buyer's Club?
(A) Visit the store before Saturday
(B) Speak with the manager
(C) Send a request by mail
(D) Contact the club president

Questions 159–161 refer to the following article.

The International Experience Project (IEP) provides young professionals with the opportunity to gain work experience abroad. IEP was founded by Margery Wilson four years ago. "When I graduated from college," she explained, "my dream was to work abroad for one or two years, learn another language, and experience living in another country. I knew I wanted to do this, but I didn't know how to find a job abroad. That was six years ago. At that time, there were no employment agencies that specialized in helping job seekers like myself. So I decided to start my own."

Since its beginnings, IEP has provided jobs for several thousand young professionals in countries all around the world. Knowing a foreign language helps, says Wilson, but it isn't a prerequisite for all jobs. In fact, many of the companies that provide employment for her clients also provide language training. IEP finds jobs for people in all fields, from economics to science to teaching. "All you need is a college degree, an interest in other countries, and an adventurous spirit," says Wilson.

159. What kind of business is IEP?
    (A) An employment agency
    (B) A travel agency
    (C) A language school
    (D) A teacher training school

160. How long ago was IEP started?
    (A) One year
    (B) Two years
    (C) Four years
    (D) Six years

161. What is a requirement for using IEP's services?
    (A) Foreign language skills
    (B) Experience living abroad
    (C) A science background
    (D) A college degree

Questions 162–163 refer to the following notice.

Norwich Office Towers
Maintenance and Cleaning Department
Notice of Painting and Repair Work

The west bank elevators will be closed for routine maintenance and repair starting Monday, August 17. Tenants and visitors are asked to use the east bank elevators or the west or east stairs during this time. The west bank elevators will be back in operation on Monday, August 24, at which time the east bank elevators will be closed. All elevator maintenance and repair work should be completed by the end of the month. Stairs and hallways will be painted during the months of September and October. A complete painting schedule will be posted before September 1.

---

162. What will the elevators be closed for?
    (A) Painting
    (B) Repair
    (C) Cleaning
    (D) Rescheduling

163. How long will the work on all the elevators take?
    (A) One week
    (B) Two weeks
    (C) One month
    (D) Two months

Questions 164–166 refer to the following advertisement.

For Sale

Fully equipped convenience store on North Main Street close to downtown. Annual sales of $2,198,456. Sells snacks, groceries, newspapers, gasoline, etc. Ample customer parking behind. Spacious two-bedroom owner's apartment on second floor. Asking $750,000. Includes building and grounds, all equipment, and $85,000 in inventory. No brokers, please. Shown by appointment only. Call Maria at White Horse Realty—243-8674.

---

164. What is above the store?
(A) A place to live
(B) A snack bar
(C) A place for equipment
(D) An office

165. How much is the store being sold for?
(A) $85,000
(B) $750,000
(C) $835,000
(D) $2,198,456

166. The word *inventory* in line 4 is closest in meaning to
(A) rents.
(B) accounts.
(C) furnishings.
(D) merchandise.

Questions 167–168 refer to the following instructions.

---

1. Remove the back cover, using a small screwdriver to loosen the screw.
2. Remove batteries and replace with two new AAA batteries. Use the + and – signs to position them correctly. Dispose of used batteries properly.
3. Replace the cover and tighten the screw with the screwdriver.
4. Reset the time using the side buttons

The GMX 200 is guaranteed to keep time accurately for one full year from date of purchase. Should it malfunction in any way during this time period, your money will be refunded in full.

---

167. What are these instructions for?
(A) Repairing a cover
(B) Setting the date
(C) Getting a refund
(D) Changing the batteries

168. What is the GMX 200?
(A) A calendar
(B) A screwdriver
(C) A clock
(D) A garbage disposal

Questions 169–172 refer to the following article.

Green Garden Café recently opened downtown and is offering a variety of handcrafted sandwiches, along with homemade soups and ice cream. All food served at the café is made from pure organic ingredients. Sandwiches are made with 100% whole-grain bread, which is baked in the café's kitchen.

Diners are lining up to try Green Garden's sandwiches for breakfast, lunch, and dinner. "One of our best sellers is our breakfast sandwich," explains café owner Melissa Whitehead. "It's not your typical bacon-and-cheese concoction. Instead, we combine eggs with fresh vegetables and serve it on fresh-baked bread. Customers can't seem to get enough of it."

You won't find the usual ham, turkey, or roast beef sandwich among the café's offered fare. In fact, all the food they serve is 100% vegetarian. Their sandwiches are filled with fresh vegetables, locally made cheese, or a combination of both. "Customers enjoy our soups and ice cream, but what they really come here for are the sandwiches," says Whitehead. "That's our most popular item."

Give the Green Garden Café a try next time you are downtown. You won't be disappointed. The café is open six days a week: Monday–Friday from 9 AM to 9 PM and Saturday from 11 AM to 4 PM.

169. What is true of the soups at Green Garden?
   (A) They are made with organic ingredients.
   (B) They are the most popular item.
   (C) They come from a factory.
   (D) They contain bacon.

170. The word *concoction* in paragraph 2, line 4 is closest in meaning to
   (A) flavor.
   (B) combination.
   (C) ingredient.
   (D) meal.

171. Which of the following sandwiches can you get at the Green Garden Cafe?
   (A) Cheese and bacon
   (B) Ham and turkey
   (C) Cheese and vegetable
   (D) Roast beef

172. On which of the following days is the café closed?
   (A) Monday
   (B) Wednesday
   (C) Friday
   (D) Sunday

Questions 173–176 refer to the following article.

A job interview is your chance to make a good impression on a potential employer, and the way you dress is an important part of the impression you make. It is not an occasion to show how fashionably you can dress. Rather, it is the time to present yourself as a serious professional who conveys a sense of confidence. The colors you wear help to give this impression. Choose dark colors such as black, navy blue, or charcoal gray, and stay away from warm browns and greens. In addition to a dark color, the suit you wear should have a conservative, neatly tailored cut.

Don't forget to pay attention to details. Your accessories are an important part of your overall look. For men this means wearing ties with simple patterns and quiet colors. Also, men should not wear any type of jewelry, even of the highest quality gold or silver, except for a wristwatch or tie clip. Women should wear plain earrings. Matching necklaces or bracelets are permissible as long as they are not gaudy or loud.

Finally, make sure your feet are dressed as well as the rest of you. Avoid any kind of fancy footwear. Your footwear should look neat and fit you comfortably. You may think that no one will look at your feet, but if you wear super-high heels, garish buckles, or bright colors on your shoes, you are calling attention to them in a way you don't want.

173. Who is this article for?
     (A) Tailors
     (B) Job hunters
     (C) Fashion designers
     (D) Clothing retailers

174. Why are dark colors recommended?
     (A) They feel warmer.
     (B) They are fashionable.
     (C) They look professional.
     (D) They show off accessories.

175. What kind of accessories are recommended?
     (A) Plain and quiet
     (B) Loud and gaudy
     (C) Gold and silver
     (D) Patterned and colorful

176. What kind of shoes should be worn?
     (A) Brightly colored
     (B) Comfortable
     (C) High heeled
     (D) Fancy

Questions 177–180 refer to the following information sheet.

INFORMATION FOR VISITORS

GETTING AROUND

- Two major bus routes, No. 34 and No. 56, pass in front of the building. Bus schedules and bus route maps are available at the front desk.
- The Market Mall subway station is five blocks away. Subway maps and information are available at the subway station.
- Taxis are available at the taxi stand near the main entrance.

MEALS

- A full-service restaurant and a café are just off the main lobby. Daily breakfast at the café is included with the price of your room.
- Ask at the front desk for a listing of local restaurants.

SHOPPING

- Market Mall, the city's premier shopping mall, is five blocks away. Whether you are looking for clothes, jewelry, books, gifts, linens, or office supplies, you are sure to find it at the Market Mall.
- The downtown shopping district, famous for its elegant fashion boutiques, is just three miles away. The downtown district is served by the No. 34 bus line.
- A pharmacy and grocery store are just across the street.

TOURISM

- The city boasts a number of fine museums, including the National History Museum and the Museum of Fine Arts. The Sun Tours Travel Company offers bus tours of historic locations around the city. Please ask at the front desk for more information.
- Hotel guests are entitled to a discount at the City Aquarium. Get your discount coupon at the front desk.

EMERGENCIES

In case of emergency, dial 01 for the hotel manager.

177. Where would you find this information sheet?
    (A) In a hotel
    (B) In a tourist agency
    (C) In a shopping mall
    (D) In an office building

178. What is five blocks away?
    (A) A pharmacy
    (B) A café
    (C) A subway station
    (D) A taxi stand

179. What can you buy in the shopping district?
    (A) Books
    (B) Office supplies
    (C) Clothes
    (D) Linens

180. Where can you probably buy cough medicine?
    (A) In the shopping district
    (B) Across the street
    (C) In the lobby
    (D) At the Market Mall

Questions 181–185 refer to the following advertisement and letter.

HELP WANTED

Busy downtown law firm seeks certified paralegal to assist three attorneys. Duties include legal research, assisting with documents, providing legal information to clients, some word processing. Requires minimum of two years' paralegal experience and word processing and database skills. Knowledge of French or Spanish desirable. Send resume and names of three references before June 1 to Martha Lee, P.O. Box 7, Williamsburg, MA 01234. No phone calls, please. We will contact you to make an appointment for an interview.

May 8, 20--

Martha Lee
P.O. Box 7
Williamsburg, MA 01234

Dear Ms. Lee,

I am writing in response to your ad in yesterday's paper for a certified paralegal. I have recently completed a paralegal training course and received my certificate last March. I am looking for a job in a small downtown firm. I am proficient with the commonly used word processing and database programs. I have a working knowledge of French and will be taking a Spanish course starting June 15. My job experience includes three years as an office assistant at an architectural firm. I have not worked for the past year, as I was busy with my paralegal training course.

I would really enjoy the opportunity to work at a firm such as yours. I am enclosing my resume and would be happy to provide you with letters of reference. I look forward to meeting with you soon.

Sincerely,

James Jones

181. When did the job ad appear in the newspaper?
    (A) May 7
    (B) May 8
    (C) June 1
    (D) June 15

182. What is one of the duties of the advertised job?
    (A) Interviewing clients
    (B) Working on legal documents
    (C) Answering phone calls
    (D) Making appointments

183. What job requirement does James Jones NOT meet?
    (A) Paralegal certificate
    (B) Knowledge of a foreign language
    (C) Computer software skills
    (D) Paralegal work experience

184. Where did James Jones work before?
    (A) At a Spanish school
    (B) At a law office
    (C) At an architectural firm
    (D) At a French company

185. What did James Jones include with his letter?
    (A) His paralegal course diploma
    (B) His resume
    (C) His French certificate
    (D) His letters of reference

Questions 186–190 refer to the following brochure and e-mail.

Computer Training Center

CLASS SCHEDULE

Word Processing Basics
Section 1: M, W 1–3
Section 2: T, Th 6–8

Advanced Word Processing
Section 1: W, F 9–12

Database Basics
Section 1: M, W 4–6
Section 2: Saturday, 9–1

Advanced Database
Section 1: M, W 1–3

INFORMATION FOR STUDENTS

- You may choose either section 1 or section 2 of any course.
- All courses last three months.
- Course fees are $300 for courses meeting four hours a week, and $500 for courses meeting six hours a week. Materials fees are $25 for word processing classes and $45 for database classes.
- Register online by visiting our website, www.computertrainingcenter.com, or call us at 456-8874.

To: marvinpeabody@nzinc.com
From: samsilliman@nzinc.com
Subject: computer training

Marvin,

I am attaching the latest schedule from the Computer Training Center. As we have discussed in person, your computer skills are not quite up to par and you would benefit from taking one of these courses. We also discussed the fact that your first-year employee probationary status is still in effect and that you are required to take some training courses during this time. Please sign up for one of these courses as soon as possible. I would encourage you to choose a beginning word processing class, as your skills in that area are woefully lacking. You have a good knowledge of database software, though you could benefit from an advanced-level class if that is what interests you most. The choice, of course, is up to you, but I recommend word processing. In choosing your class schedule, please remember that you must be present at our weekly staff meetings (Wednesday afternoons at 2:00). As soon as you have decided on a course and schedule, please contact Elizabeth Mortimer in the Human Resources Department and she will take care of the registration process for you. We at NZ, Inc. will, of course, take care of all the fees. All you have to do is attend the classes. Please e-mail me as soon as you are registered for a course.
Sam Silliman

186. Which class will Marvin probably take?
   (A) Word Processing Basics, Section 1
   (B) Word Processing Basics, Section 2
   (C) Database Basics, Section 2
   (D) Advanced Database, Section 1

187. How will Marvin register for the class?
   (A) By visiting the training center website
   (B) By calling the training center
   (C) By talking with the human resources officer
   (D) By e-mailing Sam Silliman

188. How much will Marvin pay for his course?
   (A) $0
   (B) $300
   (C) $325
   (D) $545

189. Who is Sam Silliman?
   (A) The Computer Training Center manager
   (B) Elizabeth Mortimer's employee
   (C) A computer instructor
   (D) Marvin's supervisor

190. How long has Marvin been working at NZ, Inc.?
   (A) Exactly three months
   (B) Less than one year
   (C) A little more than a year
   (D) For several years

Questions 191–195 refer to the following message and e-mail.

A MESSAGE FOR: *Simon Oliver*

DATE: *Monday, May 23*

TIME: *2:30*

FROM: *Amanda Lopez*

PHONE: *213-568-0937*

_X_ TELEPHONED   ___ CAME TO SEE YOU   ___ RETURNED YOUR CALL

MESSAGE: *Regarding your appointment with Ms. Lopez this afternoon at the City View Café, because of an emergency, she won't be able to make it. She would like to reschedule and suggests tomorrow afternoon or any time the following day. If neither of these days works, Friday might be possible. Please let her know before 6:00 this evening. Also she reminds you that she needs to see a copy of your project report.*

SIGNED: *Paulina Kraft*

To: soliver@metooinc.com
From: pkraft@metooinc.com
Subject: Message from Ms. Lopez
Date: May 23, 4:45

Mr. Oliver,

Did you get the phone message from Ms. Lopez I left on your desk? She called just five minutes after you left the office to meet her. I hope you didn't wait for her too long. I can call and reschedule with her if you'd like. I've checked your schedule and tomorrow doesn't look possible because of the conference, but you have plenty of free time the day after. I will make up a packet for you to take to her with the document she requested as well as the photos you took. Let me know about the reschedule.

Ms. Kraft

191. Why did Ms. Lopez call Mr. Oliver?
    (A) To invite him out for coffee
    (B) To ask for help in an emergency
    (C) To cancel their appointment
    (D) To tell him about a conference

192. What time did Mr. Oliver leave the office?
    (A) 2:25
    (B) 2:30
    (C) 4:45
    (D) 6:00

193. What day does Ms. Kraft suggest that Mr. Oliver meet with Ms. Lopez?
    (A) Monday
    (B) Tuesday
    (C) Wednesday
    (D) Friday

194. What will Mr. Oliver take to show to Ms. Lopez?
    (A) A report and some photos
    (B) A conference program
    (C) A schedule
    (D) A café menu

195. What is probably Ms. Kraft's job?
    (A) Photographer
    (B) Project director
    (C) Café owner
    (D) Office assistant

TOEIC Practice Test 2

Questions 196–200 refer to the following fax and price sheet.

FAX TRANSMISSION   FAX TRANSMISSION   FAX TRANSMISSION

Linton Systems, Inc.
154 North Washington Street
Bradford, NY

To: Cosmo Catering Company
17 River Road
Bradford, NY

From: Elaine Conway
Office Manager

Date: August 30

We are planning an all-day conference for October 15 and will need catering services for lunch. We expect around 40–45 people to attend. Some will be vegetarian, but we will also want some meat dishes available. We would need you to provide dishes and silverware, but we will use our own tables and chairs. Please fax menus, prices, and ordering information. Thank you.

Cosmo Catering Company
Menu and Price List

Lunch Buffets

Option 1
1 chicken entrée
1 meat entrée
salad
2 desserts

Option 2
1 chicken entrée
1 meat entrée
1 vegetarian entrée
salad
3 desserts

Option 3
2 vegetarian entrees
1 meat entree
salad
2 desserts

Prices

Up to 25 people— Option 1: $250
Option 2: $350
Option 3: $200

Up to 50 people— Option 1: $500
Option 2: $700
Option 3: $400

Up to 100 people— Option 1: $1,000
Option 2: $1,400
Option 3: $800

*Above prices include all dishes and silverware, tablecloths and napkins (white only), and setup and takedown.
*Tables and chairs are available for $2 per person.
Orders must be accompanied by a 25% deposit, local checks only. The remainder is due on the date of service.
Credit cards and cash are not accepted.

Discounts
• All orders placed a month in advance will receive a 10% discount.
• Use your own dishes and silverware and receive a 15% discount.

196. What would be the cost of the Option 2 buffet for 100 people, with tables and chairs?
    (A) $800
    (B) $1,000
    (C) $1,400
    (D) $1,600

197. Which lunch buffets would meet Elaine Conway's needs?
    (A) Options 1 and 2
    (B) Options 2 and 3
    (C) Options 1, 2, and 3
    (D) Option 2 only

198. What does Elaine Conway have to do to get a 10% discount?
    (A) Pay with cash
    (B) Rent tables and chairs
    (C) Use her own silverware
    (D) Order before September 15

199. What does she have to send with her order?
    (A) Her credit card number
    (B) Choice of tablecloth color
    (C) A check for the deposit
    (D) A dessert order

200. If she chooses Option 2, how much would she pay, without discounts?
    (A) $350
    (B) $700
    (C) $790
    (D) $1,400

Answer Key
PRACTICE TEST 2

Listening Comprehension

Part 1: Photographs

1. B	4. D	7. B	9. D
2. C	5. A	8. C	10. D
3. A	6. C		

Part 2: Question-Response

11. A	19. C	27. C	35. A
12. C	20. A	28. B	36. C
13. B	21. B	29. B	37. A
14. B	22. B	30. A	38. B
15. C	23. C	31. C	39. B
16. A	24. B	32. B	40. B
17. C	25. A	33. B	
18. A	26. A	34. A	

Part 3: Conversations

41. D	49. C	57. A	65. D
42. B	50. A	58. C	66. B
43. C	51. D	59. D	67. A
44. B	52. B	60. B	68. B
45. A	53. D	61. C	69. D
46. B	54. C	62. C	70. C
47. A	55. A	63. A	
48. D	56. B	64. B	

Part 4: Talks

71. D	79. A	87. A	95. C
72. C	80. A	88. C	96. D
73. C	81. D	89. D	97. C
74. A	82. D	90. C	98. B
75. B	83. C	91. B	99. B
76. D	84. B	92. A	100. A
77. A	85. C	93. D	
78. B	86. B	94. B	

Answer Key
PRACTICE TEST 2

Reading

Part 5: Incomplete Sentences

101. **A**	111. **B**	121. **C**	131. **D**
102. **A**	112. **D**	122. **A**	132. **B**
103. **D**	113. **D**	123. **D**	133. **A**
104. **C**	114. **A**	124. **A**	134. **C**
105. **B**	115. **A**	125. **D**	135. **D**
106. **D**	116. **A**	126. **B**	136. **C**
107. **A**	117. **D**	127. **B**	137. **B**
108. **C**	118. **B**	128. **C**	138. **A**
109. **C**	119. **C**	129. **A**	139. **B**
110. **B**	120. **B**	130. **C**	140. **D**

Part 6: Text Completion

141. **C**	144. **C**	147. **A**	150. **B**
142. **A**	145. **A**	148. **C**	151. **C**
143. **B**	146. **D**	149. **D**	152. **D**

Part 7: Reading Comprehension

153. **B**	165. **B**	177. **A**	189. **D**
154. **B**	166. **D**	178. **C**	190. **B**
155. **C**	167. **D**	179. **C**	191. **C**
156. **A**	168. **C**	180. **B**	192. **A**
157. **A**	169. **A**	181. **A**	193. **C**
158. **B**	170. **B**	182. **B**	194. **A**
159. **A**	171. **C**	183. **D**	195. **D**
160. **C**	172. **D**	184. **C**	196. **D**
161. **D**	173. **B**	185. **B**	197. **B**
162. **B**	174. **C**	186. **B**	198. **D**
163. **B**	175. **A**	187. **C**	199. **C**
164. **A**	176. **B**	188. **A**	200. **B**

TOEIC PRACTICE TEST 2—ANSWERS EXPLAINED
Listening Comprehension
PART 1: PHOTOGRAPHS

1. **(B)** This is a street scene on a snowy day. Choice (A) correctly identifies the parked car but not its location. Choice (C) associates *driving* with *car* and confuses similar sounds *snow* and *slow*. Choice (D) misidentifies what is *white*—it is *snow*, not *flowers*.

2. **(C)** A man talks about information on a blackboard while an audience listens—a professor lecturing his class. Choice (A) identifies an object in the photo—lights—but there is no janitor. Choice (B) refers to the students' books that are shown in the photo. Choice (D) refers to the blackboard.

3. **(A)** A ship holding freight is sitting in port. Choice (B) uses associated words *passenger* and *deck*. Choice (C) is incorrect because the boat is in port, not at sea. Choice (D) uses the associated word *captain*.

4. **(D)** A scientist is examining liquid in a test tube. Choice (A) refers to the liquid in the test tube, but no one is drinking it. Choice (B) refers to the scientist's mask, but she is wearing it, not removing it. Choice (C) refers to the scientist's gloves, which she is wearing, not washing.

5. **(A)** Two laptops are sitting open on a coffee table. Choice (B) refers to the curtains, which are open, not closed. Choice (C) is incorrect because it is the woman, not the man, who has a magazine. Choice (D) is incorrect because the woman is looking at her magazine, not at the man.

6. **(C)** A woman in a grocery store is picking out apples, so we can assume she plans to buy them. Choice (A) confuses similar-sounding words *fruit* and *suit*. Choice (B) refers to the apples, but they are in a store, not on a tree. Choice (D) misidentifies the action—she is *selecting* fruit not *cleaning* it.

7. **(B)** Two men shake hands as two women look on. Choice (A) confuses *drinking glasses* with *eyeglasses*, which one of the men is wearing. Choice (C) confuses similar-sounding words *smiling* and *filing*. Choice (D) refers to the stairs in the background, but no one is climbing them.

8. **(C)** Two people are looking at paintings hanging on a museum wall. Choice (A) is incorrect because they are already inside the museum. Choice (B) confuses the meaning of the word *pictures* (paintings or photos). Choice (D) refers to the bench in the photo, but no one is sitting on it.

9. **(D)** A subway train, which runs underground, is in the station. Choice (A) is incorrect because there are people and a train in the station. Choice (B) confuses similar-sounding words *train* and *plane*. Choice (C) correctly identifies the passengers in the photo but not their action.

10. **(D)** A tired businessman is lying on a bed. Choice (A) refers to the jacket that is lying across his arm and that he has probably just taken off. Choice (B) refers

to the briefcase he is holding in his hand but not opening. Choice (C) confuses similar-sounding words *lying on* and *trying on*.

PART 2: QUESTION-RESPONSE

11. **(A)** This is the common, polite response when meeting someone. Choice (B) confuses the meaning of the word *meeting*. Choice (C) confuses *meeting* with the similar-sounding word *seating*.

12. **(C)** This answers the yes/no question about where Mr. Kim works. Choice (A) repeats the word *here*. Choice (B) associates *worker* with *work*.

13. **(B)** This explains the reason for not opening the door. Choice (A) confuses similar-sounding words *door* and *more*. Choice (C) confuses similar-sounding words *door* and *floor*.

14. **(B)** This answers the question about possession. Choice (A) repeats the word *car*. Choice (C) associates *car* with *drive*.

15. **(C)** This answers the question about time. Choice (A) confuses similar-sounding words *arrive* and *drive*. Choice (B) confuses similar-sounding words *arrive* and *five*.

16. **(A)** This explains what the speaker forgot. Choice (B) confuses similar-sounding words *forget* and *get* and associates *something* with *anything*. Choice (C) confuses similar-sounding words *forget* and *get* and repeats the word *something*.

17. **(C)** This answers the question *Where?* Choice (A) repeats the word *stop*. Choice (B) associates *bus* with *ride*.

18. **(A)** This answers the question *How often?* Choice (B) would answer the question *Where?* Choice (C) confuses similar-sounding words *meeting* and *reading*.

19. **(C)** This is the information the question asks for—an address. Choice (A) repeats the word *address*. Choice (B) confuses similar-sounding words *address* and *dress*.

20. **(A)** This answers the question about phone calls. Choice (B) confuses similar-sounding words *call* and *cold* and *out* and *outside*. Choice (C) confuses similar-sounding words *call* and *tall*.

21. **(B)** A steak and some salad are what the speaker wants to eat for dinner. Choice (A) associates *dinner* with cook. Choice (C) confuses similar-sounding words *dinner* and *thinner*.

22. **(B)** The word *ten* answers the question *How many?* Choice (A) associates *books* with *read*. Choice (C) confuses similar-sounding words *books* and *looks*.

23. **(C)** *August* answers the question *When?* Choice (A) would answer the question *Where?* Choice (B) confuses similar-sounding words *vacation* and *station*.

24. **(B)** This explains the reason for not coming to lunch. Choice (A) confuses similar-sounding words *lunch* and *punch*. Choice (C) associates *lunch* with *restaurant*.

25. **(A)** Paper and envelopes are what the speaker needs from the store. Choice (B) confuses similar-sounding words *store* and *four*. Choice (C) associates *store* with *shopping*.

26. **(A)** The phrase *in my desk drawer* answers the question *Where?* Choice (B) associates *pens* with *ink*. Choice (C) repeats the word *pen*.

27. **(C)** The mention of rain prompts the second speaker to suggest an umbrella. Choice (A) confuses similar-sounding words *might* and *night* and repeats the word *soon*. Choice (B) confuses similar-sounding words *rain* and *train* and *soon* and *noon*.

28. **(B)** This describes the coat. Choices (A) and (C) repeat the word *coat*.

29. **(B)** This is a logical response to a complaint about a warm room. Choice (A) confuses similar-sounding words *warm* and *warn*. Choice (C) confuses the meaning of the word *room*.

30. **(A)** This tells where, or how close, the subway station is. Choice (B) confuses similar-sounding words *close* and *clothes*. Choice (C) repeats the word *station*.

31. **(C)** This answers the question *Where?* Choice (A) confuses *newspaper* with the similar-sounding words *new paper*. Choice (B) associates *newspaper* with *read*.

32. **(B)** *Tennis* answers the question about a favorite sport. Choice (A) confuses similar-sounding words *sport* and *port*. Choice (C) confuses similar-sounding words *favorite* and *favor*.

33. **(B)** The first speaker liked the movie and the second speaker agrees. Choice (A) confuses the related words *interesting* and *interested* and repeats the word *movies*. Choice (C) confuses similar-sounding words *movie* and *moving*.

34. **(A)** *On your desk* answers the question *Where?* Choice (B) associates *package* with *mail*. Choice (C) confuses similar-sounding words *package* and *packed*.

35. **(A)** This explains why the speaker wasn't at the workshop. Choice (B) confuses the compound word *workshop* with the two separate words *work* and *shop*. Choice (C) repeats the word *Friday*.

36. **(C)** *The whole staff* answers the question *Who?* Choice (A) confuses similar-sounding words *meeting* and *greeting*. Choice (B) repeats the word *meeting*.

37. **(A)** Because the first speaker is hungry, the second speaker suggests lunch. Choice (B) confuses *hungry* with the similar-sounding word *angry*. Choice (C) confuses *hungry* with the similar-sounding word *hurry*.

38. **(B)** This answers the question *Where?* Choice (A) confuses similar-sounding words *live* and *leave*. Choice (C) confuses similar-sounding words *live* and *give*.

39. **(B)** *This afternoon* answers the question *When?* Choice (A) would answer the question *How many?* Choice (C) repeats the words *copies*.

40. **(B)** The second speaker doesn't need more paper because there is already enough. Choice (A) repeats the word *paper*. Choice (C) associates *paper* with *write*.

PART 3: CONVERSATIONS

41. **(D)** The woman says that the meeting is at 10:00 and the man says he will arrive 15 minutes late. Choice (A) and (B) confuse *time* with the similar-sounding number *nine*. Choice (C) is the time the meeting will begin.

42. **(B)** The woman says she wants to explain the situation, which is the delayed paychecks. Choice (A) uses the word *check* out of context and confuses *accounts* with *accounting department*. Choice (C) repeats the word *pay*. Choice (D) repeats the phrase *next week*.

43. **(C)** The man says *I can't pretend not to be annoyed about it*, which means that he is annoyed. Choice (A) confuses *happen* with the similar-sounding word *happy*. Choice (B) confuses *bad* with the similar-sounding word *sad*. Choice (D) confuses *before* with the similar-sounding word *bored*.

44. **(B)** The woman asks how long the flight will last, so she has to be on an airplane. Choice (A) associates restaurant with food. Choices (C) and (D) are both associated with *ticket*.

45. **(A)** The man says that it is a *cloudless*, meaning *clear*, day. Choice (B) confuses *cloudless* with *cloudy*. Choice (C) confuses *window* with the similar-sounding word *windy*. Choice (D) confuses *know* with the similar-sounding word *snow*.

46. **(B)** The man says that food will be served *in half an hour*. Choice (A) is the row number of the woman's seat. Choice (C) confuses *half an hour* with *an hour*. Choice (D) is confused with the time the plane will arrive at its destination.

47. **(A)** The woman asks the man to help her move a desk. Choice (B) repeats the word *window*. Choice (C) confuses *room* with the similar-sounding word *broom*. Choice (D) confuses *table* with the similar-sounding word *able*.

48. **(D)** The man explains that he hurt his back and can't lift heavy things. Choice (A) is where Samantha is. Choice (B) confuses *wait* with the similar-sounding word *late*. Choice (C) repeats the word *work*.

49. **(C)** The woman decides to wait until tomorrow when she can have Samantha help her. Choice (A) confuses the word *then* with the similar-sounding number *ten*. Choice (B) is when Samantha is at a workshop. Choice (D) is not mentioned.

50. **(A)** This is what the man says he is looking for and will take. Choice (B) and (C) are things the woman offers to sell him. Choice (D) is what the woman will put the gloves in.

51. **(D)** This is the color the man says he will take. Choice (A) confuses similar-sounding words *said* and *red*. Choice (B) confuses similar-sounding words *right* and *white*. Choice (C) confuses similar-sounding words *down* and *brown*.

52. **(B)** This is the price the woman gives. Choices (A), (C), and (D) all sound similar to the correct answer.

53. **(D)** This is the number the man asks for. Choices (A), (B), and (C) all sound similar to the correct answer.

54. **(C)** He wants them for the conference tomorrow morning. Choice (A) confuses similar-sounding words *soon* and *noon*. Choice (B) repeats the word *morning*. Choice (D) confuses similar-sounding words *today* and *Tuesday*.

55. **(A)** The woman says that it is a busy day and she has several other jobs to do. Choice (B) repeats the phrase *too many*. Choice (C) confuses similar-sounding words *collated* and *late*. Choice (D) confuses related words *stapled* and *stapler*.

56. **(B)** This is what the woman says she wants to do. Choice (A) confuses homonyms *by* and *buy*. Choice (C) is what Mr. Lee is doing. Choice (D) is what the man asks the woman about.

57. **(A)** The man says that Mr. Lee is out of town. Choice (B) confuses *out of town* with *downtown*. Choice (C) confuses similar-sounding words *phone* and *home*. Choice (D) repeats the word *office*.

58. **(C)** The man says that he expects Mr. Lee to return next week. Choice (A) confuses similar-sounding words *away* and *today*. Choice (B) repeats the word *morning*. Choice (D) confuses similar-sounding words *here* and *year*.

59. **(D)** The man is afraid he'll be late for his doctor's appointment downtown. Choice (A) is not mentioned. Choice (B) is where the woman will go later. Choice (C) confuses similar-sounding words *rain* and *train*.

60. **(B)** This is where the woman says her car is. Choice (A) is where the man thinks the car is. Choice (C) confuses the meaning of the word *park*. Choice (D) is where the man has to go.

61. **(C)** The woman describes her car as an *old blue van*. Choice (A) confuses similar-sounding words *van* and *tan*. Choice (B) confuses similar-sounding words *way* and *gray*. Choice (D) confuses similar-sounding words *old* and *gold*.

62. **(C)** Ms. Jones wanted to avoid the bad traffic caused by the rain. Choice (A) confuses similar-sounding words *rain* and *train*. Choice (B) refers to the meeting she was supposed to have with the woman this afternoon. Choice (D) refers to the report that was to be discussed at the meeting.

63. **(A)** The man says that Ms. Jones left at this time. Choice (B) confuses similar-sounding words *before* and *four*. Choice (C) confuses similar-sounding words *wait* and *eight*. Choice (D) confuses similar-sounding words *then* and *ten*.

64. **(B)** Ms. Jones left the office early because of the rain. Choice (A) confuses similar-sounding words *not* and *hot*. Choice (C) confuses similar-sounding words *know* and *snow*. Choice (D) confuses similar-sounding words *call* and *cold*.

65. **(D)** This is what the woman says she mailed. Choice (A) confuses similar-sounding words *books* and *look*. Choice (B) repeats the word *report* out of context. Choice (C) confuses *photographs* with *photocopies*.

66. **(B)** This is when the woman says she mailed the photographs. Choice (A) confuses *today* with the similar-sounding phrase *two days*. Choice (C) confuses *arrive* with the similar-sounding word *five*. Choice (D) confuses *wait* with the similar-sounding word *eight*.

67. **(A)** This is what the woman says she thinks she should do. Choices (B) and (D) are what the man suggests. Choice (C) repeats the word *copies*.

68. **(B)** The woman asks the man to play tennis at the park. Choice (A) is what the man did in the morning. Choices (C) and (D) are what the man and woman will do tonight, but these are plans already in place and not what she is inviting him to do now.

69. **(D)** The man says that he is *wiped out*, or very tired. Choice (A) confuses similar-sounding words *banquet* and *bank*. Choice (B) refers to the tickets the man bought for the banquet. Choice (C) confuses similar-sounding words *better* and *letter*.

70. **(C)** The man will attend the banquet at the hotel. Choice (A) is where the man played golf. Choice (B) is where the woman will play tennis. Choice (D) confuses similar-sounding words *rest* and *restaurant*.

PART 4: TALKS

71. **(D)** Technicians are available *24 hours a day, seven days a week*, so a caller can speak with one any time he likes. Choices (A), (B), and (C) all sound similar to *24 hours a day, seven days a week*.

72. **(C)** The recording says to press 2 to make an appointment. Choice (A) is confused with *seven days a week*, which is when the business is open. Choice (B) is confused with *stay on the line*, which is the way to speak with Tech Support. Choice (D) repeats the word *office*.

73. **(C)** The recording says to press 3 for billing questions. Choice (A) is what happens if the caller stays on the line. Choice (B) is what happens if the caller presses 1. Choice (D) is what happens if the caller presses zero.

74. **(A)** Dr. Swanson will talk about small business (the topic of her book). Choice (B) is confused with the book promotion tour. Choice (C) is the topic of next month's lecture. Choice (D) is confused with the book promotion tour.

75. **(B)** The speaker says that books *will be available for sale*. Choice (A) is what the speaker says will not happen. Choice (C) uses the word *sign* out of context. Choice (D) repeats the words *speaker* and *talk*.

76. **(D)** The speaker says *Don't miss next month's lecture*. Choice (A) repeats the word *evening*. Choice (B) repeats the word *Thursday*. Choice (C) is not mentioned.

77. **(A)** The EZ Sit chair is the product advertised. Choices (B), (C), and (D) repeat other words mentioned, but they are not the product advertised for sale.

78. **(B)** This product is advertised to be used in an office. Choice (A) confuses *phone* with the similar-sounding word *home*. Choice (C) associates *show* with *theater* by confusing the meaning of the word *show* (*showroom* in the advertisement). Choice (D) confuses *roomy* with *classroom*.

79. **(A)** This is the discount mentioned. Choices (B) and (D) sound similar to the correct answer. Choice (C) is confused with the date the discount offer ends— *May 20th*.

80. **(A)** The announcer says that the drought, or spell of dry weather, will continue. Choice (B) refers to the cold front coming in on the weekend. Choices (C) and (D) are how the weather will be on Sunday.

81. **(D)** This is what the announcer says. Choice (A) confuses similar-sounding words *plenty* and *twenty*. Choice (B) is confused with the overnight temperatures mentioned—*in the high sixties*. Choice (C) sounds similar to the correct answer.

82. **(D)** The announcer predicts rain on Sunday. Choices (A) and (B) repeat words used in the talk. Choice (C) is confused with *overnight*.

83. **(C)** The speaker addresses the talk to people who *travel frequently for business*. Choice (A) mentions people who are often concerned about nutrition, the theme of the talk. Choice (B) associates travel with tourists. Choice (D) repeats the word *restaurants*.

84. **(B)** The speaker says to *make sure to eat a big breakfast*. Choices (A), (C), and (D) are foods that the speaker implies are not healthful.

85. **(C)** A big breakfast is the speaker's solution to the problem of maintaining a healthful diet while traveling. Choices (A), (B), and (D) are reasons one might choose less healthful foods.

86. **(B)** The caller is instructed to dial another number to contact the on-call dentist. Choice (A) is what the caller can do by leaving a message. Choice (C) mentions the name of the dentist whose office this is. Choice (D) repeats different words from the recording.

87. **(A)** The office is open Monday through Friday and Saturday, so it is closed on Sunday. Choices (B), (C), and (D) are days that the office is open.

88. **(C)** The caller is instructed to call back when the office is open to make an appointment. Choice (A) is what the caller can do to speak with the dentist or the office staff. Choices (B) and (D) are what the caller should do in case of emergency.

89. **(D)** The event is a job fair where job seekers can find out about job opportunities and pass out their resumes. Choice (A) repeats the word *career*. Choice (B) repeats the word *city*. Choice (C) repeats the word *hotel*.

90. **(C)** The event begins at 11:30. Choices (A) and (B) sound similar to the correct answer. Choice (D) is the time the event ends.

91. **(B)** Attendees are advised to bring copies of their resume. Choice (A) is available at the door. Choice (C) is where the event was mentioned. Choice (D) is available at the event.

92. **(A)** The speaker mentions *flight* and *flying*, so it is a plane. Choice (B) confuses similar-sounding words *rain* and *plane*. Choice (C) associates *sailing* with *boat*. Choice (D) confuses similar-sounding words *us* and *bus*.

93. **(D)** The speaker says that the travel time will be just under six hours. Choice (B) refers to the time that the flight will arrive in Mexico. Choices (A) and (C) are part of the flight number.

94. **(B)** The speaker says that the skies are clear and sunny. Choices (A) and (C) are how the weather was earlier. Choice (D) confuses similar-sounding words *windows* and *windy*.

95. **(C)** The report is about flooding caused by heavy rains and the overflowing river. Choice (A) confuses the meaning of the word *banks*. Choice (B) confuses the meaning of the word *main*. Choice (D) repeats the words *rush* and *heavy* and associates *driving* with *traffic*.

96. **(D)** The report says that *citizens are asked to stay away from downtown*. Choice (A) is incorrect because citizens are warned to *drive with caution*, not avoid driving all together. Choice (B) repeats the word *police*. Choice (C) repeats the word *clear*.

97. **(C)** This is when the speaker says the floods should recede. Choice (A) confuses similar-sounding words *few days* and *today*. Choice (B) confuses similar-sounding words *night* and *tonight*. Choice (D) repeats the word *month*.

98. **(B)** This is one of the activities mentioned. Choice (A) confuses *course* with the similar-sounding word *horse*. Choice (C) confuses *hiking* with the similar-sounding word *biking*. Choice (D) confuses the meaning of the word *course* (four-course meal) by associating it with *golf* (golf course).

99. **(B)** This is the price mentioned. Choice (A) repeats the word *one*. Choice (C) confuses similar-sounding numbers *seven* and *eleven*. Choice (D) is confused with the date when the weekend package offer begins.

100. **(A)** The resort is open April through January, so it is closed in February and March. Choice (B) is the months when the weekend package is offered. Choice (C) confuses *December* with the similar-sounding months *September* and *November*. Choice (D) is when the winter vacation specials are available.

Reading

PART 5: INCOMPLETE SENTENCES

101. **(A)** *Considered* is the main verb of the sentence, in the past tense form. Choices (B) and (C) are adjectives. Choice (D) is an adverb.

102. **(A)** This is a past unreal conditional sentence, which requires a past conditional verb in the main clause. Choice (B) is present conditional. Choice (C) is future perfect. Choice (D) is simple future.

103. **(D)** *Turned in* means *submitted*. Choices (A), (B), and (C) cannot be used in this context.

104. **(C)** *Increase* means *raise*. Samantha hoped to earn a higher salary. Choices (A), (B), and (D) look similar to the correct answer but cannot be correctly used in this context.

105. **(B)** *Since* means *because*. They needed a lot of chairs because they expected a lot of people. Choices (A), (C) , and (D) are not logical in this context.

106. **(D)** *Through* means *pass from one end to the other*. People are asked not to enter the lobby at all while it is being painted. Choices (A), (B), and (C) do not have the meaning of entering or being inside a place.

107. **(A)** This is a past perfect verb used to describe an action that happened before another action (*we got to the station*) in the past. Choice (B) is the right tense but is passive voice, and the sentence is active. Choice (C) is present perfect. Choice (D) is future perfect.

108. **(C)** This is an adjective used to describe the noun *experience*. Choices (A) and (B) are verbs. Choice (D) is a noun.

109. **(C)** *After* at the beginning of the time clause tells us that the action in the main clause happened after the action in the time clause. Choices (A), (B), and (D) all have meanings similar to *after* but cannot be used to introduce a time clause.

110. **(B)** The verb *avoid* is followed by a gerund. Choice (A) is the base or present tense form. Choice (C) is the infinitive form. Choice (D) is the past participle.

111. **(B)** This is an adverb of manner used to describe how you will work. Choices (A) and (D) are nouns. Choice (C) is an adjective.

112. **(D)** *By* in this sentence means *before*. Choices (A) and (C) don't make sense in this sentence. Choice (B) is the opposite of the correct meaning.

113. **(D)** This is an adjective used to describe the noun *offer*. Choices (A) and (B) are verbs. Choice (C) is a noun.

114. **(A)** This is a present continuous verb used to describe an action that is taking place *currently*, or now. Choice (B) is the infinitive form. Choice (C) is a past tense form. Choice (D) is a past tense form.

115. **(A)** *Impose* means to *require* or *force upon*. Choice (B), (C), and (D) look similar to the correct answer but do not fit the context of the sentence.

116. **(A)** The present tense form of the verb is used in a future time clause. Choice (B) is present continuous. Choice (C) is future. Choice (D) is simple past.

117. **(D)** The subject of the sentence, *rooms*, receives the action, so a passive-voice form is required. Choices (A), (B), and (C) are all active-voice forms.

118. **(B)** The plural verb form *are* agrees with the plural subject *chairs*. Choices (A) and (D) are singular forms. Choice (C) doesn't make sense in this sentence.

119. **(C)** This is an adverb of manner used to describe the verb *arrive*. Choice (A) is a noun. Choice (B) is a verb and belongs to a different word family. Choice (D) is an adjective.

120. **(B)** *Before* introduces the time phrase that tells when the action will take place. Choices (A) and (D) don't make sense in this sentence. Choice (C) can be used to introduce a time clause but not a time phrase.

121. **(C)** *Although* shows a contrast between the two clauses. Choices (A) and (B) are used to show a cause-and-effect relationship. Choice (D) is normally followed by a noun, not by a clause.

122. **(A)** *Expires* means *ends*. Choices (B), (C), and (D) look similar to the correct answer but cannot be used in this context.

123. **(D)** *Seldom* means *almost never*. Choices (A), (B), and (C) are all opposite in meaning.

124. **(A)** This is a non-count noun referring to g*lass* as a material. Choice (B) is a plural count noun referring to *drinking glasses* or *eyeglasses*. Choice (C) is an adjective. Choice (D) looks similar to the other choices but has a different meaning.

125. **(D)** This is an unreal conditional in the present tense, so a past tense verb is required in the *if* clause. Choice (A) is the verb form for the main clause. Choice (B) is future tense. Choice (C) is present tense.

126. **(B)** The modal *should* is followed by the base form of the verb. Choice (A) is future tense. Choice (C) is present participle or a gerund. Choice (D) is past participle.

127. **(B)** The verb *expect* is followed by an infinitive verb. Choice (A) is base form or present tense. Choice (C) is present participle or a gerund. Choice (D) is future tense.

128. **(C)** This is a noun used as the object of the verb *offers*. Choice (A) is a verb. Choice (B) is an adjective. Choice (D) is a verb.

129. **(A)** The plural noun *computers* agrees with the plural verb *have*. Choices (B), (C), and (D) are all singular nouns.

130. **(C)** *To* refers to movement in a certain direction. Choices (A), (B), and (D) refer to location.

131. **(D)** This is the correct word to use in a sentence with *nor*. Choices (A), (B), and (C) are not used with *nor*.

132. **(B)** This is a comparative adjective used in a sentence with *than* to compare one photocopier to another. Choice (A) is a superlative adjective. Choice (C) is an adverb. Choice (D) is an adjective, but not a comparative.

133. **(A)** This is an imperative verb, used for making a command or request. Choice (B) is a gerund. Choice (C) is an infinitive. Choice (D) is future tense.

134. **(C)** This is an adjective used to describe the noun *office*. Choice (A) is a noun or a verb. Choice (B) is a past tense verb. Choice (D) is a noun.

135. **(D)** The present participle verb form is used to complete the past perfect continuous verb. Choices (A) and (B) are present tense. Choice (C) is past tense.

136. **(C)** This is a superlative adjective used with *the* to compare Mr. Sato to everyone else in a group. Choice (A) is a simple adjective form. Choice (B) is a comparative adjective. Choice (D) is a noun.

137. **(B)** *Rise* is a verb that means *go up*. Choice (A) is not a verb. Choice (C) is a transitive verb; it requires an object. Choice (D) is a noun.

138. **(A)** *Audit* is a verb that tells what the accountant will do. Choices (B) and (D) are nouns. Choice (C) is an adjective.

139. **(B)** This is a past participle verb used to complete the passive causative form, *have inspected*, meaning, *We will ask another person to inspect*. Choice (A) is the base form or present tense. Choice (C) is present tense. Choice (D) is an infinitive.

140. **(D)** This present perfect verb form is used to describe an action that began in the past and continues to the present. Choice (A) is simple present. Choice (B) is simple past. Choice (C) is present continuous.

PART 6: TEXT COMPLETION

141. **(C)** A passive-voice word is required in this sentence. The action is performed *by department heads*. Choices (A), (B), and (D) are all active-voice forms.

142. **(A)** The singular third person pronoun *It* refers to the *check stub* mentioned in the previous sentence. Choices (B) and (C) are also singular third person pronouns, but they are used to refer to people, not things. Choice (D) is a plural pronoun.

143. **(B)** *Attend* means *go to* or *be present at*. Choices (A), (C), and (D) look similar to the correct answer but have different meanings.

144. **(C)** This banquet takes place once a year in the spring, so it is *annual.* Choice (A) means *once a day.* Choice (B) means *once a month.* Choice (D) means *once every two years.*

145. **(A)** The writer is discussing the place, or *location,* for the banquet. Choices (B), (C), and (D) are all things that may be part of a banquet, but they are not the topic of this paragraph.

146. **(D)** A noun is required here. Choices (A), (B), and (C) are all verb forms.

147. **(A)** A present tense verb is used in an *if* clause that refers to a future action. Choice (B) is past participle. Choice (C) is the present participle or gerund form. Choice (D) is future tense.

148. **(C)** This is a passive-voice sentence, so the past participle form of the verb is required. Choices (A) and (B) are present tense active-voice forms. Choice (D) is a noun.

149. **(D)** The plural pronoun *they* refers to the plural noun *advisers* mentioned in the previous sentence. Choices (A), (B), and (C) are all singular pronouns.

150. **(B)** This is a passive-voice sentence. Senior citizens *will be charged*, or *asked to pay* a fare. Choices (A), (C), and (D) all have the meaning of receiving money rather than paying it.

151. **(C)** *Currently* means *now*. This sentence explains the schedule that is in effect now and will change in the future. Choice (A) means *on time*. Choice (B) means *frequently*. Choice (D) means *before*.

152. **(D)** *Regarding* means *about*. Choices (A), (B), and (C) look similar to the correct answer but do not fit the context.

PART 7: READING COMPREHENSION

153. **(B)** *Just under* means the same as *a little less than*. Choice (A) is when the town meeting was held. Choice (C) misinterprets the meaning of *just under*. Choice (D) is confused with *before one more year has passed*.

154. **(B)** Clear Sound has telephone customers and also provides high-speed Internet access. Choice (A) is only part of what the company does. Choice (C) is confused with *delivers on its promises*. Choice (D) is not mentioned.

155. **(C)** Customers have *expressed great dissatisfaction* and they have complained, so they are unhappy. Choice (A) is the opposite of the correct answer. Choice (B) is confused with *welcomed with great optimism*, which is how people felt at first. Choice (D) is not mentioned.

156. **(A)** *Minor* means *small* or *unimportant*. Choices (B), (C), and (D) do not mean the same as *minor*.

157. **(A)** The ad says that paper items are on sale, so that would include envelopes. Choice (B) is confused with the mention of the *manager's desk*. Choices (C) and (D) are confused with the mention of the *computer files*.

158. **(B)** Customers are asked to go to the manager's desk for an application. Choice (A) is confused with the day the sale ends. Choice (C) is confused with the notifications that club members will receive by mail. Choice (D) is confused with *contact information*.

159. **(A)** IEP is an agency that helps people find jobs in other countries. Choice (B) is confused with the topic of going to other countries, something a travel agency might help people do. Choice (C) is something IEP specifically does not provide. Choice (D) repeats the words *teacher* and *training*.

160. **(C)** The article says that IEP was founded four years ago. Choices (A) and (B) are confused with the amount of time Margery Wilson wanted to spend abroad. Choice (D) is confused with how long ago Margery Wilson graduated from college.

161. **(D)** The service is for young professionals, people who normally have a college degree, and Margery Wilson says: *All you need is a college degree . . . .* Choice (A) is something that is mentioned as not required. Choice (B) is what will be gained by using the agency's services. Choice (C) is something a client might have but isn't required.

162. **(B)** The elevators will be closed for maintenance and repair. Choice (A) is what will be done later on in the stairs and hallways. Choice (C) is not mentioned. Choice (D) is confused with the mention of the painting schedule.

163. **(B)** The work will begin August 17 and be completed by the end of the month, which is two weeks. Choice (A) repeats the word *week*. Choices (C) and (D) repeat the word *month*.

164. **(A)** An apartment for the owner to live in is on the second floor. Choice (B) is confused with the snacks that are sold in the store. Choice (C) is confused with the equipment that is being sold with the store. Choice (D) is something that might be above a store, but it is not mentioned in the ad.

165. **(B)** The asking price is $750,000. Choice (A) is what the inventory is worth. Choice (C) is the sum of the asking price plus the value of the inventory. Choice (D) is the volume of sales.

166. **(D)** *Inventory* means *merchandise*, or the stock of items available for sale. Choices (A), (B), and (C) are all things that might be associated with the sale of a business but are not the correct answer.

167. **(D)** The instructions explain how to put new batteries into the GMX 200. Choice (A) repeats the word *cover*, which needs to be removed in order to change the batteries. Choice (B) is confused with *date of purchase*. Choice (C) is mentioned but is not the purpose of the instructions.

168. **(C)** The product is guaranteed to keep time accurately, so it is a clock. Choice (A) is confused with the mention of a date. Choice (B) is used to change the batteries. Choice (D) is confused with *dispose of used batteries properly*.

169. **(A)** All food at the café is made with organic ingredients, so that would include the soups. Choice (B) is incorrect because sandwiches are the most popular item. Choice (C) is incorrect because the soups are homemade. Choice (D) is incorrect because all the food at the café is vegetarian.

170. **(B)** *Concoction* means *combination*. Choices (A), (C), and (D) are all related to the topic of food, but they do not have the same meaning as *concoction*.

171. **(C)** Both cheese and vegetables are mentioned as sandwich ingredients. Choices (A), (B), and (D) all contain meat, which is not served at this vegetarian café.

172. **(D)** The café is open Monday through Saturday, so it is closed Sunday. Choices (A), (B), and (C) are all days the café is open.

173. **(B)** The article explains how to make a good impression at a job interview, so it is for job hunters. Choices (A), (C), and (D) are all related to the topic of clothes but are not who the article is for.

174. **(C)** The first paragraph discusses wearing dark colors to give a professional impression. Choice (A) is confused with the description of browns and greens. Choice (B) is what is mentioned as being not important. Choice (D) repeats the word *accessories*, which are discussed later, but not in relation to suit colors.

175. **(A)** Simple, quiet ties and plain earrings are recommended. Choices (B), (C), and (D) are all things that are specifically not recommended.

176. **(B)** Shoes that fit comfortably are recommended. Choices (A), (C), and (D) are all things that are specifically not recommended.

177. **(A)** The sheet contains information that would be of interest to a hotel guest. In addition, it mentions breakfast being included in the price of the room and a hotel manager, so it is information for hotel guests. Choice (B) is confused with the mention of tourism. Choice (C) is confused with the mention of a shopping mall. Choice (D) is a place where some of this information might be useful, but it is not the correct answer.

178. **(C)** The Market Mall subway station is five blocks from the hotel. Choices (A), (B), and (D) are other places mentioned in the information sheet.

179. **(C)** The downtown shopping district is famous for its fashion, or clothing, boutiques. Choices (A), (B), and (D) are all things that can be bought at the Market Mall.

180. **(B)** You can probably buy any kind of medicine at the pharmacy across the street. Choices (A), (C), and (D) are other places mentioned in the information sheet.

181. **(A)** The letter is dated May 8 and refers to the ad in *yesterday's paper,* so the ad appeared the day before May 8. Choice (B) is the date on the letter. Choice (C) is not mentioned. Choice (D) is the date James Jones's Spanish class begins.

182. **(B)** The ad mentions *assisting with documents* as one of the paralegal's duties. Choice (A) is incorrect because the duty is described as *providing legal information to clients,* not getting information from them, as in an interview. Choice (C) is confused with the request *No phone calls, please.* Choice (D) is confused with the line *We will contact you to make an appointment.*

183. **(D)** James Jones has work experience at an architectural firm, not as a paralegal, and the ad requested paralegal experience. Choices (A), (B), and (C) are all qualifications that he possesses.

184. **(C)** James Jones worked for three years at an architectural firm. Choice (A) is confused with the Spanish class he will be taking. Choice (B) is where he wants to work now. Choice (D) is confused with his knowledge of French.

185. **(B)** He mentions enclosing his resume. Choice (A) is something we can assume he has, but he doesn't say anything about enclosing it. Choice (C) is incorrect because even though he mentions knowing French, he never mentions a French certificate. Choice (D) is something he offers to send later.

186. **(B)** The courses recommended for Marvin are beginning word processing (Word Processing Basics) and Advanced Database. Of these, only Word Processing Basics, Section 2 fits his schedule because of his weekly meeting on Wednesdays at 2:00. Choices (A) and (D) are the courses that don't fit his schedule. Choice (C) is not recommended for Marvin because he already has a good knowledge of database programs.

187. **(C)** Sam Silliman tells Marvin that someone in the Human Resources Department will complete the registration process for him. Choices (A) and (B) are suggested on the course schedule materials. Choice (D) is what Sam Silliman wants Marvin to do after he has registered.

188. **(A)** Marvin will pay nothing himself because NZ, Inc. will pay all his fees for him. Choice (B) is the cost of a four-hour class. Choice (C) is the cost of a four-hour class plus materials. Choice (D) is the cost of a six-hour class plus materials.

189. **(D)** Sam Silliman is responsible for Marvin fulfilling the requirements of his probationary employment and other duties, so he must be Marvin's supervisor. Choices (A) and (C) are incorrect because Sam Silliman works for NZ, Inc., not for the Computer Training Center. Choice (B) is incorrect because Sam Silliman does not work in the Human Resources Department.

190. **(B)** Sam Silliman points out that Marvin's *first-year employee probationary status is still in effect,* which means that he has been there for less than one year. Choice (A) is incorrect because we don't know exactly how long he has been working there. Choices (C) and (D) are incorrect because he is still in his first year of employment.

191. **(C)** The message says that Ms. Lopez won't be able to make the appointment. Choice (A) is confused with the intended meeting place, a café. Choice (B) refers to the reason Ms. Lopez canceled the appointment. Choice (D) refers to what Mr. Oliver will be doing tomorrow.

192. **(A)** The phone message was left at 2:30 and, according to the e-mail, Mr. Oliver left the office five minutes before that. Choice (B) is the time the message was left. Choice (C) is the time the e-mail was sent. Choice (D) is when Ms. Lopez wants to hear back from Mr. Oliver.

193. **(C)** Today is Monday, according to the date given on the phone message. Ms. Kraft says that Mr. Oliver has free time the day after tomorrow, which would be Wednesday. Choice (A) is today. Choice (B) is tomorrow. Choice (D) is another day suggested by Ms. Lopez.

194. **(A)** In the phone message, Ms. Lopez asks to see a project report. Ms. Kraft will give that report and some photos to Mr. Oliver so that he can take them to Ms. Lopez. Choice (B) refers to the conference that Mr. Oliver will attend. Choice (C) is confused with the discussion of rescheduling the appointment. Choice (D) is confused with the meeting place.

195. **(D)** Ms. Kraft takes phone messages and schedules appointments, so she is probably an office assistant. Choice (A) is confused with the photos that Mr. Oliver took and will show Ms. Lopez. Choice (B) is confused with the project report that Ms. Lopez wants to see. Choice (C) is confused with the meeting place.

196. **(D)** The Option 2 buffet for 100 people costs $1,400, and tables and chairs for 100 people cost $200. Choice (A) is the cost of the option 3 buffet. Choice (B) is the cost of the Option 1 buffet. Choice (C) is the cost of the Option 2 buffet without tables and chairs.

197. **(B)** She wants both vegetarian and meat entrees, and Options 2 and 3 both include those. Choices (A) and (C) are incorrect because Option 1 doesn't include a vegetarian entrée. Choice (D) is incorrect because Option 2 is not the only choice that has both vegetarian and meat entrees.

198. **(D)** She would have to order a month before her conference date of October 15. Choice (A) is incorrect because the business does not accept cash. Choice (B) is something the customer has to pay extra for. Choice (C) offers a 15% discount.

199. **(C)** Orders must be accompanied by a 25% deposit, payable by check. Choice (A) is incorrect because credit cards are not accepted. Choice (B) is incorrect because there is no tablecloth color choice; they are all white. Choice (D) is included in all the options.

200. **(B)** She expects 40–45 people, so she would pay the price for up to 50 people. Choice (A) is the price for up to 25 people. Choice (C) is the price for up to 50 people plus tables and chairs, but she will use her own tables and chairs. Choice (D) is the price for up to 100 people.

Answer Sheet
TOEIC PRACTICE TEST 3

Listening Comprehension

Part 1: Photographs

1. Ⓐ Ⓑ Ⓒ Ⓓ
2. Ⓐ Ⓑ Ⓒ Ⓓ
3. Ⓐ Ⓑ Ⓒ Ⓓ

4. Ⓐ Ⓑ Ⓒ Ⓓ
5. Ⓐ Ⓑ Ⓒ Ⓓ
6. Ⓐ Ⓑ Ⓒ Ⓓ

7. Ⓐ Ⓑ Ⓒ Ⓓ
8. Ⓐ Ⓑ Ⓒ Ⓓ

9. Ⓐ Ⓑ Ⓒ Ⓓ
10. Ⓐ Ⓑ Ⓒ Ⓓ

Part 2: Question-Response

11. Ⓐ Ⓑ Ⓒ
12. Ⓐ Ⓑ Ⓒ
13. Ⓐ Ⓑ Ⓒ
14. Ⓐ Ⓑ Ⓒ
15. Ⓐ Ⓑ Ⓒ
16. Ⓐ Ⓑ Ⓒ
17. Ⓐ Ⓑ Ⓒ
18. Ⓐ Ⓑ Ⓒ

19. Ⓐ Ⓑ Ⓒ
20. Ⓐ Ⓑ Ⓒ
21. Ⓐ Ⓑ Ⓒ
22. Ⓐ Ⓑ Ⓒ
23. Ⓐ Ⓑ Ⓒ
24. Ⓐ Ⓑ Ⓒ
25. Ⓐ Ⓑ Ⓒ
26. Ⓐ Ⓑ Ⓒ

27. Ⓐ Ⓑ Ⓒ
28. Ⓐ Ⓑ Ⓒ
29. Ⓐ Ⓑ Ⓒ
30. Ⓐ Ⓑ Ⓒ
31. Ⓐ Ⓑ Ⓒ
32. Ⓐ Ⓑ Ⓒ
33. Ⓐ Ⓑ Ⓒ
34. Ⓐ Ⓑ Ⓒ

35. Ⓐ Ⓑ Ⓒ
36. Ⓐ Ⓑ Ⓒ
37. Ⓐ Ⓑ Ⓒ
38. Ⓐ Ⓑ Ⓒ
39. Ⓐ Ⓑ Ⓒ
40. Ⓐ Ⓑ Ⓒ

Part 3: Conversations

41. Ⓐ Ⓑ Ⓒ Ⓓ
42. Ⓐ Ⓑ Ⓒ Ⓓ
43. Ⓐ Ⓑ Ⓒ Ⓓ
44. Ⓐ Ⓑ Ⓒ Ⓓ
45. Ⓐ Ⓑ Ⓒ Ⓓ
46. Ⓐ Ⓑ Ⓒ Ⓓ
47. Ⓐ Ⓑ Ⓒ Ⓓ
48. Ⓐ Ⓑ Ⓒ Ⓓ

49. Ⓐ Ⓑ Ⓒ Ⓓ
50. Ⓐ Ⓑ Ⓒ Ⓓ
51. Ⓐ Ⓑ Ⓒ Ⓓ
52. Ⓐ Ⓑ Ⓒ Ⓓ
53. Ⓐ Ⓑ Ⓒ Ⓓ
54. Ⓐ Ⓑ Ⓒ Ⓓ
55. Ⓐ Ⓑ Ⓒ Ⓓ
56. Ⓐ Ⓑ Ⓒ Ⓓ

57. Ⓐ Ⓑ Ⓒ Ⓓ
58. Ⓐ Ⓑ Ⓒ Ⓓ
59. Ⓐ Ⓑ Ⓒ Ⓓ
60. Ⓐ Ⓑ Ⓒ Ⓓ
61. Ⓐ Ⓑ Ⓒ Ⓓ
62. Ⓐ Ⓑ Ⓒ Ⓓ
63. Ⓐ Ⓑ Ⓒ Ⓓ
64. Ⓐ Ⓑ Ⓒ Ⓓ

65. Ⓐ Ⓑ Ⓒ Ⓓ
66. Ⓐ Ⓑ Ⓒ Ⓓ
67. Ⓐ Ⓑ Ⓒ Ⓓ
68. Ⓐ Ⓑ Ⓒ Ⓓ
69. Ⓐ Ⓑ Ⓒ Ⓓ
70. Ⓐ Ⓑ Ⓒ Ⓓ

Part 4: Talks

71. Ⓐ Ⓑ Ⓒ Ⓓ
72. Ⓐ Ⓑ Ⓒ Ⓓ
73. Ⓐ Ⓑ Ⓒ Ⓓ
74. Ⓐ Ⓑ Ⓒ Ⓓ
75. Ⓐ Ⓑ Ⓒ Ⓓ
76. Ⓐ Ⓑ Ⓒ Ⓓ
77. Ⓐ Ⓑ Ⓒ Ⓓ
78. Ⓐ Ⓑ Ⓒ Ⓓ

79. Ⓐ Ⓑ Ⓒ Ⓓ
80. Ⓐ Ⓑ Ⓒ Ⓓ
81. Ⓐ Ⓑ Ⓒ Ⓓ
82. Ⓐ Ⓑ Ⓒ Ⓓ
83. Ⓐ Ⓑ Ⓒ Ⓓ
84. Ⓐ Ⓑ Ⓒ Ⓓ
85. Ⓐ Ⓑ Ⓒ Ⓓ
86. Ⓐ Ⓑ Ⓒ Ⓓ

87. Ⓐ Ⓑ Ⓒ Ⓓ
88. Ⓐ Ⓑ Ⓒ Ⓓ
89. Ⓐ Ⓑ Ⓒ Ⓓ
90. Ⓐ Ⓑ Ⓒ Ⓓ
91. Ⓐ Ⓑ Ⓒ Ⓓ
92. Ⓐ Ⓑ Ⓒ Ⓓ
93. Ⓐ Ⓑ Ⓒ Ⓓ
94. Ⓐ Ⓑ Ⓒ Ⓓ

95. Ⓐ Ⓑ Ⓒ Ⓓ
96. Ⓐ Ⓑ Ⓒ Ⓓ
97. Ⓐ Ⓑ Ⓒ Ⓓ
98. Ⓐ Ⓑ Ⓒ Ⓓ
99. Ⓐ Ⓑ Ⓒ Ⓓ
100. Ⓐ Ⓑ Ⓒ Ⓓ

Reading

Part 5: Incomplete Sentences

101. Ⓐ Ⓑ Ⓒ Ⓓ   112. Ⓐ Ⓑ Ⓒ Ⓓ   122. Ⓐ Ⓑ Ⓒ Ⓓ   132. Ⓐ Ⓑ Ⓒ Ⓓ
102. Ⓐ Ⓑ Ⓒ Ⓓ   113. Ⓐ Ⓑ Ⓒ Ⓓ   123. Ⓐ Ⓑ Ⓒ Ⓓ   133. Ⓐ Ⓑ Ⓒ Ⓓ
103. Ⓐ Ⓑ Ⓒ Ⓓ   114. Ⓐ Ⓑ Ⓒ Ⓓ   124. Ⓐ Ⓑ Ⓒ Ⓓ   134. Ⓐ Ⓑ Ⓒ Ⓓ
104. Ⓐ Ⓑ Ⓒ Ⓓ   115. Ⓐ Ⓑ Ⓒ Ⓓ   125. Ⓐ Ⓑ Ⓒ Ⓓ   135. Ⓐ Ⓑ Ⓒ Ⓓ
106. Ⓐ Ⓑ Ⓒ Ⓓ   116. Ⓐ Ⓑ Ⓒ Ⓓ   126. Ⓐ Ⓑ Ⓒ Ⓓ   136. Ⓐ Ⓑ Ⓒ Ⓓ
107. Ⓐ Ⓑ Ⓒ Ⓓ   117. Ⓐ Ⓑ Ⓒ Ⓓ   127. Ⓐ Ⓑ Ⓒ Ⓓ   137. Ⓐ Ⓑ Ⓒ Ⓓ
108. Ⓐ Ⓑ Ⓒ Ⓓ   118. Ⓐ Ⓑ Ⓒ Ⓓ   128. Ⓐ Ⓑ Ⓒ Ⓓ   138. Ⓐ Ⓑ Ⓒ Ⓓ
109. Ⓐ Ⓑ Ⓒ Ⓓ   119. Ⓐ Ⓑ Ⓒ Ⓓ   129. Ⓐ Ⓑ Ⓒ Ⓓ   139. Ⓐ Ⓑ Ⓒ Ⓓ
110. Ⓐ Ⓑ Ⓒ Ⓓ   120. Ⓐ Ⓑ Ⓒ Ⓓ   130. Ⓐ Ⓑ Ⓒ Ⓓ   140. Ⓐ Ⓑ Ⓒ Ⓓ
111. Ⓐ Ⓑ Ⓒ Ⓓ   121. Ⓐ Ⓑ Ⓒ Ⓓ   131. Ⓐ Ⓑ Ⓒ Ⓓ

Part 6: Text Completion

141. Ⓐ Ⓑ Ⓒ Ⓓ   144. Ⓐ Ⓑ Ⓒ Ⓓ   147. Ⓐ Ⓑ Ⓒ Ⓓ   150. Ⓐ Ⓑ Ⓒ Ⓓ
142. Ⓐ Ⓑ Ⓒ Ⓓ   145. Ⓐ Ⓑ Ⓒ Ⓓ   148. Ⓐ Ⓑ Ⓒ Ⓓ   151. Ⓐ Ⓑ Ⓒ Ⓓ
143. Ⓐ Ⓑ Ⓒ Ⓓ   146. Ⓐ Ⓑ Ⓒ Ⓓ   149. Ⓐ Ⓑ Ⓒ Ⓓ   152. Ⓐ Ⓑ Ⓒ Ⓓ

Part 7: Reading Comprehension

153. Ⓐ Ⓑ Ⓒ Ⓓ   166. Ⓐ Ⓑ Ⓒ Ⓓ   179. Ⓐ Ⓑ Ⓒ Ⓓ   192. Ⓐ Ⓑ Ⓒ Ⓓ
154. Ⓐ Ⓑ Ⓒ Ⓓ   167. Ⓐ Ⓑ Ⓒ Ⓓ   180. Ⓐ Ⓑ Ⓒ Ⓓ   193. Ⓐ Ⓑ Ⓒ Ⓓ
155. Ⓐ Ⓑ Ⓒ Ⓓ   168. Ⓐ Ⓑ Ⓒ Ⓓ   181. Ⓐ Ⓑ Ⓒ Ⓓ   194. Ⓐ Ⓑ Ⓒ Ⓓ
156. Ⓐ Ⓑ Ⓒ Ⓓ   169. Ⓐ Ⓑ Ⓒ Ⓓ   182. Ⓐ Ⓑ Ⓒ Ⓓ   195. Ⓐ Ⓑ Ⓒ Ⓓ
157. Ⓐ Ⓑ Ⓒ Ⓓ   170. Ⓐ Ⓑ Ⓒ Ⓓ   183. Ⓐ Ⓑ Ⓒ Ⓓ   196. Ⓐ Ⓑ Ⓒ Ⓓ
158. Ⓐ Ⓑ Ⓒ Ⓓ   171. Ⓐ Ⓑ Ⓒ Ⓓ   184. Ⓐ Ⓑ Ⓒ Ⓓ   197. Ⓐ Ⓑ Ⓒ Ⓓ
159. Ⓐ Ⓑ Ⓒ Ⓓ   172. Ⓐ Ⓑ Ⓒ Ⓓ   185. Ⓐ Ⓑ Ⓒ Ⓓ   198. Ⓐ Ⓑ Ⓒ Ⓓ
160. Ⓐ Ⓑ Ⓒ Ⓓ   173. Ⓐ Ⓑ Ⓒ Ⓓ   186. Ⓐ Ⓑ Ⓒ Ⓓ   199. Ⓐ Ⓑ Ⓒ Ⓓ
161. Ⓐ Ⓑ Ⓒ Ⓓ   174. Ⓐ Ⓑ Ⓒ Ⓓ   187. Ⓐ Ⓑ Ⓒ Ⓓ   200. Ⓐ Ⓑ Ⓒ Ⓓ
162. Ⓐ Ⓑ Ⓒ Ⓓ   175. Ⓐ Ⓑ Ⓒ Ⓓ   188. Ⓐ Ⓑ Ⓒ Ⓓ
163. Ⓐ Ⓑ Ⓒ Ⓓ   176. Ⓐ Ⓑ Ⓒ Ⓓ   189. Ⓐ Ⓑ Ⓒ Ⓓ
164. Ⓐ Ⓑ Ⓒ Ⓓ   177. Ⓐ Ⓑ Ⓒ Ⓓ   190. Ⓐ Ⓑ Ⓒ Ⓓ
165. Ⓐ Ⓑ Ⓒ Ⓓ   178. Ⓐ Ⓑ Ⓒ Ⓓ   191. Ⓐ Ⓑ Ⓒ Ⓓ

TOEIC Practice Test 3

LISTENING COMPREHENSION

In this section of the test, you will have the chance to show how well you understand spoken English. There are four parts to this section, with special directions for each part. You will find the Answer Sheet for Practice Test 3 on page 115. Detach it from the book and use it to record your answers. Check your answers using the Answer Key on page 152 and see the Answers Explained on page 154.

TIP

If you do not have access to an audio CD player, please refer to the audioscripts starting on page 333 when prompted to listen to an audio passage.

CD 2
TRACK
3

Part 1: Photographs

Directions: You will see a photograph. You will hear four statements about the photograph. Choose the statement that most closely matches the photograph and fill in the corresponding oval on your answer sheet.

Example

Now listen to the four statements.

Sample Answer

Ⓐ Ⓑ Ⓒ Ⓓ

Statement (B), "She's reading a magazine," best describes what you see in the picture. Therefore, you should choose answer (B).

TOEIC Practice Test 3

1.

2.

3.

4.

5.

6.

7.

9.

8.

10.

Part 2: Question-Response

Directions: You will hear a question and three possible responses. Choose the response that most closely answers the question and fill in the corresponding oval on your answer sheet.

Example

Now listen to the sample question.

You will hear:

How is the weather?

You will also hear:

(A) It's raining.
(B) He's fine, thanks.
(C) He's my boss.

The best response to the question *How is the weather?* is choice (A), *It's raining.* Therefore, you should choose answer (A).

11. Mark your answer on your answer sheet.
12. Mark your answer on your answer sheet.
13. Mark your answer on your answer sheet.
14. Mark your answer on your answer sheet.
15. Mark your answer on your answer sheet.
16. Mark your answer on your answer sheet.
17. Mark your answer on your answer sheet.
18. Mark your answer on your answer sheet.
19. Mark your answer on your answer sheet.
20. Mark your answer on your answer sheet.
21. Mark your answer on your answer sheet.
22. Mark your answer on your answer sheet.
23. Mark your answer on your answer sheet.
24. Mark your answer on your answer sheet.
25. Mark your answer on your answer sheet.

26. Mark your answer on your answer sheet.
27. Mark your answer on your answer sheet.
28. Mark your answer on your answer sheet.
29. Mark your answer on your answer sheet.
30. Mark your answer on your answer sheet.
31. Mark your answer on your answer sheet.
32. Mark your answer on your answer sheet.
33. Mark your answer on your answer sheet.
34. Mark your answer on your answer sheet.
35. Mark your answer on your answer sheet.
36. Mark your answer on your answer sheet.
37. Mark your answer on your answer sheet.
38. Mark your answer on your answer sheet.
39. Mark your answer on your answer sheet.
40. Mark your answer on your answer sheet.

Part 3: Conversations

CD 2
TRACK
5

Directions: You will hear a conversation between two people. You will see three questions on each conversation and four possible answers. Choose the best answer to each question and fill in the corresponding oval on your answer sheet.

41. What does the woman want to do?
    (A) See a TV show
    (B) Go to the movies
    (C) Take a walk
    (D) Read a book

42. Why does the man say he can't do this?
    (A) He has to catch a plane.
    (B) He wants to go to bed early.
    (C) He doesn't have tickets.
    (D) He is working late.

43. What time will the man and woman meet?
    (A) 4:00
    (B) 8:00
    (C) 9:00
    (D) 10:00

44. Why does the man want to meet with the woman?
    (A) To have lunch
    (B) To work on a report
    (C) To discuss his health
    (D) To point out some problems

45. Where will they meet?
    (A) At the man's office
    (B) In a conference room
    (C) At a restaurant
    (D) Downtown

46. When will they meet?
    (A) In the morning
    (B) At noon
    (C) In the afternoon
    (D) At night

47. Where does this conversation take place?
    (A) In a store
    (B) In an office
    (C) In an elevator
    (D) In an apartment

48. Who is the woman visiting?
    (A) A college friend
    (B) A work colleague
    (C) Her brother
    (D) The man

49. What is the man's opinion of the building?
    (A) He likes it.
    (B) It's a bad building.
    (C) It's too close to the shops.
    (D) He feels sad in it.

50. What does the man want to do?
    (A) Reserve a meeting room
    (B) Make a new schedule
    (C) Serve a luncheon
    (D) Order a book

51. What time will he finish?
    (A) 8:00
    (B) 10:00
    (C) 11:00
    (D) 1:00

52. What does the woman ask him to do?
    (A) Set up for the luncheon
    (B) Work that morning
    (C) Find a new place
    (D) Put the chairs back

53. What will be cleaned today?
(A) The conference room
(B) The hallways
(C) The office
(D) The front door

54. When will the front office be cleaned?
(A) Sunday
(B) Tuesday
(C) Wednesday
(D) Friday

55. What will the woman do next week?
(A) Give a workshop
(B) Go shopping
(C) Serve a lunch
(D) Make a schedule

56. Why is the woman going to Chicago?
(A) To see relatives
(B) To take a vacation
(C) To take care of business
(D) To visit friends

57. How long does the trip take by train?
(A) 2 hours
(B) 4 hours
(C) 9 hours
(D) 16 hours

58. Why does the woman prefer the train to the plane?
(A) She's afraid of planes.
(B) The train is more interesting.
(C) She has lots of time.
(D) The plane is expensive.

59. Why is the local post office closed?
(A) It's Sunday.
(B) The hour is late.
(C) It's a holiday.
(D) The weather is bad.

60. How far away is the main post office?
(A) Two blocks
(B) Four blocks
(C) A little less than a mile
(D) More than a mile

61. How will the man get to the post office?
(A) Walking
(B) Bus
(C) Taxi
(D) Driving

62. Who does the man eat lunch with?
(A) Nobody
(B) The woman
(C) His assistant
(D) His officemates

63. Where does the man eat lunch?
(A) At a café
(B) At his desk
(C) In the park
(D) In the cafeteria

64. How long is the lunch break?
(A) 15 minutes
(B) Half an hour
(C) 45 minutes
(D) An hour

65. How many nights will the woman stay at the hotel?
(A) 1
(B) 3
(C) 4
(D) 7

66. What does the woman want to do now?
(A) Park her car
(B) Have dinner
(C) Go to the bank
(D) Take a walk

67. What is the weather like?
    (A) Warm
    (B) Snowy
    (C) Rainy
    (D) Cool

_____

68. Where does this conversation take place?
    (A) A travel agency
    (B) A train station
    (C) A hotel
    (D) A bank

69. What time is it now?
    (A) 9:00
    (B) 10:00
    (C) 10:15
    (D) 10:30

70. What does the woman need help with?
    (A) Her book
    (B) Her ticket
    (C) Her check
    (D) Her suitcase

Part 4: Talks

Directions: You will hear a talk given by a single speaker. You will see three questions on each talk, each with four possible answers. Choose the best answer to each question and fill in the corresponding oval on your answer sheet.

71. What time does the office open?
    (A) 7:00 AM
    (B) 9:00 AM
    (C) 11:00 PM
    (D) 2:00 PM

72. How can a caller open an account?
    (A) Visit during office hours
    (B) Press 0
    (C) Stay on the line
    (D) Press 3

73. What can a caller do by pressing 2?
    (A) Leave a message
    (B) Ask a question about a bill
    (C) Hear the message in Spanish
    (D) Speak with a customer service representative

74. What is being repaired?
    (A) A tunnel
    (B) A highway
    (C) A bridge
    (D) A park

75. When will the repairs be finished?
    (A) May
    (B) September
    (C) November
    (D) December

76. When is the next traffic update?
    (A) 7:00
    (B) 9:00
    (C) 9:20
    (D) 10:00

77. What kind of job does this school train for?
    (A) Law office assistant
    (B) Computer researcher
    (C) Customer service representative
    (D) Career counselor

78. How many months does the course last?
    (A) two
    (B) four
    (C) five
    (D) six

79. How can someone get an application?
    (A) Visit the office
    (B) Call the school
    (C) Go online
    (D) Send a letter

80. Where would this announcement be heard?
    (A) Train station
    (B) Boat dock
    (C) Airport
    (D) Bus station

81. Which gate should passengers go to?
    (A) 4
    (B) 6
    (C) 7
    (D) 11

82. Who will get on first?
    (A) Passengers for Honolulu
    (B) Passengers with children
    (C) Passengers with luggage
    (D) Passengers in rows 30–35

TOEIC Practice Test 3

83. When was this announcement being made?
    (A) June
    (B) July
    (C) August
    (D) September

84. When will the festival begin?
    (A) July 15
    (B) July 16
    (C) July 18
    (D) July 20

85. What will happen on Thursday night?
    (A) There will be dancing.
    (B) Games will be free.
    (C) Food will be served.
    (D) A concert will be performed.

86. Why will airport workers go on strike?
    (A) They are working in freezing cold conditions.
    (B) They are having problems with passengers.
    (C) They won't get their salary increase.
    (D) They don't have a contract.

87. When will the strike begin?
    (A) Immediately
    (B) Tomorrow afternoon
    (C) Next week
    (D) In two months

88. Where will union leaders and airline officials meet?
    (A) In the mayor's office
    (B) At a hotel
    (C) In a boardroom
    (D) At the airport

89. How long is the trip to New York?
    (A) two hours
    (B) three hours
    (C) four hours
    (D) six hours

90. What is not allowed anywhere on the train?
    (A) Laptop computers
    (B) Loud sounds
    (C) Cell phones
    (D) Smoking

91. What will happen in 15 minutes?
    (A) Drinks will be sold.
    (B) Food service will end.
    (C) The weather will get cold.
    (D) The rear car will be closed.

92. At which one of the following times will the musical be performed?
    (A) 2:00 PM Thursday
    (B) 2:00 PM Friday
    (C) 8:00 PM Saturday
    (D) 8:00 PM Sunday.

93. What is the cost of a child's ticket to the 8:00 PM Friday show?
    (A) $12
    (B) $15
    (C) $24
    (D) $30

94. How can tickets be reserved?
    (A) Call back later
    (B) Visit the theater
    (C) Send an e-mail
    (D) Leave a message

95. What is the weather like now?
    (A) Sunny
    (B) Cloudy
    (C) Rainy
    (D) Dry

96. What will the low temperature be tonight?
    (A) 15
    (B) 50
    (C) 60
    (D) 80

97. What does the announcer recommend doing this week?
    (A) Work in the garden.
    (B) Go to the beach.
    (C) Read a book.
    (D) Cook a good meal.

98. Who is the guest speaker?
    (A) An actor
    (B) A filmmaker
    (C) A mountain climber
    (D) An equipment salesperson

99. How much does the book cost?
    (A) $4
    (B) $13
    (C) $30
    (D) $32

100. What will happen next month?
    (A) There will be a talk on diving.
    (B) A film will be shown.
    (C) There won't be a program.
    (D) Books will be discounted.

READING

In this section of the test, you will have the chance to show how well you understand written English. There are three parts to this section, with special directions for each part.

YOU WILL HAVE ONE HOUR AND FIFTEEN MINUTES TO COMPLETE PARTS 5, 6, AND 7 OF THE TEST.

Part 5: Incomplete Sentences

Directions: You will see a sentence with a missing word. Four possible answers follow the sentence. Choose the best answer to the question and fill in the corresponding oval on your answer sheet.

101. I will call you as soon as I _____.
    (A) arrive
    (B) arrives
    (C) was arriving
    (D) will arrive

102. We will have to _____ strictly to meet expenses this month.
    (A) economy
    (B) economize
    (C) economist
    (D) economical

103. You'll find the ink cartridges _____ the top shelf of the closet.
    (A) in
    (B) on
    (C) up
    (D) at

104. The missing document was _____ in an empty office.
    (A) discover
    (B) discovery
    (C) discovered
    (D) discovering

105. This report is urgent, so please turn it _____ before the end of the day.
    (A) on
    (B) up
    (C) in
    (D) over

106. If you need any help filling out the forms, _____ somebody at the front desk for assistance.
    (A) to ask
    (B) asking
    (C) asks
    (D) ask

107. We will need to think _____ in order to find a good solution to this problem.
    (A) creatively
    (B) creative
    (C) created
    (D) creator

108. This office is expensive, but it's _____ than our old office.
    (A) space
    (B) spacious
    (C) more spacious
    (D) the most spacious

109. Dr. Chin, _____ book I just showed you, works across the hall from me.
     (A) who
     (B) that
     (C) whom
     (D) whose

110. The new company headquarters is _____ Main Street.
     (A) at
     (B) on
     (C) in
     (D) to

111. I really enjoy the work that I do, _____ I have a hard time getting along with my colleagues.
     (A) but
     (B) and
     (C) as
     (D) or

112. We returned the table to the store because we _____ a small flaw on the surface.
     (A) demanded
     (B) deplored
     (C) detected
     (D) delayed

113. The old house on the corner is _____ down and needs some serious repair work.
     (A) fell
     (B) falls
     (C) fallen
     (D) falling

114. I will need these documents for the meeting tomorrow, so please have them on my desk _____ 8:00.
     (A) before
     (B) between
     (C) on
     (D) in

115. The visitor we are expecting in a few days _____ help finding a good hotel.
     (A) need
     (B) needs
     (C) have needed
     (D) are going to need

116. The _____ of our manufacturing process has saved the company a lot of money.
     (A) simplification
     (B) simplify
     (C) simply
     (D) simple

117. Ms. Lee prepared the charts, _____ Ms. Kim presented them at the meeting.
     (A) or
     (B) during
     (C) and
     (D) of

118. Everybody employed by this office _____ a professional degree.
     (A) has
     (B) have
     (C) to have
     (D) is having

119. You can expect_____ your first paycheck before the end of your first month of employment.
     (A) receive
     (B) to receive
     (C) receiving
     (D) recipient

120. It is better for the economy to buy things that are produced _____ rather than bringing in products from far away.
     (A) local
     (B) localize
     (C) locally
     (D) location

121. If you _____ your reservations earlier, you would have gotten on the flight you wanted.
     (A) made
     (B) had made
     (C) have made
     (D) would have made

122. The manager let everyone _____ the office early to attend the convention.
     (A) left
     (B) to leave
     (C) leaves
     (D) leave

123. The number of people who ask questions at the end of the lecture _____ always quite astonishing.
     (A) be
     (B) are
     (C) were
     (D) is

124. You can sign the document now, _____ you can speak to an attorney first if you prefer.
     (A) and
     (B) but
     (C) or
     (D) nor

125. You'll find the letter _____ the papers on my desk.
     (A) along
     (B) among
     (C) almost
     (D) always

126. He might _____ a discount if he pays for his ticket before next week.
     (A) get
     (B) gets
     (C) will get
     (D) going to get

127. If you lived closer to the office, you _____ trouble getting to work on time.
     (A) don't have
     (B) didn't have
     (C) won't have
     (D) wouldn't have

128. After listening to his thorough _____, I had no problems understanding how to use the software.
     (A) explains
     (B) explained
     (C) explanation
     (D) explanatory

129. He had a good reputation and was _____ as a very fair boss.
     (A) regarded
     (B) registered
     (C) regulated
     (D) regretted

130. We will review your application _____ you have submitted all your paperwork.
     (A) soon
     (B) as soon
     (C) as soon as
     (D) soon than

131. She earns more money than her coworkers _____ she works a lot of overtime hours.
     (A) although
     (B) because
     (C) despite
     (D) nevertheless

132. Prices continue to _____, causing a great deal of financial difficulty.
    (A) up
    (B) high
    (C) raise
    (D) rise

133. The walls were painted this morning, so _____ them.
    (A) touch
    (B) don't touch
    (C) touching
    (D) not to touch

134. The list of registered guests _____ sitting on the manager's desk.
    (A) have
    (B) were
    (C) are
    (D) is

135. Mr. Sato _____ here for many years and is one of our most knowledgeable employees.
    (A) is working
    (B) used to work
    (C) has been working
    (D) will have worked

136. Ms. Hansen got the job _____ she has very little experience and no college degree.
    (A) because
    (B) even though
    (C) moreover
    (D) since

137. We can't work on a solution until we _____ the source of the problem.
    (A) identification
    (B) indemnify
    (C) identity
    (D) identify

138. We discussed _____ a temporary assistant to help out with the extra work.
    (A) hire
    (B) hired
    (C) hiring
    (D) to hire

139. Very few people showed _____ for the conference.
    (A) up
    (B) to
    (C) off
    (D) through

140. The _____ of this business is a result of a lot of hard work and some solid financial support.
    (A) success
    (B) successful
    (C) succeed
    (D) successfully

Part 6: Text Completion

Directions: You will see four passages, each with three blanks. Under each blank are four answer options. Choose the word or phrase that best completes the statement.

Questions 141–143 refer to the following notice.

DISPUTING A BILL

If you have reason to believe that an item on your bill is wrong or if you need more information about any part of your bill, please contact us by writing to the Customer Service address shown on the front of this statement. We must hear from _____ within 90 days of the date on the statement. When

141. (A) us
(B) him
(C) you
(D) it

writing to us about your bill, please include your name and account number and a complete description and explanation of the error you claim. You will not have to pay the amount in question while we are _____ your claim.

142. (A) investigating
(B) interrogating
(C) intrusting
(D) invalidating

We need to receive your explanation in writing, however. If you have any questions about the procedure, please telephone the Customer Service office for _____ with making your claim.

143. (A) assists
(B) assisted
(C) assistants
(D) assistance

Questions 144–146 refer to the following letter.

February 6, 20--

To Whom It May Concern:

This is to serve as a letter of reference for Ms. Alicia Maldonado, who worked for us from January until November of last year. During her time with us, Ms. Maldonado proved herself to be a reliable and responsible worker. We _____ always count on her to get the job done well

144. (A) can
(B) could
(C) could have
(D) could never

and on time. She acquired many job skills while working with us and was capable of taking on more responsibilities. In fact, I planned to give her a _____ but, unfortunately for us, she decided to leave the

145. (A) demotion
(B) promotion
(C) probation
(D) detention

company for personal reasons. I understand that her husband's company transferred him to a position in another city. We miss Ms. Maldonado's contributions to our work and were very sorry to see _____ go.

146. (A) him
(B) us
(C) her
(D) hers

I believe Ms. Maldonado would be a great asset to any company.

Sincerely,

Maria Taylor

Questions 147–149 refer to the following memo.

To: All Personnel
From: Simon Shumlin, Office Manager
Re: Office Supply Requests

As of today, a new policy regarding the distribution of office supplies has been instituted. Unlimited entry to the supply closet is no longer allowed. Any staff member requiring supplies must make a request using the new Office Supply Request Form, available from my office. The form _____ completely and include the signature of the department

147. (A) must be filled out
     (B) must filling out
     (C) must to fill out
     (D) must fill out

head. Supplies requested by 3:00 PM Friday will be distributed by my assistant the _____ Monday.

148. (A) previous
     (B) following
     (C) foregoing
     (D) prior

We believe that this policy is the best way to ensure that everyone will have the supplies that they need available when they need them. Thank you for your _____.

149. (A) consolation
     (B) condemnation
     (C) corporation
     (D) cooperation

Questions 150–152 refer to the following article.

Many people are interested in making their homes and offices more environmentally friendly. However, they hesitate to put in alternative energy systems such as solar panels because of the high cost of installation. Alternative energy systems may actually be more _____ than is commonly believed. In looking for

150. (A) effective
     (B) affordable
     (C) polluting
     (D) popular

ways to reduce costs, it is important to start with a thorough energy analysis of your home or office. An energy expert can help you _____ how much power you actually need.

151. (A) assess
     (B) assesses
     (C) assessing
     (D) will assess

Reducing your power needs may be as _____ as buying a

152. (A) simplicity
     (B) simplify
     (C) simply
     (D) simple

few energy-efficient appliances. With reduced energy needs, you may be able to install a smaller alternative energy system, thus saving hundreds of dollars.

Part 7: Reading Comprehension

Directions: You will see single and double reading passages followed by several questions. Each question has four answer choices. Choose the best answer to the question and fill in the corresponding oval on your answer sheet.

Questions 153–154 refer to the following advertisement.

> **Office Space Available**
> **815 Enfield Street**
>
> This suite of offices is conveniently located close to downtown and major bus lines. The 3,000-square-foot floor plan has lots of potential, with space for ten offices, two conference rooms, and a large reception area. Large windows make it pleasant and sunny. Ample tenant and customer parking is in the rear of the building. Contract includes minor renovations to be made at the owner's expense prior to move-in; new tenant chooses paint and carpet colors. Call now for an appointment to see this incredible space. Melissa Soto Rental Agency, 637-2120.

153. What is true of the space for rent?
    (A) It is dark.
    (B) It will be painted.
    (C) It has a new carpet.
    (D) It doesn't include parking.

154. Who should potential tenants call to see the space?
    (A) The owner
    (B) The contractor
    (C) The rental agent
    (D) The current tenant

Questions 155–158 refer to the following advertisement.

We at the First Main Street Bank are expanding our services to help your business grow. For more than a century, we have been proudly providing the local business community with a full range of banking services, including small-business loans, special accounts, financial management services, and more. Now we are offering for the first time our free online business banking service, bringing you the convenience of paying telephone and utility bills, managing your payroll and accounts, real-time transactions, and more, all online. It's easy to set up and easy to use. Stop by any First Main Street branch to talk with the accounts manager about using online banking services to enhance your business banking experience. Call the main office at 438-0832 to find the location of a First Main Street Bank branch near you.

155. What is this advertisement announcing?
(A) A new service
(B) A new manager
(C) A new branch
(D) A new type of account

156. How can customers find out more about it?
(A) Call the main office
(B) Go online
(C) Read a brochure
(D) Visit the bank

157. How long has the bank been in business?
(A) Close to 10 years
(B) A little more than 10 years
(C) Almost 100 years
(D) More than 100 years

158. The word *enhance* in line 14 is closest in meaning to
(A) begin
(B) improve
(C) finance
(D) simplify

Questions 159–162 refer to the following letter.

To the Editor:

I read with great interest the article in your paper yesterday about the growing traffic problems in our region and how the planned construction work on a new Millers River Bridge will exacerbate the problem over the coming months. Proponents of building a new bridge, which is scheduled to begin next month and be completed within two years, claim that it will greatly alleviate the traffic problem in that part of the city once it is completed. In my opinion, that solution will be temporary at best. Allow me to propose another idea. For the past four years, a group of city planners, transportation experts, and others have been hard at work on a plan for a light rail system to serve our region. Of course, construction of a region-wide light rail train system would require a far greater investment than construction of a bridge, but it would serve a far larger percentage of our population and the effects on our traffic problems would be more far-reaching and permanent.

As discussed in yesterday's article, the new, bigger Millers River Bridge will carry more traffic than the old one, serving one small part of the city. The bridge has been artistically designed and will add beauty to our city landscape. These are small returns, in my opinion, for the expense city taxpayers will incur for the bridge construction. Clearly, investment in a regional light rail system is a better idea for our future.

Sincerely,

David Spaulding

159. Why did David Spaulding write this letter?
(A) To complain about the traffic problem
(B) To support a new light rail system
(C) To explain bridge construction
(D) To report on a city planners meeting

160. What did David Spaulding do yesterday?
(A) Read the newspaper
(B) Visited the new bridge
(C) Rode on a light rail train
(D) Met with transportation experts

161. When will the new bridge be completed?
(A) Next month
(B) In several months
(C) In two years
(D) In four years

162. What is David Spaulding's opinion of the new bridge?
(A) It's not a good solution.
(B) It won't look beautiful.
(C) It will be too big.
(D) It won't cost too much.

Questions 163–164 refer to the following notice.

Information for Building Visitors

All visitors must register at the Security Desk when entering the building. You will receive a visitor's badge. Keep it visible at all times while in the building. The security officer on duty will notify the office you are visiting, and an escort will be sent down to meet you. Please wait for your escort by the elevators. Badges are not required in the lobby and ground-floor cafeteria, which are open to the public.

The cafeteria and lobby area close at 6:30 PM, and the security officer goes off duty at 7:00 PM. All visitors must be out of the building before the security officer goes off duty. Exceptions to this rule must be arranged beforehand. For more information, speak with the security manager during normal office hours, 9:00 AM to 5:00 PM.

163. What must visitors do while in the building?
(A) Wear a visitor's badge
(B) Stay with the escort
(C) Avoid the cafeteria
(D) Remain in the lobby

164. What time should visitors leave the building?
(A) After 9:00 AM
(B) Before 5:00 PM
(C) At 6:30 PM
(D) Before 7:00 PM

Questions 165–167 refer to the following article.

Shelley Hallowell of Fairfield has been hired as the general manager for the new Harlequin Hotel in Fairfield's West Park district. Ms. Hallowell will assume her new position a month before the hotel's scheduled opening next September.

Ms. Hallowell returned to Fairfield last year after a five-year stint in the Fiji Islands as a tour guide. She held a temporary position between January and May of this year as a consultant to the local tourism board. Before moving to Fiji, she worked locally as an office assistant while studying for her degree. She is a graduate of the Hotel and Hospitality School of Fairfield.

"Ms. Hallowell has a great deal to offer our business. We feel very fortunate to have a person of her caliber working with us," said George Larue, co-owner of the Harlequin Hotel.

165. When will Ms. Hallowell begin her new job?
(A) January
(B) May
(C) August
(D) September

166. What was Ms. Hallowell's most recent job?
(A) Hotel manager
(B) Tourism consultant
(C) School instructor
(D) Office assistant

167. What did Ms. Hallowell do in the Fiji Islands?
(A) She was a student.
(B) She vacationed.
(C) She owned a hotel.
(D) She led tours.

Questions 168–170 refer to the following notice.

> **Edgemont Residents**
> **Scrap Metal and Electronics Collection**
> **Saturday, October 10, 9 ᴀᴍ–3 ᴘᴍ**
>
> Residents of the Town of Edgemont can bring their scrap metal and unwanted electronics and household appliances to the Town Recycling Center on the above date and time. This event is for town residents only. A Town of Edgemont recycling permit must be displayed on the lower right-hand side of your car's windshield to participate in this event. Permits are available at the Town Hall for $20. The following items can be recycled for free:
>
> - computers
> - computer monitors
> - printers
> - fax machines
> - VCR and DVD players
>
> There will be a $30 charge per item for the following items:
>
> - air conditioners
> - refrigerators
> - freezers
>
> Only the above-mentioned items can be recycled on this date. For information on recycling hazardous wastes such as paint, gasoline, solvents, etc., please contact the Town Hall.

168. What is required for participating in this recycling event?
(A) A permit
(B) $30
(C) A driver's license
(D) A computer

169. Which of the following items will not be accepted for recycling at this event?
(A) Old refrigerators
(B) Computer printers
(C) Paint in metal cans
(D) Used fax machines

170. The word *displayed* in line 8 is closest in meaning to
(A) shown
(B) hidden
(C) purchased
(D) submitted

Questions 171–173 refer to the following advertisement.

Are You Looking for Work?

Advertise your skills in a free "job wanted" ad in the *City Times*

This month, a 10-line classified ad is free for job seekers*
in the Monday–Friday editions of the *City Times*.

Take advantage of this onetime offer now. Send an e-mail with
your ad copy and phone number to jobads@citytimes.com.
Ads must be received by Saturday for inclusion in the following
week's editions.

*This offer is available to *City Times* subscribers only. All
others will be charged the normal fees.

---

171. What is being advertised?
    (A) A job
    (B) Skills training
    (C) Advertising space
    (D) A newspaper subscription

172. What should be included in the e-mail?
    (A) A charge card number
    (B) A telephone number
    (C) A resume
    (D) Money

173. When should the e-mail be sent?
    (A) Monday
    (B) Friday
    (C) By Saturday
    (D) Monday or Friday

Questions 174–177 refer to the following article.

Many people are not aware that plane trips pose several health hazards. This is of particular concern for business travelers who fly frequently. The more often you travel, the greater the health risk becomes. One problem with planes is that the air in the cabin is constantly recirculated. This means that instead of breathing fresh air from the outside, you breathe the same air over and over again, along with all the other passengers. This exposes you to colds, flu, or any other contagious disease that another passenger may have brought on board. You can protect yourself by making sure you get plenty of Vitamin C in the days before your flight. While on the plane, drink a lot of water. The dryness of the cabin air enhances your susceptibility to disease. Maintaining a general state of good health by eating right, exercising regularly, and getting enough sleep is also important.

Long flights pose another sort of health problem. Being forced to sit for a long time in the same position is bad for your circulation. It is particularly dangerous for people who are at risk for blood clots and other circulatory problems. You can lessen the risk by getting up from your seat every hour or so and taking a walk down the aisle. Standing up and moving around even for just a few minutes will improve your circulation and help you feel more comfortable.

Your business obligations may not allow you to fly less frequently or take shorter flights. These recommendations will help you look out for your health while traveling.

174. Who is this article for?
 (A) Flight attendants
 (B) Businesspeople
 (C) Airline companies
 (D) Doctors

175. Which of the following problems with flying is discussed in the article?
 (A) Sickness
 (B) Bad food
 (C) Plane crashes
 (D) Uncomfortable seats

176. What is advised in the article?
 (A) Don't exercise.
 (B) Stay seated.
 (C) Don't fly frequently.
 (D) Take vitamins.

177. The word *obligations* in paragraph 3, line 1 is closest in meaning to
 (A) trips
 (B) duties
 (C) budgets
 (D) managers

Questions 178–180 refer to the following memo.

MEMO

To: All personnel
From: K. Takubo, Human Resources Manager
Date: March 3, 20--
Subject: Discount on bus passes

We are pleased to announce that, because of an agreement we have made with the City Office of Public Transportation, as of next month discounted bus passes will be available to all company employees. The passes are good for two weeks of unlimited travel on any bus in the city bus system and can be purchased from us with a 25% discount. This means that instead of paying the normal price of $50, you will be charged just $37.50 for a two-week pass. We hope this will encourage more of you to come to work by bus instead of driving.

If you are interested in purchasing discounted bus passes on a regular basis, please complete a Bus Pass Request Form and submit it to your supervisor by March 24. You can pick up your first bus pass from our office on March 31. It will be valid from April 1 through April 15.

---

178. How much will company employees pay for a bus pass?
(A) $7.50
(B) $25
(C) $37.50
(D) $50

179. How can a company employee request a discounted bus pass?
(A) Ask the Office of Public Transportation
(B) Call up the bus company
(C) Send a memo to the Human Resources Office
(D) Submit a form to her supervisor

180. When can company employees start using the discounted bus passes?
(A) March 24
(B) March 31
(C) April 1
(D) April 15

Questions 181–185 refer to the following schedule and e-mail.

NATIONAL RAILWAY SYSTEMS
SCHEDULE: PIKESVILLE-WINSTON

DEPART PIKESVILLE	ARRIVE WINSTON	DEPART WINSTON	ARRIVE PIKESVILLE
5:30 AM*	8:45 AM	6:45 AM*	10:00 AM
7:45 AM	11:00 AM	8:15 AM	11:30 AM
9:30 AM	12:45 PM	10:15 AM	1:30 PM
2:30 PM*	5:45 PM	1:45 PM*	5:00 PM
4:14 PM	7:30 PM	3:30 PM	6:45 PM

*WEEKDAYS ONLY

FARE INFORMATION
WEEKDAYS: $55 EACH WAY
WEEKENDS: $43 EACH WAY

To: henry_rollins@pikesvillepaper.com
From: monica_kowalski@pikesvillepaper.com
Subject: train and hotel reservations

Henry,

Please arrange my train ticket and hotel room for the paper producer's conference in Winston next week. It begins on Wednesday with a luncheon, so I will need to arrive before noon. But please don't put me on one of those early, early trains. You know how I hate to get up too early. The conference is at the High Tower Hotel, but don't get me a room there. I'd prefer to stay at the Inn at Winston. Ask for a room with a view of the park. Book it for Wednesday and Thursday nights. I'll stay Friday night with my cousins, who live in town. Book my ticket home for Saturday. Any afternoon train will do.

Thanks.
Monica

181. What time will Monica probably leave Pikesville on Wednesday?
    (A) 5:30 AM
    (B) 7:45 AM
    (C) 9:30 AM
    (D) 11:00 AM

182. How long is the train trip between Pikesville and Winston?
    (A) 2 hours, 15 minutes
    (B) 2 hours, 45 minutes
    (C) 3 hours, 15 minutes
    (D) 3 hours, 45 minutes

183. Where does Monica want to stay on Wednesday night?
    (A) The High Tower Hotel
    (B) The Inn at Winston
    (C) Her cousins' house
    (D) At home

184. What time will she arrive home on Saturday?
    (A) 11:30 AM
    (B) 1:30 PM
    (C) 5:00 PM
    (D) 6:45 PM

185. How much will Monica's round-trip ticket cost?
    (A) $43
    (B) $55
    (C) $98
    (D) $110

Questions 186–190 refer to the following two letters.

Edward Peters
President
Whispering Pines Inn and Resort
P.O. Box 65
Upper River, New Brunswick
Canada

Dear Mr. Peters,

I am writing in regard to my recent stay at Whispering Pines. I have spent my annual summer vacation there for the past four or five years and have always enjoyed it. The comfortable accommodations and delicious menu are a big attraction for me. This year, however, the resort seemed to be lacking in the area of customer service. I enjoyed my three daily meals that came with my room. However, when on the last day of my stay I decided to try out the inn's high tea, I had a disappointing experience. The food was delicious, but the waitress was sullen and rude. Also, this year I decided to take golf lessons instead of my usual tennis lessons. I am a complete beginner and the instructor had no patience with me. He yelled at my mistakes and made me feel very uncomfortable. Despite these issues, I am not thinking about vacationing elsewhere. I plan to return to Whispering Pines and may even try another golf lesson. However, Whispering Pines is a high-quality resort, and I thought you should know about these things.

Sincerely,

Mary Kim

Whispering Pines Inn and Resort
P.O. Box 65
Upper River, New Brunswick
Canada

Mary Kim
1165 Putnam Avenue
Croton, NY

Dear Ms. Kim,

I was very sorry to hear about your recent unpleasant experience at the Whispering Pines Inn and Resort. As you know from your previous stays at Whispering Pines, we do everything possible to ensure the comfort of our guests and are widely known for our excellent accommodations and five-star menu. I sincerely regret the problems you had with your meal and your instructor. I will be in contact with the manager of the inn to discuss these issues. In the meantime, please accept the enclosed coupon. It entitles you to the same special meal you enjoyed on your last day, and I am sure next time you will have a better experience. I am glad to hear that you plan on being our guest again. You may be interested to know that in addition to golf and tennis, next year we will be adding a system of hiking trails and an indoor pool. We look forward to seeing you again at Whispering Pines.

Sincerely,

Edward Peters
President

186. Why did Ms. Kim write the letter?
   (A) To complain about some employees
   (B) To praise the accommodations
   (C) To ask about the menu
   (D) To make reservations

187. How often does Ms. Kim visit Whispering Pines?
   (A) Every week
   (B) Every month
   (C) Every year
   (D) Every four or five years

188. What will Mr. Peters do about Ms. Kim's letter?
   (A) Redo the menu
   (B) Add hiking trails
   (C) Fire an instructor
   (D) Speak to the manager

189. What can Ms. Kim get with the coupon Mr. Peters sent?
   (A) High tea
   (B) Three daily meals
   (C) A golf lesson
   (D) A room at the inn

190. What will Ms. Kim probably do on her next summer vacation?
   (A) Hike
   (B) Give up golf
   (C) Return to Whispering Pines
   (D) Go to another resort

Questions 191–195 refer to the following catalog page and order form.

Business Fashions
Fall Catalog   p. 35

Men's Dress Shirts. Solid color. Item #387
These comfortable yet elegant shirts are made of
100% combed cotton.
Colors: white, cream, light blue, light green.
Sizes S M L XL. $55

Men's Dress Shirts. Striped. Item #387A
Same as above, but with a thin stripe over a solid
background color.
Colors: red on white, blue on white, green on cream,
brown on cream.
Sizes S M L XL. $65

Striped Ties. Item #765
These stylish ties with a jaunty stripe are made of
imported silk.
Colors: burgundy red/navy blue, moss green/navy blue,
moss green/golden yellow, black/bright red.
$30

Cashmere Sweaters. Item #521
You'll feel oh-so-comfortable in these sweaters made
of 100% genuine cashmere with a chic V neck.
Colors: burgundy red, charcoal gray, midnight black.
$150

Description	Color	Size	Item No.	Quantity	Price
men's dress shirt-striped	blue/white	L	387A	2	$110
silk tie	red/blue		765	3	$90
cashmere sweater	black	L	521	1	$150
				sub total	$350
				shipping	
				total	

Payment Method*: _X_ check _____ credit card

Credit card number _____

Shipping Charges: for orders up to $200—$12.50   Please allow six weeks for delivery.
                 for orders up to $400—$20.00   *Cash and money orders not accepted.
                 for orders over $400—no charge

Send Order to

Bill Simpson
P.O. Box 78
Ardmore, IL

191. Which item is available in only three colors?
   (A) Solid color shirts
   (B) Striped shirts
   (C) Ties
   (D) Sweaters

192. What mistake did Mr. Simpson make with his shirt order?
   (A) He didn't specify a size.
   (B) He ordered a color that isn't available.
   (C) He forgot the item number.
   (D) He wrote the wrong price.

193. How many ties did Mr. Simpson order?
   (A) 1
   (B) 2
   (C) 3
   (D) 4

194. How much should Mr. Simpson pay for shipping?
   (A) $0
   (B) $12.50
   (C) $20
   (D) $22.50

195. How will Mr. Simpson pay for his order?
   (A) Cash
   (B) Check
   (C) Credit card
   (D) Money order

Questions 196–200 refer to the following notice and form.

Nugent, Inc.
Professional Development Reimbursement Policy

All Nugent employees are encouraged to take advantage of professional development opportunities that are relevant to their work. Nugent sponsors a number of professional development workshops each year, and there are also many opportunities available outside the company, including classes at the local community college, at the City Computer Training Center, and at other local institutions. Information on these and other professional development opportunities is available from the Human Resources Office.

Nugent employees are entitled to 100% reimbursement for money spent on professional development. Please note that the reimbursement is for tuition and fees only. Travel, food, and other personal expenses are the responsibility of the employee. To receive reimbursement, please obtain Form 1276 from the Human Resources Office or download one from the Nugent, Inc. website. The form must be authorized by the employee's supervisor and submitted to the Human Resources Office within one month of the last day of the class or workshop attended. Forms that are submitted late or incomplete will not result in reimbursement.

1276

Nugent, Inc
Professional Development Reimbursement Form

Name: _Muriel Hicks_   Department: _Marketing_

Title of Workshop: _Intensive French_   Location: _City Language Academy_

Dates: _August 6–August 10_

Describe how this training is relevant to your work. _We are getting more French-speaking clients from Quebec. Everyone in my department is being encouraged to learn the language._

Cost: _I spent $350 for the class plus a $20 registration fee. Also my bus fare totaled $45._

Authorizing signature: _Eleanor Lee_

196. How can a Nugent employee find
    out about professional development
    opportunities?
    (A) From the Human Resources Office
    (B) From his or her supervisor
    (C) From the Nugent, Inc. website
    (D) From a training specialist

197. Where did Muriel Hicks take a class?
    (A) Nugent
    (B) A language school
    (C) The local community college
    (D) The City Computer Training Center

198. How much money will be reimbursed
    to Ms. Hicks?
    (A) $45
    (B) $350
    (C) $370
    (D) $415

199. Who is Eleanor Lee?
    (A) A workshop organizer
    (B) A human resources officer
    (C) A French instructor
    (D) Ms. Hicks's supervisor

200. What is the last date Ms. Hicks can submit
    her reimbursement form?
    (A) August 6
    (B) August 10
    (C) September 6
    (D) September 10

Answer Key
PRACTICE TEST 3

Listening Comprehension

Part 1: Photographs

1. A	4. B	7. D	9. B
2. C	5. B	8. C	10. C
3. D	6. A		

Part 2: Question-Response

11. A	19. B	27. A	35. A
12. B	20. C	28. C	36. C
13. C	21. C	29. B	37. B
14. B	22. A	30. A	38. A
15. C	23. A	31. B	39. B
16. A	24. B	32. C	40. C
17. C	25. C	33. B	
18. A	26. B	34. B	

Part 3: Conversations

41. B	49. A	57. D	65. C
42. D	50. A	58. B	66. D
43. C	51. B	59. C	67. A
44. B	52. D	60. D	68. B
45. A	53. B	61. C	69. C
46. A	54. C	62. A	70. D
47. C	55. A	63. B	
48. B	56. A	64. C	

Part 4: Talks

71. A	79. C	87. C	95. A
72. D	80. C	88. B	96. B
73. B	81. D	89. B	97. C
74. C	82. B	90. D	98. C
75. B	83. A	91. A	99. D
76. B	84. A	92. C	100. C
77. A	85. D	93. B	
78. D	86. C	94. D	

Answer Key
PRACTICE TEST 3

Reading

Part 5: Incomplete Sentences

101. **A**	111. **A**	121. **B**	131. **B**
102. **B**	112. **C**	122. **D**	132. **D**
103. **B**	113. **D**	123. **D**	133. **B**
104. **C**	114. **A**	124. **C**	134. **D**
105. **C**	115. **B**	125. **B**	135. **C**
106. **D**	116. **A**	126. **A**	136. **B**
107. **A**	117. **C**	127. **D**	137. **D**
108. **C**	118. **A**	128. **C**	138. **C**
109. **D**	119. **B**	129. **A**	139. **A**
110. **B**	120. **C**	130. **C**	140. **A**

Part 6: Text Completion

141. **C**	144. **B**	147. **A**	150. **B**
142. **A**	145. **B**	148. **B**	151. **A**
143. **D**	146. **C**	149. **D**	152. **D**

Part 7: Reading Comprehension

153. **B**	165. **C**	177. **B**	189. **A**
154. **C**	166. **B**	178. **C**	190. **C**
155. **A**	167. **D**	179. **D**	191. **D**
156. **D**	168. **A**	180. **C**	192. **D**
157. **D**	169. **C**	181. **B**	193. **C**
158. **B**	170. **A**	182. **C**	194. **C**
159. **B**	171. **C**	183. **B**	195. **B**
160. **A**	172. **B**	184. **D**	196. **A**
161. **C**	173. **C**	185. **C**	197. **B**
162. **A**	174. **B**	186. **A**	198. **C**
163. **A**	175. **A**	187. **C**	199. **D**
164. **D**	176. **D**	188. **D**	200. **D**

TOEIC PRACTICE TEST 3—ANSWERS EXPLAINED

Listening Comprehension

PART 1: PHOTOGRAPHS

1. **(A)** A group of scientists in lab coats is gathered around a microscope. Choice (B) confuses *microscope* with *telescope*. Choice (C) correctly identifies the action, *examining*, but not the people. Choice (D) correctly identifies an object, *coats*, but no one is hanging them up.

2. **(C)** A young woman is sitting at a table writing on a laptop computer with a coffee cup beside her. Choice (A) confuses similar-sounding words *computer* and *commuter*. Choice (B) refers to the cup, but the woman is not making coffee. Choice (D) refers to the table, but no one is cleaning it.

3. **(D)** A taxi cab is moving down a crowded street. Choice (A) uses the associated word *drivers*, but none are visible in the photo. Choice (B) refers to the cars, but they are moving, not parked. Choice (C) confuses *taxi* with *taxman*.

4. **(B)** Several businesspeople are gathered around a table discussing something. Choices (A), (C), and (D) all use words that sound similar to *meeting*.

5. **(B)** Passengers are seated on an airplane. Choice (A) confuses similar-sounding words *plane* and *rain*. Choice (C) is incorrect because the aisle is empty, not crowded. Choice (D) associates bookstore with the *books* that some passengers are reading.

6. **(A)** Two businessmen are standing on steps shaking hands with each other. Choice (B) misidentifies the action they are doing with their hands. Choice (C) identifies the stairs, but the men are not walking up them. Choice (D) identifies the railing, but no one is holding on to it.

7. **(D)** A waiter is carrying a tray holding a glass and a cup. Choice (A) associates *drinks* with *glass* and *cup*. Choice (B) associates *tea* with *cup*. Choice (C) associates *drinking* with *glass* and confuses similar-sounding words *waiter* and *water*.

8. **(C)** An auto mechanic is working under the hood of a car. Choice (A) mentions a type of car *van*, but misidentifies the action. Choice (B) associates *car* with *passenger*. Choice (D) associates *car* with *driver*.

9. **(B)** A young woman is in a library next to some shelves filled with books. Choice (A) confuses similar-sounding words *books* and *cooks*. Choice (C) identifies the location, but the library is clearly open since the young woman is there. Choice (D) incorrectly identifies the woman's action—she is reading, not writing.

10. **(C)** A man in a storehouse is using a lift to put heavy items on a high shelf. Choice (A) identifies the shelf, but no one is fixing it. Choice (B) identifies the boxes on the shelf, but no one is opening them. Choice (D) identifies the man's action, but not his location.

PART 2: QUESTION-RESPONSE

11. **(A)** *Half past eleven* answers the question *What time?* Choice (B) confuses *drive* with the similar-sounding word *arrive*. Choice (C) repeats the word *time*.

12. **(B)** The speaker explains when Mr. Kim will *be back*, meaning *return*, from his vacation. Choice (A) confuses *vacation* with the similar-sounding word *station*. Choice (C) confuses *away* with the similar-sounding word *day*.

13. **(C)** The first speaker doesn't have a pen, so the second speaker offers one. Choice (A) associates *pen* with *write*. Choice (B) confuses *pen* with the similar-sounding word *open*.

14. **(B)** The phrase *in this closet* answers the question *Where?* Choice (A) confuses *coat* with the similar-sounding word *boat*. Choice (C) associates *coat* with *cold*.

15. **(C)** *Two* answers the question *How many?* Choice (A) confuses *buy* with the homonym *by*. Choice (B) confuses *books* with the similar-sounding word *looks*.

16. **(A)** The word *friend* answers the question *Who?* Choice (B) associates *lunch* with *restaurant*. Choice (C) associates *lunch* with *hungry*.

17. **(C)** *Thirty minutes* answers the question *How long?* Choice (A) confuses *meeting* with the similar-sounding word *reading*. Choice (B) repeats the word *last* out of context.

18. **(A)** The second speaker wants to leave the store because it is crowded. Choice (B) confuses *store* with the similar-sounding word *more*. Choice (C) confuses *crowded* with the similar-sounding word *cloudy*.

19. **(B)** *Five years* answers the question *How long?* Choice (A) repeats the words *work* and *here*. Choice (C) repeats the word *here*.

20. **(C)** The second speaker suggests getting the carpet cleaned because the first speaker thinks it looks dirty. Choice (A) confuses similar-sounding words *books* and *looks* and *carpet* and *car*. Choice (B) confuses similar-sounding words *carpet* and *car*.

21. **(C)** *Two hundred dollars* answers the question *How much?* Choice (A) confuses similar-sounding words *train* and *rain*. Choice (B) would answer *How long?*

22. **(A)** This answers the question about the days the bank is open. Choice (B) confuses similar-sounding words *today* and *day*. Choice (C) associates *bank* with *account*.

23. **(A)** This explains why Ms. Lee isn't here. Choice (B) confuses homonyms *here* and *hear*. Choice (C) confuses similar-sounding words *here* and *her*.

24. **(B)** *A five-minute walk* answers the question *How far?* Choice (A) associates *restaurant* with *food*. Choice (C) associates *restaurant* with *ate*.

25. **(C)** This answers the question about the topic of the meeting. Choice (A) confuses similar-sounding words *meeting* and *seating*. Choice (B) repeats the words *talk* and *meeting*.

26. **(B)** *Mr. Brown* answers the question *Who?* Choice (A) associates *photocopies* with *copy machine*. Choice (C) repeats the word *photocopies*.

27. **(A)** *A garage across the street* answers the question *Where?* Choice (B) confuses the meaning of the word *park*. Choice (C) repeats the word *car* and confuses similar-sounding words *park* and *dark*.

28. **(C)** This answers the question about a preferred place to sit. Choice (A) confuses similar-sounding words *seat* and *meat*. Choice (B) confuses similar-sounding words *prefer* and *deferred*.

29. **(B)** This is a logical response to the remark about the size of the office. Choice (A) confuses similar-sounding words *small* and *tall*. Choice (C) confuses similar-sounding words *small* and *call* and repeats the word *office*.

30. **(A)** *Ten o'clock* answers the question *When?* Choice (B) confuses similar-sounding words *arrive* and *drive*. Choice (C) would answer the question *Where?*

31. **(B)** This answers the question about the weather. Choice (A) would answer the question *Where?* Choice (C) would answer the question *How long?*.

32. **(C)** *In your office* answers the question *Where?* Choice (A) associates *newspaper* with *news*. Choice (B) associates *newspaper* with *read*.

33. **(B)** *A few old friends* answers the question *Who?* Choice (A) confuses similar-sounding words *party* and *parts*. Choice (C) associates *party* with *food* and *dancing*.

34. **(B)** *This afternoon* answers the question *When?* Choice (A) repeats the word *report*. Choice (C) confuses similar-sounding words *ready* and *reading*.

35. **(A)** This answers the question about what was served for lunch. Choice (B) repeats the word *serve* and associates *cafeteria* with *lunch*. Choice (C) confuses similar-sounding words *lunch* and *bunch*.

36. **(C)** This is a logical response to a complaint about the dark. Choice (A) uses the word *dark* out of context. Choice (B) confuses similar-sounding words *dark* and *park*.

37. **(B)** *In my office* answers the question *Where?* Choice (A) confuses similar-sounding words *afternoon* and *soon*. Choice (C) repeats the word *afternoon*.

38. **(A)** This is a logical response to the question about the sweater. Choice (B) confuses similar-sounding words *sweater* and *better*. Choice (C) associates *sweater* with *wool*.

39. **(B)** *After midnight* answers the question *What time?* Choice (A) confuses similar-sounding words *home* and *phone*. Choice (C) repeats the word *home*.

40. **(C)** This answers the question about the time. Choice (A) associates *time* with *watch*. Choice (B) confuses similar-sounding words *time* and *mine*.

PART 3: CONVERSATIONS

41. **(B)** The woman says there is a good movie at the theater and asks the man to go with her. Choice (A) repeats the word *show*. Choice (C) confuses similar-sounding words *work* and *walk*. Choice (D) confuses similar-sounding words *look* and *book*.

42. **(D)** The man says he has to work late. Choice (A) confuses similar-sounding words *plan* and *plane*. Choice (B) confuses similar-sounding words *ahead* and *bed*. Choice (C) is incorrect because the woman will buy the tickets.

43. **(C)** The man says he'll look for the woman at around 9:00. Choice (A) confuses homonyms *for* and *four*. Choice (B) confuses similar-sounding words *late* and *eight*. Choice (D) confuses similar-sounding words *then* and *ten*.

44. **(B)** The man says that they need to go over a report. Choice (A) is what the man suggests doing while they work but is not the reason for their meeting. Choice (C) associates *health* with *doctor's appointment*, which is where the woman will go in the afternoon. Choice (D) repeats the word *problem* and confuses similar-sounding words *appointment* and *point*.

45. **(A)** The man suggests meeting in his office. Choice (B) repeats the word *conference*. Choice (C) associates *lunch* with *restaurant*. Choice (D) is where the woman's doctor's appointment is.

46. **(A)** The man finally suggests meeting at 10:30 in the morning and the woman agrees. Choice (B) is the man's original suggestion. Choice (C) is when the woman will go to her doctor's appointment. Choice (D) confuses similar-sounding words *right* and *night*.

47. **(C)** The woman asks *Are you going up?* and asks the man to push the button for the tenth floor, so it is an elevator. Choice (A) repeats the word *store*. Choice (B) associates *work* with *office*. Choice (D) repeats the word *apartment*.

48. **(B)** The woman says that she is visiting a colleague from work. Choice (A) confuses similar-sounding words *colleague* and *college*. Choice (C) confuses similar-sounding words *another* and *brother*. Choice (D) is incorrect because she hadn't ever met the man before this conversation.

49. **(A)** The man says that the building isn't a bad place to live and then mentions several positive things about it. Choice (B) repeats the phrase *bad building*. Choice (C) is something he mentions as a positive thing. Choice (D) confuses similar-sounding words *bad* and *sad*.

50. **(A)** The man says he wants to *book*, or reserve, a room for a meeting on Friday. Choice (B) is confused with the man's mention of the meeting schedule. Choice (C) is confused with the event that will be taking place later that morning. Choice (D) confuses the meaning of the word *book*.

51. **(B)** The man says the meeting will finish at 10:00. Choice (A) is the time the meeting will start. Choices (C) and (D) are the start and end times for the luncheon.

52. **(D)** The woman tells the man to use the chairs and then put them back in place before he leaves. Choice (A) is confused with *the chairs will be set up for the luncheon*, that is, by somebody else. Choice (B) confuses the meaning of the word *work*. Choice (C) repeats the word *place*.

53. **(B)** The man says that the hallways will be cleaned today. Choice (A) repeats the word *conference*. Choice (C) repeats the word *office*. Choice (D) repeats the word *front*.

54. **(C)** The man says that the front office will be cleaned on Wednesday. Choice (A) confuses similar-sounding words *someday* and *Sunday*. Choice (B) confuses similar-sounding words *today* and *Tuesday*. Choice (D) is when the woman will give her workshop.

55. **(A)** The woman says she will give a workshop on Friday of next week. Choice (B) confuses *workshop* with *shop*. Choice (C) associates *cafeteria* with *lunch*. Choice (D) repeats the word *schedule*.

56. **(A)** The woman says that she is visiting relatives in Chicago next week. Choice (B) repeats the word *vacation*. Choice (C) repeats the word *business*. Choice (D) repeats the word *visit*.

57. **(D)** The man says that the train trip takes 16 hours. Choice (A) is how long the plane trip takes. Choice (B) confuses similar-sounding words *before* and *four*. Choice (C) confuses similar-sounding words *time* and *nine*.

58. **(B)** The woman says she thinks the train will be more interesting. Choice (A) repeats the word *afraid* out of context. Choice (C) repeats the word *time*. Choice (D) is what the man says.

59. **(C)** This is the reason the woman gives. Choice (A) is not mentioned. Choice (B) confuses similar-sounding words *wait* and *late*. Choice (D) is true but not the reason that the post office is closed.

60. **(D)** The woman says that the post office is *over a mile from here*. Choice (A) is the distance to the local post office. Choice (B) confuses similar-sounding words *far* and *four*. Choice (C) repeats the word *mile*.

61. **(C)** The woman will find a taxi for the man to take. Choice (A) is what the man decided not to do. Choice (B) is what the man considers doing. Choice (D) confuses similar-sounding words *try* and *drive*.

62. **(A)** The man says that he spends his lunch break alone. Choice (B) is incorrect because the woman says she eats lunch with other friends. Choice (C) is incorrect because the assistant eats in the cafeteria and the man does not. Choice (D) is incorrect because the officemates eat at a restaurant and the man does not.

63. **(B)** The man says that he eats at his desk. Choice (A) is where the woman eats. Choice (C) is where the woman takes a walk. Choice (D) is where the man's assistant eats.

64. **(C)** The man mentions 45 minutes. Choice (A) is the amount of time the woman walks in the park. Choice (B) is the amount of time the woman spends eating. Choice (D) is confused with *half an hour*.

65. **(C)** The woman reserved the room for only three nights, but now she says she needs to stay four nights. Choices (A) and (D) are confused with the room number, 107. Choice (B) is the number of nights she reserved the room for.

66. **(D)** The woman says she wants to take a walk in the park now, before dinner. Choice (A) confuses the meaning of the word *park*. Choice (B) repeats the word *dinner*. Choice (C) repeats the word *bank*.

67. **(A)** The woman says that the weather is warm. Choice (B) confuses similar-sounding words *know* and *snow*. Choice (C) confuses similar-sounding words *Main* and *rain*. Choice (D) is not mentioned.

68. **(B)** The woman is getting ready to board the train to Vancouver, so the conversation takes place in a train station. Choice (A) associates *travel agency* with the context of travel and with the word *agent*. Choice (C) associates *suitcase* with *hotel*. Choice (D) associates *bank* with *check* by confusing the meaning of the word *check* (*to check a suitcase* versus *a check for money*).

69. **(C)** The woman says that it is 10:15 now. Choice (A) is confused with the gate number. Choice (B) sounds similar to the correct answer. Choice (D) is the time the train will leave.

70. **(D)** The woman asks for someone to carry her suitcase. Choice (A) confuses the meaning of the word *book*. Choice (B) repeats the word *ticket*. Choice (C) confuses the meaning of the word *check*.

PART 4: TALKS

71. **(A)** The office is open from 7:00 AM until 9:00 PM Choice (B) is confused with the time the office closes. Choice (C) sounds similar to the correct answer. Choice (D) confuses similar-sounding words *through* and *two*.

72. **(D)** The instructions are to press 3 to open a new account. Choice (A) repeats the words *office hours*. Choice (B) is how to leave a message. Choice (C) is how to speak with a customer service representative.

73. **(B)** The instructions are to press 2 for billing questions. Choice (A) is done by pressing 0. Choice (C) is done by pressing 4. Choice (D) is done by staying on the line.

74. **(C)** The White River Bridge is closed for repairs. Choice (A) is where the bridge traffic is being rerouted. Choice (B) is where there are traffic delays. Choice (D) is confused with the name of a road—*Park Avenue*.

75. **(B)** The repairs will be completed in early September. Choice (A) confuses the meaning of the word *may*. Choices (C) and (D) sound similar to the correct answer.

76. **(B)** The speaker says to tune in for the next update at 9:00. Choice (A) confuses similar-sounding words *several* and *seven*. Choice (C) is confused with the length of the traffic delays (*20 minutes*). Choice (D) is confused with the name of the road (*Highway 10*).

77. **(A)** The Legal Training Institute trains people for a career as a legal assistant. Choices (B) and (C) are confused with the described job duties of a legal assistant. Choice (D) repeats the word *career*.

78. **(D)** The course lasts six months. Choice (A) confuses homonyms *to* and *two*. Choice (B) confuses homonyms *for* and *four*. Choice (C) is confused with the price of the course.

79. **(C)** Listeners are instructed to visit the website to get an application. Choice (A) repeats the word *career*. Choice (B) is what listeners are instructed to do if they want to find out more about the career. Choice (D) confuses similar-sounding words *better* and *letter*.

80. **(C)** The words *plane, flight,* and *fly* are mentioned, so it would be heard at an airport. Choice (A) confuses similar-sounding words *plane* and *train*. Choice (B) confuses similar-sounding words *coat* and *boat*. Choice (D) confuses similar-sounding words *us* and *bus*.

81. **(D)** The speaker announces gate number 11. Choices (A) and (B) are confused with the flight number. Choice (C) sounds similar to the correct answer. Which gate should passengers go to?

82. **(B)** The speaker says that boarding will begin with passengers with small children. Choice (A) is incorrect because it describes all the passengers. Choice (C) is mentioned, but these are not the passengers who will get on first. Choice (D) is the passengers who will get on second.

83. **(A)** The festival, to be held in July, is *coming up next month*, so the announcement is made in June. Choice (B) is the month of the festival. Choice (C) is the month after the festival. Choice (D) confuses similar-sounding words *remember* and *September*.

84. **(A)** The dates of the festival are July 15–18. Choice (B) sounds similar to the correct answer. Choice (C) is the date the festival ends. Choice (D) is confused with the $20 price of admission.

85. **(D)** On Thursday night, the opening ceremonies will be held, including a special concert. Choices (A), (B), and (C) refer to things that are part of the festival, but they are not specific to Thursday night.

86. **(C)** The reason for the strike is a salary freeze, meaning salaries will not change. Choice (A) confuses the meaning of *freeze*. Choice (B) repeats the word *passengers*. Choice (D) repeats the word *contract*.

87. **(C)** The strike is planned for next week. Choice (A) is when the salary freeze goes into effect. Choice (B) is when the meeting will take place. Choice (D)

sounds similar to *few months*, the amount of time that the airline has been having financial difficulties.

88. **(B)** The meeting will be at the Royal Hotel. Choice (A) is confused with the representatives from the mayor's office, who will attend the meeting. Choice (C) is confused with representatives from the National Transportation Board, who will also attend the meeting. Choice (D) repeats the word *airport*.

89. **(B)** The announcer says that arrival will be in just under three hours. Choice (A) confuses similar-sounding words *to* and *two*. Choice (C) confuses similar-sounding words *fourth* and *four*. Choice (D) is confused with the train number.

90. **(D)** Smoking is prohibited on all parts of the train. Choices (A), (B), and (C) refer to things not allowed in the quiet car.

91. **(A)** In 15 minutes, the food service car will open and food and drinks will be sold. Choice (B) is the opposite of the correct answer. Choice (C) repeats the word *cold*. Choice (D) repeats the words *rear car*.

92. **(C)** Show times are Saturday and Sunday at 2 PM and Thursday through Saturday at 8 PM. Choices (A), (B), and (D) do not fit into this schedule.

93. **(B)** Adult evening tickets are $30, and the child's ticket is half that price. Choice (A) is half the price of a matinee ticket. Choice (C) is the price of an adult matinee ticket. Choice (D) is the price of an adult evening ticket.

94. **(D)** Callers are asked to leave a message if they want to reserve tickets. Choices (A) and (B) are associated with the context of a phone at the theater, but are not mentioned. Choice (C) repeats the word *mail*, but because a street address is mentioned, it is traditional mail, not e-mail, that the recording refers to.

95. **(A)** The announcer describes the weather this morning as *sun and humidity*. Choices (B) and (C) are how the weather will be later. Choice (D) is how the weather was before.

96. **(B)** This is the number the announcer says. Choices (A) and (C) sound similar to the correct answer. Choice (D) is what the high temperature will be.

97. **(C)** Because the weather will be rainy, the announcer recommends staying inside with a book. Choice (A) is associated with *gardeners*, the people who will be happy about the rainy weather. Choice (B) is what the announcer recommends not doing. Choice (D) confuses similar-sounding words *book* and *cook*.

98. **(C)** The guest will talk about mountain climbing and has tried to climb Mount Everest, so he is a mountain climber. Choices (A) and (B) are associated with the fact that he appeared in a documentary film. Choice (D) repeats the word *equipment*, something the speaker will cover in his talk.

99. **(D)** This is the price mentioned. Choice (A) confuses similar-sounding words *for* and *four*. Choices (B) and (C) sound similar to the correct answer. How much does the book cost?

100. **(C)** Next month's program has been canceled, meaning it won't happen. Choice (A) is what will happen the month after next. Choice (B) is confused with the film the speaker appeared in. Choice (D) is happening tonight.

Reading

PART 5: INCOMPLETE SENTENCES

101. **(A)** The sentence is a future idea, but this verb is in the time clause so it needs to be in the present tense form. Choice (B) is present tense but doesn't agree with the subject. Choice (C) is past continuous. Choice (D) is the future form.

102. **(B)** A verb is needed to complete the future verb *will have to*. Choices (A) and (C) are nouns. Choice (D) is an adjective.

103. **(B)** *On* is used in this sentence to mean *on top of.* Choice (A) means *inside of.* Choice (C) is not a preposition of place. Choice (D) cannot be used in this context.

104. **(C)** This is a passive-voice sentence because the subject, *document,* receives the action. The past participle is used to complete the passive verb. Choice (A) is present tense or base form. Choice (B) is a noun. Choice (D) is the present participle or gerund.

105. **(C)** The verb *turn in* means *submit.* Choices (A), (B), and (D) can all also be used with *turn* but have meanings that don't fit the context.

106. **(D)** This is an imperative verb, giving a command or request. Choice (A) is the infinitive form. Choice (B) is the present participle or gerund. Choice (C) is present tense.

107. **(A)** This is an adverb of manner describing the verb *think*. Choice (B) is an adjective. Choice (C) is a verb. Choice (D) is a noun.

108. **(C)** This is a comparative adjective used to compare the new office to the old one. Choice (A) is a noun. Choice (B) is an adjective, but not comparative. Choice (D) is a superlative adjective.

109. **(D)** The relative pronoun *whose* at the beginning of the adjective clause indicates possession—the book belongs to Dr. Chin. Choices (A), (B), and (C) are all relative pronouns but do not indicate possession.

110. **(B)** The preposition *on* is used when telling the name of a street where something is located, but not the exact address. Choice (A) would be used for an exact address. Choice (C) would be used with the name of the city, but not the street or address. Choice (D) cannot be used in this context.

111. **(A)** *But* is used to show a contradiction between the two clauses of the sentence. Choice (B) would be used to add similar information. Choice (C) is used for comparatives. Choice (D) indicates a choice between two things.

112. **(C)** *Detected* means *found* or *saw.* Choices (A), (B), and (D) all look similar to the correct answer but have meanings that don't fit the context.

TOEIC Practice Test 3 **163**

113. **(D)** The present participle form is used to complete the present continuous verb in this active-voice sentence. Choice (A) is past tense. Choice (B) is simple present tense. Choice (C) is the past participle.

114. **(A)** *Before* tells when the documents should be on the desk relative to the hour of 8:00. Choice (B) would refer to two points in time. Choices (C) and (D) are not used when talking about hours of the day.

115. **(B)** The singular verb *needs* agrees with the singular subject *visitor*. Choices (A), (C), and (D) are all plural forms, so they don't agree with the subject.

116. **(A)** This is the noun form acting as the subject of the sentence. Choice (B) is a verb. Choice (C) is an adverb. Choice (D) is an adjective.

117. **(C)** *And* is used to join two clauses containing similar information. Choice (A) indicates a choice. Choices (B) and (D) cannot be used to introduce a clause.

118. **(A)** The singular verb form *has* agrees with the singular subject *everybody*. Choice (B) is a plural verb. Choice (C) is an infinitive so cannot be used as the main verb. Choice (D) is present continuous, a form usually not used with a stative verb such as *have*.

119. **(B)** The verb *expect* is followed by an infinitive verb. Choice (A) is base form or present tense. Choice (C) is a gerund or present participle. Choice (D) is a noun.

120. **(C)** *Locally* is an adverb of manner used to describe the verb *produced*. Choice (A) is an adjective. Choice (B) is a verb. Choice (D) is a noun.

121. **(B)** The past tense unreal conditional uses the past perfect form of the verb in the *if* clause. Choice (A) is simple past tense. Choice (C) is present perfect. Choice (D) is conditional, the form required for the main clause.

122. **(D)** The verb *let* is followed by a base form verb. Choice (A) is simple past tense. Choice (B) is an infinitive. Choice (C) is simple present tense.

123. **(D)** The singular verb *is* agrees with the singular subject *number*. Choice (A) is base form. Choices (B) and (C) are plural forms.

124. **(C)** In this sentence, *or* indicates a choice between two actions. Choice (A) would be used to add a clause with similar information. Choice (B) indicates a contradiction between the two clauses. Choice (D) is used in negative sentences.

125. **(B)** *Among* means *in the middle of.* Choices (A), (C), and (D) look similar to the correct answer but have meanings that don't fit the context.

126. **(A)** *Might* is a modal so it is followed by a base form verb. Choice (B) is simple present tense. Choice (C) is future tense. Choice (D) is an incomplete future form.

TOEIC Practice Test 3

127. **(D)** A present tense unreal conditional uses the conditional *would* in the main clause. Choice (A) is simple present tense. Choice (B) is simple past tense. Choice (C) is future tense.

128. **(C)** A noun is needed here as the object of the verb *listening*. Choices (A) and (B) are verbs. Choice (D) is an adjective.

129. **(A)** *Regarded* means *considered* or *seen as*. Choices (B), (C), and (D) look similar to the correct answer but have meanings that don't fit the context.

130. **(C)** *As soon as*, meaning *immediately after*, introduces the time clause. Choices (A), (B), and (D) cannot be used to introduce a time clause.

131. **(B)** *Because* indicates a cause-and-effect relationship. Choices (A), (C), and (D) indicate a contradiction.

132. **(D)** *Rise* is a verb meaning *go up*. Choices (A) and (B) are not verbs. Choice (C) is a transitive verb requiring an object.

133. **(B)** This is an imperative verb used to give a command. Choice (A) could be imperative, but the meaning of the sentence requires a negative verb. Choice (C) is a gerund and is not negative. Choice (D) is an infinitive.

134. **(D)** The singular verb *is* agrees with the singular subject *list*. Choices (A), (B), and (C) are all plural forms.

135. **(C)** The present perfect continuous verb indicates an action that began in the past and continues into the present. Choice (A) is present continuous. Choice (B) is a past tense form. Choice (D) is future perfect.

136. **(B)** *Even though* indicates a contradiction between the ideas presented in the two clauses. Choices (A) and (D) indicate a cause-and-effect relationship. Choice (C) is used to add more information.

137. **(D)** *Identify* is the main verb of the second clause in this sentence. Choice (A) is a noun. Choice (B) is a verb but belongs to a different word family and has a meaning that doesn't fit the context. Choice (C) is a noun.

138. **(C)** *Discuss* is followed by a gerund. Choice (A) is base form or present tense. Choice (B) is past tense. Choice (D) is an infinitive.

139. **(A)** *Show up* means *appear*. Choices (B), (C), and (D) can all be used after *show* but have meanings that don't fit the context.

140. **(A)** *Success* is a noun and acts as the subject of this sentence. Choice (B) is an adjective. Choice (C) is a verb. Choice (D) is an adverb.

PART 6: TEXT COMPLETION

141. **(C)** This pronoun refers to the person addressed by the notice, *you, the customer*. Choice (A) would refer to the company sending the notice. Choice (B) would refer to one man. Choice (D) would refer to a thing.

142. **(A)** *Investigating* means *studying* or *researching*. Choices (B), (C), and (D) look similar to the correct answer but have meanings that don't fit the context.

143. **(D)** *Assistance* is a noun meaning *help* and is used as the object of the preposition *for* in this sentence. Choices (A) and (B) are verbs. Choice (C) is a noun, but it refers to people, not to a service.

144. **(B)** This is a simple past tense form describing a situation that was completed in the past. Choice (A) is present tense. Choice (C) is a conditional form. Choice (D) is negative so doesn't fit the meaning of the sentence.

145. **(B)** A promotion is when an employee is given a higher-level job; since Ms. Maldonado was capable of more responsibilities, her former employer wanted to promote her. Choice (A) is the opposite of the correct answer. Choice (C) often refers to a trial period given to new employees. Choice (D) is a type of punishment.

146. **(C)** This pronoun refers to a woman, Ms. Maldonado. Choice (A) refers to a man. Choice (B) refers to the speaker. Choice (D) is a possessive pronoun, but an object pronoun is needed here as the object of the verb *see*.

147. **(A)** This is a passive verb; the form does not fill itself out but is filled out by a person. Choices (B) and (C) are constructions that don't exist, because a modal is always followed by a base form verb. Choice (D) is active voice.

148. **(B)** *Following* means *next*. Choices (A), (C), and (D) all mean *before*, which would be impossible in this context.

149. **(D)** *Cooperation* means working together. Choices (A), (B), and (C) look similar to the correct answer but have meanings that don't fit the context.

150. **(B)** *Affordable* means *reasonably priced*; the topic of this paragraph is finding ways to make alternative energy systems less expensive. Choices (A), (C), and (D) could all be used to describe alternative energy systems but don't fit the context of the sentence.

151. **(A)** The verb *help* is followed by a base form verb. Choice (B) is present tense. Choice (C) is a gerund or present participle. Choice (D) is future tense.

152. **(D)** In this sentence, the gerund *reducing* acts as the subject and is modified by the adjective *simple*. Choice (A) is a noun. Choice (B) is a verb. Choice (C) is an adverb.

PART 7: READING COMPREHENSION

153. **(B)** The new tenant will choose the paint and carpet colors as part of the renovations that will be made before move-in. Choice (A) is incorrect because the space is *pleasant and sunny*. Choice (C) is incorrect because a new carpet will be put in later, as part of the renovations. Choice (D) is incorrect because there is ample parking in the rear of the building.

154. **(C)** The phone number provided is that of a rental agency. Choice (A) is mentioned, but not as the person to call. Choice (B) is confused with the mention of the contract. Choice (D) repeats the word *tenant*.

155. **(A)** The new service advertised is online banking. Choices (B), (C), and (D) all repeat words mentioned in the advertisement.

156. **(D)** The advertisement says to *stop by*, or *visit*, any branch of the bank to talk with someone about online banking. Choice (A) is what to do to find out the locations of bank branches. Choice (B) is confused with the service being offered. Choice (C) is not mentioned.

157. **(D)** The bank has been in business *for more than a century*, and a century is 100 years. Choices (A) and (B) are incorrect because the word for a period of 10 years is *decade*, not *century*. Choice (C) is incorrect because it means *less than*, not *over* 100 years.

158. **(B)** *Enhance* means *improve*. Choices (A), (C), and (D) could fit the sentence but don't have the correct meaning.

159. **(B)** David Spaulding wrote the letter to say that a light rail system would provide a better solution to traffic problems than a new bridge. Choices (A) and (C) repeat issues mentioned in the letter but are not the purpose of the letter. Choice (D) repeats the phrase *city planners*, but there was no mention of the writer meeting with them.

160. **(A)** David Spaulding read an article about traffic problems and the new bridge in yesterday's paper. Choice (B) is incorrect because even though the bridge is discussed, there is no mention of visiting it. Choice (C) is incorrect because the light rail system has not been built yet. Choice (D) repeats the phrase *transportation experts*, but there was no mention of the writer meeting with them.

161. **(C)** The bridge is scheduled to be completed in two years. Choice (A) is when bridge construction will begin. Choice (B) is confused with the expression *over the coming months*, which is when traffic problems caused by bridge construction are expected to increase. Choice (D) is the amount of time a group of people has been working on a plan for a light rail system.

162. **(A)** David Spaulding's opinion is that a light rail system is a better solution to traffic problems than a new bridge. Choice (B) is incorrect because he says that the bridge *will add beauty to our city landscape*. Choice (C) is incorrect because even though David Spaulding mentions that the new bridge will be bigger, he doesn't express any opinion about this. Choice (D) is the opposite of his opinion.

163. **(A)** Visitors are required to keep the visitor's badge *visible at all times*. Choice (B) is incorrect because even though a visitor must wait for an escort, continuing to remain with the escort at all times is not mentioned. Choice (C) is incorrect because the cafeteria is open to the public, so anyone can go there. Choice (D) is incorrect; a visitor can leave the lobby in the company of an escort.

164. **(D)** The security officer goes off duty at 7:00 PM, and visitors must leave the building before then. Choices (A) and (B) are confused with the office hours of the security manager. Choice (C) is when the cafeteria and lobby close.

165. **(C)** The hotel will open in September, and Ms. Hallowell will begin her new job a month before then. Choices (A) and (B) are confused with the time she worked for the tourism board. Choice (D) is when the hotel will open.

166. **(B)** Ms. Hallowell worked as a consultant for the tourism board between January and May of this year. Choice (A) is what her new job will be. Choice (C) is confused with the mention of the Hotel and Hospitality School of Fairfield, where she was a student, not an instructor. Choice (D) is a job she had more than five years ago.

167. **(D)** Ms. Hallowell worked as a tour guide in the Fiji Islands. Choice (A) is what she did before that, while still living in Fairfield. Choice (B) is associated with her work in tourism. Choice (C) is associated with her new job as hotel manager.

168. **(A)** Town residents need to show a recycling permit. Choice (B) is the cost of recycling certain items such as refrigerators. Choice (C) is confused with the mention of cars. Choice (D) is an item that can be recycled.

169. **(C)** Paint is an example of a hazardous waste, which will not be accepted for recycling on this date. Choices (A), (B), and (D) are all items listed as acceptable for recycling.

170. **(A)** *Displayed* means *shown*. Choices (B), (C), and (D) are all words that might be used about a permit but don't fit the context of the sentence.

171. **(C)** This ad is aimed at job seekers who may want to place a "job wanted" ad in the newspaper. Choice (A) is associated with job seekers. Choice (B) repeats the word *skills*. Choice (D) is associated with the subscribers mentioned in the footnote.

172. **(B)** The ad says *Send an e-mail with your ad copy and phone number. . .* Choice (A) repeats the word *charge*, but is incorrect because the job-wanted ads are free. Choice (C) is associated with job seekers. Choice (D) is incorrect because the job-wanted ads are free.

173. **(C)** E-mails with ad copy should be sent by Saturday to be included in the paper the following week. Choices (A), (B), and (D) are all days a free job-wanted ad could appear in the paper.

174. **(B)** This article is for businesspeople who travel frequently by plane. Choices (A) and (C) are associated with plane travel. Choice (D) is associated with the discussion of health risks.

175. **(A)** The article discusses the problem of airplane passengers being exposed to disease. Choice (B) is confused with the advice to eat right. Choice (C) is a hazard of flying but is not mentioned. Choice (D) is confused with the mention of *being forced to sit for a long time*.

176. **(D)** Readers are advised to take Vitamin C to protect themselves from disease. Choices (A) and (B) are the opposite of pieces of advice given in the article. Choice (C) repeats the word *frequently*.

177. **(B)** *Obligations* means *duties*. Choices (A), (C), and (D) all could follow the word *business* but don't have the correct meaning.

178. **(C)** The memo explains that with the 25% discount of the normal price of $50, the bus passes will cost $37.50. Choice (A) looks similar to the correct answer. Choice (B) is confused with the size of the discount. Choice (D) is the normal price.

179. **(D)** Employees are asked to complete a form and submit it to their supervisors. Choice (A) is the agency the company made an agreement with about the bus pass discount. Choice (B) is associated with buses and bus passes. Choice (C) is where the memo about the bus passes originated.

180. **(C)** The first bus passes will be valid starting on April 1. Choice (A) is the last date to submit the request form. Choice (B) is the day bus passes can be picked up. Choice (D) is the last day the first bus passes will be valid.

181. **(B)** Monica needs to arrive before noon. She doesn't want to leave too early, so she probably won't take the 5:30 train, and the 7:45 is the only other train that will get her to Winston on time. Choice (A) is too early. Choice (C) arrives after noon. Choice (D) is the time she will arrive in Winston.

182. **(C)** The difference between each departure time and its corresponding arrival time is 3 hours, 15 minutes. Choices (A), (B), and (D) are close to the correct answer, but are not correct.

183. **(B)** Monica asks Henry to book a room for her at the Inn at Winston. Choice (A) is where she doesn't want to stay. Choice (C) is where she will stay on Friday night. Choice (D) is incorrect because she won't be home until Saturday.

184. **(D)** Monica wants to leave Winston on Saturday afternoon. The 1:45 runs on weekdays only, so her only choice is the 3:30, which arrives in Pikesville at 6:45. Choices (A) and (B) are trains that leave in the morning. Choice (C) is the arrival time for the train that runs only on weekdays.

185. **(C)** Monica will leave on Wednesday, a weekday ($55) and return on Saturday, a weekend day ($43), so her total cost is $98. Choice (A) is the one-way weekend fare. Choice (B) is the one-way weekday fare. Choice (D) is the round-trip weekday fare.

186. **(A)** Ms. Kim wrote to tell Mr. Peters about her problems with a sullen waitress and an impatient golf instructor. Choice (B) is mentioned but is not the reason for the letter. Choice (C) repeats the word *menu*. Choice (D) is associated with the context of a vacation resort.

187. **(C)** Ms. Kim spends her annual, or yearly, vacation at Whispering Pines. Choices (A) and (B) are not mentioned. Choice (D) is confused with the number of years she has been visiting the resort.

188. **(D)** Mr. Peters says he will contact the manager of the inn. Choice (A) repeats the word *menu*. Choice (B) is mentioned but not as a response to Ms. Kim's letter. Choice (C) is a reasonable response to Ms. Kim's complaint but is not what Mr. Peters will do.

189. **(A)** Mr. Peters says that Ms. Kim can enjoy the same special meal she enjoyed on her last day at the resort, which was high tea. Choices (B), (C), and (D) are all things Ms. Kim had at the resort but are not what the coupon is for.

190. **(C)** Ms. Kim has spent every summer vacation at Whispering Pines for several years and she says that she plans to return there again, so that is probably what she will do on her next vacation. Choice (A) is an activity available at the resort, but Ms. Kim never mentions it. Choices (B) and (D) are things she says she won't do.

191. **(D)** Sweaters are available in burgundy red, charcoal gray, midnight black. Choices (A), (B), and (C) are all available in four colors or color combinations.

192. **(D)** He confused the price. He ordered striped shirts, which cost $65 each or $130 for two. Choice (A) is incorrect because he specified size L. Choice (B) is incorrect because the color he ordered is listed in the catalog. Choice (C) is incorrect because he wrote the item number for striped shirts.

193. **(C)** Mr. Simpson ordered three ties for a total cost of $90. Choices (A), (B), and (D) are not the number of ties he ordered.

194. **(C)** After Mr. Simpson corrects the price mistake on his short order, his subtotal will be $370. That price is still between $200 and $400, so he should pay $20 for shipping. Choice (A) is what he would pay if his order came to more than $400. Choice (B) is what he would pay if his order were less than $200. Choice (D) is confused with Choices (B) and (D).

195. **(B)** On the order form, Mr. Simpson indicated that he will pay by check. Choices (A) and (D) are not accepted by the company. Choice (C) is an option, but Mr. Simpson didn't choose it.

196. **(A)** The notice says that this information is available from the Human Resources Office. Choice (B) is the person who has to authorize the reimbursement form. Choice (C) is the place to find the reimbursement form. Choice (D) is related to the topic of professional development but is not mentioned.

197. **(B)** Muriel Hicks took a French class at the City Language Academy. Choices (A), (C), and (D) are all places where professional development opportunities are available but are not where she took a class.

198. **(C)** Ms. Hicks will be reimbursed for her tuition ($350) plus fees ($20). Choice (A) is the cost of the bus fare. Choice (B) is the cost of tuition only. Choice (D) is the cost of tuition, fees, and bus fare, but the bus fare is not reimbursable.

199. **(D)** The notice says that the form must be authorized by the employee's supervisor, and Eleanor Lee is the one who authorized the form. Choice (A) is related to the topic of professional development but is not mentioned. Choice (B) is the person who will receive the form. Choice (C) is the person who gave the class.

200. **(D)** The form must be submitted within one month of the last day of the class, August 10, and one month from that date is September 10. Choice (A) is the day the class began. Choice (B) is the last day of class. Choice (C) is one month from the first day of class.

Answer Sheet
TOEIC PRACTICE TEST 4

Listening Comprehension

Part 1: Photographs

1. Ⓐ Ⓑ Ⓒ Ⓓ
2. Ⓐ Ⓑ Ⓒ Ⓓ
3. Ⓐ Ⓑ Ⓒ Ⓓ
4. Ⓐ Ⓑ Ⓒ Ⓓ
5. Ⓐ Ⓑ Ⓒ Ⓓ
6. Ⓐ Ⓑ Ⓒ Ⓓ
7. Ⓐ Ⓑ Ⓒ Ⓓ
8. Ⓐ Ⓑ Ⓒ Ⓓ
9. Ⓐ Ⓑ Ⓒ Ⓓ
10. Ⓐ Ⓑ Ⓒ Ⓓ

Part 2: Question-Response

11. Ⓐ Ⓑ Ⓒ
12. Ⓐ Ⓑ Ⓒ
13. Ⓐ Ⓑ Ⓒ
14. Ⓐ Ⓑ Ⓒ
15. Ⓐ Ⓑ Ⓒ
16. Ⓐ Ⓑ Ⓒ
17. Ⓐ Ⓑ Ⓒ
18. Ⓐ Ⓑ Ⓒ
19. Ⓐ Ⓑ Ⓒ
20. Ⓐ Ⓑ Ⓒ
21. Ⓐ Ⓑ Ⓒ
22. Ⓐ Ⓑ Ⓒ
23. Ⓐ Ⓑ Ⓒ
24. Ⓐ Ⓑ Ⓒ
25. Ⓐ Ⓑ Ⓒ
26. Ⓐ Ⓑ Ⓒ
27. Ⓐ Ⓑ Ⓒ
28. Ⓐ Ⓑ Ⓒ
29. Ⓐ Ⓑ Ⓒ
30. Ⓐ Ⓑ Ⓒ
31. Ⓐ Ⓑ Ⓒ
32. Ⓐ Ⓑ Ⓒ
33. Ⓐ Ⓑ Ⓒ
34. Ⓐ Ⓑ Ⓒ
35. Ⓐ Ⓑ Ⓒ
36. Ⓐ Ⓑ Ⓒ
37. Ⓐ Ⓑ Ⓒ
38. Ⓐ Ⓑ Ⓒ
39. Ⓐ Ⓑ Ⓒ
40. Ⓐ Ⓑ Ⓒ

Part 3: Conversations

41. Ⓐ Ⓑ Ⓒ Ⓓ
42. Ⓐ Ⓑ Ⓒ Ⓓ
43. Ⓐ Ⓑ Ⓒ Ⓓ
44. Ⓐ Ⓑ Ⓒ Ⓓ
45. Ⓐ Ⓑ Ⓒ Ⓓ
46. Ⓐ Ⓑ Ⓒ Ⓓ
47. Ⓐ Ⓑ Ⓒ Ⓓ
48. Ⓐ Ⓑ Ⓒ Ⓓ
49. Ⓐ Ⓑ Ⓒ Ⓓ
50. Ⓐ Ⓑ Ⓒ Ⓓ
51. Ⓐ Ⓑ Ⓒ Ⓓ
52. Ⓐ Ⓑ Ⓒ Ⓓ
53. Ⓐ Ⓑ Ⓒ Ⓓ
54. Ⓐ Ⓑ Ⓒ Ⓓ
55. Ⓐ Ⓑ Ⓒ Ⓓ
56. Ⓐ Ⓑ Ⓒ Ⓓ
57. Ⓐ Ⓑ Ⓒ Ⓓ
58. Ⓐ Ⓑ Ⓒ Ⓓ
59. Ⓐ Ⓑ Ⓒ Ⓓ
60. Ⓐ Ⓑ Ⓒ Ⓓ
61. Ⓐ Ⓑ Ⓒ Ⓓ
62. Ⓐ Ⓑ Ⓒ Ⓓ
63. Ⓐ Ⓑ Ⓒ Ⓓ
64. Ⓐ Ⓑ Ⓒ Ⓓ
65. Ⓐ Ⓑ Ⓒ Ⓓ
66. Ⓐ Ⓑ Ⓒ Ⓓ
67. Ⓐ Ⓑ Ⓒ Ⓓ
68. Ⓐ Ⓑ Ⓒ Ⓓ
69. Ⓐ Ⓑ Ⓒ Ⓓ
70. Ⓐ Ⓑ Ⓒ Ⓓ

Part 4: Talks

71. Ⓐ Ⓑ Ⓒ Ⓓ
72. Ⓐ Ⓑ Ⓒ Ⓓ
73. Ⓐ Ⓑ Ⓒ Ⓓ
74. Ⓐ Ⓑ Ⓒ Ⓓ
75. Ⓐ Ⓑ Ⓒ Ⓓ
76. Ⓐ Ⓑ Ⓒ Ⓓ
77. Ⓐ Ⓑ Ⓒ Ⓓ
78. Ⓐ Ⓑ Ⓒ Ⓓ
79. Ⓐ Ⓑ Ⓒ Ⓓ
80. Ⓐ Ⓑ Ⓒ Ⓓ
81. Ⓐ Ⓑ Ⓒ Ⓓ
82. Ⓐ Ⓑ Ⓒ Ⓓ
83. Ⓐ Ⓑ Ⓒ Ⓓ
84. Ⓐ Ⓑ Ⓒ Ⓓ
85. Ⓐ Ⓑ Ⓒ Ⓓ
86. Ⓐ Ⓑ Ⓒ Ⓓ
87. Ⓐ Ⓑ Ⓒ Ⓓ
88. Ⓐ Ⓑ Ⓒ Ⓓ
89. Ⓐ Ⓑ Ⓒ Ⓓ
90. Ⓐ Ⓑ Ⓒ Ⓓ
91. Ⓐ Ⓑ Ⓒ Ⓓ
92. Ⓐ Ⓑ Ⓒ Ⓓ
93. Ⓐ Ⓑ Ⓒ Ⓓ
94. Ⓐ Ⓑ Ⓒ Ⓓ
95. Ⓐ Ⓑ Ⓒ Ⓓ
96. Ⓐ Ⓑ Ⓒ Ⓓ
97. Ⓐ Ⓑ Ⓒ Ⓓ
98. Ⓐ Ⓑ Ⓒ Ⓓ
99. Ⓐ Ⓑ Ⓒ Ⓓ
100. Ⓐ Ⓑ Ⓒ Ⓓ

Answer Sheet
TOEIC PRACTICE TEST 4

Reading

Part 5: Incomplete Sentences

101. Ⓐ Ⓑ Ⓒ Ⓓ 112. Ⓐ Ⓑ Ⓒ Ⓓ 122. Ⓐ Ⓑ Ⓒ Ⓓ 132. Ⓐ Ⓑ Ⓒ Ⓓ
102. Ⓐ Ⓑ Ⓒ Ⓓ 113. Ⓐ Ⓑ Ⓒ Ⓓ 123. Ⓐ Ⓑ Ⓒ Ⓓ 133. Ⓐ Ⓑ Ⓒ Ⓓ
103. Ⓐ Ⓑ Ⓒ Ⓓ 114. Ⓐ Ⓑ Ⓒ Ⓓ 124. Ⓐ Ⓑ Ⓒ Ⓓ 134. Ⓐ Ⓑ Ⓒ Ⓓ
104. Ⓐ Ⓑ Ⓒ Ⓓ 115. Ⓐ Ⓑ Ⓒ Ⓓ 125. Ⓐ Ⓑ Ⓒ Ⓓ 135. Ⓐ Ⓑ Ⓒ Ⓓ
106. Ⓐ Ⓑ Ⓒ Ⓓ 116. Ⓐ Ⓑ Ⓒ Ⓓ 126. Ⓐ Ⓑ Ⓒ Ⓓ 136. Ⓐ Ⓑ Ⓒ Ⓓ
107. Ⓐ Ⓑ Ⓒ Ⓓ 117. Ⓐ Ⓑ Ⓒ Ⓓ 127. Ⓐ Ⓑ Ⓒ Ⓓ 137. Ⓐ Ⓑ Ⓒ Ⓓ
108. Ⓐ Ⓑ Ⓒ Ⓓ 118. Ⓐ Ⓑ Ⓒ Ⓓ 128. Ⓐ Ⓑ Ⓒ Ⓓ 138. Ⓐ Ⓑ Ⓒ Ⓓ
109. Ⓐ Ⓑ Ⓒ Ⓓ 119. Ⓐ Ⓑ Ⓒ Ⓓ 129. Ⓐ Ⓑ Ⓒ Ⓓ 139. Ⓐ Ⓑ Ⓒ Ⓓ
110. Ⓐ Ⓑ Ⓒ Ⓓ 120. Ⓐ Ⓑ Ⓒ Ⓓ 130. Ⓐ Ⓑ Ⓒ Ⓓ 140. Ⓐ Ⓑ Ⓒ Ⓓ
111. Ⓐ Ⓑ Ⓒ Ⓓ 121. Ⓐ Ⓑ Ⓒ Ⓓ 131. Ⓐ Ⓑ Ⓒ Ⓓ

Part 6: Text Completion

141. Ⓐ Ⓑ Ⓒ Ⓓ 144. Ⓐ Ⓑ Ⓒ Ⓓ 147. Ⓐ Ⓑ Ⓒ Ⓓ 150. Ⓐ Ⓑ Ⓒ Ⓓ
142. Ⓐ Ⓑ Ⓒ Ⓓ 145. Ⓐ Ⓑ Ⓒ Ⓓ 148. Ⓐ Ⓑ Ⓒ Ⓓ 151. Ⓐ Ⓑ Ⓒ Ⓓ
143. Ⓐ Ⓑ Ⓒ Ⓓ 146. Ⓐ Ⓑ Ⓒ Ⓓ 149. Ⓐ Ⓑ Ⓒ Ⓓ 152. Ⓐ Ⓑ Ⓒ Ⓓ

Part 7: Reading Comprehension

153. Ⓐ Ⓑ Ⓒ Ⓓ 166. Ⓐ Ⓑ Ⓒ Ⓓ 179. Ⓐ Ⓑ Ⓒ Ⓓ 192. Ⓐ Ⓑ Ⓒ Ⓓ
154. Ⓐ Ⓑ Ⓒ Ⓓ 167. Ⓐ Ⓑ Ⓒ Ⓓ 180. Ⓐ Ⓑ Ⓒ Ⓓ 193. Ⓐ Ⓑ Ⓒ Ⓓ
155. Ⓐ Ⓑ Ⓒ Ⓓ 168. Ⓐ Ⓑ Ⓒ Ⓓ 181. Ⓐ Ⓑ Ⓒ Ⓓ 194. Ⓐ Ⓑ Ⓒ Ⓓ
156. Ⓐ Ⓑ Ⓒ Ⓓ 169. Ⓐ Ⓑ Ⓒ Ⓓ 182. Ⓐ Ⓑ Ⓒ Ⓓ 195. Ⓐ Ⓑ Ⓒ Ⓓ
157. Ⓐ Ⓑ Ⓒ Ⓓ 170. Ⓐ Ⓑ Ⓒ Ⓓ 183. Ⓐ Ⓑ Ⓒ Ⓓ 196. Ⓐ Ⓑ Ⓒ Ⓓ
158. Ⓐ Ⓑ Ⓒ Ⓓ 171. Ⓐ Ⓑ Ⓒ Ⓓ 184. Ⓐ Ⓑ Ⓒ Ⓓ 197. Ⓐ Ⓑ Ⓒ Ⓓ
159. Ⓐ Ⓑ Ⓒ Ⓓ 172. Ⓐ Ⓑ Ⓒ Ⓓ 185. Ⓐ Ⓑ Ⓒ Ⓓ 198. Ⓐ Ⓑ Ⓒ Ⓓ
160. Ⓐ Ⓑ Ⓒ Ⓓ 173. Ⓐ Ⓑ Ⓒ Ⓓ 186. Ⓐ Ⓑ Ⓒ Ⓓ 199. Ⓐ Ⓑ Ⓒ Ⓓ
161. Ⓐ Ⓑ Ⓒ Ⓓ 174. Ⓐ Ⓑ Ⓒ Ⓓ 187. Ⓐ Ⓑ Ⓒ Ⓓ 200. Ⓐ Ⓑ Ⓒ Ⓓ
162. Ⓐ Ⓑ Ⓒ Ⓓ 175. Ⓐ Ⓑ Ⓒ Ⓓ 188. Ⓐ Ⓑ Ⓒ Ⓓ
163. Ⓐ Ⓑ Ⓒ Ⓓ 176. Ⓐ Ⓑ Ⓒ Ⓓ 189. Ⓐ Ⓑ Ⓒ Ⓓ
164. Ⓐ Ⓑ Ⓒ Ⓓ 177. Ⓐ Ⓑ Ⓒ Ⓓ 190. Ⓐ Ⓑ Ⓒ Ⓓ
165. Ⓐ Ⓑ Ⓒ Ⓓ 178. Ⓐ Ⓑ Ⓒ Ⓓ 191. Ⓐ Ⓑ Ⓒ Ⓓ

TOEIC Practice Test 4

LISTENING COMPREHENSION

In this section of the test, you will have the chance to show how well you understand spoken English. There are four parts to this section, with special directions for each part. You will find the Answer Sheet for Practice Test 4 on page 171. Detach it from the book and use it to record your answers. Check your answers using the Answer Key on page 207 and see the Answers Explained on page 209.

TIP

If you do not have access to an audio CD player, please refer to the audio-scripts starting on page 333 when prompted to listen to an audio passage.

Part 1: Photographs

Directions: You will see a photograph. You will hear four statements about the photograph. Choose the statement that most closely matches the photograph and fill in the corresponding oval on your answer sheet.

Example

Now listen to the four statements.

Sample Answer

(A) (B) (C) (D)

Statement (B), "She's reading a magazine," best describes what you see in the picture. Therefore, you should choose answer (B).

1.

2.

3.

4.

5.

6.

9.

7.

10.

8.

Part 2: Question-Response

Directions: You will hear a question and three possible responses. Choose the response that most closely answers the question and fill in the corresponding oval on your answer sheet.

Example

Now listen to the sample question.

You will hear:

How is the weather?

You will also hear:

(A) It's raining.
(B) He's fine, thanks.
(C) He's my boss.

The best response to the question *How is the weather?* is choice (A), *It's raining.* Therefore, you should choose answer (A).

11. Mark your answer on your answer sheet.	26. Mark your answer on your answer sheet.
12. Mark your answer on your answer sheet.	27. Mark your answer on your answer sheet.
13. Mark your answer on your answer sheet.	28. Mark your answer on your answer sheet.
14. Mark your answer on your answer sheet.	29. Mark your answer on your answer sheet.
15. Mark your answer on your answer sheet.	30. Mark your answer on your answer sheet.
16. Mark your answer on your answer sheet.	31. Mark your answer on your answer sheet.
17. Mark your answer on your answer sheet.	32. Mark your answer on your answer sheet.
18. Mark your answer on your answer sheet.	33. Mark your answer on your answer sheet.
19. Mark your answer on your answer sheet.	34. Mark your answer on your answer sheet.
20. Mark your answer on your answer sheet.	35. Mark your answer on your answer sheet.
21. Mark your answer on your answer sheet.	36. Mark your answer on your answer sheet.
22. Mark your answer on your answer sheet.	37. Mark your answer on your answer sheet.
23. Mark your answer on your answer sheet.	38. Mark your answer on your answer sheet.
24. Mark your answer on your answer sheet.	39. Mark your answer on your answer sheet.
25. Mark your answer on your answer sheet.	40. Mark your answer on your answer sheet.

Part 3: Conversations

Directions: You will hear a conversation between two people. You will see three questions on each conversation and four possible answers. Choose the best answer to each question and fill in the corresponding oval on your answer sheet.

41. When was the phone call made?
    (A) Two minutes ago
    (B) A few minutes ago
    (C) At 4:00
    (D) Before noon

42. Who called?
    (A) The man's boss
    (B) The woman's assistant
    (C) The accountant
    (D) The budget director

43. Why did this person call?
    (A) To discuss the budget
    (B) To announce a salary raise
    (C) To ask the man to go to work early
    (D) To go over the accounts

44. Where does this conversation take place?
    (A) At a country club
    (B) At a restaurant
    (C) At a gym
    (D) At a hotel

45. How much will the woman pay?
    (A) $65
    (B) $155
    (C) $165
    (D) $220

46. What will the woman do now?
    (A) Read a book
    (B) Look at the room
    (C) Play tennis
    (D) Eat something

47. Where is Mr. Wing now?
    (A) On vacation
    (B) At a meeting
    (C) On a business trip
    (D) At the train station

48. When will he return to the office?
    (A) Tomorrow
    (B) On Friday
    (C) Next week
    (D) In three weeks

49. Who will help the woman with her project?
    (A) The man
    (B) Her boss
    (C) Mr. Wing
    (D) Mr. Wing's assistant

50. What is the man's complaint?
    (A) He didn't see any art
    (B) The tickets were expensive
    (C) The hotel is far away
    (D) The museum is closed at night

51. What time is it now?
    (A) 3:00
    (B) 4:00
    (C) 9:00
    (D) 10:00

52. What will they do now?
    (A) Work
    (B) Go to the hotel
    (C) Park the car
    (D) Eat something

53. How is the weather today?
    (A) Cloudy
    (B) Rainy
    (C) Sunny
    (D) Icy

54. What are the speakers doing?
    (A) Working
    (B) Walking
    (C) Taking the train
    (D) Going to the store

55. When will the weather change?
    (A) Tomorrow
    (B) In two days
    (C) On the weekend
    (D) In a week

56. Why is the woman late?
    (A) She didn't have the bus fare.
    (B) She had to walk to the bus stop.
    (C) She missed the bus.
    (D) The bus was delayed.

57. How does the man get to work?
    (A) Bus
    (B) Car
    (C) Subway
    (D) Walking

58. How much is the bus fare?
    (A) $1.50
    (B) $2.00
    (C) $2.50
    (D) $4.00

59. Where does the man want to go?
    (A) A restaurant
    (B) A grocery store
    (C) A post office
    (D) A bank

60. How many blocks away is it?
    (A) One
    (B) Two
    (C) Three
    (D) Four

61. What time is it now?
    (A) 1:00
    (B) Just before 1:30
    (C) Just after 1:30
    (D) 2:00

62. Why did the man leave his old job?
    (A) He didn't get enough vacation time.
    (B) It wasn't close to home.
    (C) The work was too slow.
    (D) The pay was too low.

63. How does he feel about his new job?
    (A) Happy
    (B) Unsure
    (C) Bad
    (D) Sad

64. How many weeks of vacation does he get?
    (A) One
    (B) Two
    (C) Three
    (D) Six

65. Where are the speakers going?
    (A) A park
    (B) A garage
    (C) The office
    (D) The theater

66. What time does the man want to leave?
    (A) 10:00
    (B) 5:45
    (C) 6:15
    (D) 9:00

67. Where will they go later?
    (A) A restaurant
    (B) A party
    (C) A game
    (D) Home

68. What does the man want to drink?
    (A) Coffee
    (B) Hot tea
    (C) Iced tea
    (D) Water

69. How does the man feel?
    (A) Thirsty
    (B) Tired
    (C) Hungry
    (D) Angry

70. What does the woman offer the man?
    (A) A book
    (B) Some cake
    (C) Some magazines
    (D) A ride

Part 4: Talks

CD 3
TRACK 4

Directions: You will hear a talk given by a single speaker. You will see three questions on each talk, each with four possible answers. Choose the best answer to each question and fill in the corresponding oval on your answer sheet.

71. What time will the flight to Caracas leave?
    (A) 2:00
    (B) 3:00
    (C) 5:00
    (D) 7:00

72. What is offered to the passengers?
    (A) A free meal
    (B) A book
    (C) A suitcase
    (D) A refund check

73. How can passengers take advantage of the offer?
    (A) Board the plane
    (B) Talk to the gate agent
    (C) Wait in the lounge
    (D) Go to the baggage claim area

74. What place is opening?
    (A) A garden
    (B) An office
    (C) A store
    (D) An apartment

75. When will the opening take place?
    (A) Sunday
    (B) Monday
    (C) Friday
    (D) Saturday

76. Where is this place?
    (A) Next to the train station
    (B) Downtown
    (C) Beside a park
    (D) Across from a mall

77. What is the weather like?
    (A) Rainy
    (B) Snowy
    (C) Sunny
    (D) Warm

78. How many cars were in the accident?
    (A) 2
    (B) 5
    (C) 7
    (D) 11

79. When will the weather change?
    (A) This morning
    (B) In the afternoon
    (C) In the evening
    (D) Tomorrow

80. What are the tickets for?
    (A) A play
    (B) A circus
    (C) A movie
    (D) A TV show

81. How much do the tickets cost?
    (A) $15
    (B) $16
    (C) $37
    (D) $50

82. How can you get a free ticket?
    (A) Go to the theater
    (B) Send a postcard
    (C) Make a phone call
    (D) Visit a website

83. What was destroyed by a fire?
    (A) A tool shed
    (B) A park
    (C) A school
    (D) A bookstore

84. What time was the fire reported?
    (A) 4:00
    (B) 5:00
    (C) 7:00
    (D) 9:00

85. Who was hurt in the fire?
    (A) Ethel Rogers
    (B) A firefighter
    (C) Some children
    (D) No one

86. When can passengers get on the train?
    (A) In 3 minutes
    (B) In 5 minutes
    (C) In 6 minutes
    (D) In 10 minutes

87. What must passengers have to get on the train?
    (A) An information form
    (B) A passport
    (C) A reservation
    (D) A first-class ticket

88. What are passengers not allowed to take on the train?
    (A) Photographs
    (B) Two or more carry-on bags
    (C) Coats and purses
    (D) Meat

89. How long does the radio program last?
    (A) 15 minutes
    (B) 45 minutes
    (C) 1 hour
    (D) 2 hours

90. What will Dr. Silva talk about?
    (A) Office workers' health and fitness problems
    (B) The importance of business clothes that fit
    (C) How to give business talks
    (D) Writing books

91. What will Dr. Silva do after his talk?
    (A) Answer questions
    (B) Ask questions
    (C) Read the news
    (D) Go to the bank

92. What did the president do this afternoon?
    (A) Flew in a plane
    (B) Watched TV
    (C) Gave a speech
    (D) Had a meeting

93. Where will the president go tomorrow?
    (A) The capital city
    (B) Tokyo
    (C) Australia
    (D) Home

94. How long will his trip last?
    (A) 2 weeks
    (B) 3 weeks
    (C) 1 month
    (D) 4 months

95. At which one of the following times is the bank open?
    (A) Monday at 8:30 AM
    (B) Tuesday at 9:30 AM
    (C) Friday at 5:30 PM
    (D) Saturday at 4:30 PM

96. How can a customer find out the balance of his savings account?
    (A) Press 1
    (B) Press 2
    (C) Press 3
    (D) Press 4

97. What happens when a customer presses 0?
    (A) She can open a new account.
    (B) She can apply for a loan.
    (C) She can get a credit card.
    (D) She can hear the message again.

98. According to the speaker, what is the best place to look for a job?
    (A) Career counseling offices
    (B) Employment agencies
    (C) The Internet
    (D) Newspapers

99. What kinds of jobs can be found in this place?
    (A) Educational jobs only
    (B) Medical jobs only
    (C) Engineering jobs only
    (D) Any kind of job

100. According to the speaker, what is a job seeker's most important tool?
    (A) A resume
    (B) A degree
    (C) Interview skills
    (D) Work experience

READING

In this section of the test, you will have the chance to show how well you understand written English. There are three parts to this section, with special directions for each part.

YOU WILL HAVE ONE HOUR AND FIFTEEN MINUTES TO COMPLETE PARTS 5, 6, AND 7 OF THE TEST.

Part 5: Incomplete Sentences

Directions: You will see a sentence with a missing word. Four possible answers follow the sentence. Choose the best answer to the question and fill in the corresponding oval on your answer sheet.

101. When Ms. Song gets here, we _____ the meeting.
 (A) start
 (B) will start
 (C) have started
 (D) are starting

102. Don't forget to sign the application form _____ you submit it.
 (A) while
 (B) after
 (C) as soon as
 (D) before

103. The final report should be sent _____ the company's main office before the end of the month.
 (A) in
 (B) to
 (C) on
 (D) at

104. All employees _____ to attend next Friday's staff meeting.
 (A) encourage
 (B) will encourage
 (C) are encouraged
 (D) are encouraging

105. We _____ each staff member to do his or her part to get this project completed on time.
 (A) expect
 (B) expel
 (C) expend
 (D) expedite

106. The association conference will take place _____ December.
 (A) in
 (B) on
 (C) at
 (D) of

107. Mr. Lutz is _____ to take on such a big responsibility because he doesn't feel prepared for it at this time.
 (A) relieved
 (B) reluctant
 (C) reliable
 (D) relocated

108. The current _____ of this office plans to leave before the end of the month.
 (A) occupancy
 (B) occupying
 (C) occupy
 (D) occupant

109. We are looking for ways to reduce expenses _____ our financial situation is not good.
(A) although
(B) but
(C) because
(D) or

110. The office closes _____ noon on Saturdays.
(A) at
(B) on
(C) in
(D) to

111. The director says that she _____ to hire several new staff members next year.
(A) plan
(B) plans
(C) planning
(D) planned

112. Mr. Chan _____ in charge of operations since the beginning of last year.
(A) is
(B) was
(C) has been
(D) will be

113. Replacement cartridges for the printer can be found _____ the top shelf of the supply closet.
(A) on
(B) in
(C) at
(D) between

114. Both lunch _____ dinner are served in the company cafeteria.
(A) or
(B) either
(C) but
(D) and

115. Requests for extra time off must _____ by the employee's supervisor.
(A) approve
(B) be approved
(C) be approving
(D) approval

116. The board of directors agreed _____ Ms. Silva's contract for another year.
(A) renew
(B) to renew
(C) renewing
(D) will renew

117. It is important to dress _____ when going on a job interview.
(A) profess
(B) profession
(C) professional
(D) professionally

118. Ms. Toth slipped and fell _____ she was walking on the icy sidewalk in front of the building.
(A) while
(B) during
(C) although
(D) but

119. We prohibit _____ in any part of the building or grounds.
(A) smoke
(B) to smoke
(C) smoking
(D) will smoke

120. All packages, bags, and bundles will be _____ by a security officer before leaving the building.
(A) respected
(B) inspected
(C) prospected
(D) suspected

121. The new office is _____ 151 North Main Street.
(A) on
(B) at
(C) in
(D) for

122. We are concerned _____ the high rate of absenteeism among our employees.
(A) on
(B) for
(C) about
(D) of

123. The new building will be dedicated _____ June 30.
(A) on
(B) in
(C) at
(D) to

124. The rent on this office is _____ than the rent we have been paying at our old place.
(A) high
(B) higher
(C) highly
(D) highest

125. _____ we were careful with expenses, we still went over our budget this year.
(A) If
(B) Since
(C) Because
(D) Even though

126. She delayed _____ the contract until she had a chance to speak with her attorney.
(A) sign
(B) signing
(C) to sign
(D) signature

127. The woman _____ rents this office uses it only a few days a month.
(A) who's
(B) whose
(C) who
(D) whom

128. If your passport is no longer _____, then you should use some other form of identification.
(A) valid
(B) validate
(C) validating
(D) validation

129. He _____ about that issue for last month's report.
(A) writes
(B) wrote
(C) is writing
(D) written

130. _____ your supervisor if you plan to be away from the office for any length of time during the day.
(A) Notify
(B) Notifying
(C) Should notify
(D) Will notify

131. Mr. Carlo was very upset when he learned that he had been passed _____ for the promotion.
(A) in
(B) out
(C) over
(D) through

132. We have spent too much money and will have to _____ for the rest of the year.
(A) economy
(B) economize
(C) economist
(D) economically

133. Time is short and we will have to work very hard to _____ our goals by the end of the year.
    (A) perceive
    (B) receive
    (C) conceive
    (D) achieve

134. You can choose to have your paycheck mailed to you, _____ you can have your salary deposited directly into your bank account.
    (A) or
    (B) if
    (C) but
    (D) so

135. This building, _____ was built more than 100 years ago, is scheduled for demolition next month.
    (A) it
    (B) that
    (C) was
    (D) which

136. If you _____ your application tomorrow, you will still be eligible for the job.
    (A) to submit
    (B) submitted
    (C) submit
    (D) submits

137. We _____ in the elevator when the electricity went out, and we were stuck there for almost an hour.
    (A) rode
    (B) were riding
    (C) ridden
    (D) had ridden

138. You must _____ every item on the form or your application will not be considered.
    (A) complete
    (B) to complete
    (C) completing
    (D) will complete

139. We feel _____ about coming to an agreement on this issue soon.
    (A) hoping
    (B) hopeful
    (C) hopefully
    (D) to hope

140. _____ in today's business world is difficult, and many new businesses fail.
    (A) Compete
    (B) To compete
    (C) Competing
    (D) Have competed

Part 6: Text Completion

Directions: You will see four passages, each with three blanks. Under each blank are four answer options. Choose the word or phrase that best completes the statement.

Questions 141–143 refer to the following memo.

MEMO

To: All staff
From: D. Rivera
Re: Office Dress Code

It has come to our attention that a number of staff members have been coming to work in inappropriate _____. Please be reminded that this is a place of

141. (A) attire
(B) transportation
(C) schedules
(D) attitudes

business and that staff members are expected to dress professionally. This means that casual clothing such as shorts, T-shirts, sandals, and sneakers should not _____ in the office. This is of particular importance when

142. (A) wear
(B) worn
(C) be wearing
(D) be worn

meeting with clients. Remember that each one of you represents the company and needs to keep in mind the impression that you give to clients and potential clients.

If you have any questions or concerns about this policy, please let _____ know.

143. (A) I
(B) him
(C) you
(D) me

I will be happy to clarify any issues for you and listen to your concerns. Thank you for your cooperation.

Questions 144–146 refer to the following article.

As we age, it becomes more and more important to get regular exercise. At the same time, our work lives may become more and more _____.

144. (A) vacant
     (B) relaxed
     (C) hectic
     (D) dull

How can a busy professional find time for exercise in an already overscheduled life? The answer is to exercise a little bit at a time over the course of the day. It all adds up, and you may find that by the end of the day you have gotten thirty minutes of exercise or more just by finding small opportunities here and there. The possibilities are endless. For example, _____ you park your car farther away from

145. (A) so
     (B) if
     (C) because
     (D) although

your office than you normally do, you can get several minutes of walking time in, both on the way to and from the office. If you work in a tall building, skip the elevator and take the stairs, at least for part of the way. _____ stairs provides good

146. (A) Climb
     (B) Climbs
     (C) Climbing
     (D) To climb

aerobic exercise. There are many more possibilities. How many can you think of?

Questions 147–149 refer to the following notice.

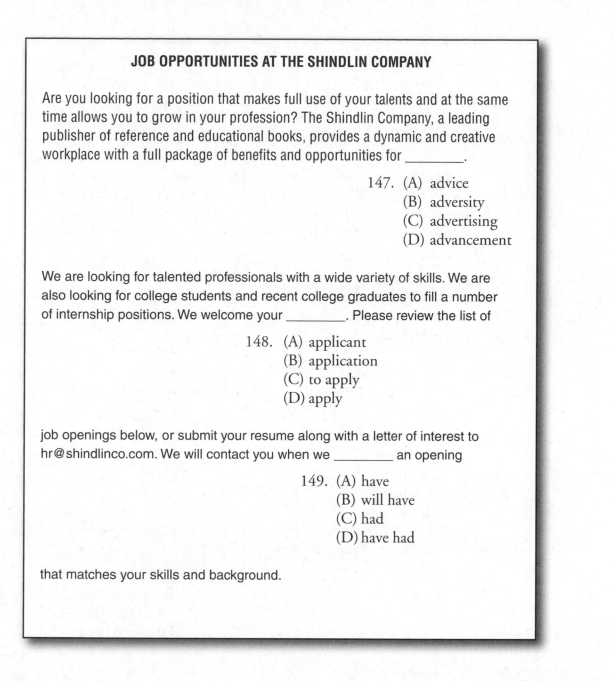

JOB OPPORTUNITIES AT THE SHINDLIN COMPANY

Are you looking for a position that makes full use of your talents and at the same time allows you to grow in your profession? The Shindlin Company, a leading publisher of reference and educational books, provides a dynamic and creative workplace with a full package of benefits and opportunities for _____.

147. (A) advice
(B) adversity
(C) advertising
(D) advancement

We are looking for talented professionals with a wide variety of skills. We are also looking for college students and recent college graduates to fill a number of internship positions. We welcome your _____. Please review the list of

148. (A) applicant
(B) application
(C) to apply
(D) apply

job openings below, or submit your resume along with a letter of interest to hr@shindlinco.com. We will contact you when we _____ an opening

149. (A) have
(B) will have
(C) had
(D) have had

that matches your skills and background.

Questions 150–152 refer to the following e-mail.

To: Mi Ja Kim
From: Eun Hee Cho
Subject: Help with workshop

Hello, Ms. Kim,

I am working on the logistics for next week's workshop, and
I need some help with planning the lunch. I've looked over
the budget, and it appears that we don't have a great deal
of money to spend for this. I am having a hard time finding
a good _____ service that doesn't charge too

150. (A) accounting
     (B) banking
     (C) catering
     (D) organizing

much. Can you suggest one that can serve a decent meal at a
decent price? I also need your suggestions for a place to
serve the lunch. Mr. Song suggested one of the conference
rooms, but _____ all seem too small to me. Do you think

151. (A) them
     (B) they
     (C) he
     (D) it

we could use the cafeteria? I would really _____ your

152. (A) appreciate
     (B) appreciative
     (C) appreciation
     (D) appreciated

ideas and suggestions.

Thank you very much.
Eun Hee Cho

Part 7: Reading Comprehension

Directions: You will see single and double reading passages followed by several questions. Each question has four answer choices. Choose the best answer to the question and fill in the corresponding oval on your answer sheet.

Questions 153–154 refer to the following advertisement.

Does your business need more business?

Advertise in the *Daily Herald*'s Business Directory

Your ad will reach over 75,000 readers who need your services. Carpenters, plumbers, landscapers, bookkeepers, cleaners, and organizers are just some of the service providers who have found advertising in the *Daily Herald* newspaper to be a worthwhile investment.

Call 482-9872 to place your ad.
Ads are just $.50 per line per day.

153. Who would be interested in this ad?
    (A) Business owners
    (B) Investment advisers
    (C) Homeowners
    (D) Newspaper reporters

154. What would be the cost to run a 10-line ad for five days?
    (A) $.50
    (B) $2.50
    (C) $5.00
    (D) $25.00

Questions 155–157 refer to the following article.

The Business and Industry Association will host a meeting to discuss business policy with local government officials next week. This event, which takes place each November, gives business and political leaders the opportunity to discuss business and economic concerns that will have an impact over the coming year, and to set the agenda for the next year's business regulation policy. A summary of the discussion will be provided to all members of the Business and Industry Association as well as to political representatives, and will be reported in this newsletter as well.

The meeting will take place at the Tinmouth Hotel on November 15 from 9:00 AM until noon. After the meeting, a luncheon will be served to all participants. Afterward Dr. Myrtle Pleasance of the Business Research Institute will address the audience on the topic of Analyzing Client Behavior. All members of the Business and Industry Association are encouraged to attend and can register by calling 583-9261 or visiting www.busind.org.

155. How often does the meeting take place?
(A) Once a week
(B) Once a month
(C) Once a year
(D) Twice a year

156. Who will participate in the discussion?
(A) Researchers
(B) Business leaders
(C) The governor
(D) Hotel administrators

157. What will happen right after the luncheon?
(A) The discussion will continue.
(B) There will be a speaker.
(C) Everyone will go home.
(D) Members will call the Business and Industry Association.

Questions 158–161 refer to the following form.

Chester Corp. Credit Card
Disputed Item Claim Form

Please complete all items on this form and sign it before mailing. Do not include your credit card payment. This claim form must be sent in a separate envelope.

Name *Helga Larsen*

Date *March 25, 20--*

Amount Disputed *$115*

Merchant *Online Office Supplies, Inc.*

I have examined my statement and am disputing a charge made to my account for the following reason:

____ This purchase was not made by me or by any other person authorized to use my card.

_X_ The amount shown on my statement is different from the amount I was charged at the time of purchase. Amount charged at time of purchase was ___*$75*___ . (Enclose a copy of the sales receipt.)

____ The item was to be shipped to me by mail. Expected delivery date _____. (This claim cannot be made until 30 days after the expected delivery date.)

____ The merchandise I purchased was defective and returned by me to the merchant.

Return date _____. (Enclose copy of return receipt or postal receipt.)

Signature *Helga Larsen*

---

158. What is this form for?
    (A) To apply for a credit card
    (B) To make a purchase
    (C) To report a billing error
    (D) To ask for a refund

159. What should Ms. Larsen enclose with the form?
    (A) Payment
    (B) A sales receipt
    (C) An extra envelope
    (D) Defective merchandise

160. The word *examined* in line 9 is closest in meaning to
    (A) paid.
    (B) sent in.
    (C) copied.
    (D) looked at.

161. According to Ms. Larsen, how much should she pay?
    (A) $15
    (B) $75
    (C) $115
    (D) $175

Questions 162–163 refer to the following letter.

Ming & Associates
1800 Pacific Boulevard
Sydney

April 10, 20--

Harold Ungemach
Box 86449
Sydney

Dear Mr. Ungemach,

Thank you for sending us your resume. Your qualifications are impressive. Unfortunately, we are rarely in the position of hiring full-time employees. We do, however, frequently have a need for consultants to work on temporary assignments. We are often looking for professionals with your background and skills to work on certain projects. If you would be interested in a temporary consulting position, please let me know. I will then keep your resume on file and notify you when a suitable assignment becomes available. Again, thank you for thinking of us. I will look forward to hearing from you.

Sincerely,

Mara Knightly
Human Resources Coordinator

---

162. Why did Mr. Ungemach write to the Ming & Associates company?
    (A) To order a product
    (B) To apply for a full-time job
    (C) To offer to help with a project
    (D) To develop his skills

163. What does Ms. Knightly ask Mr. Ungemach to do?
    (A) Send her his resume
    (B) Select a professional assignment
    (C) Notify her when he is available
    (D) Indicate his interest in a consulting position

Questions 164–167 refer to the following notice.

Central Power Company
Account #4885 9965 0066 43
Notification of Discontinuation of Service

Payment on your electric bill is now more than 30 days overdue. In compliance with National Regulation #50504, if we do not receive payment within 10 business days, we will discontinue your service. We must receive payment of $85 due on your bill plus a $15 late fee before August 31 to avoid interruption of service. Once disconnection has occurred, all outstanding charges must be paid in addition to a $50 reconnection fee before we can resume your service. You may be eligible for a monthly installment plan. Please contact our Customer Service office to discuss financing options.

See the reverse side of this notice for a complete explanation
of our rights and obligations under National Regulation #50504.

---

164. What is the purpose of this notice?
(A) To request an overdue payment
(B) To explain charges on an electric bill
(C) To clarify a national regulation
(D) To offer a financial service

165. If the customer pays before August 31, how much will he owe?
(A) $15
(B) $85
(C) $100
(D) $150

166. How can the customer find out about financing?
(A) Read the other side of the notice
(B) Call the Customer Service office
(C) Study National Regulation #50504
(D) Write to the power company

167. The word *resume* in line 8 is closest in meaning to
(A) add to.
(B) improve.
(C) restart.
(D) cut off.

Questions 168–171 refer to the following article.

Local officials have finally reached an agreement with the Smithson Development Company regarding the construction of a new shopping mall in the Billings Bay neighborhood. A contract was signed last night, and construction is slated to begin in six months. The Smithson Development Company originally purchased the land for the mall four years ago from a horse farmer. The road to approval has been a long one. Plans for the mall have been protested by environmental groups and local residents. However, after modifying plans several times and including many environmentally friendly features as part of the construction, Smithson was finally able to win the approval of the city council.

The Billings Bay Mall will be the largest by far in our area. Space is planned for 250 retail shops as well as two large department stores, 20 restaurants, cafés, and snack shops, a 10-screen movie theater, an indoor play area, classroom space for the local community college, and a small walk-in health clinic. There will also be a 750-car underground parking garage, as well as space for at least twice as many cars in outdoor parking areas. Smithson estimates that construction will take no more than one year. Plans for a grand opening are already under way.

168. Who is not in favor of the new shopping mall?
(A) Local residents
(B) The city council
(C) A horse farmer
(D) Mr. Smithson

169. Which one of the following things will customers NOT be able to do at the mall?
(A) Take a class
(B) Buy a car
(C) Watch a movie
(D) See a doctor

170. How many cars will be able to park in the outdoor parking lot?
(A) 250
(B) 500
(C) 750
(D) 1,500

171. When will construction of the mall probably be completed?
(A) 6 months from now
(B) 1 year from now
(C) 1½ years from now
(D) 4 years from now

Questions 172–174 refer to the following ad.

Sale!   Sale!
Sale!

Pinkerton's announces its biggest sale of the year.
We have slashed prices on select items throughout the store.

- Printer ink cartridges—Buy one at $30, get the second one at 50% off
- Photocopier paper—Buy one pack of 500 sheets, get the second one free
- Jumbo pack notebooks—25% each pack of 10
- Desk organizers—Assorted colors, 15% off
- Office desks and computer stands—35% off
- Super-Comfort brand desk chairs—Assorted colors, 50% off

Hurry on down to Pinkerton's.
With deals like these, items will fly right off the shelves!

Sale ends Saturday.

172. What kind of business is Pinkerton's?
(A) Office supply store
(B) Printing company
(C) Furniture store
(D) Photocopy service

173. How much would a customer spend for
two ink cartridges?
(A) $15
(B) $30
(C) $45
(D) $50

174. What item is 25% off?
(A) Photocopier paper
(B) Notebooks
(C) Desks
(D) Chairs

Questions 175–178 refer to the following letter.

Eastman Energy Associates
54 East Putnam Avenue
Riverside

June 8, 20--

Priscilla Pavlis
Pavlis and Company
P.O. Box 16
Riverside

Dear Ms. Pavlis,

Thank you for your letter of May 25. I am very happy to respond to your questions about our services. Eastman Energy Associates conducts energy audits of businesses with the aim of helping our customers heat and cool their buildings more efficiently. Typically, we begin by inspecting furnaces, air-conditioning units, and heating and cooling ducts for efficient operation and compatibility with the building and with your heating and cooling needs. We then conduct a thorough inspection of the building itself, both inside and outside, for places where air can enter and escape. We focus on outside doors and windows, outside walls, and the roof.

Within a week of our visit, we send a complete written report with an evaluation of your building's strengths and weaknesses. We also include a list of suggested upgrades with their estimated costs as well as estimated savings in heating/cooling costs. We follow up with a phone call to ensure that you understand each detail and to address any concerns you may have. An audit of a building of your size would take about eight hours to complete. We would charge $1,500 for the audit, including the written report and follow-up call. Any further consulting you may require beyond that would be charged at our hourly rate of $175 an hour.

Please let me know if you have any further questions. You can reach me by phone at 492-0983. Call that same number if you would like to schedule an audit for your building. We are currently making appointments for next month. Thank you for contacting Eastman.

Sincerely,

Karla Heinz
Energy Consultant

175. Why did Ms. Heinz write this letter?
    (A) To advertise her business
    (B) To follow up on a consultation
    (C) To reply to Ms. Pavlis's letter
    (D) To explain charges on a bill

176. What does Ms. Pavlis want to do?
    (A) Save money on heating and cooling
    (B) Construct a new building
    (C) Get new windows and doors
    (D) Repair her roof

177. How much will Ms. Pavlis pay if she gets the service as outlined in the letter?
    (A) $175
    (B) $1,500
    (C) $1,575
    (D) $1,675

178. The word *upgrades* in paragraph 2, line 2 is closest in meaning to
    (A) materials.
    (B) systems.
    (C) builders.
    (D) improvements.

Questions 179–180 refer to the following advertisement.

HELP WANTED

We are seeking an experienced financial professional to manage the accounting office at a rapidly growing financial services company. Responsibilities of the position include coordinating the work of a six-person accounting department, managing business accounts, and reviewing client financial information. This position reports to the chief financial officer (CFO). Requirements: university degree in accounting, a minimum of three years' management experience, up-to-date knowledge of accounting software, strong organizational and interpersonal skills. Benefits include health and dental insurance, vacation and sick leave, and a retirement plan. Interested candidates should send a resume and letter of interest to

Magus Finance, Inc.
Attn: Simona Santarelli, HR Coordinator
Box 4828
Marlboro
Or e-mail: s_santarelli@magus.com
No phone calls, please.

---

179. Who should apply for this job?
    (A) A dentist
    (B) An accountant
    (C) A software engineer
    (D) A health care manager

180. How can someone apply for this job?
    (A) Call the HR coordinator
    (B) Write a letter to the CFO
    (C) Send a resume to Ms. Santarelli
    (D) Visit the Magus Finance, Inc. office

Questions 181–185 refer to the following bill and letter.

CRISP COMPANY

New charges for: Byron & Farrar Law Offices, account #2095687
From 03/01 to 03/31 20--

Previous

Balance from last bill: $125
Payments received: $0
Previous balance due: $125

Current

Local phone service: $50
Long distance phone charges: $39
Internet services: $35
Tax: $8
Current charges: $132

Total due: Please pay this amount: $257

Payments received after March 25 are not applied to this statement.
To dispute a charge, contact our customer service office in writing:

Crisp Company
Customer Service Office
45 Mountain View Road
Wilmington

April 18, 20--

Crisp Company
Customer Service Office
45 Mountain View Road
Wilmington

Dear Customer Service,

I am writing in regard to the recent bill from your company sent to us at Byron and Farrar Law Offices, account #2095687. In this bill we were charged for two months of service. This is incorrect since we owe only for this month's service. I personally paid last month's bill. According to my records, I wrote a check to your company for $125 and mailed it on March 26. I have contacted my bank and have been informed that that check has been processed and your company has received the funds. They will be providing me with a copy of the check before the end of the week, which I will then forward to you. Tomorrow I will be sending you a check for the amount owed for this month's charges only. Please correct your records to show the payment already made on last month's bill. Thank you for your attention. I expect the next bill will show the correct charges.

Sincerely,

Robert Krumholz
Office Manager

181. What kind of services does Crisp Company offer?
(A) Law
(B) Delivery
(C) Phone and Internet
(D) Accounting

182. Why did Mr. Krumholz write the letter?
(A) He disagrees with a charge.
(B) He forgot his account number.
(C) He needs a copy of a check.
(D) He requires more services.

183. What mistake did Mr. Krumholz make?
(A) He wrote the wrong amount on the check.
(B) He didn't have enough money in the bank.
(C) He added the figures incorrectly.
(D) He sent in last month's payment late.

184. According to Mr. Krumholz, how much does he owe the company now?
(A) $50
(B) $125
(C) $132
(D) $257

185. What will Mr. Krumholz do tomorrow?
(A) Contact his bank
(B) Mail a check
(C) Get a copy of a check
(D) Write a letter to Crisp Company

Questions 186–190 refer to the schedule and e-mail.

WORKSHOP SCHEDULE—DRAFT			
Time	**Location**	**Presentation**	**Presenter**
9:30	Room B	Changing World Markets	L. Chang
11:00	Room C	Cross-Cultural Considerations in Marketing	J. H. Lee
12:15	Room C	Lunch	
1:30	Room D	Analyzing Demographics	I. A. Kim
3:00	Room A	Internet Marketing	D. Wang
4:00	Room A	Open Discussion	All

To: F. Bao
From: J. S. Park
Subject: Workshop logistics
Date: Monday, June 10
attch: Workshop schedule

Ms. Bao,

I have attached a draft of the schedule for the upcoming workshop. I wish we had scheduled it for a week from today instead of for the day after tomorrow. There is still so much to do to get ready; however, we can't change the date now. I really appreciate your support in getting things ready.

Here are some things I need you to take care of. Tea and snacks should be served immediately after Mr. Chang's presentation. He plans to talk for just an hour, so there will be time for this before the next presentation begins. Also, the room that we have scheduled for lunch is one of the smaller rooms, and serving a meal there would be difficult. In addition, we have a workshop scheduled in the same place right before lunch, so there would be no time to set up. See if you can exchange places with the Demographics workshop. The room we have scheduled for that seems more convenient and comfortable for eating.

Please make sure there are enough chairs in each room for everyone. So far, 45 people have registered for the workshop, but a few more registrations could come in today or tomorrow. You should have 15 extra chairs in each room just to be safe. There is one last schedule change. Mr. Wang will have to leave right after lunch, so please give him Ms. Lee's time slot, and she can take Mr. Wang's afternoon time slot. Send me the revised schedule this afternoon. Thank you.

Jae Sun Park

186. When will the workshop take place?
(A) June 10
(B) June 11
(C) June 12
(D) June 17

187. What time will tea and snacks be served?
(A) 9:30
(B) 10:30
(C) 11:00
(D) 12:15

188. Where does Mr. Park want the lunch served?
(A) Room A
(B) Room B
(C) Room C
(D) Room D

189. How many chairs should there be in each room?
(A) 15
(B) 30
(C) 45
(D) 60

190. Who will present at 3:00?
(A) L. Chang
(B) J. H. Lee
(C) I. A. Kim
(D) D. Wang

Questions 191–195 refer to the following employee manual page and form.

Annual Leave

All employees of the Howland Corporation are entitled to annual leave, or vacation days, according to their length of service at Howland, as follows:

Years Employed at Howland	Number of Annual Leave Days
0–2	10
3–5	15
6–10	20
11 or more	25

Annual leave days must be used up by the end of the calendar year or they will be forfeited. The actual dates when leave days may be taken are dependent on permission from the employee's supervisor. To apply to use annual leave days, the employee must complete form number 465, obtain the supervisor's permission and signature, and submit the form to the human resources director no later than 21 calendar days before the date when the requested leave will begin. Incomplete or late requests will not be reviewed and leave will not be granted.

Form No. 465

The Howland Corporation
Annual Leave Request Form

Name: *Daniel Ortiz*

Department: *Research and Development*

Number of annual leave days allowed: *15*

Number of leave days requested: *5*

Dates: *July 21 – July 25*   Name of Supervisor: *Nestor Perez*

Authorizing signature: _____

Please submit this form to Daisy Ortega, Room 14.

191. What is the maximum number of annual leave days a Howland employee can take?
    (A) 10
    (B) 15
    (C) 20
    (D) 25

192. How long has Daniel Ortiz probably worked at the Howland Corporation?
    (A) No more than 2 years
    (B) At least 3 years
    (C) At least 6 years
    (D) More than 11 years

193. What is the latest date Daniel Ortiz can submit this form?
    (A) July 1
    (B) July 15
    (C) July 21
    (D) July 26

194. Who has to sign the form?
    (A) Daniel Ortiz
    (B) Daisy Ortega
    (C) Nestor Perez
    (D) Mr. Howland

195. Who is Daisy Ortega?
    (A) President of the Howland Corporation
    (B) Head of the Research and Development Department
    (C) Human Resources Director
    (D) Daniel Ortiz's assistant

Questions 196–200 refer to the following advertisement and e-mail.

FOR RENT

Large, sunny office in convenient downtown location, near two bus routes, ample parking in rear. 900 sq. feet divided into two private offices and comfortable reception area, small kitchen, one bathroom. Modern 10-story building with two elevators. $1,750/month. First month's rent and security deposit equal to one month's rent required to move in. To see, call City Office Rentals at 382-0838 between 8:30 and 4:30, Tues.–Sat.

To: Marilyn Sawyer
From: Paul Lebowski
Subject: Office rental
Date: Tuesday, October 3

Marilyn,
Here's a link to an office rental ad I found online: www.offices.com/10-01. I think it's worth looking at even though the rent is a bit high. I know it is a good deal more than we are paying now, but look at the size. It's twice as big as our current office, and I'm sure we can use the space. And it has a kitchen and bathroom and a reception area just like we have now. Unfortunately it is nowhere near a subway station. That is a convenience I would miss having, but it does have parking, unlike our current office. I'm sure our clients would appreciate that. It would also be good to be in a building with an elevator. I'm really tired of using the stairs. I'd like to see the space as soon as possible. Could you call and make an appointment? Try and get one for tomorrow if you can, because after that I'll be away until next Monday, as you know. Thanks.
Paul

196. How big is Marilyn and Paul's current office?
(A) 450 square feet
(B) 750 square feet
(C) 900 square feet
(D) 1,750 square feet

197. What is true of Marilyn and Paul's current office?
(A) It costs more than the advertised office.
(B) It is near the subway.
(C) It is in a building with an elevator.
(D) It is in a 10-story building.

198. When does Paul want to see the office?
(A) Monday
(B) Tuesday
(C) Wednesday
(D) Thursday

199. What does the advertised office have that the current office doesn't?
(A) A kitchen
(B) A bathroom
(C) A parking area
(D) A reception area

200. How much would Marilyn and Paul have to pay before moving into the advertised office?
(A) $900
(B) $1,750
(C) $1,800
(D) $3,500

Answer Key
PRACTICE TEST 4

Listening Comprehension

Part 1: Photographs

1. D	4. C	7. D	9. C
2. B	5. C	8. B	10. A
3. A	6. A		

Part 2: Question-Response

11. B	19. B	27. A	35. B
12. A	20. B	28. C	36. A
13. C	21. C	29. A	37. A
14. C	22. A	30. C	38. C
15. A	23. A	31. B	39. A
16. B	24. C	32. A	40. C
17. A	25. B	33. C	
18. C	26. A	34. C	

Part 3: Conversations

41. B	49. D	57. C	65. D
42. A	50. B	58. C	66. B
43. C	51. A	59. A	67. D
44. D	52. D	60. B	68. D
45. C	53. C	61. B	69. A
46. B	54. B	62. D	70. B
47. A	55. A	63. A	
48. C	56. D	64. C	

Part 4: Talks

71. D	79. D	87. C	95. B
72. A	80. B	88. B	96. A
73. B	81. A	89. B	97. D
74. C	82. B	90. A	98. C
75. D	83. C	91. A	99. D
76. D	84. D	92. D	100. A
77. B	85. D	93. B	
78. C	86. A	94. B	

Answer Key
PRACTICE TEST 4

Reading

Part 5: Incomplete Sentences

101. B	111. B	121. B	131. C
102. D	112. C	122. C	132. B
103. B	113. A	123. A	133. D
104. C	114. D	124. B	134. A
105. A	115. B	125. D	135. D
106. A	116. B	126. B	136. C
107. B	117. D	127. C	137. B
108. D	118. A	128. A	138. A
109. C	119. C	129. B	139. B
110. A	120. B	130. A	140. C

Part 6: Text Completion

141. A	144. C	147. D	150. C
142. D	145. B	148. B	151. B
143. D	146. C	149. A	152. A

Part 7: Reading Comprehension

153. A	165. C	177. B	189. D
154. D	166. B	178. D	190. B
155. C	167. C	179. B	191. D
156. B	168. A	180. C	192. B
157. B	169. B	181. C	193. A
158. C	170. D	182. A	194. C
159. B	171. C	183. D	195. C
160. D	172. A	184. C	196. A
161. B	173. C	185. B	197. B
162. B	174. B	186. C	198. C
163. D	175. C	187. B	199. C
164. A	176. A	188. D	200. D

TOEIC PRACTICE TEST 4—ANSWERS EXPLAINED

Listening Comprehension

PART 1: PHOTOGRAPHS

1. **(D)** A group of businesspeople is riding down an escalator. Choice (A) confuses the papers they are holding with newspapers. Choice (B) confuses similar-sounding words *escalator* and *elevator*. Choice (C) refers to the documents they are holding, but no one is signing them.

2. **(B)** A ferry with cars on deck is crossing the water. Choice (A) is incorrect because the photo shows a ferry, not a bridge, crossing the water. Choice (C) is incorrect because the ferry is nowhere near a dock. Choice (D) is incorrect because the cars are on a ferry, not a highway.

3. **(A)** People are crossing the street on the painted lines, or the pedestrian crosswalk. Choice (B) confuses similar-sounding words *walking* and *talking*. Choice (C) identifies the correct location but not the action. Choice (D) confuses *crosswalk* with *sidewalk*.

4. **(C)** Two men in chef's hats are cooking food in a restaurant kitchen. Choice (A) associates *restaurant* with *kitchen*. Choice (B) confuses similar-sounding words *kitchen* and *chicken*. Choice (D) associates *kitchen* with *food*.

5. **(C)** A man holding several shopping bags is looking in a store window. Choice (A) mentions the window and confuses similar-sounding words *bags* and *rags*. Choice (B) mentions the door, but the man is not walking through it. Choice (D) is incorrect because the man is outside the store, not inside it.

6. **(A)** A group of young people is sitting at a café table holding coffee cups, and one of them is laughing. Choice (B) confuses similar-sounding words *coffee* and *coughing*. Choice (C) confuses similar-sounding words *smiling* and *filing*. Choice (D) mentions the cups, but they are not broken.

7. **(D)** A man is walking through a place that has signs directing people to boarding areas and gates, so he must be in an airport. Choice (A) associates *round-trip ticket* with *airport*. Choice (B) confuses similar-sounding words *airport* and *court*. Choice (C) is incorrect because the man's suitcase is already packed.

8. **(B)** Two men are at a construction site and one is pointing something out to the other. Choice (A) is incorrect because their hats are on their heads, not in their hands. Choice (C) mentions the other man's phone, but no desk is visible in this outdoor scene. Choice (D) confuses similar-sounding words *pointing* and *painting*.

9. **(C)** A businessman is talking on the phone and looking at some papers. Choice (A) confuses similar-sounding words *talking* and *walking* and *phone* and *home*. Choice (B) associates *dialing* with *phone*. Choice (D) confuses similar-sounding words *looking* and *cooking*.

10. **(A)** A group of businesspeople is having a discussion around a table that has three computers, some drinking glasses, and some papers on it. Choice (B) confuses the drinking glasses with eyeglasses. Choice (C) is incorrect because it is a conference table, not a dinner table. Choice (D) mentions the papers, but no one is reading them.

PART 2: QUESTION-RESPONSE

11. **(B)** *My boss* answers the question *Who?* Choice (A) would answer *Whose?* Choice (C) would answer *Where?*

12. **(A)** The second speaker is *starving*, or very hungry, so agrees to the first speaker's suggestion of having lunch now. Choice (B) repeats the words *hour* and *lunch*. Choice (C) associates *lunch* with *restaurant*.

13. **(C)** *At the end of the week* answers the question *When?* Choice (A) confuses similar-sounding words *report* and *import*. Choice (B) confuses similar-sounding words *due* and *two*.

14. **(C)** *Across the street* answers the question *Where?* Choice (A) confuses similar-sounding words *bank* and *back*. Choice (B) confuses similar-sounding words *bank* and *thank*.

15. **(A)** *The small blue one* answers the question *Which?* Choice (B) confuses similar-sounding words *car* and *far*. Choice (C) confuses similar-sounding words *yours* and *tour*.

16. **(B)** This explains why John left early. Choice (A) repeats the word *leave*. Choice (C) repeats the word *early*.

17. **(A)** *Boring* answers the question *How?* Choice (B) associates *movie* with *tickets*. Choice (C) confuses similar-sounding words *movie* and *move*.

18. **(C)** This is a reason why the second speaker cannot respond to the first speaker's request for help. Choice (A) confuses similar-sounding words *copy* and *shopping*. Choice (B) repeats the word *documents*.

19. **(B)** This answers the question about possession. Choice (A) associates *coat* with *closet*. Choice (C) repeats the word *coat*.

20. **(B)** The first speaker offers coffee, but the second speaker prefers tea. Choice (A) confuses similar-sounding words *coffee* and *coughing*. Choice (C) associates *coffee* with *cups*.

21. **(C)** *This one* answers the question *Which?* Choice (A) confuses similar-sounding words *seat* and *meat*. Choice (B) associates *seat* with *chair*.

22. **(A)** *An hour or so* answers the question *How long?* Choice (B) confuses the meaning of the word *long*. Choice (C) confuses similar-sounding words *take* and *cake* and repeats the word *there*.

23. **(A)** This explains what the second speaker did with the package. Choice (B) repeats the word *package*. Choice (C) confuses similar-sounding words *package* and *packing*.

24. **(C)** This answers the yes-no question about the meeting. Choice (A) confuses similar-sounding words *meeting* and *eating*. Choice (B) repeats the word *meeting*.

25. **(B)** This answers the question *Where?* Choice (A) confuses similar-sounding words *ink* and *think*. Choice (C) repeats the word *printer*.

26. **(A)** This is a logical response to the complaint about the rainy weather. Choice (B) confuses similar-sounding words *rain* and *train* and related words *tired* and *tiring*. Choice (C) confuses similar-sounding words *weather* and *leather*.

27. **(A)** *I* answers the question *Who?* Choice (B) confuses *papers* with *newspaper*. Choice (C) confuses the meaning of the word *sign*.

28. **(C)** This is a logical response to the question about the broken photocopy machine. Choice (A) associates *photocopy machine* with *copies*. Choice (B) confuses similar-sounding words *broken* and *spoken*.

29. **(A)** The first speaker needs a ride and the second speaker offers one. Choice (B) associates *airport* with *plane*. Choice (C) repeats the word *airport*.

30. **(C)** This answers the question about the time. Choice (A) repeats the word *time*. Choice (B) confuses similar-sounding words *time* and *fine*.

31. **(B)** *This one* answers the question *Which?* Choice (A) confuses similar-sounding words *suit* and *fruit*. Choice (C) confuses homonyms *wear* and *where*.

32. **(A)** *John's* answers the question *Whose?* Choice (B) repeats the word *car*. Choice (C) confuses the meaning of the word *park* and also confuses similar-sounding words *car* and *far*.

33. **(C)** *Next September* answers the question *When?* Choice (A) confuses similar-sounding words *conference* and *preference*. Choice (B) would answer the question *Where?*

34. **(C)** This explains the reason for going to the office. Choice (A) repeats the word *office*. Choice (B) repeats the word *Saturday*.

35. **(B)** This answers the tag question about possession. Choices (A) and (C) repeat the word *desk*.

36. **(A)** This explains what can be seen from the window. Choice (B) confuses *window* with the similar-sounding word *windy*. Choice (C) repeats the word *window*.

37. **(A)** *A cafeteria on the first floor* answers the question *Where?* Choice (B) confuses similar-sounding words *quick* and *pick*. Choice (C) confuses similar-sounding words *lunch* and *crunch*.

38. **(C)** *Three or four days* answers the question *How long?* Choice (A) confuses similar-sounding words *plan* and *plane*. Choice (B) repeats the word *stay*.

39. **(A)** This is a logical response to the question about finishing work. Choice (B) confuses similar-sounding words *budget* and *budge*. Choice (C) repeats the word *report*.

40. **(C)** This is a logical response to a remark about chilly weather. Choice (A) repeats the word *outside*. Choice (B) confuses similar-sounding words *chilly* and *hilly*.

PART 3: CONVERSATIONS

41. **(B)** The woman heard the phone ringing a few minutes ago. Choice (A) confuses similar-sounding words *few* and *two*. Choice (C) confuses similar-sounding words *before* and *four*. Choice (D) is when the report for the accountant needs to be finished.

42. **(A)** The man says it was his boss on the phone. Choice (B) is the person the woman is expecting to call. Choice (C) is the person the man has to prepare a report for. Choice (D) repeats the word *budget*, which is what the woman's assistant is supposed to call about.

43. **(C)** The man's boss called to ask him to go to work early tomorrow to help with the report for the accountant. Choice (A) repeats the word *budget*. Choice (B) is what the woman would like the man's boss to do. Choice (D) associates *accounts* with *accountant*.

44. **(D)** The woman has a suitcase and is getting a room for the night, so she is at a hotel. Choice (A) associates the *pool, exercise room*, and *tennis courts* with a *country club*. Choice (B) associates *eat* with *restaurant*. Choice (C) associates *exercise room* with *gym*.

45. **(C)** The man says that the room costs $165. Choices (A) and (B) sound similar to the correct answer. Choice (D) is the room number.

46. **(B)** The woman says she will take her suitcase up and look at the room. Choice (A) confuses similar-sounding words *look* and *book*. Choice (C) is impossible because the tennis courts are closed. Choice (D) is what she will do after looking at the room.

47. **(A)** The man says that Mr. Wing is on vacation. Choice (B) is where the woman expected to see him. Choice (C) repeats the word *trip*. Choice (D) confuses similar-sounding words *vacation* and *station*.

48. **(C)** The man says Mr. Wing will be away until next week. Choice (A) is when Mr. Wing's assistant will be in the office. Choice (B) is when the woman's project is due. Choice (D) confuses similar-sounding words *see* and *three*.

49. **(D)** The man says that Mr. Wing's assistant will help the woman. Choice (A), one of the speakers, does not offer to help. Choice (B) is the person the work will be submitted to. Choice (C) is the person the woman wanted to ask for help.

50. **(B)** The man is complaining about how much the tickets cost. Choice (A) is incorrect because the man and woman agree that they enjoyed seeing the paintings. Choice (C) repeats the words *hotel* and *far*. Choice (D) confuses *right* with the similar-sounding word *night*.

51. **(A)** This is the time that the woman says. Choice (B) confuses similar-sounding words *before* and *four*. Choice (C) confuses similar-sounding words *fine* and *nine*. Choice (D) confuses similar-sounding words *then* and *ten*.

52. **(D)** The woman says, *Let's get a snack*, that is, something to eat. Choice (A) confuses the meaning of the word *work*. Choice (B) repeats the word *hotel*. Choice (C) confuses the meaning of the word *park* as well as the similar-sounding words *far* and *car*.

53. **(C)** The man mentions the sunny day. Choice (A) is incorrect because the woman says that there is not a cloud in the sky. Choice (B) is how the weather was last week. Choice (D) confuses similar-sounding words *nice* and *ice*.

54. **(B)** The speakers are discussing the walk they are enjoying in the nice weather. Choice (A) confuses similar-sounding words *walk* and *work*. Choice (C) confuses similar-sounding words *rain* and *train*. Choice (D) confuses similar-sounding words *more* and *store*.

55. **(A)** The woman says that it will rain tomorrow. Choice (B) confuses similar-sounding words *today* and *two days*. Choice (C) confuses similar-sounding words *end* and *weekend*. Choice (D) repeats the word *week*.

56. **(D)** This is the explanation the woman gives. Choice (A) repeats the phrase *bus fare*. Choice (B) is incorrect because it takes the woman only two minutes to walk to the bus stop. Choice (C) is not mentioned.

57. **(C)** The man says that he takes the subway to work. Choice (A) is how the woman gets to work. Choice (B) confuses similar-sounding words *far* and *car*. Choice (D) is related to the word *walk*, the way the woman gets to the bus stop.

58. **(C)** This is what the man says the bus fare is. Choice (A) is the difference between the bus fare and the subway fare. Choice (B) sounds similar to the correct answer. Choice (D) is the subway fare.

59. **(A)** The man is hungry and asks for directions to a restaurant. Choices (B), (C), and (D) are places he will see on the way to the restaurant.

60. **(B)** The woman says it is two blocks away. Choice (A) is how far it is from the corner. Choice (C) is not mentioned. Choice (D) confuses similar-sounding words *before* and *four*.

61. **(B)** The woman says that it is *almost 1:30*. Choices (A) and (C) sound similar to the correct answer. Choice (D) is when the restaurant stops serving lunch.

62. **(D)** The man says he had to leave his job because of the low pay. Choice (A) is his complaint about the new job. Choice (B) is the opposite of what he says. Choice (C) confuses similar-sounding words *low* and *slow*.

63. **(A)** The woman says that the man is happy with his new job, and he agrees. Choice (B) confuses similar-sounding words *sure* and *unsure*. Choice (C) repeats the word *bad* from the woman's phrase *That's too bad*. Choice (D) confuses similar-sounding words *bad* and *sad*.

64. **(C)** This is the number the man says. Choice (A) repeats the word *one* from the woman's phrase *I need every one of them*. Choice (B) confuses similar-sounding words *too* and *two*. Choice (D) is the number of weeks vacation the woman gets.

65. **(D)** They are going to the theater to see a play. Choice (A) confuses the meaning of the word *park*. Choice (B) repeats the word *garage*. Choice (C) is where they are now.

66. **(B)** This is the time the man says. Choice (A) sounds similar to the correct answer. Choice (C) is when the woman wants to leave. Choice (D) confuses similar-sounding words *time* and *nine*.

67. **(D)** The man says that they will go home when the play is over. Choice (A) confuses similar-sounding words *rest* and *restaurant*. Choice (B) confuses similar-sounding words *part* and *party*. Choice (C) confuses the meaning of the word *play* by associating it with *game*.

68. **(D)** This is what the man says he wants. Choices (A) and (B) are what the woman offers. Choice (C) repeats the words *ice* and *tea*.

69. **(A)** The man says that he is thirsty. Choice (B) confuses similar-sounding words *tried* and *tired*. Choice (C) is how the man says he does not feel. Choice (D) sounds similar to *hungry*.

70. **(B)** The woman offers the man a slice of cake. Choice (A) confuses similar-sounding words *look* and *book*. Choice (C) is where the woman found the cake recipe. Choice (D) confuses similar-sounding words *tried* and *ride*.

PART 4: TALKS

71. **(D)** The flight was originally scheduled to leave at 5:00 but has been delayed and will leave two hours later. Choice (A) is confused with the length of the delay. Choice (B) sounds similar to the flight number—43. Choice (C) is the originally scheduled departure time.

72. **(A)** Passengers are invited to enjoy a complimentary, or free, meal at a restaurant in the airport. Choice (B) confuses the meaning of the word *book*. Choice (C) is what the passengers will have to pick up if they choose to rebook on another flight. Choice (D) confuses the meaning of the work *check*.

73. **(B)** Passengers have to show their boarding passes to the gate agent to get a meal ticket. Choice (A) is associated with *boarding pass*. Choice (C) repeats the word *lounge*, which is used to describe the location of the ticket office. Choice (D) is what passengers who rebook on a different flight will have to do.

74. **(C)** The place is the Mayflower and Company Department Store. Choice (A) is confused with the store's *garden supplies* department and is associated with the name of the store. Choice (B) is confused with the store's *office supplies* department. Choice (D) confuses similar-sounding words *department* and *apartment*.

75. **(D)** The grand opening is being celebrated *next Saturday*. Choices (A) and (B) sound similar to the phrase *one day*, the length of the opening event. Choice (C) is not mentioned.

76. **(D)** The store is *across the road from City Mall*. Choice (A) confuses similar-sounding words *rain* and *train*. Choice (B) is ten minutes away. Choice (C) confuses the meaning of the word *park*.

77. **(B)** Snow is falling, which has led to dangerous road conditions. Choice (A) confuses similar-sounding words *train* and *rain*. Choices (C) and (D) describe how the weather will be tomorrow.

78. **(C)** It was a seven-car accident. Choice (A) confuses similar-sounding words *to* and *two*. Choice (B) confuses similar-sounding words *drive* and *five*. Choice (D) sounds similar to the correct answer.

79. **(D)** Snow will continue to fall throughout the afternoon and evening, but tomorrow will be sunny and warmer. Choices (A), (B), and (C) are all included in the period of snowfall.

80. **(B)** The announcement is about a circus that will be performing at the City Center Theater. Choices (A) and (C) are associated with the theater. Choice (D) repeats the word *show*.

81. **(A)** The announcer says that the tickets cost $15. Choices (B) and (D) sound similar to the correct answer. Choice (C) is confused with the show times: 3 PM and 7 PM.

82. **(B)** People who want a free ticket should send a postcard to the circus owners in care of the theater. Choice (A) repeats the word *theater*. Choice (C) is how to order paid tickets. Choice (D) is not mentioned.

83. **(C)** The Riverside Park Elementary School was destroyed. Choice (A) confuses similar-sounding words *school* and *tool*. Choice (B) is confused with the name of the school. Choice (D) is mentioned as a place near the school.

84. **(D)** Ethel Rogers saw and reported the fire when she left her bookstore around 9:00. Choice (A) confuses similar-sounding words *for* and *four*. Choice (B) is confused with the number of hours firefighters worked to put out the fire. Choice (C) confuses similar-sounding words *several* and *seven*.

85. **(D)** According to the report, there were no injuries. Choice (A) is the person who reported the fire. Choice (B) is who put out the fire. Choice (C) is confused with the schoolchildren who safely left the building hours before the fire.

86. **(A)** The announcer says that passengers can begin boarding in three minutes. Choices (B) and (C) are confused with the train number (56). Choice (D) is confused with the gate number.

87. **(C)** The announcer says that only passengers with reserved seats can get on the train. Choice (A) confuses the meaning of the word *form*. Choice (B) is suggested but not required—passengers must show a form of photo ID but could use a driver's license or something else. Choice (D) is associated with first-class passengers, who are asked to line up to the right of the gate.

88. **(B)** Passengers are allowed only one carry-on item. Choice (A) is confused with the required photo identification. Choice (C) is allowed. Choice (D) confuses similar-sounding words *seat* and *meat*.

89. **(B)** The program goes from 1:15 until 2:00. Choices (A) and (C) sound similar to the starting time. Choice (D) sounds similar to the ending time.

90. **(A)** Dr. Silva will talk about *health and fitness issues facing office workers*. Choice (B) repeats the word *business* and confuses the meaning of the word *fit*. Choice (C) is confused with the name of the program, *Business Talks*. Choice (D) is associated with the fact that Dr. Silva has written a book, but his talk is about the contents of the book, not about writing it.

91. **(A)** Dr. Silva will answer phone calls from listeners who have questions. Choice (B) repeats the word *questions*. Choice (C) is confused with the contents of following programs. Choice (D) is confused with the topic of tomorrow's program.

92. **(D)** The president met with world leaders. Choice (A) is what he will do tomorrow. Choices (B) and (C) are confused with the speech he will give on TV tonight.

93. **(B)** The president will fly to Tokyo tomorrow. Choice (A) is where he is today. Choice (C) is another place he will visit on his trip. Choice (D) is where he will go when the trip is over.

94. **(B)** He will do a three-week tour of Asia and Australia. Choice (A) confuses similar-sounding words *to* and *two*. Choice (C) repeats the word *month*. Choice (D) confuses similar-sounding words *for* and *four*.

95. **(B)** The bank is open from 9:00 AM until 4:30 PM Monday through Friday; therefore, it is already open by 9:30 AM on Tuesday. Choices (A), (C), and (D) are all times that the bank is not open.

96. **(A)** Customers are told to press 1 to get *information on an existing checking or savings account*. Choice (B) is what to do to open a new account. Choice (C) is what to do to apply for a credit card. Choice (D) is what to do for information on loans.

97. **(D)** The recording says to press 0 *to repeat this menu*. Choice (A) is what happens by pressing 2. Choice (B) is what happens by pressing 4. Choice (C) is what happens by pressing 3.

98. **(C)** The speaker says that the Internet is the best place to look for a job. Choices (A), (B), and (D) are other places to look for a job, but they aren't the best place.

99. **(D)** According to the speaker, there is *something for everyone* on the Internet. Choices (A), (B), and (C) are all examples of some of the types of jobs that can be found on the Internet.

100. **(A)** This is what the speaker says is the most important job-seeking tool. Choices (B), (C), and (D) are other examples of tools for job seekers.

Reading

PART 5: INCOMPLETE SENTENCES

101. **(B)** This is a sentence about the future with present tense in the time clause and future tense in the main clause. Choice (A) is simple present. Choice (C) is present perfect. Choice (D) is present continuous.

102. **(D)** *Before* in this position means that first the form will be signed, and then it will be submitted. Choice (A) means *at the same time as*. Choices (B) and (C) would indicate the opposite order of events—submit the form first, then sign it—which isn't logical.

103. **(B)** *To* is the correct preposition to use after *send*. Choices (A), (C), and (D) cannot logically be used in this sentence.

104. **(C)** This is a passive-voice sentence. The subject, *employees*, don't perform the actions; somebody else encourages them. Choices (A), (B), and (D) are all active-voice forms.

105. **(A)** *Expect* in this context means *require*. Choices (B), (C), and (D) look similar to the correct answer but have meanings that don't fit the context of the sentence.

106. **(A)** *In* is the correct preposition to use with a month. Choices (B), (C), and (D) are not used with the name of a month.

107. **(B)** *Reluctant* means *unwilling*. Mr. Lutz is unwilling to take on a responsibility for which he is unprepared. Choices (A), (C), and (D) look similar to the correct answer but have meanings that don't fit the context of the sentence.

108. **(D)** *Occupant* is a noun referring to a person who occupies a place. Choice (A) is a noun referring to a situation. Choice (B) is a gerund. Choice (C) is a base form verb.

109. **(C)** *Because* indicates a cause-and-effect relationship. Choices (A) and (B) indicate a contradiction. Choice (D) indicates a choice.

110. **(A)** *At* is used with the exact time of day. Choices (B), (C), and (D) are not used when stating the exact time of day.

111. **(B)** This simple present verb agrees with the third person singular subject, *she*. Choice (A) does not agree with the subject. Choice (C) is a gerund and cannot be used as the main verb of the clause. Choice (D) is simple past tense.

112. **(C)** This is a present perfect verb indicating an action that began in the past and continues to the present. Choice (A) is simple present. Choice (B) is simple past. Choice (D) is future.

113. **(A)** *On* means *on top of*, so is the logical choice to indicate the position of something relative to a shelf. Choices (B), (C), and (D) are not logical.

114. **(D)** *And* is used to add similar information. Choices (A) and (B) indicate a choice. Choice (C) indicates a contradiction.

115. **(B)** This is a passive idea. The subject, *requests*, receives the action of approval by the supervisor. Choices (A) and (C) are active-voice forms. Choice (D) is a noun.

116. **(B)** The main verb *agree* is followed by an infinitive. Choice (A) is base form or simple present tense. Choice (C) is a gerund. Choice (D) is future tense.

117. **(D)** This is an adverb of manner modifying the verb *dress*. Choice (A) is a verb. Choice (B) is a noun. Choice (C) is an adjective.

118. **(A)** *While* means *at the same time as*. Choice (B) cannot be used to introduce a clause. Choices (C) and (D) indicate a contradiction.

119. **(C)** *Prohibit* is followed by a gerund. Choice (A) is base form or simple present tense. Choice (B) is an infinitive. Choice (D) is future tense.

120. **(B)** *Inspected* means *examined*. Choices (A), (C), and (D) look similar to the correct answer but have meanings that don't fit the context of the sentence.

121. **(B)** *At* is used for an exact address. Choices (A), (C), and (D) are not used for an exact address.

122. **(C)** The adjective *concerned* is used with the preposition *about*. Choices (A), (B), and (D) are not usually used with *concerned*.

123. **(A)** The preposition *on* is used to indicate the exact date when something will occur. Choices (B), (C), and (D) are not used in this context.

124. **(B)** This is a comparative adjective used to compare the rent of the two offices. Choice (A) is a simple adjective form. Choice (C) is an adverb. Choice (D) is a superlative adjective.

125. **(D)** *Even though* is used to indicate a contradiction. Choice (A) indicates a condition. Choice (B) and (C) indicate cause and effect.

126. **(B)** The verb *delay* is followed by a gerund. Choice (A) is base form or simple present tense. Choice (C) is an infinitive. Choice (D) is a noun.

127. **(C)** *Who* is a relative pronoun used to refer to the noun *the woman* and acts as the subject of the adjective clause. Choice (A) is a contraction of *who* and *is*. Choice (B) is possessive. Choice (D) is an object pronoun.

128. **(A)** This is an adjective used to describe the word *passport*. Choice (B) is a verb. Choice (C) is a gerund. Choice (D) is a noun.

129. **(B)** This is a simple past tense verb that describes an action that happened last month. Choice (A) is simple present. Choice (C) is present continuous. Choice (D) is a past participle.

130. **(A)** This is an imperative verb form that is used to give a command and does not require the mention of the subject. Choice (B) is a gerund. Choices (C) and (D) require the mention of the subject.

131. **(C)** *Pass over* means *ignore* or *not choose*. Choice (A) would form *pass in*, meaning *submit*. Choice (B) would form *pass out*, meaning *distribute* or *lose consciousness*. Choice (D) would form *pass through*, meaning *go through*.

132. **(B)** The verb form is required here. Choices (A) and (C) are nouns. Choice (D) is an adverb.

133. **(D)** *Achieve* means *reach*. Choices (A), (B), and (C) look similar to the correct answer but have meanings that don't fit the context.

134. **(A)** *Or* indicates a choice. Choice (B) indicates a condition. Choice (C) indicates a contradiction. Choice (D) indicates a result.

135. **(D)** *Which* is a relative pronoun referring to the noun *building* and acts as the subject of the nonrestrictive adjective clause. Choice (A) is a pronoun, but not a relative pronoun. Choice (B) is a relative pronoun used in restrictive clauses. Choice (C) is a verb.

136. **(C)** This sentence is a future real conditional idea and requires a present tense verb in the *if* clause. Choice (A) is an infinitive. Choice (B) is past tense. Choice (D) is present tense but doesn't agree with the subject.

137. **(B)** The past continuous form indicates an action that was in progress when another action (*the electricity went out*) occurred. Choice (A) is simple past tense. Choice (C) is past participle. Choice (D) is past perfect.

138. **(A)** *Must* is a modal so it is followed by the base form of the verb. Choice (B) is an infinitive. Choice (C) is a gerund. Choice (D) is future tense.

139. **(B)** *Hopeful* is an adjective describing how we feel. Choice (A) is a gerund. Choice (C) is an adverb. Choice (D) is an infinitive.

140. **(C)** This is a gerund used as the subject of the sentence. Choice (A) is a base form verb. Choice (B) is an infinitive. Choice (D) is present perfect tense.

PART 6: TEXT COMPLETION

141. **(A)** *Attire* means *clothes*, and this memo is about the right clothes to wear to work. Choices (B), (C), and (D) could fit the sentence but don't fit the context of the memo.

142. **(D)** This is a passive-voice sentence—the clothes mentioned do not wear themselves; they are worn by people. Choices (A), (B), and (C) are all active-voice forms.

143. **(D)** This is a first person object pronoun referring to the writer of the memo, who is the one who will discuss problems and concerns about the dress policy. Choice (A) is a subject pronoun. Choice (B) is third person. Choice (C) is second person.

144. **(C)** *Hectic* means *very busy*. Choices (A), (B), and (D) could fit the sentence but don't fit the context of the article.

145. **(B)** This is a present tense real conditional and *if* introduces the condition. Choice (A) introduces a result. Choice (C) introduces a reason. Choice (D) introduces a contradiction.

146. **(C)** The gerund *climbing* acts as the subject of the sentence. Choices (A) and (B) are present tense forms. Choice (D) is an infinitive.

147. **(D)** *Opportunities for advancement* is something a company is likely to offer potential employees. Choices (A), (B), and (C) are not things a company would normally offer to job applicants.

148. **(B)** This is a noun referring to the process of asking for a job. In this sentence it acts as the object of the verb *welcome*. Choice (A) is a noun referring to the person who asks for a job. Choices (C) and (D) are verbs.

149. **(A)** A future time clause requires a present tense verb. Choice (B) is future tense. Choice (C) is past tense. Choice (D) is present perfect.

150. **(C)** Ms. Cho is looking for a service to prepare and serve lunch, that is, a catering service. Choices (A), (B), and (D) could fit the sentence but don't fit the context of the e-mail message.

151. **(B)** This is a subject pronoun acting as the subject of the clause and referring to the plural noun *rooms*. Choice (A) is an object pronoun. Choices (C) and (D) are singular pronouns.

152. **(A)** This is a base form verb following the modal *would*. Choice (B) is an adjective. Choice (C) is a noun. Choice (D) is a past tense verb.

PART 7: READING COMPREHENSION

153. **(A)** The ad is asking business owners to advertise their businesses in the *Daily Herald* newspaper. Choice (B) repeats the word *investment*. Choice (C) is some of the people who might want to use the services business owners would advertise. Choice (D) repeats the word *newspaper*.

154. **(D)** Ten lines cost $5.00 a day, so the cost would be $25 for five days. Choice (A) is the cost of one line for one day. Choice (B) is the cost of one line for five days. Choice (C) is the cost of ten lines for one day.

155. **(C)** The meeting takes place every November, or once a year. Choice (A) repeats the word *week*. Choice (B) associates *November* with the word *month*. Choice (D) is incorrect because the meeting takes place only once each November.

156. **(B)** According to the article, business and political leaders will discuss business and economic concerns. Choice (A) is confused with the after-lunch speaker. Choice (C) is confused with *government officials*. Choice (D) is confused with the location of the meeting.

157. **(B)** Dr. Myrtle Pleasance of the Business Research Institute will speak. Choices (A) and (C) are logical possibilities but are not correct. Choice (D) is what should be done to register for the meeting before it takes place.

158. **(C)** The form is to dispute an item, that is, disagree about a charge, on a credit card bill. Choices (A), (B), and (D) are all actions related to credit cards but are not the purpose of the form.

159. **(B)** Ms. Larsen is claiming that she was charged the wrong amount, and the form asks for a sales receipt in that situation. Choice (A) is incorrect because the form says to send payments separately. Choices (C) and (D) repeat words used on the form.

160. **(D)** *Examined* means *looked at*. Choices (A), (B), and (C) are all things one might do with a credit card statement but are not the correct answer.

161. **(B)** This is the amount Ms. Larsen says she was charged at the time she made the purchase. Choice (A) looks similar to the amount she was charged on the credit card statement. Choice (C) is the amount she was charged on the credit card statement. Choice (D) looks similar to the amount she was charged at the time of purchase.

162. **(B)** Ms. Knightly writes: *Unfortunately, we are rarely in the position of hiring full-time employees,* so we can assume that this is what Mr. Ungemach asked for. Choice (A) is a logical reason why someone might write to a company but is not the correct answer. Choice (C) repeats the word *product*. Choice (D) repeats the word *skills*.

163. **(D)** Ms. Knightly asks Mr. Ungemach to let her know if he would be interested in a temporary assignment as a consultant. Choice (A) is incorrect because Mr. Ungemach has already done this. Choice (B) repeats the words *professional* and *assignment*. Choice (C) is confused with Ms. Knightly's offer to notify Mr. Ungemach when a position becomes available.

164. **(A)** The notice asks for payment on an electric bill that is more than 30 days overdue. Choice (B) is incorrect because although the notice explains some charges, that is not the main purpose. Choice (C) is on the back of the notice, but not its main purpose. Choice (D) is confused with the financing options that can be discussed with Customer Service.

165. **(C)** The customer will owe the $85 already owed for electric service and a $15 late fee. Choice (A) is the late fee only. Choice (B) is the electric service charge only. Choice (D) includes the reconnection charge and is what would be owed after August 31.

166. **(B)** The customer is invited to call the Customer Service office to find out about financing options. Choice (A) is how to find out more about National

Regulation #50504. Choice (C) is on the reverse of the notice but is not about financing. Choice (D) is not mentioned.

167. **(C)** *Resume* means *restart*. The other words could fit the sentence but do not have the correct meaning.

168. **(A)** Local residents, together with environmental groups, protested the mall. Choice (B) gave official approval for the mall. Choice (C) is the person who sold the land to the development company to build the mall. Choice (D) is probably the owner of the development company that will build the mall.

169. **(B)** Customers will be able to park cars but there is no mention of any business selling cars. Choice (A) is possible because there will be classroom space for the local community college. Choice (C) is possible because there will be a movie theater. Choice (D) is possible because there will be a clinic.

170. **(D)** Twice as many cars will fit outdoors as in the garage (where 750 will fit). Choice (A) is the number of stores. Choice (B) is twice the number of stores. Choice (C) is the number of cars that will fit in the garage.

171. **(C)** Construction will begin in six months and take about a year. Choice (A) is when construction will begin. Choice (B) is confused with the length of time construction will take. Choice (D) is confused with how long ago Smithson bought the land for the mall.

172. **(A)** All the items listed for sale are used in offices. Choice (B) is associated with the printer ink cartridges. Choice (C) is incorrect because even though Pinkerton's sells some furniture, it sells other kinds of things as well. Choice (D) is associated with the photocopier paper.

173. **(C)** The first ink cartridge costs $30, and the second is 50% of that, or $15. Choice (A) is the cost of the second cartridge only. Choice (B) is the cost of the first cartridge only. Choice (D) is confused with the size of the discount.

174. **(B)** Notebooks are 25% off. Choices (A), (C), and (D) have different discounts.

175. **(C)** She wrote the letter to respond to questions Ms. Pavlis had sent in a letter on May 25. Choice (A) is incorrect because Ms. Pavlis wrote to ask for information so this is not really an advertisement. Choice (B) will happen after the audit takes place. Choice (D) is confused with the mention of costs that may have to be made to save on heating and cooling.

176. **(A)** The service offered by Eastman Energy Associates is an audit to show businesses how they can save money on heating and cooling costs. Choice (B) is confused with the discussion of different parts of the building. Choices (C) and (D) repeat words mentioned in the letter.

177. **(B)** Ms. Heinz says the audit costs $1,500, including everything. Choice (A) is the cost of one hour of consulting. Choice (C) looks similar to the costs mentioned. Choice (D) is the cost of the audit plus one hour of consulting.

178. **(D)** *Upgrades* means *improvements*. Choices (A), (B), and (C) could fit the sentence but don't have the right meaning.

179. **(B)** The job is for someone with an accounting degree to manage an accounting office. Choice (A) is associated with dental insurance, one of the job benefits. Choices (C) and (D) repeat words used on the advertisement.

180. **(C)** Interested candidates should send a letter and resume to Simona Santarelli. Choice (A) is incorrect because the ad asks for no phone calls. Choice (B) mentions the person who will supervise whoever is hired for the position, but this is not the person who is accepting resumes. Choice (D) repeats the name of the company, but visiting the office is not mentioned.

181. **(C)** The bill shows charges for phone and Internet services. Choice (A) is the kind of business Mr. Krumholz works for. Choice (B) is not mentioned. Choice (D) is associated with *tax*.

182. **(A)** Mr. Krumholz believes that he owes for only one month's service when he was charged for two. Choice (B) is incorrect because he included the account number in his letter. Choice (C) is what he will get from his bank, not from Crisp Company. Choice (D) is a logical reason to write a letter to a company but is not the correct answer.

183. **(D)** Mr. Krumholz sent the payment on March 26 and the bill says that it shows only charges made until March 25. Choice (A) is incorrect because even though the check was sent late, it did have the correct amount ($125). Choice (B) repeats the word *bank*. Choice (C) is a mistake someone might make with a bill but is not the correct answer.

184. **(C)** He believes he owes the current charges only, which are $132 according to the bill. Choice (A) is what he owes for local phone service only. Choice (B) is what he owed last month. Choice (D) is what he owes according to the bill.

185. **(B)** Tomorrow he will mail a check to cover the current charges. Choice (A) is something he has already done. Choice (C) will happen before the end of the week. Choice (D) is what he is doing today.

186. **(C)** Today is June 10, and the workshop will take place the day after tomorrow. Choice (A) is today's date. Choice (B) is tomorrow's date. Choice (D) is a week from today, when Mr. Park wishes the workshop was going to take place.

187. **(B)** Tea and snacks will be served as soon as Mr. Chang finishes his hour-long presentation, scheduled to begin at 9:30. Choice (A) is when Mr. Chang's presentation begins. Choice (C) is when the next presentation begins. Choice (D) is when lunch will be served.

188. **(D)** Mr. Park wants lunch served in the room that is currently scheduled for the Analyzing Demographics presentation. Choices (A), (B), and (C) are rooms where other workshop activities will take place.

189. **(D)** There are currently 45 people registered for the workshop, and Mr. Park wants there to be 15 more chairs than that in each room. Choice (A) is the

number of extra chairs. Choice (B) is 15 less than the number of people registered. Choice (C) is the number of people registered.

190. **(B)** Mr. Wang has to leave early, so Mr. Park wants to give him Ms. Lee's scheduled presentation time, and Ms. Lee will take Mr. Wang's time. Choices (A), (C), and (D) are people who will present at other times.

191. **(D)** Employees who have worked at Howland for 11 or more years can take 25 annual leave days. Choices (A), (B), and (C) are the amounts of leave allowed for employees who have worked at the company for less time.

192. **(B)** According to the form, Daniel Ortiz is allowed 15 days of annual leave, which is the amount allowed for employees who have worked at Howland for three to five years. Choice (A) describes employees who get 10 days of annual leave. Choices (C) and (D) describe employees who get more than 15 days of annual leave.

193. **(A)** Daniel Ortiz wants to begin his vacation on July 21, and he must submit the form 21 days ahead of time. Choice (B) is confused with the number of leave days he is allowed. Choices (C) and (D) are confused with the dates of his vacation.

194. **(C)** The form has to be signed by Daniel Ortiz's supervisor, who, according to the form, is Nestor Perez. Choice (A) is the person requesting leave. Choice (B) is the person to whom the form should be submitted. Choice (D) is confused with the name of the company.

195. **(C)** The manual says that the form should be submitted to the human resources director, and the form says that it should be submitted to Daisy Ortega. Choices (A), (B), and (D) repeat words found on the form but are not the correct answer.

196. **(A)** The advertised office at 900 square feet is twice the size of the current office. Choices (B) and (D) are confused with the cost of the rent. Choice (C) is the size of the advertised office.

197. **(B)** The advertised office is not near the subway, and Paul says that is a convenience he would miss, so we can assume that the current office is near the subway. Choice (A) is incorrect because Paul says that the advertised office is the more expensive one. Choices (C) and (D) are true of the advertised office.

198. **(C)** Paul wants to see the office *tomorrow*, and today is Tuesday, so he wants to see it on Wednesday. Choice (A) is when Paul will return after being away. Choice (B) is today. Choice (D) is not mentioned.

199. **(C)** Paul points out that the advertised office has parking, *unlike our current office*. Choices (A), (B), and (D) are all things that can be found in both offices.

200. **(D)** The monthly rent is $1,750, and they would have to pay twice that—once for the first month's rent, and again for the security deposit. Choice (A) is confused with the size of the office. Choice (B) is one month's rent. Choice (C) is not mentioned.

Answer Sheet
TOEIC PRACTICE TEST 5

Listening Comprehension

Part 1: Photographs

1. Ⓐ Ⓑ Ⓒ Ⓓ
2. Ⓐ Ⓑ Ⓒ Ⓓ
3. Ⓐ Ⓑ Ⓒ Ⓓ
4. Ⓐ Ⓑ Ⓒ Ⓓ
5. Ⓐ Ⓑ Ⓒ Ⓓ
6. Ⓐ Ⓑ Ⓒ Ⓓ
7. Ⓐ Ⓑ Ⓒ Ⓓ
8. Ⓐ Ⓑ Ⓒ Ⓓ
9. Ⓐ Ⓑ Ⓒ Ⓓ
10. Ⓐ Ⓑ Ⓒ Ⓓ

Part 2: Question-Response

11. Ⓐ Ⓑ Ⓒ
12. Ⓐ Ⓑ Ⓒ
13. Ⓐ Ⓑ Ⓒ
14. Ⓐ Ⓑ Ⓒ
15. Ⓐ Ⓑ Ⓒ
16. Ⓐ Ⓑ Ⓒ
17. Ⓐ Ⓑ Ⓒ
18. Ⓐ Ⓑ Ⓒ
19. Ⓐ Ⓑ Ⓒ
20. Ⓐ Ⓑ Ⓒ
21. Ⓐ Ⓑ Ⓒ
22. Ⓐ Ⓑ Ⓒ
23. Ⓐ Ⓑ Ⓒ
24. Ⓐ Ⓑ Ⓒ
25. Ⓐ Ⓑ Ⓒ
26. Ⓐ Ⓑ Ⓒ
27. Ⓐ Ⓑ Ⓒ
28. Ⓐ Ⓑ Ⓒ
29. Ⓐ Ⓑ Ⓒ
30. Ⓐ Ⓑ Ⓒ
31. Ⓐ Ⓑ Ⓒ
32. Ⓐ Ⓑ Ⓒ
33. Ⓐ Ⓑ Ⓒ
34. Ⓐ Ⓑ Ⓒ
35. Ⓐ Ⓑ Ⓒ
36. Ⓐ Ⓑ Ⓒ
37. Ⓐ Ⓑ Ⓒ
38. Ⓐ Ⓑ Ⓒ
39. Ⓐ Ⓑ Ⓒ
40. Ⓐ Ⓑ Ⓒ

Part 3: Conversations

41. Ⓐ Ⓑ Ⓒ Ⓓ
42. Ⓐ Ⓑ Ⓒ Ⓓ
43. Ⓐ Ⓑ Ⓒ Ⓓ
44. Ⓐ Ⓑ Ⓒ Ⓓ
45. Ⓐ Ⓑ Ⓒ Ⓓ
46. Ⓐ Ⓑ Ⓒ Ⓓ
47. Ⓐ Ⓑ Ⓒ Ⓓ
48. Ⓐ Ⓑ Ⓒ Ⓓ
49. Ⓐ Ⓑ Ⓒ Ⓓ
50. Ⓐ Ⓑ Ⓒ Ⓓ
51. Ⓐ Ⓑ Ⓒ Ⓓ
52. Ⓐ Ⓑ Ⓒ Ⓓ
53. Ⓐ Ⓑ Ⓒ Ⓓ
54. Ⓐ Ⓑ Ⓒ Ⓓ
55. Ⓐ Ⓑ Ⓒ Ⓓ
56. Ⓐ Ⓑ Ⓒ Ⓓ
57. Ⓐ Ⓑ Ⓒ Ⓓ
58. Ⓐ Ⓑ Ⓒ Ⓓ
59. Ⓐ Ⓑ Ⓒ Ⓓ
60. Ⓐ Ⓑ Ⓒ Ⓓ
61. Ⓐ Ⓑ Ⓒ Ⓓ
62. Ⓐ Ⓑ Ⓒ Ⓓ
63. Ⓐ Ⓑ Ⓒ Ⓓ
64. Ⓐ Ⓑ Ⓒ Ⓓ
65. Ⓐ Ⓑ Ⓒ Ⓓ
66. Ⓐ Ⓑ Ⓒ Ⓓ
67. Ⓐ Ⓑ Ⓒ Ⓓ
68. Ⓐ Ⓑ Ⓒ Ⓓ
69. Ⓐ Ⓑ Ⓒ Ⓓ
70. Ⓐ Ⓑ Ⓒ Ⓓ

Part 4: Talks

71. Ⓐ Ⓑ Ⓒ Ⓓ
72. Ⓐ Ⓑ Ⓒ Ⓓ
73. Ⓐ Ⓑ Ⓒ Ⓓ
74. Ⓐ Ⓑ Ⓒ Ⓓ
75. Ⓐ Ⓑ Ⓒ Ⓓ
76. Ⓐ Ⓑ Ⓒ Ⓓ
77. Ⓐ Ⓑ Ⓒ Ⓓ
78. Ⓐ Ⓑ Ⓒ Ⓓ
79. Ⓐ Ⓑ Ⓒ Ⓓ
80. Ⓐ Ⓑ Ⓒ Ⓓ
81. Ⓐ Ⓑ Ⓒ Ⓓ
82. Ⓐ Ⓑ Ⓒ Ⓓ
83. Ⓐ Ⓑ Ⓒ Ⓓ
84. Ⓐ Ⓑ Ⓒ Ⓓ
85. Ⓐ Ⓑ Ⓒ Ⓓ
86. Ⓐ Ⓑ Ⓒ Ⓓ
87. Ⓐ Ⓑ Ⓒ Ⓓ
88. Ⓐ Ⓑ Ⓒ Ⓓ
89. Ⓐ Ⓑ Ⓒ Ⓓ
90. Ⓐ Ⓑ Ⓒ Ⓓ
91. Ⓐ Ⓑ Ⓒ Ⓓ
92. Ⓐ Ⓑ Ⓒ Ⓓ
93. Ⓐ Ⓑ Ⓒ Ⓓ
94. Ⓐ Ⓑ Ⓒ Ⓓ
95. Ⓐ Ⓑ Ⓒ Ⓓ
96. Ⓐ Ⓑ Ⓒ Ⓓ
97. Ⓐ Ⓑ Ⓒ Ⓓ
98. Ⓐ Ⓑ Ⓒ Ⓓ
99. Ⓐ Ⓑ Ⓒ Ⓓ
100. Ⓐ Ⓑ Ⓒ Ⓓ

Answer Sheet
TOEIC PRACTICE TEST 5

Reading

Part 5: Incomplete Sentences

101. Ⓐ Ⓑ Ⓒ Ⓓ	112. Ⓐ Ⓑ Ⓒ Ⓓ	122. Ⓐ Ⓑ Ⓒ Ⓓ	132. Ⓐ Ⓑ Ⓒ Ⓓ
102. Ⓐ Ⓑ Ⓒ Ⓓ	113. Ⓐ Ⓑ Ⓒ Ⓓ	123. Ⓐ Ⓑ Ⓒ Ⓓ	133. Ⓐ Ⓑ Ⓒ Ⓓ
103. Ⓐ Ⓑ Ⓒ Ⓓ	114. Ⓐ Ⓑ Ⓒ Ⓓ	124. Ⓐ Ⓑ Ⓒ Ⓓ	134. Ⓐ Ⓑ Ⓒ Ⓓ
104. Ⓐ Ⓑ Ⓒ Ⓓ	115. Ⓐ Ⓑ Ⓒ Ⓓ	125. Ⓐ Ⓑ Ⓒ Ⓓ	135. Ⓐ Ⓑ Ⓒ Ⓓ
106. Ⓐ Ⓑ Ⓒ Ⓓ	116. Ⓐ Ⓑ Ⓒ Ⓓ	126. Ⓐ Ⓑ Ⓒ Ⓓ	136. Ⓐ Ⓑ Ⓒ Ⓓ
107. Ⓐ Ⓑ Ⓒ Ⓓ	117. Ⓐ Ⓑ Ⓒ Ⓓ	127. Ⓐ Ⓑ Ⓒ Ⓓ	137. Ⓐ Ⓑ Ⓒ Ⓓ
108. Ⓐ Ⓑ Ⓒ Ⓓ	118. Ⓐ Ⓑ Ⓒ Ⓓ	128. Ⓐ Ⓑ Ⓒ Ⓓ	138. Ⓐ Ⓑ Ⓒ Ⓓ
109. Ⓐ Ⓑ Ⓒ Ⓓ	119. Ⓐ Ⓑ Ⓒ Ⓓ	129. Ⓐ Ⓑ Ⓒ Ⓓ	139. Ⓐ Ⓑ Ⓒ Ⓓ
110. Ⓐ Ⓑ Ⓒ Ⓓ	120. Ⓐ Ⓑ Ⓒ Ⓓ	130. Ⓐ Ⓑ Ⓒ Ⓓ	140. Ⓐ Ⓑ Ⓒ Ⓓ
111. Ⓐ Ⓑ Ⓒ Ⓓ	121. Ⓐ Ⓑ Ⓒ Ⓓ	131. Ⓐ Ⓑ Ⓒ Ⓓ	

Part 6: Text Completion

141. Ⓐ Ⓑ Ⓒ Ⓓ	144. Ⓐ Ⓑ Ⓒ Ⓓ	147. Ⓐ Ⓑ Ⓒ Ⓓ	150. Ⓐ Ⓑ Ⓒ Ⓓ
142. Ⓐ Ⓑ Ⓒ Ⓓ	145. Ⓐ Ⓑ Ⓒ Ⓓ	148. Ⓐ Ⓑ Ⓒ Ⓓ	151. Ⓐ Ⓑ Ⓒ Ⓓ
143. Ⓐ Ⓑ Ⓒ Ⓓ	146. Ⓐ Ⓑ Ⓒ Ⓓ	149. Ⓐ Ⓑ Ⓒ Ⓓ	152. Ⓐ Ⓑ Ⓒ Ⓓ

Part 7: Reading Comprehension

153. Ⓐ Ⓑ Ⓒ Ⓓ	166. Ⓐ Ⓑ Ⓒ Ⓓ	179. Ⓐ Ⓑ Ⓒ Ⓓ	192. Ⓐ Ⓑ Ⓒ Ⓓ
154. Ⓐ Ⓑ Ⓒ Ⓓ	167. Ⓐ Ⓑ Ⓒ Ⓓ	180. Ⓐ Ⓑ Ⓒ Ⓓ	193. Ⓐ Ⓑ Ⓒ Ⓓ
155. Ⓐ Ⓑ Ⓒ Ⓓ	168. Ⓐ Ⓑ Ⓒ Ⓓ	181. Ⓐ Ⓑ Ⓒ Ⓓ	194. Ⓐ Ⓑ Ⓒ Ⓓ
156. Ⓐ Ⓑ Ⓒ Ⓓ	169. Ⓐ Ⓑ Ⓒ Ⓓ	182. Ⓐ Ⓑ Ⓒ Ⓓ	195. Ⓐ Ⓑ Ⓒ Ⓓ
157. Ⓐ Ⓑ Ⓒ Ⓓ	170. Ⓐ Ⓑ Ⓒ Ⓓ	183. Ⓐ Ⓑ Ⓒ Ⓓ	196. Ⓐ Ⓑ Ⓒ Ⓓ
158. Ⓐ Ⓑ Ⓒ Ⓓ	171. Ⓐ Ⓑ Ⓒ Ⓓ	184. Ⓐ Ⓑ Ⓒ Ⓓ	197. Ⓐ Ⓑ Ⓒ Ⓓ
159. Ⓐ Ⓑ Ⓒ Ⓓ	172. Ⓐ Ⓑ Ⓒ Ⓓ	185. Ⓐ Ⓑ Ⓒ Ⓓ	198. Ⓐ Ⓑ Ⓒ Ⓓ
160. Ⓐ Ⓑ Ⓒ Ⓓ	173. Ⓐ Ⓑ Ⓒ Ⓓ	186. Ⓐ Ⓑ Ⓒ Ⓓ	199. Ⓐ Ⓑ Ⓒ Ⓓ
161. Ⓐ Ⓑ Ⓒ Ⓓ	174. Ⓐ Ⓑ Ⓒ Ⓓ	187. Ⓐ Ⓑ Ⓒ Ⓓ	200. Ⓐ Ⓑ Ⓒ Ⓓ
162. Ⓐ Ⓑ Ⓒ Ⓓ	175. Ⓐ Ⓑ Ⓒ Ⓓ	188. Ⓐ Ⓑ Ⓒ Ⓓ	
163. Ⓐ Ⓑ Ⓒ Ⓓ	176. Ⓐ Ⓑ Ⓒ Ⓓ	189. Ⓐ Ⓑ Ⓒ Ⓓ	
164. Ⓐ Ⓑ Ⓒ Ⓓ	177. Ⓐ Ⓑ Ⓒ Ⓓ	190. Ⓐ Ⓑ Ⓒ Ⓓ	
165. Ⓐ Ⓑ Ⓒ Ⓓ	178. Ⓐ Ⓑ Ⓒ Ⓓ	191. Ⓐ Ⓑ Ⓒ Ⓓ	

TOEIC Practice Test 5

LISTENING COMPREHENSION

In this section of the test, you will have the chance to show how well you understand spoken English. There are four parts to this section, with special directions for each part. You will find the Answer Sheet for Practice Test 5 on page 225. Detach it from the book and use it to record your answers. Check your answers using the Answer Key on page 260 and see the Answers Explained on page 262.

TIP

If you do not have access to an audio CD player, please refer to the audio-scripts starting on page 333 when prompted to listen to an audio passage.

CD 3
TRACK
5

Part 1: Photographs

Directions: You will see a photograph. You will hear four statements about the photograph. Choose the statement that most closely matches the photograph and fill in the corresponding oval on your answer sheet.

Example

Now listen to the four statements.

Sample Answer

Ⓐ Ⓑ Ⓒ Ⓓ

Statement (B), "She's reading a magazine," best describes what you see in the picture. Therefore, you should choose answer (B).

TOEIC Practice Test 5

1.

2.

3.

4.

5.

6.

7.

8.

9.

10.

Part 2: Question-Response

Directions: You will hear a question and three possible responses. Choose the response that most closely answers the question and fill in the corresponding oval on your answer sheet.

Example

Now listen to the sample question.

You will hear:

How is the weather?

You will also hear:

(A) It's raining.
(B) He's fine, thanks.
(C) He's my boss.

The best response to the question *How is the weather?* is choice (A), *It's raining.* Therefore, you should choose answer (A).

11. Mark your answer on your answer sheet.

12. Mark your answer on your answer sheet.

13. Mark your answer on your answer sheet.

14. Mark your answer on your answer sheet.

15. Mark your answer on your answer sheet.

16. Mark your answer on your answer sheet.

17. Mark your answer on your answer sheet.

18. Mark your answer on your answer sheet.

19. Mark your answer on your answer sheet.

20. Mark your answer on your answer sheet.

21. Mark your answer on your answer sheet.

22. Mark your answer on your answer sheet.

23. Mark your answer on your answer sheet.

24. Mark your answer on your answer sheet.

25. Mark your answer on your answer sheet.

26. Mark your answer on your answer sheet.

27. Mark your answer on your answer sheet.

28. Mark your answer on your answer sheet.

29. Mark your answer on your answer sheet.

30. Mark your answer on your answer sheet.

31. Mark your answer on your answer sheet.

32. Mark your answer on your answer sheet.

33. Mark your answer on your answer sheet.

34. Mark your answer on your answer sheet.

35. Mark your answer on your answer sheet.

36. Mark your answer on your answer sheet.

37. Mark your answer on your answer sheet.

38. Mark your answer on your answer sheet.

39. Mark your answer on your answer sheet.

40. Mark your answer on your answer sheet.

Part 3: Conversations

Directions: You will hear a conversation between two people. You will see three questions on each conversation and four possible answers. Choose the best answer to each question and fill in the corresponding oval on your answer sheet.

41. What is the woman's room number?
    (A) 62
    (B) 64
    (C) 624
    (D) 642

42. What will the desk clerk do?
    (A) Bring a new TV
    (B) Get someone to fix the TV
    (C) Take the TV away
    (D) Put the TV in the right room

43. When will the woman go out?
    (A) In 10 minutes
    (B) In 30 minutes
    (C) In an hour
    (D) At 10:00

44. What does the woman want to do?
    (A) Clean the coffeepot
    (B) Change her skirt
    (C) Wash the kitchen
    (D) Sweep the floor

45. Where is the kitchen?
    (A) On the fifth floor
    (B) On the sixth floor
    (C) On the ninth floor
    (D) On the sixteenth floor

46. What does the man want to drink?
    (A) Milk
    (B) Cocoa
    (C) Coffee
    (D) Cola

47. Where does this conversation take place?
    (A) In a cab
    (B) On a plane
    (C) At the airport
    (D) At the subway station

48. Why is the man annoyed?
    (A) They have to wait for the woman's baggage.
    (B) They can't find his baggage.
    (C) They're stuck in traffic.
    (D) They can't get a cab.

49. How many suitcases does the woman have?
    (A) One
    (B) Two
    (C) Three
    (D) Four

50. Where are they going to eat?
    (A) On the sidewalk
    (B) In the park
    (C) At a café
    (D) At home

51. What are they going to eat?
    (A) Sandwiches
    (B) Ice cream
    (C) Salads
    (D) Meat

52. Where will the man wait for the woman?
    (A) At the gate
    (B) By the lake
    (C) On the lawn
    (D) By the fountain

53. How does the woman feel about her office?
    (A) Worried
    (B) Lucky
    (C) Bad
    (D) Sad

54. What is true of the man's office?
    (A) It's too dark.
    (B) It's near a park.
    (C) It faces a vacant lot.
    (D) It overlooks a parking lot.

55. How long has the man been at his company?
    (A) 2 months
    (B) 4 months
    (C) 7 months
    (D) 11 months

56. What is the man's job?
    (A) Bus driver
    (B) Tour guide
    (C) Singer
    (D) Artist

57. What time will they meet tomorrow?
    (A) 2:00
    (B) 5:00
    (C) 8:00
    (D) 9:00

58. What should people bring?
    (A) A dress
    (B) Cold drinks
    (C) Some books
    (D) Warm clothes

59. How many nights did the woman stay at the hotel?
    (A) One
    (B) Two
    (C) Three
    (D) Four

60. Why was there a problem with her bill?
    (A) The man's addition was incorrect.
    (B) The man gave her the wrong bill.
    (C) The woman read the bill wrong.
    (D) The woman lost the bill.

61. How will the woman pay the bill?
    (A) Cash
    (B) Check
    (C) Credit card
    (D) Charge account

62. Where does this conversation take place?
    (A) At home
    (B) On a plane
    (C) In a restaurant
    (D) At a grocery store

63. When is breakfast over?
    (A) 7:00
    (B) 7:30
    (C) 11:00
    (D) 11:30

64. What does the woman order?
    (A) Ice cream
    (B) Roast beef
    (C) Waffles
    (D) Black coffee

65. What does the man do in his spare time?
    (A) Write books
    (B) Play golf
    (C) Go to plays
    (D) Go hiking

66. What does the woman like to do?
    (A) Eat
    (B) Read
    (C) Cook
    (D) Run

67. When does the woman want to have a meal with the man?
    (A) This afternoon
    (B) Tomorrow
    (C) Friday
    (D) Saturday

68. What is the woman borrowing?
    (A) A book
    (B) A video
    (C) A magazine
    (D) A newspaper

69. What is the maximum time she can have it without paying a fine?
    (A) Three weeks
    (B) Four weeks
    (C) Six weeks
    (D) Eight weeks

70. What is the charge for overdue books?
    (A) 5 cents a day
    (B) 9 cents a day
    (C) 20 cents a day
    (D) 25 cents a day

CD 4
TRACK 2

Part 4: Talks

Directions: You will hear a talk given by a single speaker. You will see three questions on each talk, each with four possible answers. Choose the best answer to each question and fill in the corresponding oval on your answer sheet.

71. What time does this business open in the morning?
(A) 6:00
(B) 6:30
(C) 8:00
(D) 8:30

72. What happens if a caller presses 1?
(A) He can leave a message.
(B) He can speak to a specific person.
(C) He will get directions to the office.
(D) He will learn about financial services.

73. How can a caller speak to an adviser?
(A) Press 0
(B) Press 2
(C) Stay on the line
(D) Dial an extension number.

74. What kind of subway station is Downtown Central?
(A) A suburban station
(B) A transfer station
(C) A through station
(D) A rural station

75. Where do passengers catch the East–West line?
(A) On the lower-level platform
(B) On the upper-level platform
(C) On the same platform
(D) On the outside platform

76. Why are East–West line subways behind schedule?
(A) It's a rainy day.
(B) Conditions are icy.
(C) The track is being fixed.
(D) The drivers are in training.

77. What will the weather be like today?
(A) Stormy
(B) Partly sunny
(C) Rainy
(D) Cold

78. What will increase during the afternoon?
(A) Storms
(B) Rain
(C) Wind
(D) Cold

79. When can you hear the next weather report?
(A) This morning
(B) This afternoon
(C) This evening
(D) Tomorrow

80. What new service is being offered?
(A) Payment of handling charges
(B) Two-day delivery
(C) High-quality service
(D) Telephone orders

81. What is different about the service for customers in Alaska?
(A) They have to pay more.
(B) They get delivery in three days.
(C) The service isn't offered there.
(D) They must ship with another company.

82. What is the minimum order size to qualify for this service?
(A) $100
(B) $115
(C) $150
(D) $160

83. What is the purpose of this hotline?
(A) To tell about special events
(B) To give sports news
(C) To give weather updates
(D) To suggest restaurants

84. What additional information does the hotline provide?
(A) Information about new city ordinances
(B) Public transportation information
(C) Breaking news
(D) Movie reviews

85. Who gets free movie tickets?
(A) The first caller of the day
(B) The third caller of the day
(C) The first 10 callers of the day
(D) The first teen callers of the day

86. What is the first thing the receptionist should do for a visitor?
(A) Say hello
(B) Ask his name
(C) Have him sign the book
(D) Call the person he is visiting

87. Where should the visitor wait?
(A) By the desk
(B) Outside
(C) In the office
(D) In the lobby

88. What should visitors never do?
(A) Carry books
(B) Wait too long
(C) Eat in the lobby
(D) Walk around alone

89. What change is planned for buses on this route?
(A) They will leave four minutes sooner.
(B) They will arrive four minutes later.
(C) They will make fewer trips.
(D) They will make more trips.

90. When will this change take place?
(A) Immediately
(B) June 5
(C) June 15
(D) June 21

91. What is true about bus fares?
(A) They must be paid with exact change.
(B) They won't go up this year.
(C) They will be raised 10 cents.
(D) They go up every year.

92. What is the largest group that the conference center can handle?
(A) 10
(B) 20
(C) 100
(D) 200

93. Where do participants stay while attending the conference?
(A) At a nearby hotel
(B) At their own homes
(C) In the center's guest rooms
(D) In town

94. Where is the conference center probably located?
    (A) In the country
    (B) In the city
    (C) In the suburbs
    (D) In a park

95. What problem is occurring?
    (A) There is a power failure.
    (B) There is a water problem.
    (C) There is a gas shortage.
    (D) There is flooding.

96. What has caused the problem?
    (A) An accident
    (B) A snowstorm
    (C) A thunderstorm
    (D) A fire

97. What are residents asked to do?
    (A) Stay indoors
    (B) Light candles
    (C) Call for help
    (D) Turn off electrical appliances

98. How many floors did the old library have?
    (A) 2
    (B) 5
    (C) 6
    (D) 10

99. On which floor can you find novels for adults?
    (A) Third
    (B) Fourth
    (C) Fifth
    (D) Sixth

100. What is on the tenth floor?
    (A) Offices
    (B) Magazines and periodicals
    (C) Books about houses
    (D) Tapes, CDs, and DVDs

READING

In this section of the test, you will have the chance to show how well you understand written English. There are three parts to this section, with special directions for each part.

**YOU WILL HAVE ONE HOUR AND FIFTEEN MINUTES
TO COMPLETE PARTS 5, 6, AND 7 OF THE TEST.**

Part 5: Incomplete Sentences

Directions: You will see a sentence with a missing word. Four possible answers follow the sentence. Choose the best answer to the question and fill in the corresponding oval on your answer sheet.

101. If your meal is unsatisfactory, we _____ it without question.
(A) will replace
(B) replaces
(C) are replacing
(D) replaced

102. _____ the manager's suggestions were reasonable, the supervisor agreed with them.
(A) Until
(B) Although
(C) Because
(D) Even though

103. The proposal is due at the client's office _____ Thursday.
(A) with
(B) on
(C) at
(D) for

104. The results of the traveler preference survey are _____.
(A) surprised
(B) surprises
(C) surprise
(D) surprising

105. We cannot ship the order now because our _____ is low.
(A) invitation
(B) inventory
(C) invention
(D) invoice

106. The train from Madrid arrives _____ noon.
(A) in
(B) on
(C) over
(D) at

107. The company has quit _____ in that magazine.
(A) to advertise
(B) advertise
(C) advertising
(D) advertisement

108. Western Components, Inc. is _____ than Consolidated Electronics Company.
(A) as reliable
(B) most reliable
(C) the reliable
(D) more reliable

109. The project has been completed, _____ the final report is not ready yet.
    (A) because
    (B) but
    (C) or
    (D) since

110. Most cruise passengers will board the ship _____ 4:00 and 5:00.
    (A) between
    (B) at
    (C) until
    (D) with

111. The technicians in the research division _____ the process confidential.
    (A) is keeping
    (B) are keeping
    (C) to keep
    (D) has kept

112. A good waiter _____ to explain the menu.
    (A) is never too busy
    (B) never too busy is
    (C) is too busy never
    (D) being never too busy

113. The laundry bag is _____ the cabinet.
    (A) within
    (B) among
    (C) inside
    (D) between

114. The name of our company symbolizes tradition _____ experience.
    (A) nor
    (B) but
    (C) or
    (D) and

115. Mr. Fong had the client _____ her questions in writing.
    (A) submit
    (B) submitted
    (C) submitting
    (D) submits

116. Ms. Ripola is _____ an accountant when totaling the receipts.
    (A) careful as
    (B) as careful
    (C) as careful as
    (D) careful than

117. _____ the seminar, the audience had trouble hearing the speaker.
    (A) Since
    (B) During
    (C) Although
    (D) While

118. Reductions in the budget require us _____ our costs for international travel.
    (A) limit
    (B) to limit
    (C) limiting
    (D) limit

119. Hiring temporary workers can be very _____.
    (A) economize
    (B) economically
    (C) economy
    (D) economical

120. Marketing costs are _____ the department predicted.
    (A) higher than
    (B) high as
    (C) highest
    (D) highest than

121. The housekeeping staff comes on duty
     _____ 2:00.
     (A) in
     (B) on
     (C) at
     (D) with

122. We missed the deadline _____ our
     computer malfunctioned.
     (A) until
     (B) because
     (C) if
     (D) though

123. Our representative will meet you
     _____ Rome.
     (A) on
     (B) for
     (C) in
     (D) to

124. Computer software is a _____
     market.
     (A) competitor
     (B) competitive
     (C) competition
     (D) competitively

125. We will not send the payment_____
     the invoice is corrected.
     (A) until
     (B) because
     (C) since
     (D) once

126. Most of the employees _____ in the
     company cafeteria.
     (A) eating
     (B) eats
     (C) eat
     (D) to eat

127. Salespeople _____ attract new clients
     receive a bonus.
     (A) whose
     (B) which
     (C) whom
     (D) who

128. The new instructions are _____ the
     old ones.
     (A) more difficult
     (B) difficult as
     (C) difficult than
     (D) more difficult than

129. Mr. Meisel _____ to get to work
     early.
     (A) is liking
     (B) likes
     (C) would be liking
     (D) like

130. The ticket holders may be _____
     about the change in date.
     (A) confusing
     (B) confuse
     (C) confused
     (D) confuses

131. The corporate office is _____ the
     Jamieson building.
     (A) on
     (B) under
     (C) in
     (D) over

132. Our service technicians receive
     _____ training available.
     (A) better
     (B) as good
     (C) best
     (D) the best

133. Your room has been reserved _____ two nights.
(A) in
(B) for
(C) with
(D) at

134. The price of the equipment is low, _____ the maintenance costs can be high.
(A) or
(B) but
(C) and
(D) either

135. The conference _____ was scheduled for next week has been postponed.
(A) that
(B) whose
(C) it
(D) who

136. Mr. Ho's assistant _____ his mail while he was away.
(A) will answer
(B) answered
(C) answers
(D) answering

137. The reception clerk _____ on the telephone when the phone went dead.
(A) talked
(B) is talking
(C) was talking
(D) would talk

138. Overnight mail is _____ way to send a package.
(A) faster
(B) the fastest
(C) faster than
(D) as fast as

139. The latest version of the software _____ with your new computer.
(A) includes
(B) is included
(C) is including
(D) included

140. The hotel offers guests a continental breakfast in the lobby _____ a full breakfast in the restaurant.
(A) with
(B) since
(C) either
(D) or

Part 6: Text Completion

Directions: You will see four passages, each with three blanks. Under each blank are four answer options. Choose the word or phrase that best completes the statement.

Questions 141–143 refer to the following passage.

How to Send a Fax _____ the Airport

    141. (A) by
          (B) for
          (C) from
          (D) to

This fax machine is provided for the convenience of airport passengers.
To send a fax, follow these simple instructions:

1) Lift the telephone. Enter "2" on the keypad.

2) Insert your credit card. You _____ $5 for the first 10 minutes on

    142. (A) will charge
          (B) will be charged
          (C) are going to charge
          (D) have been charging

domestic faxes, and $10 for the first 10 minutes on international faxes.
Each additional minute costs $1 extra.

3) Place your _____ in the tray. Press "1" to approve the charge to

    143. (A) billfold
          (B) demand
          (C) currency
          (D) document

your credit card.

4) Listen for the dial tone and enter the fax number.

5) The paper will pass from the tray into the machine. After the fax is sent,
you should receive a "Fax Sent" confirmation message

Questions 144–146 refer to the following advertisement.

DO YOU TRAVEL _____ ON BUSINESS?

144. (A) rarely
(B) uncommonly
(C) frequently
(D) occasionally

CALL ATA, THE ASIAN TRAVEL AGENCY.

We're the place for busy travelers like you. We take care of the logistics so you can focus on your job. We handle airline, hotel, and rental-car reservations throughout Asia, and we always offer the _____ prices. Our regular

145. (A) low
(B) lower
(C) lowly
(D) lowest

business clients receive a 5% discount on every order. Our _____ staff

146. (A) multilingual
(B) multiplied
(C) multitude
(D) multifold

is ready to serve you in English, Chinese, Japanese, Korean, and Thai.

For excellent service, call ATA to learn more.

Questions 147–149 refer to the following e-mail.

To: yi-fangwu@techworld.tw
From: shih-yismith@techworld.tw
Subject: Technology conference

Are you interested in going to the IFT conference in Taipei in December? _____ topic is technology of the future. Everyone says this is

147. (A) Its
    (B) It's
    (C) Our
    (D) His

one of the best technology conferences around. I wanted to go last year, but I _____ fit it into my schedule. If you want to go, then we

148. (A) can't
    (B) mustn't
    (C) couldn't
    (D) shouldn't

should talk to our _____ soon. I want to be sure that we can get

149. (A) supervisors
    (B) coworkers
    (C) assistants
    (D) customers

permission to go. I haven't heard anyone else talk about it, so we have a good chance of getting approval.

Reply soon!
Shih-Yi

Questions 150–152 refer to the following e-mail.

To: jamesw@procomp.com
From: pamelah@procomp.com
Subject: Office supplies

James,

Office Express is having a big sale this week. We might as well take advantage and _____ some money. They're selling printer paper at 50% off, so

150. (A) earn
     (B) save
     (C) borrow
     (D) lose

please pick up several boxes. Also, get some printer ink cartridges because they're on sale, too. I've noticed that we're running _____ paper for

151. (A) out of
     (B) into
     (C) over
     (D) up to

the photocopier. Last I checked there was just one pack left, so get some of that, whatever the price. Also, our coffeemaker doesn't seem to be working well, and I think we should replace _____ soon. If you

152. (A) him
     (B) her
     (C) it
     (D) us

see one at a good price, get it. Have them charge everything to our account. Go today if you can, because you know how fast they sell out of things when there's a sale.

Pamela

Part 7: Reading Comprehension

Directions: You will see single and double reading passages followed by several questions. Each question has four answer choices. Choose the best answer to the question and fill in the corresponding oval on your answer sheet.

Questions 153–155 refer to the following advertisement.

THE ADVANTAGE THAT MADE US #1 IN ASIA
YES! Please send me your student travel catalog.

Experience
We have the most experience in overseas travel: 47 years of discovering the best sights and events, the best hotels and restaurants, the best staff here and abroad—all priced for a student's budget.

Popularity
More students choose our Out to Asia trips than any other.

References
We stand by our reputation. We'll give you the names of past participants so you can get a firsthand impression.

Savings
We can pass on greater volume discounts, so your dollars will buy you more.

Member, Association of World Travel Organizations

---

153. Why should someone choose Out to Asia?
     (A) It offers varied travel packages.
     (B) It has a good safety record.
     (C) Its packages are all-inclusive.
     (D) Other people like it.

154. Who is offered as a reference?
     (A) Members of the Association of World Travel Organizations
     (B) Asian students
     (C) Former Out to Asia travelers
     (D) Staff members

155. What describes the cost of Out to Asia tours?
     (A) They're very expensive because they include study opportunities.
     (B) They're quite expensive, but everything's the best.
     (C) They're cheap because they're planned for big numbers.
     (D) They're in the middle price range.

Questions 156–158 refer to the following table.

LOW AIRFARES

New York	Berlin	$349
New York	San Francisco	$239
New York	Bombay	$699
Washington	Rome	$575
San Francisco	Paris	$735

All flights make at least one stop with a change of aircraft. These prices available only on a two-week advance purchase. Alterations made after ticketing will be subject to $25 fee. No refunds.

156. If you go from New York to Berlin, what happens?
(A) You get a refund.
(B) You change planes.
(C) You are charged an extra fee.
(D) Your fare costs $239.

157. How early do you have to purchase your ticket to get the lowest fare?
(A) 1 day
(B) 1 week
(C) 10 days
(D) 14 days

158. If you want to change your ticket, what do you have to do?
(A) Trade tickets at the airport
(B) Buy a new ticket
(C) Pay a $25 charge
(D) Fly with another airline

Questions 159–162 refer to the following information.

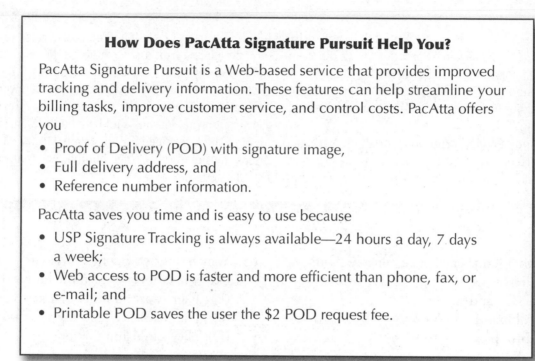

> ### How Does PacAtta Signature Pursuit Help You?
>
> PacAtta Signature Pursuit is a Web-based service that provides improved tracking and delivery information. These features can help streamline your billing tasks, improve customer service, and control costs. PacAtta offers you
>
> - Proof of Delivery (POD) with signature image,
> - Full delivery address, and
> - Reference number information.
>
> PacAtta saves you time and is easy to use because
>
> - USP Signature Tracking is always available—24 hours a day, 7 days a week;
> - Web access to POD is faster and more efficient than phone, fax, or e-mail; and
> - Printable POD saves the user the $2 POD request fee.

159. What is Signature Pursuit?
 (A) A delivery service
 (B) A tracking system
 (C) A billing program
 (D) A mailing system

160. The word *streamline* in paragraph 1, line 2, is closest in meaning to
 (A) complete.
 (B) simplify.
 (C) calculate.
 (D) complicate.

161. What information can you get from PacAtta?
 (A) The current location of a package
 (B) The sender's address
 (C) Who signed for the package
 (D) An account number

162. What is NOT a benefit of using Signature Pursuit?
 (A) It simplifies billing procedures.
 (B) It saves time and money.
 (C) It makes customer service better.
 (D) It increases the odds of successful delivery.

Questions 163–166 refer to the following article.

Delicious Foods Corporation said it will raise prices an average of 3 percent for 19 different brands of jams and jellies. This is the second increase in eight months. The company attributes this recent rise to higher fruit prices resulting from the drought last spring.

Delicious Foods Corporation products with the higher prices will appear on supermarket shelves early next month. Other companies are expected to follow the lead of Delicious Foods and raise prices on their canned fruit and vegetable products before the end of the year. Consumers should expect their pocketbooks to take a big hit throughout the winter. "We can only hope that the weather will improve in the next growing season," said Louella Pearson, president of the Consumer United group. "If not, and if prices continue to rise, some families will really suffer," she added.

163. On what foods have prices already risen?
(A) Preserves
(B) Cakes and sweets
(C) All brands of foods
(D) Fruit pies

164. How many price increases has Delicious Foods recently made?
(A) One increase in 3 months
(B) Two increases in 8 months
(C) One increase in 19 months
(D) Two increases in 18 months

165. Why has the price of fruits risen?
(A) The farmers want more money.
(B) There was too much rain last year.
(C) The weather last spring was dry.
(D) They can't ship the food.

166. What will happen next month?
(A) The weather will improve.
(B) Other companies will raise their prices.
(C) Consumers will buy more pocketbooks.
(D) The higher-priced products will arrive in stores.

Questions 167–168 refer to the following advertisement.

CARLYLE DEPARTMENT STORE
would like to thank its customers!

More than 14,000 satisfied customers from across the city
visit Carlyle Department Store every week.

Because of our valued customers, Carlyle has maintained
a steady profit margin during the current recession.

As a special thank-you, we at Carlyle announce the following offer: The first
100 customers who spend $1,000 in the 10-day period beginning tomorrow,
May 10, will receive a 10% discount on their next purchase over $100.

Come shop at Carlyle and see why thousands
of satisfied customers keep coming back.

167. What is the present state of the economy?
 (A) It is weak.
 (B) It is strong.
 (C) It is growing.
 (D) It is stable.

168. What is being offered?
 (A) A free gift
 (B) A price reduction
 (C) $100 cash
 (D) A rebate

Questions 169–172 refer to the following article.

If you want to advance in your career, you will have to make some careful decisions about which jobs you take. Evaluate a job offer for the value it has to your career. You may have to make some sacrifices at first. You may have to move to a different region or even to a different country to take a job that is right for you. You may have to work late hours, at least temporarily. You might even have to take a lower salary for a job that offers you the experience that you need. But you should never accept a job if it is not related to your career goals.

Accepting a job that is not within your career path will not give you the training or experience you need or want. You will find yourself frustrated in such a position and consequently, you will not perform your best. This will have an effect on the people around you, who will feel as if you are not acting as part of the team. Therefore, the best advice to follow is to think carefully before accepting any position and make sure that the job you accept is the job you want to have.

169. What is the most significant factor in evaluating a job?
 (A) Good location
 (B) High salary
 (C) Value to your career
 (D) How much you will like it

170. Which of the following is NOT mentioned as a possible sacrifice?
 (A) Moving
 (B) No benefits
 (C) Long hours
 (D) Low salary

171. What kind of job should you never accept?
 (A) One not related to your career goals
 (B) One that requires a long commute
 (C) One that has a negative effect on others
 (D) One that makes you work hard

172. What is wrong with taking a job outside your career path?
 (A) You will earn less.
 (B) You won't perform as well.
 (C) You won't get good advice.
 (D) You will be stuck on a team.

TOEIC Practice Test 5

Questions 173–175 refer to the following form.

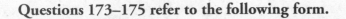

Palmer Towers
285 Hamilton Boulevard
Springfield

Providing our guests with excellent service since 1925

Room Type and Daily Rate (tax not included)

1 Double $186.00 per night

Number of Guests _____ 2 _____

Arrival Date _____ 4/25 _____   Departure Date _____ 4/28 _____

Arrival time _____ 5:00 PM _____   Confirmation Number _____ 24-0726 _____

Check-in time is after 3:00 PM.
Check-out time is 1:00 PM.
Reservations will be held until 9:00 PM.

Guest Name _____ Mr. and Mrs. R. Wolf _____

---

173. What is this form for?
    (A) To register at a hotel
    (B) To reserve hotel meeting space
    (C) To receive messages for hotel guests
    (D) To check out of a hotel

174. How many rooms do Mr. and Mrs. Wolf have?
    (A) 1
    (B) 2
    (C) 4
    (D) 5

175. What will be added to the daily rate?
    (A) A service fee
    (B) A reservation charge
    (C) Tips for the maid
    (D) Tax

Questions 176–180 refer to the following memorandum.

MEMORANDUM

To: All personnel being transferred to the Paris office
From: A. Scheider
Re: Preparation for Paris transfer

Every day my inbox is full of messages concerning this move. Rather than responding to each of you individually, I am forwarding this memo to all of you. Please read and follow the instructions below carefully. Do not omit any steps, and please do not ask me these questions again.

- Pack all items in and on your desk in boxes.
- Label all boxes clearly with your name and company ID number.
- Notify maintenance to clean your desk so it will be ready for the next occupant.
- Retrieve and delete all messages in your voicemail box.
- Change the outgoing message in your voicemail to notify clients of your transfer.
- Provide the network manager with your old password and computer ID number.
- Notify clients by e-mail of your new location and phone number.

---

176. Why was this memo written?
(A) To respond to several queries about the move
(B) To train the new staff in Paris
(C) To suggest ways to use the computer
(D) To propose procedures for using the telephone

177. The word *omit* in paragraph 1, line 3, is closest in meaning to
(A) obey.
(B) forget.
(C) follow.
(D) question.

178. What should each employee pack?
(A) Documents from the files
(B) Things on the desk
(C) The computer system
(D) The voicemail equipment

179. What should each employee do for the person who will occupy his desk next?
(A) Have the desk cleaned
(B) Get a computer password
(C) Move boxes to the edge of the room
(D) Notify clients of the new occupant

180. What should each employee give to the network manager?
(A) His computer equipment
(B) His computer files
(C) His computer ID number
(D) His computer manual

Questions 181–185 refer to the following notice and memo.

COMMUTER TRANSIT PASS INFORMATION
City of Springfield

Now it is easier and more affordable than ever to commute using the City of Springfield Public Transportation System (CSPTS). Three options are available:

SUBWAY PASS

This pass is good for unlimited rides on any CSPTS subway, any time of day or night, any day of the week.

Two-week pass: $60
Six-month pass: $650

BUS PASS

This pass is good for unlimited rides on any bus in the CSPTS bus system, any time of day or night, any day of the week.

Two-week pass: $45
Six-month pass: $500

SUBWAY-BUS PASS

If your commute involves taking both bus and subway, then this is the pass for you. It is good for unlimited rides on any CSPTS subway or bus, any time of day or night, any day of the week.

Two-week pass: $75
Six-month pass: $850

All passes entitle the bearer to a 25% discount on parking in CSPTS subway station parking lots. Simply show the pass to the parking lot attendant to receive your discount.

Passes are available for sale at all CSPTS subway stations, at the CSPTS downtown office, and at designated banks throughout the city.

MEMO

To: All staff
From: James Jones, HR
Re: Transit passes

As an incentive to drive less and use public transportation more, we are offering all staff members here at the Smith Company a special 50% discount on CSPTS transit passes. These are good for bus or subway travel on all routes in the CSPTS system. To apply for the special discounted pass, obtain a Transit Pass Request Form from the Human Resources office. Complete the form, have it authorized by your department head, and submit it to me before the end of the month. You can choose between a two-week pass and a six-month pass. However, please keep in mind that a new form will have to be submitted each time you need a new pass. As an added incentive to those of you who normally drive to work, please be advised that the cost to park in our building's garage will increase to $7 a day starting the first of next month.

181. Who can get a discounted transit pass?
(A) People who work at the Smith Company
(B) CSPTS employees
(C) Anyone who lives in Springfield
(D) People who currently drive to work

182. Where are the discounted passes available?
(A) In any subway station
(B) In the CSPTS downtown office
(C) In certain banks
(D) In James Jones's office

183. What is the cost of a discounted six-month bus-only pass?
(A) $250
(B) $325
(C) $425
(D) $850

184. Which is the least expensive pass?
(A) A regular two-week subway-only pass
(B) A regular two-week bus-only pass
(C) A discounted two-week subway-bus pass
(D) A discounted six-month subway-only pass

185. If it normally costs $10 to park at a subway station, how much would a pass holder pay?
(A) $2.50
(B) $7.00
(C) $7.50
(D) $25.00

Questions 186–190 refer to the following memo and e-mail.

MEMO

For: All Staff
From: Management
Re: Computers

We will purchase 20 new laptop computers for the lending library next month. Management has received numerous e-mails regarding the computers we currently have in the library. Some have keys that stick, and others are not reliable for saving data. These computers will be replaced. Many others just need to be cleared out because they have no memory left. We can continue to use them.

Please report any problems you have with a borrowed computer. Make sure to note the equipment number, the year, and make of the computer, and e-mail this information to Kwan. He needs to keep track of the machines that need replacing and the ones that need repairing. Thank you for your cooperation.

Jin

REMINDER: Please do not store names, addresses, or phone numbers on company computers. Always use a disk.

To: tech1@smithson.org
From: chongdae@smithson.org
Subject: Laptop #3VB7

Hi, Kwan,

I'm away on business right now, so I can't come into your office to speak with you about my computer problems. I am using laptop #3VB7 from the lending library. It's a new model from this year. I've taken it on several business trips over the past few months and have never had any problems with it. However, this morning, I noticed a large crack on the cover. I don't know whether it was mishandled by one of the flight attendants or if it is just getting old and needs replacing. So far, it still seems to be working, but I don't know if I should be saving important data on it.

Can you let me know if I should buy a temporary storage disk for my data, or whether you think this hard drive will be okay until I get back to the office? I'm worried that I will lose all of my notes from the meetings and, more important, the contact information that I have been collecting.

Thanks,
Dae

186. What needs to be replaced?
(A) Unreliable laptops
(B) Library books
(C) Desktop computers
(D) Outdated technology

187. Which of the following is NOT mentioned as a problem with some of the computers?
(A) Some of the buttons are unreliable.
(B) They have no room for new information.
(C) Saving data is not always possible.
(D) The screens are difficult to see.

188. What is Dae's main problem?
(A) She doesn't know if her laptop is reliable.
(B) Her computer doesn't have enough storage space.
(C) Her technician is in an important meeting.
(D) She doesn't have a computer to take on her trip.

189. What information did Dae forget to mention in her e-mail that she was supposed to include?
(A) The equipment number on the laptop
(B) The company that made the laptop
(C) The size of the laptop
(D) The year the laptop was made

190. What company policy did Dae break?
(A) She took a laptop on a business trip.
(B) She saved contact information on the computer.
(C) She wrote e-mail on company time.
(D) She borrowed the same laptop many times.

Questions 191–195 refer to the following invoice and letter.

CARTER, MILLER, WOOD & HUBERT
Attorneys-at-Law
Jaxman Building, 234-99
Phone: (603) 763-9999

INVOICE

Angela Harris   January 7, 20--
448 Main St.
Willowdale, NH

Re: Legal Services

The following fees apply for:
(1) Declaration of identity for emergency travel

Our Fees:

Form 889	$75.00
Next-day service	$50.00
Notarized photographs	no charge
Tax	$4.50
Amount due:	**$129.50**

Please submit payment within 30 days from the date of this bill. $5 will be added to the bill each day after the due date.

Thank you.

Gerald Miller

ANGELA HARRIS
448 MAIN ST.
WILLOWDALE, NH

January 15, 20--

Gerald Miller
Jaxman Building, 234-99
Newman Grove, NH

Dear Mr. Miller,

I received a bill from your office this week, and I'm concerned about the fee. First, nobody mentioned the extra charge for one-day service. Your receptionist asked when I wanted the document, and I said that I was leaving town the next day. I also said that you could mail me the forms after they were signed if that would be easier. My business trip is not for another six weeks, so the extra charge for next-day service is outrageous.

Second, I was very surprised that you charged me $25 for Form 889. I recently looked online and discovered that anyone can download this form free of charge. I realize that I would have to fill this information out myself, but I don't think it's fair to charge so much for something I could have done online for free.

Finally, it was not you who I dealt with originally. I had an appointment with Terrance Wood, and my form and photograph were signed by Alain Carter. Now, it is you who is sending me this invoice. To whom should I write the check?

Please contact me by e-mail at aharris@freemail.com before the end of the week to discuss this matter.

Angela Harris

191. How much does this firm charge to have a document prepared in one day?
(A) $5
(B) $50
(C) $75
(D) $129.50

192. What does Form 889 provide?
(A) Proof of identity for travel purposes
(B) Medical insurance for emergency travel
(C) Dates and times related to a travel itinerary
(D) Permission to work in a foreign country

193. When is Harris leaving on her trip?
(A) In one day
(B) At the end of the week
(C) In 30 days
(D) In six weeks

194. Why is Harris upset by this invoice?
(A) She could have printed her own form for free.
(B) She didn't want to pay for her photograph.
(C) She thinks 30 days isn't enough time to pay the bill.
(D) She was hoping to pay by cash, not check.

195. Which of the lawyers did Harris have no contact with?
(A) Wood
(B) Carter
(C) Hubert
(D) Miller

Questions 196–200 refer to the following letter and chart.

ATLAS INSURANCE CORPORATION
6-9-9 Ginza Chuo-ku
Tokyo, 170-557

February 6, 20--

Watanabe Naoki
1-4-6 Marunouchi Chiyoda-ku
Tokyo, 100-0008

Dear Watanabe Naoki,

Because you are a valued customer of Atlas Insurance, we are sending this courtesy letter to remind you that your vehicle license sticker and insurance expire on March 18, 20--. All drivers in Tokyo must renew their driver's license and insurance annually. License plates need to be replaced only once every ten years. You will receive an attached notice if you need a new plate for your vehicle.

Please renew by following one of the procedures below:

A) Take the enclosed notice to your local insurance broker by the date specified above.

B) Complete the form on the reverse of this notice, and mail it to your local broker at least five days before your vehicle plate sticker and insurance expire.*

NEW: As of April 1, 20--, city authorities will be forbidden by law to offer any lenience regarding expired license plate stickers or insurance.

Thank you for choosing Atlas Insurance.

Sincerely,

The Atlas Insurance Group, Tokyo

*This option is NOT available for customers who want to pay premiums on a monthly payment plan.

PG 2.
Principal operator: Watanabe Naoki
Type of Insurance: Personal *

Basic Insurance Coverage	Type of Discount	Your fee
1 year	Safe Driver Discount (25%)	¥82,000

Optional Insurance

Liability		¥8,000
Collision (¥ 25,000 deductible)		¥9,000
Comprehension (¥ 25,000 deductible)		¥9,250

Other

New plates		N/A

TOTAL COST (1 year)		**¥108,250**

Explanation of terms:

*This insurance does NOT cover business use. Business use means using your vehicle to get to your place of employment more than five times in one month. If your driving patterns change, please call your insurance agent to discuss upgrades to your insurance plan.

196. How far in advance did this customer receive his notice of expiration?
  (A) About five days
  (B) Just under one month
  (C) Just over one month
  (D) At least one year

197. When must Watanabe mail his renewal in?
  (A) Before February 6th
  (B) By March 13th
  (C) By March 18th
  (D) After April 1st

198. Which of the following changed this year according to Watanabe's notice?
  (A) A law in Tokyo
  (B) The price of insurance
  (C) The discount for safe drivers
  (D) A renewal method

199. What should Watanabe do if he begins using his car for business?
  (A) Nothing.
  (B) Notify city authorities.
  (C) Change his insurance plan.
  (D) Get a new license plate.

200. Which is definitely true about Watanabe?
  (A) He has never had an accident.
  (B) He never drives his vehicle to work.
  (C) His insurance payments are collected monthly.
  (D) His vehicle license plate is less than ten years old.

Answer Key
PRACTICE TEST 5

Listening Comprehension

Part 1: Photographs

1. A	4. C	7. B	9. B
2. D	5. C	8. D	10. D
3. B	6. A		

Part 2: Question-Response

11. A	19. B	27. A	35. C
12. B	20. A	28. B	36. B
13. B	21. B	29. A	37. A
14. C	22. C	30. A	38. A
15. B	23. A	31. B	39. A
16. C	24. A	32. C	40. B
17. B	25. B	33. B	
18. C	26. C	34. B	

Part 3: Conversations

41. C	49. A	57. D	65. B
42. B	50. B	58. D	66. A
43. B	51. A	59. A	67. C
44. A	52. D	60. B	68. A
45. B	53. B	61. C	69. C
46. B	54. D	62. C	70. D
47. C	55. C	63. D	
48. A	56. B	64. D	

Part 4: Talks

71. D	79. A	87. D	95. A
72. C	80. B	88. D	96. C
73. C	81. A	89. B	97. D
74. B	82. C	90. B	98. B
75. A	83. A	91. B	99. B
76. C	84. B	92. D	100. A
77. B	85. C	93. C	
78. C	86. A	94. A	

Answer Key
PRACTICE TEST 5

Reading

Part 5: Incomplete Sentences

101. **A**	111. **B**	121. **C**	131. **C**
102. **C**	112. **A**	122. **B**	132. **D**
103. **B**	113. **C**	123. **C**	133. **B**
104. **D**	114. **D**	124. **B**	134. **B**
105. **B**	115. **A**	125. **A**	135. **A**
106. **D**	116. **C**	126. **C**	136. **B**
107. **C**	117. **B**	127. **D**	137. **C**
108. **D**	118. **B**	128. **D**	138. **B**
109. **B**	119. **D**	129. **B**	139. **B**
110. **A**	120. **A**	130. **C**	140. **D**

Part 6: Text Completion

141. **C**	144. **C**	147. **A**	150. **B**
142. **B**	145. **D**	148. **C**	151. **A**
143. **D**	146. **A**	149. **A**	152. **C**

Part 7: Reading Comprehension

153. **D**	165. **C**	177. **B**	189. **B**
154. **C**	166. **D**	178. **B**	190. **B**
155. **C**	167. **A**	179. **A**	191. **B**
156. **B**	168. **B**	180. **C**	192. **A**
157. **D**	169. **C**	181. **A**	193. **D**
158. **C**	170. **B**	182. **D**	194. **A**
159. **B**	171. **A**	183. **A**	195. **C**
160. **B**	172. **B**	184. **C**	196. **C**
161. **C**	173. **A**	185. **C**	197. **B**
162. **D**	174. **A**	186. **A**	198. **A**
163. **A**	175. **D**	187. **D**	199. **C**
164. **B**	176. **A**	188. **A**	200. **D**

TOEIC PRACTICE TEST 5—ANSWERS EXPLAINED
Listening Comprehension
PART 1: PHOTOGRAPHS

1. **(A)** A man is loading boxes onto a plane. Choices (B), (C), and (D) all use words that sound similar to *plane*.

2. **(D)** An office scene shows a lamp behind a desk chair. Choice (A) is incorrect because the computer is open. Choice (B) is impossible because no one is in the chair. Choice (C) is incorrect because the books are on the desk.

3. **(B)** A carpenter is measuring a board in a partially built house. Choice (A) correctly identifies the action but not the object or the person. Choice (C) confuses the carpenter's hardhat with a helmet. Choice (D) is impossible because the walls are still being built.

4. **(C)** A group of businesspeople is sitting around a table looking at a couple of computers. Choice (A) confuses similar-sounding words *working* and *walking*. Choice (B) confuses similar-sounding words *working* and *cooking*. Choice (D) uses the word *looking*, but no one is looking out the window.

5. **(C)** Some people are standing on a sidewalk on a rainy day holding open umbrellas. Choice (A) associates *raincoats* with *umbrellas*. Choice (B) confuses similar-sounding words *rain* and *train*. Choice (D) correctly identifies the location but not the action.

6. **(A)** A man in a factory is looking at wires in a box. Choice (B) is incorrect because the door is open. Choice (C) correctly identifies the location but confuses similar-sounding words *wire* and *fire*. Choice (D) correctly identifies the gloves but not their location.

7. **(B)** A man waiting in an airport lounge is working on his computer. Choice (A) correctly identifies the action but not the location. Choice (C) refers to the briefcase, but the man is not opening it. Choice (D) refers to the computer, but the man is not buying it.

8. **(D)** Food and dishes are on the table, including fruit on a plate. Choices (A), (B), and (C) correctly identify objects in the photo but not their location.

9. **(B)** A pilot is looking at a map. Choices (A), (C), and (D) all use words that sound similar to *map*.

10. **(D)** Three men are gathered around a table and one of them is signing a document. Choice (A) is incorrect because one man is not wearing a jacket. Choice (B) confuses the meaning of the word *sign*. Choice (C) is incorrect because one man is holding a pair of eyeglasses is his hand, but no one is wearing them.

PART 2: QUESTION-RESPONSE

11. **(A)** This is a logical response to a question about location. Choice (B) confuses similar-sounding words *waiting* and *weigh*. Choice (C) confuses similar-sounding words *waiting* and *raining*.

12. **(B)** This is a logical response to a question about location. Choice (A) associates *books* and *library*. Choice (C) repeats the words *books* and *children*.

13. **(B)** This is a logical response to a dinner invitation. Choice (A) repeats the word *join*. Choice (C) confuses similar-sounding words *join* and *coin* and *dinner* and *thinner*.

14. **(C)** The second speaker offers to heat the coffee because the first speaker complains that it is cold. Choice (A) confuses the meaning of the word *cold*. Choice (B) confuses *old* with the similar-sounding word *cold*, and *copies* with the similar-sounding word *coffee*.

15. **(B)** This is a logical response to a question about plans. Choice (A) confuses similar-sounding words *plan* and *plane* and *noon* and *afternoon*. Choice (C) uses the related word *planning*.

16. **(C)** This is a logical response to the question about identifying the train. Choice (A) repeats the word *express*. Choice (B) could answer *excuse me* when it means permission to leave a room.

17. **(B)** This is a logical response to the question about package delivery. Choice (A) confuses related words *package* and *packed*. Choice (C) confuses similar sounding words *package* and *age*.

18. **(C)** This is a logical response to a question about getting to the airport. Choice (A) uses the related word *plane* but does not answer the question. Choice (B) confuses similar-sounding words *airport* and *port* and *get* and *met*.

19. **(B)** The second speaker decides not to take the call now but to return it later. Choice (A) confuses *hall* with the similar-sounding word *call*. Choice (C) associates *phone number* with *phone call*.

20. **(A)** *After lunch* answers the question *When?* Choice (B) confuses the meaning of the word *return*. Choice (C) confuses similar-sounding words return and *right turn*.

21. **(B)** This answers the question about *often*. Choice (A) confuses similar-sounding words *stay* and *play*. Choice (C) associates *hotel* with *bill*.

22. **(C)** This is a logical response to a question about movies. Choice (A) confuses similar-sounding words *movies* and *moving*. Choice (B) repeats the word *like*.

23. **(A)** This explains the reason the flight was canceled. Choice (B) repeats the word *flight* but does not answer the question. Choice (C) confuses similar-sounding words *canceled* and *can sell*.

24. **(A)** This answers the question about possession. Choice (B) confuses similar-sounding words *suitcase* and *suit*. Choice (C) confuses the meaning of the word *case*.

25. **(B)** *In the room* answers the question *Where?* Choice (A) confuses similar-sounding words *kept* and *swept*. Choice (C) confuses similar-sounding words *supplies* and *supper*.

26. **(C)** *Very relaxing* answers the question *How?* Choice (A) confuses similar-sounding words *vacation* and *vacant*. Choice (B) confuses similar-sounding words *vacation* and *nation*.

27. **(A)** This answers the question about turning off the computer. Choice (B) repeats *turn off*. Choice (C) repeats the word *computer*.

28. **(B)** *Senior management* answers the question *Who?* Choice (A) confuses the meaning of the word *attend*. Choice (C) confuses similar-sounding words *attend* and *at ten*.

29. **(A)** This answers the question about lunch. Choice (B) would answer the question *When?* Choice (C) associates *lunch* with *guests*.

30. **(A)** The first speaker complains of tight shoes so the second speaker suggests a larger size. Choice (B) confuses the phrase *good night* with the similar-sounding phrase *too tight*. Choice (C) confuses *news* with the similar-sounding word *shoes*.

31. **(B)** *On the bookshelf* answers the question *Where?* Choice (A) confuses *software* with similar sounding words *wearing* and *soft*. Choice (C) confuses *manual* with the similar-sounding phrase *man you know well*.

32. **(C)** *Two days ago* answers the question *When?* Choice (A) relates *gas* and *oil*. Choice (B) confuses similar-sounding words *last* and *elastic* and *car* and *far*.

33. **(B)** This answers the question about the cause of the forest fire. Choice (A) confuses the meaning of the word *fire*. Choice (C) confuses *forest* with the similar-sounding phrase *for a rest*.

34. **(B)** The second speaker has been waiting for the bus so is glad to hear that it will arrive soon. Choice (A) confuses *afternoon* with the similar-sounding word *soon*. Choice (C) confuses *spoon* with the similar-sounding word *afternoon*.

35. **(C)** This explains the reason for not writing. Choice (A) associates *writing* and *letters*. Choice (B) uses the related word *write*.

36. **(B)** The first speaker suggests leaving and the second speaker agrees. Choice (A) repeats the word *rain* and confuses the meaning of the word *leave*. Choice (C) repeats the word *rain*.

37. **(A)** *Every day* answers the question *How often?* Choice (B) repeats the word *call*. Choice (C) associates *calls* with *phones*.

38. **(A)** The second speaker is happy to hear about the snow because it provides the opportunity to go skiing. Choice (B) confuses *weak* with the similar-sounding word *week*. Choice (C) confuses *know* with the similar-sounding word *snow*.

39. **(A)** *Any day next week* answers the question *When?* Choice (B) confuses homonyms *would* and *wood.* Choice (C) uses the related word *came* and confuses similar-sounding words *would* and *could.*

40. **(B)** This answers the request for permission to sit down. Choice (A) confuses the modal auxiliary *may* with the name of the month *May.* Choice (C) associates *sit* with *cushion* and confuses the meaning of the word *down.*

PART 3: CONVERSATIONS

41. **(C)** The woman says her room number is 624. Choices (A), (B), and (D) sound similar to the correct answer.

42. **(B)** The woman calls to complain about a broken TV, and the desk clerk says he'll send someone to her room, we can assume to fix it. The other choices are plausible responses to the situation but are not the meaning of his answer.

43. **(B)** The woman says that she is going out in half an hour. Choices (A) and (D) confuse *ten* with the similar-sounding word *then.* Choice (C) repeats the word *hour.*

44. **(A)** The woman is complaining about the dirty coffeepot. Choice (B) confuses *skirt* with the similar-sounding word *dirty.* Choice (C) confuses *watch* with the similar-sounding word *wash* and repeats the word *kitchen.* Choice (D) uses the word *floor* out of context.

45. **(B)** The man says that the kitchen is on the sixth floor. Choices (A) and (D) sound similar to the correct answer. Choice (C) confuses *ninth* with the similar-sounding word *mind.*

46. **(B)** The man asks for cocoa. Choice (A) repeats the word *milk*, which will be used for making the cocoa. Choice (C) is what the woman offers. Choice (D) sounds similar to the correct answer.

47. **(C)** The speakers just got off a plane and need to pick up baggage, so they are at the airport. Choices (A), (B), and (D) repeat words used in the conversation.

48. **(A)** The man thinks he will have to wait a long time while the woman gets her baggage. Choice (B) is incorrect because it is the woman, not the man, who has baggage. Choice (C) repeats the word *stuck* and associates *traffic* with *cab.* Choice (D) repeats the word *cab.*

49. **(A)** The woman says that she has one bag. Choice (B) confuses *two* with the similar-sounding word *too.* Choice (C) is not mentioned. Choice (D) confuses *four* with the similar-sounding word *for.*

50. **(B)** The speakers agree to have lunch in the park. Choice (A) is confused with *sidewalk café.* Choice (C) is the woman's suggestion. Choice (D) is where the man made his sandwich.

51. **(A)** The man brought a sandwich from home, and the woman is going to buy one. Choice (B) confuses *ice* with the similar-sounding word *nice*. Choice (C) is the woman's suggestion. Choice (D) confuses *meat* with the similar-sounding word *meet*.

52. **(D)** The man says that he will wait by the fountain. Choice (A) confuses *gate* with the similar-sounding word *wait*. Choice (B) confuses *lake* with the similar-sounding word *take*. Choice (C) confuses *lawn* with the similar-sounding word *long*.

53. **(B)** The woman says *I'm lucky*. Choice (A) is confused with the man's saying, *I shouldn't worry*. Choice (C) is confused with the woman's saying, *Don't feel too bad*. Choice (D) confuses *sad* with the similar-sounding word *bad*.

54. **(D)** The man says that his office faces a parking lot. Choice (A) confuses *dark* with the similar-sounding word *park*. Choice (B) describes the woman's office. Choice (C) confuses *vacant lot* with *parking lot*.

55. **(C)** According to the woman, the man has been there for seven months. Choice (A) confuses *two* with the similar-sounding word *too*. Choice (B) confuses *four* with the similar-sounding word *for*. Choice (D) sounds similar to the correct answer.

56. **(B)** The man is organizing a group for a bus tour of the river valley. Choice (A) associates *bus driver* with *bus*. Choice (C) confuses *singer* with the similar-sounding word *bring*. Choice (D) associates *artist* with *landscapes*.

57. **(D)** The man says that they will meet at 9:00. Choice (A) confuses *two* with the similar-sounding word *tomorrow*. Choice (B) confuses *five* with the similar-sounding word *drive*. Choice (C) confuses *eight* with the similar-sounding word *late*.

58. **(D)** The man says to *dress warmly*. Choice (A) uses *dress* as a noun instead of as a verb. Choice (B) repeats the word *cold*. Choice (C) confuses *books* with the similar-sounding word *look*.

59. **(A)** The woman says she stayed only one night. Choice (B) is confused with *$200*, the amount of money she was charged. Choice (C) is the number of nights she was charged for. Choice (D) confuses *four* with the similar-sounding word *for*.

60. **(B)** The man apologizes for giving the woman the wrong bill. Choice (A) is the man's original guess. Choice (C) repeats the word *wrong*. Choice (D) is not mentioned.

61. **(C)** The man says that credit card is the only acceptable method of payment. Choice (A) is mentioned by the man as an unacceptable method of payment. Choice (B) is how the woman wants to pay. Choice (D) uses the word *account* out of context.

62. **(C)** The woman is ordering breakfast, so the conversation takes place in a restaurant. Choices (A), (B), and (D) are places associated with food or meals but are not the correct answer.

63. **(D)** The man says breakfast is served until 11:30. Choices (A), (B), and (C) sound similar to the correct answer.

64. **(D)** The woman wants coffee without cream or sugar. Choice (A) confuses *ice cream* with *cream*. Choice (B) confuses *roast* with the similar-sounding word *toast*. Choice (C) confuses *waffles* with the similar-sounding word *wonderful*.

65. **(B)** The man says that he plays golf. Choice (A) confuses *books* with the similar-sounding word *cook*. Choice (C) uses the word *plays* out of context. Choice (D) confuses *hiking* with the similar-sounding word *like*.

66. **(A)** The woman says that she loves to eat. Choice (B) confuses *read* with the similar-sounding word *eat*. Choice (C) is what the man likes to do. Choice (D) confuses *run* with the similar-sounding word *fun*.

67. **(C)** The woman suggests Friday. Choice (A) confuses *afternoon* with the similar-sounding word *soon*. Choice (B) is the man's suggestion. Choice (D) is when the man plays golf.

68. **(A)** The woman says that she is borrowing a book. Choices (B), (C), and (D) are other items mentioned by the librarian.

69. **(C)** A book can be borrowed for three weeks and renewed for three more weeks, making a total of six weeks. Choice (A) is the initial loan period. Choice (B) confuses *four* with the similar-sounding word *more*. Choice (D) confuses *eight* with the similar-sounding word *late*.

70. **(D)** The librarian says that the charge is 25 cents a day. Choice (A) and (C) sound similar to the correct answer. Choice (B) confuses *nine* with the similar-sounding word *fine*.

PART 4: TALKS

71. **(D)** Business hours are from 8:30 AM to 6:30 PM. Choices (A) and (B) are confused with the closing time. Choice (C) sounds similar to the correct answer.

72. **(C)** The caller is instructed to press 1 for directions. Choices (A) and (B) are confused with the instructions to dial an extension number to leave a message for a specific person. Choice (D) is what will happen if the caller presses 2.

73. **(C)** Callers are asked to stay on the line to speak with a financial adviser. Choice (A) will let the caller hear this message again. Choice (B) will let the caller hear about financial services. Choice (D) will allow the caller to leave a message for a specific person.

74. **(B)** This station is a *transfer point*, or *transfer station*, where passengers can connect with other trains. Choices (A) and (D) are contradicted by *Downtown Central*. Choice (C) is contradicted by *transfer point*.

75. **(A)** The platform is on the *lower level*. Choice (B) is the opposite. Choice (C) is contradicted by *take the elevator or stairs*. Choice (D) is not mentioned.

76. **(C)** The announcer says that the trains are behind schedule *because of repair work on the tracks*. Choice (A) confuses *rainy* with the similar-sounding word *trains*. Choice (B) confuses *icy* with the similar-sounding word *advised*. Choice (D) uses the word *train* out of context.

77. **(B)** It will be *partly sunny*. Choices (A) and (C) are contradicted by *sunny*. Choice (D) is contradicted by *72 degrees*.

78. **(C)** *Get stronger* means *increase*. Choice (A) is incorrect because it is sunny already. Choice (B) is contradicted by *sunny*. Choice (D) is not logical if the temperature is 72 degrees.

79. **(A)** The next weather report will be at 11:00 AM. Choice (B) is when the wind will get stronger. Choice (C) is when the wind will calm down. Choice (D) is when the weather will be cool and cloudy.

80. **(B)** The new service is delivery within *two days*. Choice (A) is not a new service. Choices (C) and (D) are not mentioned.

81. **(A)** Customers in Alaska pay $19 instead of $9. Choices (B), (C), and (D) are contradicted by *the same two-day service*.

82. **(C)** The offer is available for orders of at least $150. Choices (A), (B), and (D) sound similar to the correct answer.

83. **(A)** The hotline tells about events. Choices (B), (C), and (D) are not considered events.

84. **(B)** The hotline provides information on special events as well as public transportation routes. Choices (A), (C), and (D) are not mentioned.

85. **(C)** Free movie tickets are given to the first 10 callers every day. Choices (A), (B), and (D) sound similar to the correct answer.

86. **(A)** *Hello* is the first thing the receptionist should say. Choices (B), (C), and (D) all occur afterward.

87. **(D)** He should wait *in the lobby*. Choices (A) and (C) are contradicted by *take a seat in the lobby*. Choice (B) is not logical.

88. **(D)** The speaker says that visitors must be escorted to the office they will visit, and should not be allowed to walk around the building alone. Choice (A) repeats the word *book*. Choice (B) confuses *long* with the similar-sounding word *alone*. Choice (C) sounds similar to *take a seat in the lobby*.

89. **(B)** They'll arrive *later*. Choice (A) is the opposite of the correct answer. Choices (C) and (D) are contradicted by no change in the number of scheduled trips.

90. **(B)** The change will take place on June 5. Choice (A) is not mentioned. Choice (C) sounds similar to the correct answer. Choice (D) is confused with the number of the bus route.

91. **(B)** The speaker says that bus fares will *stay the same at least until the end of the year.* Choice (A) confuses the meaning of the word *change.* Choice (C) confuses *ten* with the similar-sounding word *end.* Choice (D) repeats the word *year.*

92. **(D)** It handles groups to *200.* Choice (A) is the smallest group it will serve. Choices (B) and (C) fall within the limits.

93. **(C)** The advertisement describes *our guest rooms.* Choices (A), (B), and (D) are not logical if the center provides rooms.

94. **(A)** Because the guest rooms *overlook the countryside,* the conference center is in the country. Choices (B) and (C) are contradicted by *countryside.* Choice (D) is not mentioned.

95. **(A)** *Have lost electrical power* means *a power failure.* Choices (B), (C), and (D) would be possible but are not the correct answer.

96. **(C)** The problem has been caused by a *violent thunderstorm.* Choices (A), (B), and (D) are possible causes of a power failure but are not the correct answer.

97. **(D)** Residents should *turn off appliances.* Choices (A) and (B) are not mentioned. Choice (C) is contradicted by *service crews are already working.*

98. **(B)** The new library has 10 floors, which is twice as many as the old library had. Choices (A) and (C) are not mentioned. Choice (D) is the number of floors in the new library.

99. **(B)** Adult fiction is on the fourth floor. Choice (A) is the floor for books for teenagers. Choices (C) and (D) are the floors for adult nonfiction.

100. **(A)** The administrative offices are on the tenth floor. Choice (B) is what is found on the eighth floor. Choice (C) uses the word *houses* out of context. Choice (D) is what is found on the seventh floor.

Reading

PART 5: INCOMPLETE SENTENCES

101. **(A)** This is a real future conditional, so a future tense verb is required in the main clause. Choice (B) is present tense and doesn't agree with the subject. Choice (C) is present continuous. Choice (D) is past.

102. **(C)** *Because* establishes a cause-and-effect relationship. Choices (A), (B), and (D) are not logical.

103. **(B)** *On* is used with days of the week. Choice (A) means *together.* Choice (C) is used with hours of the day. Choice (D) indicates a recipient.

104. **(D)** The *results* surprise others; it is active, so the present participle is used. Choice (A) is the past participle. Choice (B) is the present tense. Choice (C) is the base form of the verb.

105. **(B)** *Inventory* means *stock*. Choices (A), (C), and (D) look similar to the correct answer but don't have the correct meaning.

106. **(D)** *At* is used with hours of the day. Choice (A) means *inside*. Choice (B) is used with days of the week. Choice (C) means *above*.

107. **(C)** *Quit* is followed by a gerund. Choice (A) is an infinitive. Choice (B) is base form. Choice (D) is a noun.

108. **(D)** This is a comparative adjective using *more* and *than*. Choices (A), (B), and (C) are not used with *than*.

109. **(B)** *But* indicates a contrast. Choices (A) and (D) indicate cause and effect. Choice (C) indicates a choice.

110. **(A)** *Between* is used here to indicate the beginning and end points of a time frame. Choice (B) is used to indicate one specific point in time. Choice (C) indicates the end point of a time frame. Choice (D) means *together*.

111. **(B)** This agrees with the plural subject *technicians*. Choices (A) and (D) are singular. Choice (C) is an infinitive.

112. **(A)** The adverb *never* follows the verb *to be*. Choices (B) and (C) have the wrong word order. Choice (D) has the wrong form of the verb.

113. **(C)** This indicates the position of the laundry bag. Choice (A) is not normally used as a preposition of place. Choices (B) and (D) require more than one item as a reference point.

114. **(D)** *And* is used to connect two similar ideas. Choice (A) is used with *neither*. Choice (B) indicates a contrast. Choice (C) indicates a choice.

115. **(A)** The causative *had* is followed by the base form of the verb. Choice (B) is past tense. Choice (C) is a gerund. Choice (D) is present tense.

116. **(C)** Equal comparisons require *as* on both sides of the adjective. Choice (A) omits the first *as*. Choice (B) omits the second *as*. Choice (D) uses *than*.

117. **(B)** *During* is logical and is used with noun phrases. Choice (A) is not logical. Choices (C) and (D) are used to introduce clauses, not noun phrases.

118. **(B)** *Require* is followed by an infinitive verb. Choice (A) is present tense. Choice (C) is a gerund. Choice (D) is base form.

119. **(D)** *Economical* is an adjective used to modify the subject *hiring*. Choice (A) is a verb. Choice (B) is an adverb. Choice (C) is a noun.

120. **(A)** This is a comparative form using *–er* and *than*. Choice (B) is an incomplete equal comparison. Choice (C) is an incomplete superlative. Choice (D) incorrectly uses *than* with a superlative adjective.

121. **(C)** *At* is used with specific hours of the day. Choice (A) means *inside*. Choice (B) is used with days of the week. Choice (D) means *together*.

122. **(B)** *Because* indicates a cause-and-effect relationship. Choices (A), (C), and (D) are not logical.

123. **(C)** *In* is used with cities. Choice (A) is used with days of the week. Choice (B) indicates a recipient. Choice (D) indicates a destination.

124. **(B)** This is an adjective used to modify the noun *market*. Choices (A) and (C) are nouns. Choice (D) is an adverb.

125. **(A)** This indicates when the payment will be sent. Choices (B), (C), and (D) are not logical.

126. **(C)** Habitual action is expressed with the simple present tense. Choice (A) is a gerund. Choice (B) is base form. Choice (D) is an infinitive.

127. **(D)** The relative pronoun *who* refers to *salespeople* and acts as the subject of the clause. Choice (A) is possessive. Choice (B) is used to refer to things. Choice (C) is used as an object, not a subject.

128. **(D)** The comparative, using *more* and *than*, is used to compare the new instructions with the old ones. Choice (A) omits *than*. Choice (B) is an incomplete equal comparison. Choice (C) omits *more*.

129. **(B)** Habitual action is expressed by the present tense. Choices (A) and (C) are incorrect because *like* is a stative verb and therefore is not used with a continuous tense. Choice (D) does not agree with the subject.

130. **(C)** The *change* is causing the ticket holders to be confused; use the past participle. Choice (A) is present participle. Choice (B) is base form. Choice (D) is present tense.

131. **(C)** *In* is used for locations inside buildings. Choice (A) is used for floor locations inside buildings. Choice (B) means *below*. Choice (D) means *above*.

132. **(D)** The superlative form is used to indicate one out of many. Choice (A) is the comparative form. Choice (B) is an incomplete equal comparison. Choice (C) omits *the*.

133. **(B)** *For* is used with periods of time. Choice (A) means *inside*. Choice (C) means *together*. Choice (D) is used to indicate a specific hour of the day.

134. **(B)** *But* indicates a contrast. Choice (A) indicates a choice. Choice (C) connects two similar ideas. Choice (D) is used with *or*.

135. **(A)** The relative pronoun *that* refers to *conference*. Choice (B) is possessive. Choice (C) is not a relative pronoun so cannot be used to introduce an adjective clause. Choice (D) refers to people.

136. **(B)** The sentence is about an action that occurred in the past. Choice (A) is future tense. Choice (C) is present tense. Choice (D) is a gerund.

137. **(C)** The past continuous is used to refer to an action that was in progress when it was interrupted by another action in the past. Choice (A) is simple past tense. Choice (B) is present continuous. Choice (D) is conditional.

138. **(B)** The superlative is used to indicate one out of many. Choice (A) is a comparative omitting *than*. Choice (C) is a comparative, not a superlative. Choice (D) is an equal comparison.

139. **(B)** Someone else included the software; use the past participle. Choice (A) is present tense. Choice (C) is present continuous. Choice (D) is past tense.

140. **(D)** *Or* indicates a choice. Choices (A) and (B) are not logical. Choice (C) cannot be used without *or*.

PART 6: TEXT COMPLETION

141. **(C)** The fax machine is at the airport, so the instructions are for sending a fax *from* the airport to another place. Choices (A) and (B) cannot be used in this context. Choice (D) is used to indicate where or who would receive, not send, a fax.

142. **(B)** A passive-voice form is required because the subject is not active; the owner of the fax machine charges the user (*You*) to use it. Choices (A), (C), and (D) are active-voice forms.

143. **(D)** You will place your *document* in the tray in order to send it by fax. Choices (A) and (C) are items that cannot be sent by fax. Choice (B) is not a concrete object.

144. **(C)** The ad is directed toward people who travel often or *frequently*. Choices (A), (B), and (D) have the opposite of the correct meaning.

145. **(D)** A superlative adjective is required here after the article *the*. Choices (A) and (B) are adjectives but are not superlative. Choice (C) is an adjective with a completely different meaning.

146. **(A)** *Multilingual* means *speaking many languages*. Choices (B), (C), and (D) look similar to the correct answer but have very different meanings.

147. **(A)** This is a possessive adjective referring to the noun *conference*. Choice (B) is a contraction of *it is*. Choices (C) and (D) are possessive adjectives that refer to people.

148. **(C)** The writer *wasn't able to*, or *couldn't*, fit the conference into his schedule. Choices (A), (B), and (D) are present ideas, but the writer is talking about the past.

149. **(A)** The writer suggests talking to their supervisors in order to get permission to attend the conference. Choices (B), (C), and (D) are not people who can give permission.

150. **(B)** Items on sale have a lower price than usual so shoppers save money by spending less. Choices (A), (C), and (D) are all things that can be done with money, but they don't fit the context.

151. **(A)** *Run out of* means to *finish your supply of something*. Choices (B), (C), and (D) can all be used with *run* but create meanings that don't fit the context.

152. **(C)** This pronoun refers to a thing, *coffeemaker*. Choices (A), (B), and (D) all refer to people.

PART 7: READING COMPREHENSION

153. **(D)** People should choose Out to Asia because of its *popularity*, that is, because many people like it. Choices (A), (B), and (C) are not mentioned.

154. **(C)** *Past participants*, or former travelers with the program, are offered as references. Choices (A) and (D) are mentioned in the ad but are not offered as references. Choice (B) repeats the word *students*.

155. **(C)** They can pass on greater volume discounts, so your dollars can buy you more. Choices (A), (B), and (D) are not mentioned.

156. **(B)** You have to change planes. Choice (A) is incorrect because the information says that there are no refunds. Choice (C) is required only if you change an already scheduled flight. Choice (D) is not mentioned.

157. **(D)** The low prices are based on a *two-week advance purchase*. Choices (A), (B), and (C) are less than two weeks.

158. **(C)** There is a $25 fee for changing flights after the ticket has been purchased. Choices (A), (B), and (D) are not mentioned.

159. **(B)** PacAtta provides *improved tracking and delivery information,* so it is a tracking system. Choice (A) repeats the word *delivery*. Choice (C) repeats the word *billing*. Choice (D) is confused with *e-mail*.

160. **(B)** *Streamline* means *make simpler*. Choices (A) and (C) could fit the sentence but don't have the right meaning. Choice (D) is the opposite of the correct answer.

161. **(C)** A *signature image* would show who signed for the package. Choices (A), (B), and (D) are information one could get from a tracking system but are not mentioned in this information.

162. **(D)** The information does not mention improved delivery as a result of Signature Pursuit. Choices (A), (B), and (C) are all mentioned as benefits of Signature Pursuit.

163. **(A)** Jams and jellies are preserves. Choice (B) is not mentioned. Choice (C) repeats the word *brands*. Choice (D) repeats the word *fruit*.

164. **(B)** *The second increase in eight months* means that there have been two increases in eight months. Choice (A) repeats the word *three*. Choice (C) repeats the word *nineteen*. Choice (D) confuses *eight* with *eighteen*.

165. **(C)** A drought, or a period of dry weather, is the cause of higher fruit prices. Choices (A) and (D) are possible but not mentioned. Choice (B) is the opposite of the correct answer.

166. **(D)** We will see the higher-priced products in supermarkets next month. Choice (A) is what Louella Pearson says everyone hopes for next season. Choice (B) is what will happen before the end of the year. Choice (C) uses the word *pocketbooks* out of context.

167. **(A)** A recession means that *the economy is weak*. Choices (B), (C), and (D) do not describe a recession.

168. **(B)** The first 100 customers who spend $1,000 in a 10-day period will get a 10% discount on their next purchase over $100. Choice (A) is not mentioned. Choice (C) repeats the number *100*. Choice (D) is not mentioned.

169. **(C)** The value of the job to your career is the most important. Choices (A) and (B) are things you might have to sacrifice. Choice (D) is plausible but is not mentioned.

170. **(B)** Benefits are not mentioned. Choices (A), (C), and (D) are all mentioned.

171. **(A)** The article advises never to take a job that *is not related to your career goals*. Choice (B) is not given as a reason for refusing jobs. Choice (C) is a possible consequence of taking the wrong kind of job. Choice (D) is not given as a reason for refusing jobs.

172. **(B)** According to the article, taking the wrong kind of job will cause you to feel frustrated and to not perform your best. Choices (A), (C), and (D) all repeat words used in the article.

173. **(A)** The form gives the names of the guests and describes their room and dates of their stay, so it is a hotel registration form. Choices (B), (C), and (D) are all forms one might see at a hotel but are not the correct answer.

174. **(A)** The form shows that they have one double room. Choice (B) is confused with the number of guests. Choice (C) is confused with the arrival and departure dates. Choice (D) is confused with the arrival time.

175. **(D)** *Tax not included* means that tax will be added to the daily rate. Choice (A) repeats the word *service*. Choices (B) and (C) are not mentioned.

176. **(A)** The memo was written in response to many messages asking questions about the move to Paris. Choices (B), (C), and (D) repeat words used in the memo but are not the correct answer.

177. **(B)** *Omit* means *leave out* or *forget*; the writer wants his staff to remember to follow all the steps. Choices (A) and (C) have the opposite of the correct meaning. Choice (D) fits the context but does not have the right meaning.

178. **(B)** Employees are instructed to *pack all items in and on your desk*. Choice (A) is not mentioned. Choices (C) and (D) are things employees will have to deal with but are not things that will be packed.

179. **(A)** Employees are asked to notify maintenance to have the desk cleaned for the next occupant. Choice (B) will be given to the network manager. Choice (C) repeats the word *boxes*. Choice (D) repeats the word *clients*.

180. **(C)** Employees are asked to provide the network manager with their password and computer ID number. Choices (A), (B), and (D) are all related to computers but are not the correct answer.

181. **(A)** The memo is to offer discounted passes to staff members at the Smith Company. Choice (B) mentions the name of the transit company, but there is no information about discounts for its employees. Choices (C) and (D) are people who can get a regular transit pass, without a discount.

182. **(D)** James Jones, who works in the Smith Company Human Resources office, is the person who receives the forms requesting the discounted passes. Choices (A), (B), and (C) are places where regular passes are for sale.

183. **(A)** A regular six-month bus-only pass costs $500, so with the 50% discount it costs $250. Choice (B) is the cost of a discounted subway-only pass. Choice (C) is the cost of a discounted subway-bus pass. Choice (D) is the cost of a regular subway-bus pass.

184. **(C)** A discounted two-week subway-bus pass costs 50% of $75, or $37.50. Choice (A) costs $60. Choice (B) costs $45. Choice (D) costs $325.

185. **(C)** A pass holder gets a 25% discount on parking at a subway station. Choices (A) and (D) are confused with the size of the discount. Choice (B) is what it will cost to park in the Smith Company building garage starting next month.

186. **(A)** The memo is about buying new laptop computers to replace older ones that are not reliable. Choice (B) repeats the word *library*, but the library lends computers, not books. Choice (C) is incorrect because only laptop computers are mentioned. Choice (D) is not mentioned.

187. **(D)** Computer screens are not mentioned. Choices (A), (B), and (C) are all mentioned as problems with the computers.

188. **(A)** Dae is not sure whether it is safe to save data on her computer's hard drive. Choice (B) is incorrect because although Dae mentions saving data, she never says that there is not enough space to store it. Choice (C) is not mentioned. Choice (D) is incorrect because Dae's e-mail is all about the computer she has with her on a trip.

189. **(B)** The memo asks users to include the make of the computer when reporting problems. Choices (A) and (D) are mentioned in Dae's e-mail. Choice (C) is not required information.

190. **(B)** Dae is collecting contact information on her borrowed laptop, but the memo reminds staff not to save names, addresses, and phone numbers directly

on computers. Choices (A), (C), and (D) are not mentioned as things that staff are not allowed to do.

191. **(B)** *Next-day service* costs $50. Choice (A) is the charge per day for late payment of bills. Choice (C) was the charge for preparing Form 889. Choice (D) is the total amount that Angela Harris owes.

192. **(A)** The invoice says that the service provided was for *Declaration of identity for emergency travel.* Choice (B) repeats the phrase *emergency travel,* but there is no mention in the text of medical insurance. Choices (C) and (D) are related to traveling but are not mentioned.

193. **(D)** In her letter, Harris says that she is leaving in six weeks. Choice (A) is confused with the charge for one-day service. Choice (B) is confused with when Harris wants to hear back from the attorneys. Choice (C) is the amount of time she has to pay her bill.

194. **(A)** After visiting the lawyer's office, Harris went online and found that she could get the form for free. Choice (B) is incorrect because there was no charge for the photographs. Choice (C) isn't something she is complaining about. Choice (D) is not mentioned.

195. **(C)** Hubert is the only lawyer Harris doesn't mention. Choice (A) is the one she had her appointment with. Choice (B) is the one who signed her document and photographs. Choice (D) is the one who signed the invoice and to whom she addressed the letter.

196. **(C)** The notice is dated February 6 and the expiration date is March 18. Choices (A), (B), and (D) don't correspond with these dates.

197. **(B)** The renewal must be mailed in at least five days before the March 18 expiration date. Choice (A) is confused with the date of the notice. Choice (C) is the expiration date. Choice (D) is the date a new law goes into effect.

198. **(A)** A law that prohibits leniency with expired stickers and insurance goes into effect on April 1. Choices (B), (C), and (D) are all mentioned in the text, but there is no change mentioned about any of them.

199. **(C)** Watanabe's current insurance plan covers personal use of his car; if he wants to use his car differently, the notice says to call his insurance agent to discuss changing his insurance plan. Choice (A) is contradicted by the correct answer. Choice (B) is confused with the people who are affected by the new law. Choice (D) is necessary only every 10 years.

200. **(D)** New license plates are required every 10 years, and according to the form Watanabe doesn't need new plates yet. Choice (A) is not definite; Watanabe qualifies for the safe driver discount, but we don't know if this means he has never had an accident. Choice (B) is not definite because Watanabe's insurance covers using the car for work up to five days a month. Choice (C) is true of some insurance customers, but Watanabe is not one of them.

Answer Sheet

TOEIC PRACTICE TEST 6

Listening Comprehension

Part 1: Photographs

1. Ⓐ Ⓑ Ⓒ Ⓓ
2. Ⓐ Ⓑ Ⓒ Ⓓ
3. Ⓐ Ⓑ Ⓒ Ⓓ
4. Ⓐ Ⓑ Ⓒ Ⓓ
5. Ⓐ Ⓑ Ⓒ Ⓓ
6. Ⓐ Ⓑ Ⓒ Ⓓ
7. Ⓐ Ⓑ Ⓒ Ⓓ
8. Ⓐ Ⓑ Ⓒ Ⓓ
9. Ⓐ Ⓑ Ⓒ Ⓓ
10. Ⓐ Ⓑ Ⓒ Ⓓ

Part 2: Question-Response

11. Ⓐ Ⓑ Ⓒ
12. Ⓐ Ⓑ Ⓒ
13. Ⓐ Ⓑ Ⓒ
14. Ⓐ Ⓑ Ⓒ
15. Ⓐ Ⓑ Ⓒ
16. Ⓐ Ⓑ Ⓒ
17. Ⓐ Ⓑ Ⓒ
18. Ⓐ Ⓑ Ⓒ
19. Ⓐ Ⓑ Ⓒ
20. Ⓐ Ⓑ Ⓒ
21. Ⓐ Ⓑ Ⓒ
22. Ⓐ Ⓑ Ⓒ
23. Ⓐ Ⓑ Ⓒ
24. Ⓐ Ⓑ Ⓒ
25. Ⓐ Ⓑ Ⓒ
26. Ⓐ Ⓑ Ⓒ
27. Ⓐ Ⓑ Ⓒ
28. Ⓐ Ⓑ Ⓒ
29. Ⓐ Ⓑ Ⓒ
30. Ⓐ Ⓑ Ⓒ
31. Ⓐ Ⓑ Ⓒ
32. Ⓐ Ⓑ Ⓒ
33. Ⓐ Ⓑ Ⓒ
34. Ⓐ Ⓑ Ⓒ
35. Ⓐ Ⓑ Ⓒ
36. Ⓐ Ⓑ Ⓒ
37. Ⓐ Ⓑ Ⓒ
38. Ⓐ Ⓑ Ⓒ
39. Ⓐ Ⓑ Ⓒ
40. Ⓐ Ⓑ Ⓒ

Part 3: Conversations

41. Ⓐ Ⓑ Ⓒ Ⓓ
42. Ⓐ Ⓑ Ⓒ Ⓓ
43. Ⓐ Ⓑ Ⓒ Ⓓ
44. Ⓐ Ⓑ Ⓒ Ⓓ
45. Ⓐ Ⓑ Ⓒ Ⓓ
46. Ⓐ Ⓑ Ⓒ Ⓓ
47. Ⓐ Ⓑ Ⓒ Ⓓ
48. Ⓐ Ⓑ Ⓒ Ⓓ
49. Ⓐ Ⓑ Ⓒ Ⓓ
50. Ⓐ Ⓑ Ⓒ Ⓓ
51. Ⓐ Ⓑ Ⓒ Ⓓ
52. Ⓐ Ⓑ Ⓒ Ⓓ
53. Ⓐ Ⓑ Ⓒ Ⓓ
54. Ⓐ Ⓑ Ⓒ Ⓓ
55. Ⓐ Ⓑ Ⓒ Ⓓ
56. Ⓐ Ⓑ Ⓒ Ⓓ
57. Ⓐ Ⓑ Ⓒ Ⓓ
58. Ⓐ Ⓑ Ⓒ Ⓓ
59. Ⓐ Ⓑ Ⓒ Ⓓ
60. Ⓐ Ⓑ Ⓒ Ⓓ
61. Ⓐ Ⓑ Ⓒ Ⓓ
62. Ⓐ Ⓑ Ⓒ Ⓓ
63. Ⓐ Ⓑ Ⓒ Ⓓ
64. Ⓐ Ⓑ Ⓒ Ⓓ
65. Ⓐ Ⓑ Ⓒ Ⓓ
66. Ⓐ Ⓑ Ⓒ Ⓓ
67. Ⓐ Ⓑ Ⓒ Ⓓ
68. Ⓐ Ⓑ Ⓒ Ⓓ
69. Ⓐ Ⓑ Ⓒ Ⓓ
70. Ⓐ Ⓑ Ⓒ Ⓓ

Part 4: Talks

71. Ⓐ Ⓑ Ⓒ Ⓓ
72. Ⓐ Ⓑ Ⓒ Ⓓ
73. Ⓐ Ⓑ Ⓒ Ⓓ
74. Ⓐ Ⓑ Ⓒ Ⓓ
75. Ⓐ Ⓑ Ⓒ Ⓓ
76. Ⓐ Ⓑ Ⓒ Ⓓ
77. Ⓐ Ⓑ Ⓒ Ⓓ
78. Ⓐ Ⓑ Ⓒ Ⓓ
79. Ⓐ Ⓑ Ⓒ Ⓓ
80. Ⓐ Ⓑ Ⓒ Ⓓ
81. Ⓐ Ⓑ Ⓒ Ⓓ
82. Ⓐ Ⓑ Ⓒ Ⓓ
83. Ⓐ Ⓑ Ⓒ Ⓓ
84. Ⓐ Ⓑ Ⓒ Ⓓ
85. Ⓐ Ⓑ Ⓒ Ⓓ
86. Ⓐ Ⓑ Ⓒ Ⓓ
87. Ⓐ Ⓑ Ⓒ Ⓓ
88. Ⓐ Ⓑ Ⓒ Ⓓ
89. Ⓐ Ⓑ Ⓒ Ⓓ
90. Ⓐ Ⓑ Ⓒ Ⓓ
91. Ⓐ Ⓑ Ⓒ Ⓓ
92. Ⓐ Ⓑ Ⓒ Ⓓ
93. Ⓐ Ⓑ Ⓒ Ⓓ
94. Ⓐ Ⓑ Ⓒ Ⓓ
95. Ⓐ Ⓑ Ⓒ Ⓓ
96. Ⓐ Ⓑ Ⓒ Ⓓ
97. Ⓐ Ⓑ Ⓒ Ⓓ
98. Ⓐ Ⓑ Ⓒ Ⓓ
99. Ⓐ Ⓑ Ⓒ Ⓓ
100. Ⓐ Ⓑ Ⓒ Ⓓ

Answer Sheet
TOEIC PRACTICE TEST 6

Reading

Part 5: Incomplete Sentences

101. Ⓐ Ⓑ Ⓒ Ⓓ
102. Ⓐ Ⓑ Ⓒ Ⓓ
103. Ⓐ Ⓑ Ⓒ Ⓓ
104. Ⓐ Ⓑ Ⓒ Ⓓ
106. Ⓐ Ⓑ Ⓒ Ⓓ
107. Ⓐ Ⓑ Ⓒ Ⓓ
108. Ⓐ Ⓑ Ⓒ Ⓓ
109. Ⓐ Ⓑ Ⓒ Ⓓ
110. Ⓐ Ⓑ Ⓒ Ⓓ
111. Ⓐ Ⓑ Ⓒ Ⓓ

112. Ⓐ Ⓑ Ⓒ Ⓓ
113. Ⓐ Ⓑ Ⓒ Ⓓ
114. Ⓐ Ⓑ Ⓒ Ⓓ
115. Ⓐ Ⓑ Ⓒ Ⓓ
116. Ⓐ Ⓑ Ⓒ Ⓓ
117. Ⓐ Ⓑ Ⓒ Ⓓ
118. Ⓐ Ⓑ Ⓒ Ⓓ
119. Ⓐ Ⓑ Ⓒ Ⓓ
120. Ⓐ Ⓑ Ⓒ Ⓓ
121. Ⓐ Ⓑ Ⓒ Ⓓ

122. Ⓐ Ⓑ Ⓒ Ⓓ
123. Ⓐ Ⓑ Ⓒ Ⓓ
124. Ⓐ Ⓑ Ⓒ Ⓓ
125. Ⓐ Ⓑ Ⓒ Ⓓ
126. Ⓐ Ⓑ Ⓒ Ⓓ
127. Ⓐ Ⓑ Ⓒ Ⓓ
128. Ⓐ Ⓑ Ⓒ Ⓓ
129. Ⓐ Ⓑ Ⓒ Ⓓ
130. Ⓐ Ⓑ Ⓒ Ⓓ
131. Ⓐ Ⓑ Ⓒ Ⓓ

132. Ⓐ Ⓑ Ⓒ Ⓓ
133. Ⓐ Ⓑ Ⓒ Ⓓ
134. Ⓐ Ⓑ Ⓒ Ⓓ
135. Ⓐ Ⓑ Ⓒ Ⓓ
136. Ⓐ Ⓑ Ⓒ Ⓓ
137. Ⓐ Ⓑ Ⓒ Ⓓ
138. Ⓐ Ⓑ Ⓒ Ⓓ
139. Ⓐ Ⓑ Ⓒ Ⓓ
140. Ⓐ Ⓑ Ⓒ Ⓓ

Part 6: Text Completion

141. Ⓐ Ⓑ Ⓒ Ⓓ
142. Ⓐ Ⓑ Ⓒ Ⓓ
143. Ⓐ Ⓑ Ⓒ Ⓓ

144. Ⓐ Ⓑ Ⓒ Ⓓ
145. Ⓐ Ⓑ Ⓒ Ⓓ
146. Ⓐ Ⓑ Ⓒ Ⓓ

147. Ⓐ Ⓑ Ⓒ Ⓓ
148. Ⓐ Ⓑ Ⓒ Ⓓ
149. Ⓐ Ⓑ Ⓒ Ⓓ

150. Ⓐ Ⓑ Ⓒ Ⓓ
151. Ⓐ Ⓑ Ⓒ Ⓓ
152. Ⓐ Ⓑ Ⓒ Ⓓ

Part 7: Reading Comprehension

153. Ⓐ Ⓑ Ⓒ Ⓓ
154. Ⓐ Ⓑ Ⓒ Ⓓ
155. Ⓐ Ⓑ Ⓒ Ⓓ
156. Ⓐ Ⓑ Ⓒ Ⓓ
157. Ⓐ Ⓑ Ⓒ Ⓓ
158. Ⓐ Ⓑ Ⓒ Ⓓ
159. Ⓐ Ⓑ Ⓒ Ⓓ
160. Ⓐ Ⓑ Ⓒ Ⓓ
161. Ⓐ Ⓑ Ⓒ Ⓓ
162. Ⓐ Ⓑ Ⓒ Ⓓ
163. Ⓐ Ⓑ Ⓒ Ⓓ
164. Ⓐ Ⓑ Ⓒ Ⓓ
165. Ⓐ Ⓑ Ⓒ Ⓓ

166. Ⓐ Ⓑ Ⓒ Ⓓ
167. Ⓐ Ⓑ Ⓒ Ⓓ
168. Ⓐ Ⓑ Ⓒ Ⓓ
169. Ⓐ Ⓑ Ⓒ Ⓓ
170. Ⓐ Ⓑ Ⓒ Ⓓ
171. Ⓐ Ⓑ Ⓒ Ⓓ
172. Ⓐ Ⓑ Ⓒ Ⓓ
173. Ⓐ Ⓑ Ⓒ Ⓓ
174. Ⓐ Ⓑ Ⓒ Ⓓ
175. Ⓐ Ⓑ Ⓒ Ⓓ
176. Ⓐ Ⓑ Ⓒ Ⓓ
177. Ⓐ Ⓑ Ⓒ Ⓓ
178. Ⓐ Ⓑ Ⓒ Ⓓ

179. Ⓐ Ⓑ Ⓒ Ⓓ
180. Ⓐ Ⓑ Ⓒ Ⓓ
181. Ⓐ Ⓑ Ⓒ Ⓓ
182. Ⓐ Ⓑ Ⓒ Ⓓ
183. Ⓐ Ⓑ Ⓒ Ⓓ
184. Ⓐ Ⓑ Ⓒ Ⓓ
185. Ⓐ Ⓑ Ⓒ Ⓓ
186. Ⓐ Ⓑ Ⓒ Ⓓ
187. Ⓐ Ⓑ Ⓒ Ⓓ
188. Ⓐ Ⓑ Ⓒ Ⓓ
189. Ⓐ Ⓑ Ⓒ Ⓓ
190. Ⓐ Ⓑ Ⓒ Ⓓ
191. Ⓐ Ⓑ Ⓒ Ⓓ

192. Ⓐ Ⓑ Ⓒ Ⓓ
193. Ⓐ Ⓑ Ⓒ Ⓓ
194. Ⓐ Ⓑ Ⓒ Ⓓ
195. Ⓐ Ⓑ Ⓒ Ⓓ
196. Ⓐ Ⓑ Ⓒ Ⓓ
197. Ⓐ Ⓑ Ⓒ Ⓓ
198. Ⓐ Ⓑ Ⓒ Ⓓ
199. Ⓐ Ⓑ Ⓒ Ⓓ
200. Ⓐ Ⓑ Ⓒ Ⓓ

TOEIC Practice Test 6

LISTENING COMPREHENSION

In this section of the test, you will have the chance to show how well you understand spoken English. There are four parts to this section, with special directions for each part. You will find the Answer Sheet for Practice Test 6 on page 277. Detach it from the book and use it to record your answers. Check your answers using the Answer Key on page 314 and see the Answers Explained on page 316.

TIP

If you do not have access to an audio CD player, please refer to the audio-scripts starting on page 333 when prompted to listen to an audio passage.

CD 4
TRACK 3

Part 1: Photographs

Directions: You will see a photograph. You will hear four statements about the photograph. Choose the statement that most closely matches the photograph and fill in the corresponding oval on your answer sheet.

Example

Now listen to the four statements.

Sample Answer

Ⓐ Ⓑ Ⓒ Ⓓ

Statement (B), "She's reading a magazine," best describes what you see in the picture. Therefore, you should choose answer (B).

TOEIC Practice Test 6

1.

2.

3.

4.

5.

6.

7.

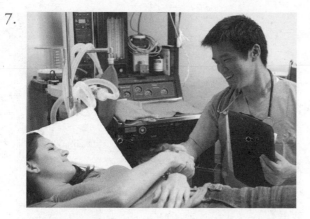

8.

9.

10.

Part 2: Question-Response

Directions: You will hear a question and three possible responses. Choose the response that most closely answers the question and fill in the corresponding oval on your answer sheet.

Example

Now listen to the sample question.

You will hear:

How is the weather?

You will also hear:

(A) It's raining.
(B) He's fine, thanks.
(C) He's my boss.

The best response to the question *How is the weather?* is choice (A), *It's raining.* Therefore, you should choose answer (A).

11. Mark your answer on your answer sheet.

12. Mark your answer on your answer sheet.

13. Mark your answer on your answer sheet.

14. Mark your answer on your answer sheet.

15. Mark your answer on your answer sheet.

16. Mark your answer on your answer sheet.

17. Mark your answer on your answer sheet.

18. Mark your answer on your answer sheet.

19. Mark your answer on your answer sheet.

20. Mark your answer on your answer sheet.

21. Mark your answer on your answer sheet.

22. Mark your answer on your answer sheet.

23. Mark your answer on your answer sheet.

24. Mark your answer on your answer sheet.

25. Mark your answer on your answer sheet.

26. Mark your answer on your answer sheet.

27. Mark your answer on your answer sheet.

28. Mark your answer on your answer sheet.

29. Mark your answer on your answer sheet.

30. Mark your answer on your answer sheet.

31. Mark your answer on your answer sheet.

32. Mark your answer on your answer sheet.

33. Mark your answer on your answer sheet.

34. Mark your answer on your answer sheet.

35. Mark your answer on your answer sheet.

36. Mark your answer on your answer sheet.

37. Mark your answer on your answer sheet.

38. Mark your answer on your answer sheet.

39. Mark your answer on your answer sheet.

40. Mark your answer on your answer sheet.

TOEIC Practice Test 6

Part 3: Conversations

Directions: You will hear a conversation between two people. You will see three questions on each conversation and four possible answers. Choose the best answer to each question and fill in the corresponding oval on your answer sheet.

41. What is the man's room number?
    (A) 57
    (B) 74
    (C) 574
    (D) 754

42. What does the man want to eat?
    (A) Cake
    (B) Steak
    (C) Fish
    (D) Rice

43. How will he pay for his meal?
    (A) He will pay cash.
    (B) The woman will take a check.
    (C) He will use a money order.
    (D) It will be charged to his room.

44. How is the man traveling?
    (A) By bus
    (B) By train
    (C) By plane
    (D) By subway

45. Which gate will he leave from?
    (A) 4
    (B) 20
    (C) 24
    (D) 30

46. Where is the gate?
    (A) Next to the café
    (B) Near the newsstand
    (C) Across from the bank
    (D) Next to the bandstand

47. What is the problem?
    (A) The man is tired.
    (B) The woman feels sick.
    (C) They have a flat tire.
    (D) They forgot the date.

48. What time is it now?
    (A) 5:00
    (B) 5:30
    (C) 6:30
    (D) 7:00

49. What is the woman going to do right now?
    (A) Have dinner
    (B) Make a phone call
    (C) Look in her briefcase
    (D) Cancel her appointment

50. What time is the woman's appointment?
    (A) Noon
    (B) 1:00
    (C) 3:00
    (D) 8:00

51. How will she get to her appointment?
    (A) Walk
    (B) Train
    (C) Bus
    (D) Cab

52. How is the weather now?
    (A) Rain
    (B) Sun
    (C) Snow
    (D) Hail

53. What is the problem?
    (A) The supplies are the wrong size.
    (B) The supplies weren't paid for.
    (C) The supplies haven't arrived.
    (D) The supplies are always late.

54. What supplies were ordered?
    (A) Paper and ink
    (B) Computers
    (C) Printers
    (D) Drinks

55. When will the woman call the supplier again?
    (A) This morning
    (B) At 5:00 today
    (C) Tomorrow morning
    (D) On Wednesday

56. What will the woman do by 5:00?
    (A) Finish her work
    (B) Take a walk
    (C) Take a break
    (D) Make a sandwich

57. Where will the woman eat lunch?
    (A) At a sandwich shop
    (B) At the cafeteria
    (C) At her desk
    (D) At home

58. What does the man offer to do for the woman?
    (A) Take her to the hospital
    (B) Bring her some food
    (C) Help her with her work
    (D) Drive her home

59. When did the man move into his new office?
    (A) Sunday
    (B) Monday
    (C) Wednesday
    (D) Friday

60. Why is it better than his old office?
    (A) It is bigger.
    (B) It isn't as cold.
    (C) It's closer to his boss.
    (D) It is lighter.

61. Where is the new office?
    (A) In the basement
    (B) Next to the parking lot
    (C) Close to the health club
    (D) Near the park

62. Where does this conversation take place?
    (A) At a museum
    (B) At a map store
    (C) At an art school
    (D) At a travel agency

63. What does the woman give the man?
    (A) An exhibit
    (B) A brochure
    (C) A painting
    (D) A tour

64. How much does the man have to pay for it?
    (A) $0
    (B) $3.00
    (C) $4.00
    (D) $33.00

65. What day does the man have off work?
    (A) Friday
    (B) Saturday
    (C) Sunday
    (D) Monday

66. What does the man want to do on his day off?
    (A) See a movie
    (B) Walk in the park
    (C) Go to a concert
    (D) Take a rest

67. Why doesn't the man want to eat at the restaurant?
    (A) It's too dark.
    (B) He prefers to stay home.
    (C) It's outdoors.
    (D) He's trying to lose weight.

68. When does the tour start?
    (A) In 10 minutes
    (B) In 15 minutes
    (C) At 4:00
    (D) At 9:00

69. What will the tour members do first?
    (A) Visit the museum
    (B) See the plaza
    (C) Go inside the houses
    (D) Park the bus

70. What does the man want to look at in the houses?
    (A) The art
    (B) The clothes
    (C) The gardens
    (D) The architecture

Part 4: Talks

Directions: You will hear a talk given by a single speaker. You will see three questions on each talk, each with four possible answers. Choose the best answer to each question and fill in the corresponding oval on your answer sheet.

71. Where would you hear this message?
    (A) At a store
    (B) At a bank
    (C) At an accountant's office
    (D) At a telephone company

72. How can you hear information about your account?
    (A) Press 1
    (B) Press your account number
    (C) Dial an extension number
    (D) Stay on the line

73. What happens if you press 2?
    (A) You will speak to a customer service representative.
    (B) You can leave a message for a staff member.
    (C) You can find out an extension number.
    (D) You will hear about the services offered by the company.

74. What has this study found?
    (A) Secretaries are more efficient than managers.
    (B) Managers are more efficient than secretaries.
    (C) Secretaries ask managers for help.
    (D) Secretaries do too much work.

75. What do managers say?
    (A) Their secretaries are hardworking.
    (B) Secretaries take more time off.
    (C) Secretaries ease a manager's workload.
    (D) Secretaries have more work.

76. How many people participated in the study?
    (A) 75
    (B) 100
    (C) 250
    (D) 350

77. What is the fastest way to order over the phone?
    (A) Look through the catalog
    (B) Fill out the order form
    (C) Give the item number
    (D) Give the page number

78. What else is needed to complete the order?
    (A) A money order
    (B) A check
    (C) Cash
    (D) A credit card

79. How long will the caller have to wait to place an order?
    (A) 6 minutes
    (B) 8 minutes
    (C) 15 minutes
    (D) 16 minutes

80. Which of the following jobs is NOT advertised?
    (A) Cook
    (B) Waiter
    (C) Dishwasher
    (D) Hostess

81. What sort of experience should applicants have?
    (A) Experience with the public
    (B) Sales experience
    (C) Experience in food service
    (D) Grocery store experience

82. When is a good time to call to apply for a job?
    (A) Monday morning
    (B) Friday night
    (C) Saturday afternoon
    (D) Sunday morning

83. What weather condition will develop by noon?
    (A) Rain
    (B) Snow
    (C) Sleet
    (D) Ice

84. What problem can drivers expect tonight?
    (A) Icy roads
    (B) Wet roads
    (C) Low visibility
    (D) Frozen engines

85. When will there be another storm?
    (A) Tomorrow
    (B) In two days
    (C) On Sunday
    (D) On Monday

86. Where would you hear this announcement?
    (A) On an airplane
    (B) On a bus
    (C) On a train
    (D) On a ship

87. Where will the passengers get off?
    (A) Gate 5
    (B) Gate 9
    (C) Gate 15
    (D) Gate 29

88. What should passengers do to prepare?
    (A) Pack their bags
    (B) Secure their luggage
    (C) Change their seats
    (D) Get out their tickets

89. Why should you go to this store?
    (A) The prices are low.
    (B) The quality is high.
    (C) The store is nearby.
    (D) They're having a sale.

90. What can you do if you need help?
    (A) Wait in line
    (B) Consult a design specialist
    (C) Come back next week
    (D) Read a book

91. How long does it take for an order to be ready?
    (A) One day
    (B) Three days
    (C) One week
    (D) Three weeks

92. What is wrong at the station?
    (A) The elevator is broken.
    (B) The escalator isn't working.
    (C) The stairs are closed.
    (D) The exits are blocked.

93. How has the problem been solved for passengers in need?
    (A) They can get a wheelchair.
    (B) They can take a taxi.
    (C) They can take a bus.
    (D) They can get a refund.

94. What does the announcer do at the end of the statement?
    (A) Thanks the passengers
    (B) Apologizes to the passengers
    (C) Warns the passengers
    (D) Advises the passengers

95. Why is there a high demand for electric
    power?
    (A) The weather is extremely hot.
    (B) The weather is colder than usual.
    (C) More people are using appliances.
    (D) Residents are staying in their houses.

96. What is the public asked to do?
    (A) Use less electricity
    (B) Take food to the poor
    (C) Avoid the cold
    (D) Produce their own power

97. What temperature should residents keep
    their houses at?
    (A) 15 degrees
    (B) 16 degrees
    (C) 50 degrees
    (D) 60 degrees

98. When will the new restaurant have its
    grand opening?
    (A) Tuesday
    (B) Friday
    (C) Saturday
    (D) Sunday

99. What kind of food is served at the
    restaurant?
    (A) Pizza
    (B) Pastry
    (C) Rice dishes
    (D) Veal

100. Who gets a discount?
     (A) Children
     (B) Older adults
     (C) Lunchtime customers
     (D) All local citizens

READING

In this section of the test, you will have the chance to show how well you understand written English. There are three parts to this section, with special directions for each part.

**YOU WILL HAVE ONE HOUR AND FIFTEEN MINUTES
TO COMPLETE PARTS 5, 6, AND 7 OF THE TEST.**

Part 5: Incomplete Sentences

Directions: You will see a sentence with a missing word. Four possible answers follow the sentence. Choose the best answer to the question and fill in the corresponding oval on your answer sheet.

101. The price of all cruises _____ airfare and all transfers.
  (A) have included
  (B) includes
  (C) are including
  (D) include

102. Mr. Brett missed the plane _____ he was working late.
  (A) before
  (B) until
  (C) because
  (D) and

103. Many customers have requested that we _____ them notice of our sales.
  (A) send
  (B) sends
  (C) sent
  (D) sending

104. The workers were loading the truck when the boxes _____.
  (A) have fallen
  (B) fall
  (C) fell
  (D) are falling

105. The new manager, _____ was just hired, will start tomorrow.
  (A) she
  (B) he
  (C) which
  (D) who

106. Mr. Kumar_____ if he had been delayed.
  (A) would call
  (B) would have called
  (C) will be calling
  (D) will calling

107. Our _____ are trying to hire our best employees.
  (A) competition
  (B) competitive
  (C) competitors
  (D) competitively

108. Of all our tour ships, this one is our _____.
  (A) more bigger
  (B) big
  (C) bigger
  (D) biggest

109. The purser got his assistant _____ the passenger orientation.
    (A) conducting
    (B) to conduct
    (C) conducted
    (D) conducts

110. All travel arrangements must be completed _____ December 5.
    (A) with
    (B) in
    (C) for
    (D) by

111. The bookcase is _____ the door.
    (A) beside
    (B) among
    (C) between
    (D) across

112. Ms. Mosley is _____ member of our advertising team.
    (A) creative
    (B) most creative
    (C) more creative
    (D) the most creative

113. Meetings are scheduled _____ in the first-floor auditorium.
    (A) always
    (B) sometimes
    (C) rarely
    (D) every month

114. _____ 5:00, the subway becomes very crowded.
    (A) When
    (B) After
    (C) Since
    (D) While

115. The airport was _____ Mr. Debionne had expected.
    (A) the busiest
    (B) busier than
    (C) busy as
    (D) as busy

116. A good chef is always ready to _____ recipes.
    (A) adapt
    (B) adoption
    (C) adept
    (D) adjourn

117. The personnel director screened the job applicants_____ arranging interviews.
    (A) because
    (B) until
    (C) since
    (D) before

118. The board of directors will meet _____ October 10.
    (A) for
    (B) to
    (C) on
    (D) in

119. Ms. Nyen was giving her speech when the microphone _____.
    (A) is failing
    (B) fails
    (C) had failed
    (D) failed

120. The clerk _____ the computer manual from the secretary.
    (A) lent
    (B) to loan
    (C) loaned
    (D) borrowed

121. The status report _____ the financial projections were both late.
(A) or
(B) and
(C) but
(D) nor

122. A firm will not _____ if its employees are unhappy.
(A) prosper
(B) prosperous
(C) prosperity
(D) prospering

123. The intern _____ a fax machine before coming to work at our office.
(A) had used never
(B) had never used
(C) never had used
(D) used had never

124. If there _____ some restaurants near the hotel, we would not have to spend time and money on taxis.
(A) were
(B) was
(C) will
(D) would be

125. The Mid America Airlines flight _____ Phoenix will be arriving at Gate 9 in five minutes.
(A) from
(B) in
(C) by
(D) on

126. Every morning, a member of the kitchen staff turns on the ovens and _____ the coffee.
(A) brewing
(B) has brewed
(C) brews
(D) brewed

127. The _____ speech made the audience restless.
(A) boring
(B) bored
(C) bores
(D) bore

128. This year the annual meeting takes place _____ Toronto.
(A) on
(B) for
(C) by
(D) in

129. _____ we were late, we could not enter the conference hall.
(A) Although
(B) Because
(C) Therefore
(D) However

130. If the traffic is bad, _____ a bus.
(A) take
(B) takes
(C) taking
(D) will take

131. There is not much agriculture in this area because the _____ yearly rainfall is so low.
(A) available
(B) avenging
(C) avaricious
(D) average

132. Please use the parking spaces that _____ for visitors.
(A) designates
(B) designated
(C) are designating
(D) have been designated

133. Participants _____ fly to the convention can get a group rate.
(A) they
(B) who
(C) which
(D) whom

134. The department requires someone with _____ in international law.
(A) exploration
(B) experience
(C) explanation
(D) expectancy

135. If the smoke alarm rings, _____ the building quickly.
(A) leaves
(B) will leave
(C) is leaving
(D) leave

136. Pens and stationery _____ kept in the top drawer.
(A) are
(B) is
(C) was
(D) am

137. The chief engineer is knowledgeable and _____.
(A) industrious
(B) industry
(C) industrial
(D) industries

138. Ms. Neil _____ the general manager of the hotel since 2004.
(A) is
(B) has been
(C) had been
(D) had

139. We read about Mr. Moriwaki's promotion _____ the company newsletter.
(A) in
(B) of
(C) on
(D) to

140. Mr. Ross promised _____ the charts before tomorrow's staff meeting.
(A) to prepare
(B) preparing
(C) prepare
(D) prepared

Part 6: Text Completion

Directions: You will see four passages, each with three blanks. Under each blank are four answer options. Choose the word or phrase that best completes the statement.

Questions 141–143 refer to the following memorandum.

From: Karin O'Flaherty, Program Coordinator
To: Indira Singh
Re: Program procedures

Welcome to our school! We look forward to a successful year.
Please _____ the following rules.

141. (A) revise
    (B) review
    (C) revert
    (D) revenge

Computer Lab: The lab is in Room 107. Thirty computers are available for the use of our students and teachers. If you plan to take your class to the lab, you must let the lab coordinator know ahead of time. To make sure you get the time slot you want, reserve your lab time at least one week _____.

142. (A) succeeding
    (B) subsequent
    (C) in advance
    (D) in the syllabus

Copying: We have student assistants available to do all of your copying. Just place your papers in the "copying" box in the main office one day ahead of time. If you want to make copies yourself, you can use the machine in Room 110.

Food: _____ in the classrooms is strictly prohibited. Please use the

143. (A) Eat
    (B) Eaten
    (C) Eating
    (D) To eat

teacher's room, or you may eat in the cafeteria with the students.

Daily Schedule: Please plan to arrive at your classroom in the morning before 8:00. You may leave any time after 3:00.
Let me know if you have any questions.

Questions 144–146 refer to the following e-mail.

From: Theresa Schultz [Theresa@bbsb.com]
To: Daniel Lee [Dan@bbsb.com]
Subject: Lunch arrangements

I will be having a business lunch with Ms. Yu and Mr. Bao tomorrow. Please call the Fountainhead Restaurant and make reservations for three. _____ a table near the fountain. Anytime between

144. (A) Require
(B) Request
(C) Requisite
(D) Requisition

noon and two is fine.

_____ you have made the arrangements, please call Ms. Yu

145. (A) During
(B) Prior to
(C) As soon as
(D) Meantime

and Mr. Bao and let them know the time and place. Also, remind them to bring their copies of the annual report, as I plan to go over it with them during lunch.

I'll be back from my trip late tonight. I'd like you to type up the notes from my trip tomorrow morning, if possible. My supervisor would like to see them before next week's board meeting, so I want to hand them _____ before the end of the week.

146. (A) in
(B) on
(C) to
(D) out

Thanks for everything.

Questions 147–149 refer to the following notice.

SHOPPERS' WORLD

Returned Items Policy

We must receive returned items within 30 days of the date of purchase. Please make sure that the receipt is included and check that the price tags are still attached. Items may _____ for cash or store credit.

       147. (A) return
                (B) returning
                (C) be returned
                (D) be returning

If the customer _____ the receipt but the price tags are still

       148. (A) had lost
                (B) has lost
                (C) will lose
                (D) is losing

attached and the item is in good condition, you may offer the customer store credit only. Items that are damaged or dirtied in any way or that have missing price tags cannot be returned.

If you have any questions _____ this policy or if you need help

       149. (A) regarding
                (B) answering
                (C) disagreeing
                (D) following

processing a return, please contact your supervisor.

Questions 150–152 refer to the following notice.

Dr. I. M. Lee, world-renowned _____ on international economics,

150. (A) expert
(B) experiment
(C) experience
(D) expeller

will be reading from his newest book, *Money in the New Millenium*, at the Central Bookstore on Wednesday, October 14. Dr. Lee has recently returned from a tour of Asia, _____ he met with leading regional economic

151. (A) who
(B) whom
(C) which
(D) where

experts. After his reading, he will share highlights from his trip and discuss Asia's role in the new world economy. *Money in the New Millenium* and other titles by Dr. Lee will be on sale after his talk, and Dr. Lee will be available to sign the books. _____ to this event is free, but early arrival is

152. (A) Admit
(B) Admitted
(C) Admission
(D) Admissible

recommended in order to secure a seat.

Part 7: Reading Comprehension

Directions: You will see single and double reading passages followed by several questions. Each question has four answer choices. Choose the best answer to the question and fill in the corresponding oval on your answer sheet.

Questions 153–154 refer to the following form.

MOVING?

Fill out this card and mail it to the businesses and publications who send you mail.
For best results, mail this card at least one month before your moving date.

Date _____ *April 12* _____

Your Name _____ *John Carpenter* _____

Old Address _____ *268 Monroe Highway* _____
(Number and Street)

Salem, _____ *South Carolina* _____ *29702* _____
(City)   (State)   (Zip Code)

New Address _____ *764 Alston Street* _____
(Number and Street)

Columbia, _____ *South Carolina* _____ *29805* _____
(City)   (State)   (Zip Code)

New address is effective _____ *immediately* _____

---

153. What is the purpose of this form?
    (A) To apply for a new address
    (B) To notify businesses of an address change
    (C) To order a publication
    (D) To find the location of a business

154. When is the form effective?
    (A) March 12
    (B) April 12
    (C) May 12
    (D) In 12 days

Questions 155–156 refer to the following advertisement.

155. What is offered at no charge?
    (A) A TV
    (B) A purse
    (C) A dictionary
    (D) A language textbook

156. How can you get this item?
    (A) Take a class
    (B) Visit a store
    (C) Watch a TV show
    (D) Buy a language program

Questions 157–159 refer to the following announcement.

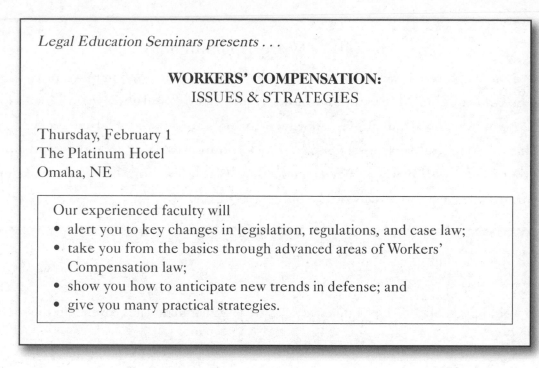

Legal Education Seminars presents . . .

WORKERS' COMPENSATION:
ISSUES & STRATEGIES

Thursday, February 1
The Platinum Hotel
Omaha, NE

Our experienced faculty will
- alert you to key changes in legislation, regulations, and case law;
- take you from the basics through advanced areas of Workers' Compensation law;
- show you how to anticipate new trends in defense; and
- give you many practical strategies.

157. Who would be likely to attend this seminar?
(A) Workers
(B) Legislators
(C) Lawyers
(D) Doctors

158. What will be taught?
(A) Information about payment to injured workers
(B) How employment and hiring laws are made
(C) How to strategize to keep employees healthy
(D) Ways to communicate with employees

159. What else can you learn?
(A) Arguments being used by the defense
(B) How to influence the law
(C) How to advance your career
(D) Where to practice your new skills

Questions 160–161 refer to the following advertisement.

The Office Writer's Handbook

is a necessary reference work for anyone who has to write for business purposes. It states the rules of English grammar accurately and clearly, and shows you how to apply them to your writing. It also gives approved formats for business letters, reports, and even charts. A special section covers the most common writing mistakes and how to avoid them. *The Office Writer's Handbook* is available in most bookstores, or order yours online at www.referenceworks.com.

---

160. Who would probably NOT be interested in this book?
    (A) Students
    (B) Legal assistants
    (C) Hotel managers
    (D) Airline executives

161. What material is covered in the special section?
    (A) Sample charts
    (B) Writing formats
    (C) Business letters
    (D) Common mistakes

Questions 162–164 refer to the following letter.

GARDENS BY HOK
P.O. Box 687
1103 Lisbon, Portugal

September 8, 20--

Guy Williams
Landscape Design Magazine
Ottho Heldringstraat 2
1066 AZ Amsterdam
The Netherlands

Dear Mr. Williams,

Thank you for sending the advertising information we requested. After careful consideration, we have decided not to place an ad in the December issue. Because of the nature of our business, we generally spend more of our advertising dollars during the warmer months of the year. We will probably, however, want to advertise with you in your next issue in March in anticipation of the spring rush. We will be in touch with you closer to that time to discuss pricing, placement, etc. Thank you for your assistance.

Sincerely yours,

Sov Hok

162. What is Sov Hok's business?
(A) Magazine publication
(B) Garden design
(C) Advertising
(D) Magazine sales

163. Why did Mr. Hok write this letter?
(A) To find out about magazine subscriptions
(B) To ask for a job
(C) To discuss placing an ad
(D) To ask about pricing

164. How often does *Landscape Design Magazine* come out?
(A) Weekly
(B) Monthly
(C) Bi-monthly
(D) Quarterly

Questions 165–168 refer to the following report.

Food products account for the largest portion of our agricultural exports, although it is traditionally thought that pesticides and other agricultural chemicals are in the lead. The value of food product exports has increased in recent years, with the increased interest among consumers in more exotic food products. Our growers have responded to the demand, and we have established one million hectares as a special development region for these products. Our low nighttime temperatures, combined with the fact that we have little rain and plenty of sun during the daytime, gives us a competitive edge over growers in other regions.

Our exports of native tropical fruits and root vegetables have increased from less than 2% to more than 5% of total agricultural exports in the past two years, and growth is expected to continue. But we continue to anticipate new food trends and will be ready to respond as the market changes.

165. What is exported the most?
(A) Pesticides
(B) Fibers
(C) Foods
(D) Chemicals

166. Why has the value of food product exports increased?
(A) Increased interest in unfamiliar foods
(B) Drought in other countries
(C) Higher prices
(D) More affluent consumers

167. What trend is expected to continue?
(A) Regulations on agricultural exports
(B) High demand for exotic fruits and vegetables
(C) High prices for foods
(D) Desire to produce more

168. The word *anticipate* in paragraph 2, line 4, is closest in meaning to
(A) fear.
(B) enjoy.
(C) expect.
(D) develop.

Questions 169–172 refer to the following magazine article.

Business travelers usually find that they have little time to exercise, especially when their schedules are suddenly changed by late meetings or late flights. But everyone should get some exercise. There are ways to make exercise part of your day even when you cannot make it to the hotel's exercise room. Experts suggest stretching your neck, arms, back, and shoulders while sitting in your airplane seat. At your hotel, you can stretch your legs and abdominal muscles. Then you can run in place for a good aerobic workout.

Exercise is not just for your body. It is for your mind as well. The mind-body connection has long been established by professional medical associations. People who exercise regularly perform more efficiently at work and perform more effectively than their colleagues who don't exercise. So to get ahead of everyone else, try to exercise every day, even when traveling.

169. Who is this article for?
(A) Overweight people
(B) Frequent vacationers
(C) Business travelers
(D) Pilots and flight attendants

170. Why is it difficult for travelers to get exercise?
(A) Their schedules change unexpectedly
(B) They work too hard
(C) There are no places to exercise
(D) They don't want to exercise

171. Where can travelers exercise?
(A) At meetings
(B) In an airplane seat
(C) In a car
(D) In the hotel lobby

172. According to the article, what is a benefit of exercise?
(A) Improved work performance
(B) Weight loss
(C) Feeling younger
(D) Better relationships with colleagues

Questions 173–177 refer to the following fax.

FAX TRANSMISSION

Kleanit
Bravo Murillo, 320
Portal 4-20
28020 Madrid
Spain

Dear fellow computer user,

A word of advice: It's time to clean out your computer. If you're like me, you don't remove documents that are no longer necessary. You never know when you may need a file so you don't throw it away, right? E-mail messages pile up, too, creating a huge warehouse of obscure file names.

I found that a simple software package called Kleanit gets rid of everything I don't need and keeps the things I do. I was so impressed with this package that I decided to share it with others.

No longer do those bothersome extra messages and computer files waste processing time and cause my computer to perform inefficiently. Kleanit makes sure that the only files in my computer are files that relate to my current projects or routine tasks.

Why don't you try it? I'll send you a trial copy and if you aren't satisfied, you can send it back. If you are as impressed as I am, and you will be, send your check for $32.50 at your earliest convenience.

Have a nice day

Robert Horstma
CEO

---

173. According to the fax, what prompted Mr. Horstma to sell Kleanit?
(A) His e-mail responses
(B) His poor computer skills
(C) His need for money
(D) His satisfaction with the product

174. What suggestion is made in his fax?
(A) To buy new computers
(B) To send less mail
(C) To print out documents
(D) To purchase new software

175. The word *obscure* in paragraph 1, line 3, is closest in meaning to
(A) useful.
(B) unclear.
(C) unusual.
(D) understood.

176. According to the fax, what effect does clutter have on a computer?
(A) It operates slowly.
(B) It runs out of space.
(C) It stops working.
(D) It erases files.

177. Which documents does the software leave
     in your computer?
     (A) Duplicate files
     (B) Current and routine files
     (C) Files from last year
     (D) Files others have sent you

Questions 178–180 refer to the following introduction.

Darla K. Wise received her BA degree from Arizona State University in 1980 and her Doctorate of Jurisprudence from Harvard University in 1987.

She represented self-insured employers in central New York for five years before joining the law firm of Corman, Hagan, Wallis and White, where she has been a principal since 1990. Her practice emphasizes the representation of corporate interests in libel suits.

Ms. Wise is a member of the New York Bar Association and the New York Trial Lawyers Association.

The continuing education foundation of the New York Bar Association is pleased to have Ms. Wise speak to us today.

178. What is Ms. Wise's profession?
     (A) Lawyer
     (B) University professor
     (C) School principal
     (D) Bar and restaurant manager

179. What is her highest educational degree?
     (A) Associate's degree
     (B) Bachelor's degree
     (C) Master's degree
     (D) Doctoral degree

180. What is she doing today?
     (A) Taking the bar exam
     (B) Giving a talk
     (C) Buying a suit
     (D) Assisting at a trial

Questions 181–185 refer to the following advertisement and e-mail.

GENERAL HOSPITAL
UPCOMING WORKSHOPS

October 8   Keep Your Heart Healthy
October 10   Walk for Fitness
October 12   Delicious Low-Calorie Meals*

Workshops are free unless otherwise noted. All workshops are held from 10:00 AM until noon in Conference Room A. We welcome people ages 15 and up. Advance registration is recommended. E-mail *workshops@gh.com* to register. There is a $3 fee for same-day registration, which is permitted on a space-available basis.

For the October 10 workshop, wear comfortable shoes. For all of the workshops, bring extra money if you would like to purchase any items. We will sell cookbooks, tapes, and DVDs.

*This workshop has a $10 materials fee to cover the cost of ingredients. Participants will cook and eat a three-course meal.

From:	Mona Cappadona [Mona@gh.com]
To:	Khalid Mahmod [Khalid@gh.com]
Subject:	Report on October Workshops

The October workshops were very successful. All together 65 people attended. Fifteen people participated in Keep Your Heart Healthy, twice that number participated in Walk for Fitness, and 22 people showed up for Delicious Low-Calorie Meals. We collected $60 in same-day registration fees.

I recommend that we offer these workshops again in January with a few minor changes. First, we need to increase the Meals workshop fee by $2. The fee we charged this last time didn't quite cover the cost of the ingredients. Second, we should provide a telephone number in our advertisement. Some people don't have e-mail. Third, we need to improve our scheduling. Someone scheduled our group and another group in the same room at the same time, and we had to move the October 8 workshop to Room C. Fortunately, it was available. The Meals workshop should meet in the kitchen.

The October 10 workshop was very popular. I would like to offer a workshop on the same topic, but for children ages 5–14. Are you available on Friday morning to discuss this?

181. How much would it cost to take the Keep Your Heart Healthy class if you registered on October 5?
(A) $0
(B) $3
(C) $15
(D) $60

182. What can you buy at a workshop?
(A) Exercise clothes
(B) Adhesive tape
(C) Recipes
(D) Shoes

183. How many people paid the same-day registration fee?
(A) 20
(B) 22
(C) 60
(D) 65

184. What will be the new fee for the Delicious Low-Calorie Meals workshop?
(A) $2
(B) $10
(C) $12
(D) $20

185. What workshop will be offered for children?
(A) Keep Your Heart Healthy
(B) Walk for Fitness
(C) Delicious Low-Calorie Meals
(D) Delicious Meals for Children

TOEIC Practice Test 6

Questions 186–190 refer to the following bulletin and e-mail.

We are starting an Internship Program in Information Technology. We will offer 10 internships for undergraduate and graduate students as well as for recent graduates who have finished their degrees within the last 12 months. All of the interns will receive an hourly salary plus a bonus at the end of the internship.

The first internships will begin on June 1. They will last for a minimum of two months.

Every intern will work on projects with a supervisor. These projects include Networking, Business Software, and Computer Maintenance—Crash Prevention. Applicants who speak a second language are encouraged to apply and will be assigned to our special Global Communications project.

First preference will be given to employees' children and relatives. The application deadline is April 15. Write to interns@excel.com to learn more about the internships and to request an application.

From:	Jon Samuels [Jon@gomail.com]
To:	Excel Company [interns@excel.com]
Sent:	Friday, April 1, 20-- 1:29 PM
Subject:	Application for Internship Program

I would like to learn more about the Internship Program in Information Technology. My mother, who works as an electrical engineer at your company, told me about this opportunity.

I am a junior at National University. Although my major is business administration, I am also interested in information technology and am considering studying this subject in graduate school. Can business majors apply for the internship?

I will be leaving for a trip to Korea in May to visit relatives and brush up on my second language, Korean. I won't return from my trip until four days after the first internships begin. Could I start my internship then? I can work until the beginning of September.

If I qualify for the internship, please send me an application as soon as possible, as well as any other information I may need.

Thank you.

186. What qualification docs Jon have that will give him preference over other applicants?
(A) His mother works for the company.
(B) He is majoring in business administration.
(C) He speaks Korean.
(D) He took classes in electrical engineering.

187. How long does Jon have to complete his application?
(A) 2 weeks
(B) 3 weeks
(C) 2 months
(D) 12 months

188. What does Jon want to study in graduate school?
(A) Business administration
(B) Information technology
(C) Communications
(D) Korean language

189. What project will Jon probably be assigned to work on?
(A) Networking
(B) Business Software
(C) Computer Maintenance
(D) Global Communications

190. When does Jon want to start his internship?
(A) May 1
(B) June 1
(C) June 5
(D) September 4

Questions 191–195 refer to the following fax and phone message.

FAX COVER SHEET

Moon Computer Supplies
NO. 110-9 Zhongshan Road
Xindian City 608
Taipei, Taiwan

Tel: (886) 2-7668-9506
Fax: (886) 2-7668-9507

To: Angie Shan
From: Jamie Wu, Account Representative
Date: April 12, 20--
Pages: 1
Ref: order confirmation

Message:
Angie, we shipped your items a few days ago. You should receive them by April 14. We had to divide the shipment into two boxes, but they both should arrive the same day. The items shipped are as follows:

Item 1 2 LCD Monitors
Item 2 1 PC Case, Black
Item 3 5 Keyboards, Ivory
Item 4 4 200 GB Hard Drives
Item 5 8 Headphones

Please contact us if you have any questions. I will be out on a business trip, but you can communicate with my assistant, Marcia. You know her.

DATE   April 17, 20--

TIME   11:07 AM ✔____ PM ____

FOR   Ms. Lee
RECEIVED BY   Wei

CALLER   Angie
PHONE NUMBER   2-7684-3267

MESSAGE There is a problem with her order. She received items 1, 2, and 4, but they arrived two days after the expected date. The other items have not arrived. The PC case received is the wrong color; she ordered blue. The hard drives are also not as she ordered them. They are 100 GB less than she wanted. These problems need to be fixed immediately. Please call her today.

CALL BACK REQUESTED?   YES ✔____   NO ____

DATE/TIME COMPLETED   ____/____/____

                       ____ : ____ AM ____ PM ____

191. What is Ms. Lee's first name?
(A) Jamie
(B) Angie
(C) Marcia
(D) Wei

192. When did the first box arrive?
(A) April 12
(B) April 14
(C) April 16
(D) April 17

193. Which of the following items has Ms. Shan not yet received?
(A) Headphones
(B) Monitors
(C) PC case
(D) Hard drives

194. What size hard drive did Ms. Shan order?
(A) 100 GB
(B) 200 GB
(C) 300 GB
(D) 400 GB

195. What color PC case did Ms. Shan want?
(A) Black
(B) Ivory
(C) Blue
(D) White

Questions 196–200 refer to the following e-mails.

From: Mark Connors [Mark@realtors.com]
To: Alana Dorrian [Alana@realtors.com]
Subject: Company expenses

Alana, I would like you to research ways to reduce our expenses. The real estate market is not doing well now. Also, we expect high utility bills later this year. So, we need to spend less money. Please investigate these ideas and submit a report to me within one week. Thank you.

1. Rent: Can we get a better price from our landlord? We can sign a lease for a longer time period and ask for a cheaper rate. Ask him for a 10% reduction if we sign the lease for three years.

2. Space: Do we need all five rooms? Can we rent one to another company?

3. Utility bills: Should we add extra insulation? If it will save us at least $500 a year, I think it would be worth it. Also, our office temperature is 70 degrees. Can we lower it and still be comfortable?

4. Other ideas: Can you think of another way to save money?

From: Alana Dorrian [Alana@realtors.com]
To: Mark Connors [Mark@realtors.com]
Subject: Re: Company expenses

Here are my findings about how to reduce our office overhead.

1. I talked to Mr. Stanley. The amount of reduction is too high for him. However, he is willing to reduce the rent by half of what you request.
2. We don't need all of our rooms. Stavros and Kama have different schedules and can share a room, so we can rent one to another company. The mailing company next door is interested in renting the space.
3. I called the utility company. They say that by adding extra insulation we will save twice the amount that you wanted to save. They also said that it will make a difference if we set the thermostat two degrees lower.
4. Finally, to reduce our electric bills, we should encourage all staff to turn off their computers and office lights at the end of the day.

196. What is the landlord's name?
    (A) Mr. Connors
    (B) Mr. Stanley
    (C) Mr. Stavros
    (D) Mr. Kama

197. How many rooms will Mark's company
    continue to use for its own business?
    (A) One
    (B) Two
    (C) Four
    (D) Five

198. How much money will the extra insulation
    save the company?
    (A) $250
    (B) $500
    (C) $1,000
    (D) $2,000

199. What temperature does the utility
    company recommend for the office?
    (A) 66 degrees
    (B) 68 degrees
    (C) 70 degrees
    (D) 72 degrees

200. What cost-saving idea does Alana suggest?
    (A) Turning off lights and computers
    (B) Giving everyone a different schedule
    (C) Calling the utility company
    (D) Renting out a room

Answer Key

PRACTICE TEST 6

Listening Comprehension

Part 1: Photographs

1. B	4. D	7. B	9. B
2. A	5. C	8. D	10. C
3. C	6. A		

Part 2: Question-Response

11. A	19. B	27. C	35. B
12. C	20. C	28. B	36. A
13. A	21. B	29. C	37. C
14. B	22. C	30. C	38. C
15. C	23. C	31. A	39. B
16. B	24. B	32. A	40. C
17. A	25. A	33. A	
18. A	26. B	34. C	

Part 3: Conversations

41. C	49. B	57. C	65. C
42. B	50. C	58. B	66. C
43. D	51. C	59. C	67. D
44. C	52. A	60. A	68. B
45. C	53. C	61. C	69. A
46. B	54. A	62. A	70. D
47. C	55. C	63. B	
48. B	56. A	64. A	

Part 4: Talks

71. B	79. D	87. D	95. B
72. A	80. C	88. B	96. A
73. D	81. C	89. A	97. D
74. A	82. D	90. B	98. B
75. C	83. B	91. C	99. A
76. D	84. C	92. A	100. B
77. B	85. C	93. C	
78. D	86. A	94. B	

Answer Key
PRACTICE TEST 6

Reading

Part 5: Incomplete Sentences

101. **B**	111. **A**	121. **B**	131. **D**
102. **C**	112. **D**	122. **A**	132. **D**
103. **A**	113. **D**	123. **B**	133. **B**
104. **C**	114. **B**	124. **A**	134. **B**
105. **D**	115. **B**	125. **A**	135. **D**
106. **B**	116. **A**	126. **C**	136. **A**
107. **C**	117. **D**	127. **A**	137. **A**
108. **D**	118. **C**	128. **D**	138. **B**
109. **B**	119. **D**	129. **B**	139. **A**
110. **D**	120. **D**	130. **A**	140. **A**

Part 6: Text Completion

141. **B**	144. **B**	147. **C**	150. **A**
142. **C**	145. **C**	148. **B**	151. **D**
143. **C**	146. **A**	149. **A**	152. **C**

Part 7: Reading Comprehension

153. **B**	165. **C**	177. **B**	189. **D**
154. **B**	166. **A**	178. **A**	190. **C**
155. **C**	167. **B**	179. **D**	191. **C**
156. **D**	168. **C**	180. **B**	192. **C**
157. **C**	169. **C**	181. **A**	193. **A**
158. **A**	170. **A**	182. **C**	194. **C**
159. **A**	171. **B**	183. **A**	195. **C**
160. **A**	172. **A**	184. **C**	196. **B**
161. **D**	173. **D**	185. **B**	197. **C**
162. **B**	174. **D**	186. **A**	198. **C**
163. **C**	175. **B**	187. **A**	199. **B**
164. **D**	176. **A**	188. **B**	200. **A**

TOEIC PRACTICE TEST 6—ANSWERS EXPLAINED

Listening Comprehension

PART 1: PHOTOGRAPHS

1. **(B)** People are eating at an outdoor café. Choice (A) mentions the chairs, but no one is putting them inside. Choice (C) mentions the tables, but no one is moving them around. Choice (D) confuses *outdoors* with *doors*.

2. **(A)** A cargo ship is in the middle of the ocean. Choice (B) confuses similar-sounding words *boat* and *coat* and associates the *water* with *wet*. Choice (C) associates *ship* with *captain* and *deck*, but no captain is visible. Choice (D) is incorrect because the ocean surface is smooth and calm.

3. **(C)** A young woman is reading a book in a library. Choice (A) confuses similar-sounding words *book* and *cook*. Choice (B) confuses similar-sounding words *reading* and *meeting*. Choice (D) confuses similar-sounding words *pages* and *cages*.

4. **(D)** A group of people is walking down the street carrying different kinds of bags. Choice (A) refers to the buildings in the background, but no one is entering them. Choice (B) confuses similar-sounding words *walking* and *working*. Choice (C) confuses similar-sounding words *walking* and *talking*.

5. **(C)** A man is painting a picture of an outdoor scene. Choice (A) uses the word *brush* out of context. Choice (B) uses the word *picture* out of context. Choice (D) repeats the word *painter*, but this painter is an artist, not a house painter preparing a wall to be painted.

6. **(A)** Some people are listening to a presentation in a hotel conference room. Choice (B) correctly identifies the screen but not the action and confuses similar-sounding words *sitting* and *setting*. Choice (C) correctly identifies the location but not the action. Choice (D) correctly identifies the action but not the object.

7. **(B)** A doctor holding a medical record or file is chatting with a patient. Choice (A) correctly identifies the medical record but not its location. Choice (C) correctly identifies the patient, but she is not getting out of bed. Choice (D) identifies the hospital but it is not closed.

8. **(D)** A man is sitting on a bed in a hotel room working on a computer. Choice (A) correctly identifies the action but not the location. Choice (B) correctly identifies the location but not the action. Choice (C) correctly identifies the location but not the action.

9. **(B)** The photo shows a receptionist's desk with a plant on the counter above the desk. Choice (A) correctly identifies the location, but there is no person visible in the photo. Choice (C) correctly identifies the chairs but not their location. Choice (D) is incorrect because there is nothing on the wall.

10. **(C)** A truck is going over a highway bridge. Choice (A) confuses similar-sounding words *truck* and *duck* and associates *bridge* with *river*. Choice (B) is incorrect because there is almost no traffic on the road. Choice (D) associates *truck* with *driver*, but no driver is visible in the photo.

PART 2: QUESTION-RESPONSE

11. **(A)** The second speaker is starving, so is happy to hear that dinner will be ready soon. Choice (B) confuses *read* with the similar-sounding word *ready*, and *afternoon* with the similar-sounding word *soon*. Choice (C) confuses *thinner* with the similar-sounding word *dinner*.

12. **(C)** *Wilson Boulevard* answers the question about an address. Choice (A) confuses similar-sounding words *address* and *dress*. Choice (B) confuses similar-sounding words *address* and *adding*.

13. **(A)** *A cleaning company* answers the question *Who?* Choice (B) repeats the word *office*. Choice (C) confuses *office* with the similar-sounding phrase *his voice*.

14. **(B)** *On the bus* answers the question *Where?* Choice (A) associates *umbrella* with *raining*. Choice (C) confuses *leave* with *leisure*.

15. **(C)** Because the printer ran out of paper, the second speaker says that there is more paper in the closet. Choice (A) repeats the word *printer*. Choice (B) confuses *newspaper* with *paper*.

16. **(B)** This is a logical response to the suggestion made by the first speaker. Choices (A) and (C) repeat the word *newspaper*.

17. **(A)** *Once* answers the question *How many times?* Choice (B) confuses the meaning of the word *China* by associating it with *dishes*. Choice (C) confuses the meaning of the word *time*.

18. **(A)** This is a logical response to a question about a past action. Choice (B) confuses similar-sounding words *fax* and *facts*. Choice (C) confuses similar-sounding words *sent* and *rent*.

19. **(B)** *Sales staff* answers the question *Who?* Choice (A) confuses *marketing* with *market*. Choice (C) confuses the meaning of the word *develop*.

20. **(C)** This is a time clause used to answer the question *When?* Choice (A) confuses *purpose* with *purchase*. Choice (B) confuses similar-sounding words *computer* and *commuter*.

21. **(B)** *Summer* answers the question about a season. Choice (A) confuses similar-sounding words *season* and *reason*. Choice (C) confuses the meaning of the word *fall*, using it as a verb, not as the name of a season.

22. **(C)** This explains the reason for being late. Choice (A) confuses similar-sounding words *late* and *ate*. Choice (B) confuses similar-sounding words *late* and *date*.

23. **(C)** This describes the more comfortable chair. Choice (A) confuses similar-sounding words *chair* and *there* and repeats the word *more*. Choice (B) confuses similar-sounding words *comfortable* and *table*.

24. **(B)** The first speaker wants an appointment with Ms. Park, and the second speaker suggests a convenient time. Choice (A) confuses *pointed* with the similar-sounding word *appointment*. Choice (C) confuses *dark* with the similar-sounding word *Park*.

25. **(A)** *Across from the bank* answers the question *Where?* Choice (B) associates *post office* with *letter* and repeats the word *office*. Choice (C) associates *post office* with *postal workers*.

26. **(B)** This is a polite response to the request. Choice (A) repeats the word *pass*. Choice (C) confuses similar-sounding words *salt* and *insulted*.

27. **(C)** This explains the purpose of the visit. Choice (A) uses the related word *visitors*. Choice (B) confuses similar-sounding words *purpose* and *porpoise*.

28. **(B)** This is a logical response to the suggestion to take a break. Choice (A) confuses the noun *break* with the verb *break* by relating it to *broken*. Choice (C) repeats the word *take*.

29. **(C)** This explains the reason for postponing the meeting. Choice (A) confuses similar-sounding words *postponed* and *phone*. Choice (B) confuses similar-sounding words *meeting* and *meat*.

30. **(C)** This answers the question *When?* Choice (A) confuses similar-sounding words *memo* and *menu*. Choice (B) associates *computer* with *written*.

31. **(A)** *In the hall closet* answers the question *Where?* Choice (B) confuses *suitcase* with the similar-sounding phrase *in case*. Choice (C) confuses *suitcases* with *suits*.

32. **(A)** The second speaker offers to pick Susan up at her 4:30 train. Choice (B) associates *tickets* with *train*. Choice (C) confuses *stain* with the similar-sounding word *train*.

33. **(A)** This answers the question about languages. Choice (B) associates *languages* with *linguist*. Choice (C) repeats the word *speak*.

34. **(C)** This is a logical response to the question about retirement plans. Choice (A) confuses the use of the verb *retire*, making it mean *go to bed* rather than *stop working*. Choice (B) confuses similar-sounding words *retire* and *tire*.

35. **(B)** *Another two weeks* answers the question *When?* Choice (A) uses the related word *exhibit*. Choice (C) confuses homonyms *close* and *clothes*.

36. **(A)** This gives a reason for high airfares. Choice (B) confuses similar sounds *air* and *hair* and associates the words *expensive* and *cost*. Choice (C) associates *airfares* with *airport*.

37. **(C)** *The newsstand in the lobby* answers the question *Where?* Choice (A) repeats *paper*. Choice (B) repeats *news*.

38. **(C)** Because the first speaker got home so late, the second speaker guesses that he is very tired now. Choice (A) confuses *phone* with the similar-sounding word *home* and repeats the word *night*. Choice (B) associates *clock* with *midnight*.

39. **(B)** This is a logical response to the suggestion to take a walk. Choice (A) repeats the word *let*. Choice (C) uses the expression *take a walk* with the literal meaning of *take*.

40. **(C)** *Ten o'clock* answers the question *When?* Choice (A) confuses the meaning of the word *over*. Choice (B) confuses similar-sounding words *concert* and *concerned*.

PART 3: CONVERSATIONS

41. **(C)** The man says his room number is 574. Choices (A), (B), and (D) sound similar to the correct answer.

42. **(B)** The man orders *steak*. Choice (A) confuses *cake* with the similar-sounding word *steak*. Choice (C) confuses *fish* with the similar-sounding word *dish*. Choice (D) confuses *rice* with the similar-sounding word *ice*.

43. **(D)** The woman says that all orders are charged to the customer's room. Choices (A) and (B) are forms of payment that the woman says are not accepted. Choice (C) uses the word *order* out of context.

44. **(C)** The woman mentions the man's *flight*. Choice (A) confuses *bus* with the similar-sounding word *just*. Choice (B) confuses *train* with the similar-sounding word *main*. Choice (D) confuses *subway* with *way*.

45. **(C)** The woman says that the man's flight leaves from Gate 24. Choices (A) and (B) sound similar to the correct answer. Choice (D) is confused with the time the flight will leave.

46. **(B)** The woman tells the man the gate is *across from the main newsstand*. Choice (A) is where the man should turn left. Choice (C) repeats the word *across* and confuses *bank* with the similar-sounding word *thank*. Choice (D) confuses *bandstand* with *newsstand*.

47. **(C)** The man says that they have a flat tire. Choice (A) confuses *tired* with the similar-sounding word *tire*. Choice (B) confuses *sick* with the similar-sounding word *fix*. Choice (D) confuses *date* with the similar-sounding word *late*.

48. **(B)** The woman says that it is 5:30. Choice (A) sounds similar to the correct answer. Choice (C) confuses *six* with the similar-sounding word *fix*. Choice (D) is the time that they have to arrive at their dinner.

49. **(B)** The woman is going to call the people they have a date with to let them know that they might arrive late. Choice (A) is what the speakers will do later. Choice (C) uses the word *case* out of context. Choice (D) confuses the word *appointment* with the similar-sounding word *disappoint*.

50. **(C)** The woman says that her appointment is at 3:00 this afternoon. Choice (A) confuses *noon* with *afternoon*. Choice (B) confuses *one* with the similar-sounding word *fun*. Choice (D) confuses *eight* with the similar-sounding word *take*.

51. **(C)** The woman decides to take the bus because of the rain. Choice (A) is her original plan. Choice (B) confuses *train* with the similar-sounding word *rain*. Choice (D) is not mentioned.

52. **(A)** The man says *it's starting to rain*. Choice (B) confuses *sun* with the similar-sounding word *fun*. Choice (C) confuses *snow* with the similar-sounding word *know*. Choice (D) confuses *hail* with the similar-sounding word *sales*.

53. **(C)** The woman says that the supplies haven't arrived yet. Choice (A) associates *size* with *big*. Choice (B) confuses *paid* with the similar-sounding word *delayed*. Choice (D) is incorrect because there is no indication that the supplies arrive late every time even though they are late this time.

54. **(A)** The woman says that she ordered compter paper and printer ink. Choice (B) repeats the word *computer*. Choice (C) repeats the word *printer*. Choice (D) confuses *drinks* with the similar-sounding word *ink*.

55. **(C)** The woman says that she will call tomorrow morning. Choice (A) repeats the word *morning*. Choice (B) confuses *five* with the similar-sounding word *arrive*. Choice (D) is the day that she originally ordered the supplies.

56. **(A)** The woman says that she has to get her work done by 5:00. Choice (B) confuses *walk* with the similar-sounding word *work*. Choice (C) is the man's suggestion. Choice (D) repeats the word *sandwich*, which is what the woman will have for lunch.

57. **(C)** The woman says that she will eat at her desk. Choice (A) repeats the word *sandwich*. Choice (B) repeats the word *cafeteria*. Choice (D) repeats the word *home*.

58. **(B)** The man offers to bring the woman some lunch from the cafeteria. Choice (A) associates *hospital* with *sick*. Choice (C) repeats the word *work*. Choice (D) uses the word *drive* out of context.

59. **(C)** The man says that he moved on *Wednesday*. Choices (A) and (B) confuse *Sunday* and *Monday* with the similar-sounding word *someday*. Choice (D) confuses *Friday* with the similar-sounding word *finally*.

60. **(A)** The man says he likes the office because it has more room. Choice (B) confuses *cold* with the similar-sounding word *old*. Choice (C) confuses *boss* with the similar-sounding word *across*. Choice (D) confuses *light* with the similar-sounding word *like*.

61. **(C)** The woman mentions that the office is close to the company health club. Choices (A) and (B) describe the location of the old office. Choice (D) confuses *park* with *parking lot*.

62. **(A)** The woman offers the man a brochure with a map of the museum. Choice (B) repeats the word *map*. Choice (C) repeats the word *art*. Choice (D) associates *travel agency* with *tours* and *map*.

63. **(B)** The man wants a guided tour, but instead the woman gives him a brochure with information about the museum exhibits. Choice (A) repeats the word *exhibit*. Choice (C) associates *painting* with *art*. Choice (D) is what the man asked for.

64. **(A)** The woman says that there is no charge for the brochure. Choices (B) and (D) confuse *three* with the similar-sounding word *free*. Choice (C) confuses *four* with the similar-sounding word *for*.

65. **(C)** The man says that he is free on Sunday. Choice (A) confuses the phrase *free day* with the similar-sounding word *Friday*. Choice (B) is a day the man has to work. Choice (D) confuses *Monday* with the similar-sounding word *Sunday*.

66. **(C)** The man suggests going to a concert in the park. Choice (A) is what the woman wants to do. Choice (B) confuses *walk* with the similar-sounding word *work*. Choice (D) confuses *rest* with the similar-sounding word *restaurant*.

67. **(D)** The man says he can't eat at the restaurant because he is on a diet. Choice (A) confuses *dark* with the similar-sounding word *park*. Choice (B) is what the woman says they'll do since they can't agree on anything. Choice (C) is the reason the woman doesn't like the concert.

68. **(B)** The woman says the tour begins in 15 minutes. Choice (A) confuses *ten* with the similar-sounding word *then*. Choice (C) confuses *four* with the similar-sounding word *our*. Choice (D) confuses *nine* with the similar-sounding word *time*.

69. **(A)** The tour begins at the art museum. Choice (B) is what they will do second. Choice (C) is what they can't do because the houses are closed to the public. Choice (D) uses the word *park* out of context.

70. **(D)** The man says he wants to see the interior architecture. Choice (A) is what they will see in the museum. Choice (B) confuses *clothes* with the similar-sounding word *closed*. Choice (C) is what the woman mentions.

PART 4: TALKS

71. **(B)** By calling this number, a person can get information about his or her savings or checking account or leave a message for a bank staff member, so it must be a bank. Choice (A) associates *store* with *customer*. Choice (C) associates *accountant* with *account*. Choice (D) associates *telephone* with *message*.

72. **(A)** The message instructs callers to press 1 to access their account information. Choice (B) is information the caller should have available. Choice (C) is the

way to leave a message. Choice (D) is the way to speak to a customer service representative.

73. **(D)** Callers are instructed to press 2 to learn about the bank's services. Choice (A) is what happens if you stay on the line. Choice (B) is what you can do by dialing an extension number. Choice (C) is what happens if you press 3.

74. **(A)** The speaker says that secretaries are more efficient. Choice (B) is the opposite of the correct answer. Choice (C) is not likely, given that secretaries are more efficient. Choice (D) is possible but is not part of the study.

75. **(C)** Managers admit that work is easier with their secretaries' help. Choice (A) confuses *efficiency* with *hard work*. Choices (B) and (D) are related to the information but are not mentioned.

76. **(D)** The study included 250 secretaries and 100 managers. Choice (A) is the number of businesses in the study. Choice (B) is the number of managers only. Choice (C) is the number of secretaries only.

77. **(B)** *Fill out* means *complete*. Choice (A) won't help you order faster. Choice (C) is only part of the information needed. Choice (D) confuses *item number* with *page number*.

78. **(D)** The speaker says to have your credit card handy. Choices (A), (B), and (C) are payment methods but wouldn't work for a phone order.

79. **(D)** The message says that the wait time is 16 minutes. Choices (A) and (C) sound similar to the correct answer. Choice (B) confuses *eight* with the similar-sounding word *wait*.

80. **(C)** *Dishwasher* is associated with a restaurant but is not mentioned. Choices (A), (B), and (D) are all mentioned in the advertisement.

81. **(C)** Food service experience. Choices (A) and (B) may be useful but are not mentioned. Choice (D) associates *food* with *grocery store*.

82. **(D)** The ad says to call Monday through Friday in the afternoon, or weekends in the morning. Choices (A), (B), and (C) do not follow this advice.

83. **(B)** Snow. Choices (A) and (C) will fall in the morning. Choice (D) is not mentioned.

84. **(C)** *Low visibility* is a *visibility hazard*. Choices (A) and (B) are probably true but are not mentioned. Choice (D) associates *drivers* with *engines*.

85. **(C)** The report says that another storm is expected on Sunday. Choice (A) is when the skies will clear up. Choice (B) confuses in *two days* with the similar-sounding phrase *in a few days*. Choice (D) sounds similar to the correct answer.

86. **(A)** *Landing* suggests a plane. Choices (B) and (C) are places where one might hear a similar announcement. Choice (D) associates *ship* and *cabin*.

87. **(D)** The plane will land at Gate 29. Choices (A) and (C) are confused with *15 minutes*, when the plane will land. Choice (B) sounds similar to the correct answer.

88. **(B)** Passengers are asked to put their luggage under the seat. Choice (A) associates *luggage* and *bags*. Choice (C) repeats the word *seats*. Choice (D) is something passengers might be asked to do but is not mentioned.

89. **(A)** They have *the lowest prices available*. Choices (B), (C), and (D) are plausible reasons but are not the correct answer.

90. **(B)** The advertisement suggests talking to a design specialist to help pick out something from the samples. Choice (A) confuses similar-sounding words *design* and *line*. Choice (C) repeats the phrase *next week*. Choice (D) confuses similar-sounding words *look* and *book*.

91. **(C)** An order is guaranteed to be ready in one week. Choice (A) confuses *day* with the similar-sounding word *today*. Choices (B) and (D) confuse *three* with the similar-sounding word *free*.

92. **(A)** *Broken* means *not in service*. Choice (B) repeats the word *escalators*. Choice (C) repeats the word *stairs*. Choice (D) repeats the word *exit*.

93. **(C)** They can go to the next station, use the elevator there, and then take a bus. Choices (A), (B), and (D) are plausible but are not the correct answer.

94. **(B)** The phrase *We regret* is a form of apology. Choices (A) and (C) are plausible but are not the correct answer. Choice (D) is confused with the phrase *Please be advised*.

95. **(B)** The demand for power is caused by *the extremely cold weather*. Choice (A) is the opposite of the correct answer. Choice (C) repeats the word *appliances*. Choice (D) repeats the word *residents*.

96. **(A)** The public is asked to use less electricity by lowering their household heat and turning off appliances. Choice (B) associates *consumption* and *food* and confuses similar-sounding words *power* and *poor*. Choice (C) repeats the words *avoid* and *weather*. Choice (D) confuses similar-sounding words *reduce* and *produce* and repeats the word *power*.

97. **(D)** Residents are asked to lower their household heat to 60 degrees (Fahrenheit). Choices (A), (B), and (C) all sound similar to the correct answer.

98. **(B)** The restaurant will open on Friday. Choice (A) confuses Tuesday with the similar-sounding phrase *two days*. Choices (C) and (D) are when brunch is served.

99. **(A)** The restaurant serves *the city's best pizza and pasta*. Choice (B) confuses *pastry* with the similar-sounding word *pasta*. Choice (C) confuses *rice* with the similar-sounding word *prizes*. Choice (D) confuses *veal* with the similar-sounding word *meal*.

100. **(B)** There is a senior citizens discount for adults aged 65 and over. Choice (A) is confused with the special menu for children. Choice (C) is confused with the people who will get free drinks and prizes at the grand opening. Choice (D) repeats the word *citizens*.

Reading

PART 5: INCOMPLETE SENTENCES

101. **(B)** This agrees with the singular subject *price.* Choices (A), (C), and (D) are all plural.

102. **(C)** *Because* indicates a cause-and-effect relationship. Choices (A), (B), and (D) are not logical.

103. **(A)** The causative verb *request* is followed by a base form verb. Choice (B) is present tense. Choice (C) is past tense. Choice (D) is a gerund.

104. **(C)** The simple past tense is used here to indicate an action that interrupted another action in progress in the past. Choice (A) is present perfect. Choice (B) is present tense. Choice (D) is present continuous.

105. **(D)** The relative pronoun *who* introduces the adjective clause and refers to a person, the new manager. Choices (A) and (B) are not relative pronouns. Choice (C) is used to refer to a thing.

106. **(B)** This is a past unreal conditional, so it uses *would + have + a past participle verb* in the main clause. Choices (A), (C), and (D) are verb forms not used for a past unreal conditional.

107. **(C)** *Competitors* is a noun referring to people that acts as the subject of this sentence. Choice (A) is a noun that refers to a situation, not to people. Choice (B) is an adjective. Choice (D) is an adverb.

108. **(D)** Superlative adjectives use *most* or *–est.* Choice (A) is an incorrect comparative form. Choice (B) is a simple adjective form. Choice (C) is the comparative form.

109. **(B)** The causative *get* is followed by an infinitive verb. Choice (A) is a gerund. Choice (C) is past tense. Choice (D) is present tense.

110. **(D)** *By* is used with deadlines or schedules. Choice (A) means *together.* Choice (B) means *inside.* Choice (C) indicates a recipient.

111. **(A)** *Beside* means *next to.* Choices (B) and (C) require more than one reference point. Choice (D) should be *across from.*

112. **(D)** The superlative comparison in the sentences uses *the* and *–est.* Choice (A) is the simple form of the verb. Choice (B) omits *the.* Choice (C) is the comparative form.

113. **(D)** The time phrase *every month* can follow the main verb. Choices (A), (B), and (C) cannot follow the main verb.

114. **(B)** *After* establishes a logical time reference. Choices (A), (C), and (D) are not logical.

115. **(B)** Comparisons of two things use *more* or *–er* and *than.* Choice (A) is the superlative form. Choices (C) and (D) are equal comparisons that each omit one *as.*

116. **(A)** *Adapt* means *modify.* Choices (B), (C), and (D) look similar to the correct answer but do not fit the context of the sentence.

117. **(D)** *Before* establishes a logical time relationship between the clauses. Choices (A), (B), and (C) are not logical.

118. **(C)** *On* is used with specific dates. Choice (A) indicates a purpose. Choice (B) indicates destination. Choice (D) means *inside.*

119. **(D)** The simple past tense is used here to indicate an action that interrupted another action in progress in the past. Choice (A) is present continuous. Choice (B) is present tense. Choice (C) is past perfect.

120. **(D)** *Borrow* is used with *from.* This sentence means that the manual belonged to the secretary and the clerk used it. Choices (A), (B), and (C) would use *to* instead of *from* and would indicate that the manual belonged to the clerk and the secretary used it.

121. **(B)** *Both* is used with *and* to connect two similar ideas. Choice (A) indicates a choice. Choice (C) indicates a *contradiction* or *contrast.* Choice (D) is used with *neither.*

122. **(A)** The verb form is needed here to complete the future tense with *will.* Choice (B) is an adjective. Choice (C) is a noun. Choice (D) is a gerund.

123. **(B)** *Never* goes between the auxiliary and the main verb. Choices (A), (C), and (D) place *never* in the wrong position.

124. **(A)** In an unreal present conditional, *were* is the correct form of the verb *be* in the *if* clause. Choices (B), (C), and (D) are the wrong form to use in the *if* clause.

125. **(A)** *From* is used to indicate the departure point. Choices (B), (C), and (D) cannot be used in this context.

126. **(C)** Use the simple present form to match the first verb, *turns on,* and indicate a habitual action in the present. Choice (A) is a gerund. Choice (B) is present perfect. Choice (D) is past tense.

127. **(A)** The speech causes the audience to feel restless; it is active so uses the present participle. Choice (B) is the past participle. Choice (C) is present tense. Choice (D) is base form or present tense.

128. **(D)** Use *in* with city locations. Choice (A) is used with dates. Choice (B) indicates a recipient. Choice (C) means *next to.*

129. **(B)** *Because* establishes a cause-and-effect relationship. Choice (A) indicates a contrast. Choices (C) and (D) are used with clauses expressing a result.

130. **(A)** Commands require the base form of the verb. Choice (B) is present tense. Choice (C) is present participle. Choice (D) is future.

131. **(D)** *Average* means *typical amount.* Choices (A), (B), and (C) look similar to the correct answer but do not fit the context of the sentence.

132. **(D)** Someone else has designated the spaces, so passive voice is needed. Choices (A), (B), and (C) are all active voice.

133. **(B)** The relative pronoun *who* acts as the subject of the adjective clause and refers to *participants.* Choice (A) is not a relative pronoun. Choice (C) is used to refer to things, not people. Choice (D) is an object pronoun.

134. **(B)** The department needs someone with a background, or experience, in international law. Choices (A), (C), and (D) look similar to the correct answer but do not fit the context of the sentence.

135. **(D)** Commands require the base form of the verb. Choice (A) is present tense. Choice (B) is future. Choice (C) is present continuous.

136. **(A)** The plural verb *are* agrees with the plural subject *pens and stationery.* Choices (B), (C), and (D) are all singular forms.

137. **(A)** The adjective *industrious* describes the noun *engineer.* Choices (B) and (D) are nouns. Choice (C) is an adjective but is not used to describe people.

138. **(B)** This is a present perfect verb used to describe a situation that started in the past and continues to the present. Choice (A) is simple present tense. Choice (C) is past perfect. Choice (D) is simple past.

139. **(A)** *In* is used for publications. Choices (B), (C), and (D) cannot be used in this context.

140. **(A)** The verb *promise* is followed by an infinitive. Choice (B) is a gerund. Choice (C) is base form. Choice (D) is simple past tense.

PART 6: TEXT COMPLETION

141. **(B)** *Review* means to *look over.* Choices (A), (C), and (D) look similar to the correct answer but don't have the correct meaning.

142. **(C)** *In advance* means *ahead of time.* Choices (A) and (B) mean the opposite of the correct answer. Choice (D) is related to school but does not fit the sentence.

143. **(C)** This is a gerund used as the subject of the sentence. Choice (A) is a base form verb. Choice (B) is a past participle form. Choice (D) is an infinitive verb.

144. **(B)** Ms. Schultz wants her assistant to ask for or request a certain table. Choices (A), (C), and (D) look similar to the correct answer but don't have the correct meaning.

145. **(C)** *As soon as* means *immediately after.* Choices (A) and (D) mean *at the same time.* Choice (B) means *before.*

146. **(A)** *Hand in* means *submit*. Choice (B) would create a word that doesn't have any meaning. Choice (C) would create a word that means *put in someone's hand*. Choice (D) would create a word that means *distribute*.

147. **(C)** A passive form is required here because the subject, *items*, is not active. Choices (A), (B), and (D) are active forms.

148. **(B)** The present perfect tense is used to refer to an action that occurred at an indefinite time in the past. Choice (A) is past perfect tense. Choice (C) is future. Choice (D) is present progressive.

149. **(A)** *Regarding* means *about*. Choices (B), (C), and (D) do not fit the context.

150. **(A)** An *expert* is a person who knows a lot about something. Choices (B), (C), and (D) look similar to the correct answer but cannot be used in this context.

151. **(D)** *Where* is a relative pronoun referring to a place, in this case, *Asia*. Choices (A) and (B) are used to refer to a person. Choice (C) is used to refer to a thing.

152. **(C)** *Admission* is a noun and acts as the subject in this sentence. Choices (A) and (B) are verbs. Choice (D) is an adjective.

PART 7: READING COMPREHENSION

153. **(B)** This card is for people who are moving to notify others of their new address. Choice (A) repeats the phrase *new address*. Choice (C) is incorrect because this form will be sent to publications that the person already has ordered. Choice (D) associates *address* with *location*.

154. **(B)** The date the form was filled out is April 12 and it is effective *immediately*, that is, on the same date it was filled out. Choice (A) is a month before the date the form was filled out and is confused with the recommendation to mail the form a month ahead of time. Choice (C) is a month after the date on the card. Choice (D) is confused with the date, April *12*.

155. **(C)** An electronic bilingual dictionary is offered for free to purchasers of the language program. Choice (A) is one place the program has been advertised. Choice (B) is one way you can carry the dictionary. Choice (D) is confused with the language program.

156. **(D)** When you order the language program, the free dictionary will be sent to you. Choice (A) is associated with the context of learning a language. Choice (B) is a place one might buy a language program. Choice (C) repeats the word *TV*.

157. **(C)** Lawyers would be likely to attend Legal Education seminars. Choice (A) confuses *workers* with the subject of workers' compensation. Choices (B) and (D) are not likely to be interested.

158. **(A)** Workers' Compensation is payment to injured workers. Choices (B), (C), and (D) use words from the announcement but are not mentioned.

159. **(A)** The faculty will discuss how to anticipate new trends in defense. Choices (B), (C), and (D) are not mentioned.

160. **(A)** Students generally write for academic purposes, not business purposes, so would probably not be interested in this book. Choices (B), (C), and (D) are all people who generally do write for business purposes.

161. **(D)** The special section covers *common writing mistakes*. Choices (A), (B), and (C) are covered in other sections of the book.

162. **(B)** The name of Sov Hok's business is Gardens by Hok, and he is interested in advertising in *Landscape Design Magazine*, so he is probably a garden designer. Choices (A), (C), and (D) are related to Guy Williams's business.

163. **(C)** In his letter, Mr. Hok informs Mr. Williams that he won't place an ad in the magazine now but may want to later. Choices (A) and (B) are reasons someone might write to a magazine but are not the correct answer. Choice (D) is something Mr. Hok says he will do later.

164. **(D)** *Quarterly* means *every three months*. If the current issue under discussion is December and the next issue is March, the magazine comes out every three months. Choices (A), (B), and (C) are plausible but are not the correct answer.

165. **(C)** According to the article, foods *account for the largest portion of our agricultural exports*. Choices (A) and (D) are what many think is exported the most. Choice (B) is not mentioned.

166. **(A)** It has increased because of increased *interest among consumers in more exotic food products*. Choice (B) is confused with *the fact that we have little rain*. Choices (C) and (D) are plausible but are not mentioned.

167. **(B)** According to the last paragraph, the increase in exports of tropical fruits and root vegetables is expected to continue. Choice (A) repeats the phrase *agricultural exports*. Choices (C) and (D) are results of the trend.

168. **(C)** *Anticipate* means to *expect something to happen*. Choices (A), (B), and (D) could fit the context but don't have the correct meaning.

169. **(C)** The article is specifically directed toward business travelers. Choice (A) is people who might be interested in the topic of exercise. Choices (B) and (D) are other people who travel frequently.

170. **(A)** The article says *their schedules are suddenly changed*. Choices (B), (C), and (D) are plausible reasons but are not mentioned.

171. **(B)** The article advises exercising in an airplane seat. Choices (A), (C), and (D) are places where a business traveler might be but are not mentioned.

172. **(A)** People who exercise regularly perform *more efficiently at work*. Choices (B) and (C) are possible benefits but are not mentioned. Choice (D) repeats the word *colleagues*.

173. **(D)** Mr. Horstma writes that he was *so impressed with the product that he decided to share it with others*. Choice (A) repeats the word *e-mail*. Choice (B)

is related to the topic of computers but is not mentioned. Choice (C) is plausible but is not mentioned.

174. **(D)** The purpose of the fax is to suggest that people buy the Kleanit software package. Choice (A) is related to the topic but is not mentioned. Choice (B) confuses *e-mail* with *mail.* Choice (C) repeats the word *documents.*

175. **(B)** *Obscure* means *unclear;* when your computer is cluttered with many old files, it is unclear what the file names refer to. Choices (A), (C), and (D) look similar to the correct answer but have very different meanings.

176. **(A)** The computer will operate *inefficiently.* Choices (B), (C), and (D) are plausible but are not mentioned.

177. **(B)** Mr. Horstma writes that after using Kleanit, *the only files in my computer are files that relate to my current projects or routine tasks.* Choices (A), (C), and (D) are examples of files you might delete.

178. **(A)** Ms. Wise has a law degree, works at a law firm, is a member of the Bar Association, and represents clients, so she must be a lawyer. Choice (B) is confused with the mention of the universities where she studied. Choice (C) confuses the meaning of the word *principal.* Choice (D) confuses the meaning of the word *bar.*

179. **(D)** Ms. Wise earned a Doctorate of Jurisprudence from Harvard University in 1987. Choice (A) is confused with the word *association.* Choice (B) is a degree she got in 1980, before working on her doctorate. Choice (C) is not mentioned.

180. **(B)** The continuing education foundation *is pleased to have Ms. Wise speak to us today.* Choice (A) is something she has already done. Choice (C) confuses the meaning of the word *suit.* Choice (D) is something she has done at other times.

181. **(A)** All workshops are free. Choice (B) is the same-day registration fee, charged if you register for this workshop on October 8. Choice (C) is confused with the number of participants in the class. Choice (D) is the total amount collected in late registration fees.

182. **(C)** The advertisement says that cookbooks are for sale. Choice (A) associates *exercise clothes* with *walking for fitness.* Choice (B) uses the word *tape* out of context; it is audiotapes that are for sale. Choice (D) is what participants in the walking class should bring with them to class.

183. **(A)** The fee is $3 per person and $60 total were collected. Choice (B) is confused with the number of participants in the Low Calorie Meals class. Choice (C) is the amount of money collected. Choice (D) is confused with the amount of people who attended.

184. **(C)** The original fee was $10, and Mona plans to add $2 to that. Choice (A) is the amount by which the fee will be raised. Choice (B) is the original fee. Choice (D) is not mentioned.

185. **(B)** The October 10 class was Walk for Fitness, and Mona wants to offer a similar one for children. Choices (A) and (C) are the other classes offered. Choice (D) looks similar to the other classes but is not mentioned.

186. **(A)** Jon's mother works as an electrical engineer at the company, and the ad says that preference will be given to employees' children. Choices (B) and (C) are true about Jon but are not things that will give him preference. Choice (D) is confused with Jon's mother's profession.

187. **(A)** Jon's e-mail is dated April 1, and the application deadline is April 15. Choice (B) is not mentioned. Choice (C) is confused with the minimum length of the internships. Choice (D) is confused with the maximum time following graduation that a person can apply to become an intern.

188. **(B)** Jon is thinking about studying information technology. Choice (A) is what he is studying now as an undergraduate. Choice (C) is confused with the Global Communications project. Choice (D) is confused with Jon's second language.

189. **(D)** Interns who speak a second language will be assigned to the Global Communications project. Choices (A), (B), and (C) are other projects that interns may be assigned to.

190. **(C)** June 1 is when the first internships start, and Jon wants to start when he returns from Korea, four days after that. Choice (A) is confused with when Jon will go to Korea. Choice (B) is when the first internships start. Choice (D) is confused with when Jon wants to finish his internship.

191. **(C)** Mr. Wu asked Ms. Shan to contact his assistant, Marcia, and Ms. Shan left a message for Ms. Lee; we can assume they are the same person. Choices (A), (B), and (D) are the first names of other people mentioned in the texts.

192. **(C)** The box arrived two days after the expected April 14 date. Choice (A) is the date of the fax. Choice (B) is the expected arrival date. Choice (D) is the date of the phone message.

193. **(A)** Ms. Shan says she received items 1, 2, and 4; therefore, she did not receive item 5, which is the headphones. Choice (B) is item 1. Choice (C) is item 2. Choice (D) is item 4.

194. **(C)** Ms. Shan received 200 GB hard drives, which were 100 GB smaller than she ordered. Choice (A) is confused with 100 GB smaller. Choice (B) is the size hard drive she received. Choice (D) is confused with the number of hard drives she received.

195. **(C)** The message says that Ms. Shan wanted a blue PC case. Choice (A) is the color she received. Choice (B) is the color of the keyboards. Choice (D) is not mentioned.

196. **(B)** Mr. Stanley is the name of the person Alana talked to about the rent. Choice (A) is the name of Alana's boss. Choices (C) and (D) are two other people who work for the company.

197. **(C)** The company has a total of five rooms and will rent out one to a mailing company. Choice (A) is the number of rooms they will rent to the other company. Choice (B) is not mentioned. Choice (D) is the total number of rooms they have.

198. **(C)** Mark wanted to save $500, and the insulation will save twice as much. Choice (A) is half, not twice, what Mark wanted to save. Choice (B) is what Mark wanted to save. Choice (D) is twice what will be saved.

199. **(B)** The office temperature is currently 70 degrees, and the utility company recommends setting it two degrees lower. Choice (A) is two degrees lower than the recommendation. Choice (C) is the current temperature. Choice (D) is two degrees higher than the current temperature.

200. **(A)** Alana suggests reminding the staff to turn off lights and computers at the end of the day. Choice (B) is confused with the fact that two of the staff members have different schedules. Choice (C) is what she did to research one of Mark's ideas. Choice (D) is another of Mark's ideas.

Audioscripts for the
TOEIC Practice Tests Parts 1–4

The audioscripts for the Listening Comprehension section of the six Practice Tests in this book follow. Each Listening Comprehension section has four parts, and each part has separate instructions.

You should use the compact discs when you take the Listening Comprehension sections. If you do not have the compact discs available, someone can read the Listening Comprehension sections to you.

TOEIC PRACTICE TEST 1

Listening Comprehension

Part 1: Photographs

Directions: You will see a photograph. You will hear four statements about the photograph. Choose the statement that most closely matches the photograph and fill in the corresponding oval on your answer sheet.

Example

Now listen to the four statements.

(A) She's getting on a plane.
(B) She's reading a magazine.
(C) She's taking a nap.
(D) She's holding a glass.

Statement (B), "She's reading a magazine," best describes what you see in the picture. Therefore, you should choose answer (B).

1. Look at the photo marked number 1 in your test book.
   (A) They're shaking hands.
   (B) They're filling their glasses.
   (C) They're applauding the speaker.
   (D) They're waving to their friends.

   [5 second pause]

2. Look at the photo marked number 2 in your test book.
   (A) The train is moving fast.
   (B) It's a rainy day.
   (C) Their umbrellas are in the closet.
   (D) They're walking on the sidewalk.

   [5 second pause]

3. Look at the photo marked number 3 in your test book.
   (A) The carpenter is using a drill.
   (B) The patient is sitting up.
   (C) The driver is wearing gloves.
   (D) The dentist is examining the man.

   [5 second pause]

4. Look at the photo marked number 4 in your test book.
   (A) They're talking about the house.
   (B) They're closing the window.
   (C) They're printing the plans.
   (D) They're catching a mouse.

   [5 second pause]

5. Look at the photo marked number 5 in your test book.
   (A) The plane has already landed.
   (B) The passengers are ready to board.
   (C) The train has left the station.
   (D) The pilot has a uniform.

   [5 second pause]

6. Look at the photo marked number 6 in your test book.
   (A) Their hats are in their hands.
   (B) The window is broken.
   (C) Their bags are in the car.
   (D) They're looking at clothes in the window.

   [5 second pause]

7. Look at the photo marked number 7 in your test book.
   (A) He's walking down the hall.
   (B) He's wearing a bathing suit.
   (C) He's talking to his colleagues.
   (D) He's looking out the window.

   [5 second pause]

8. Look at the photo marked number 8 in your test book.
   (A) The customers are sitting inside.
   (B) The chairs are on the sidewalk.
   (C) The waiter is standing by the window.
   (D) The tables are in the kitchen.

   [5 second pause]

9. Look at the photo marked number 9 in your test book.
   (A) She's reading a newspaper.
   (B) She's eating a meal.
   (C) She's looking at new shoes.
   (D) She's reporting the news.

   [5 second pause]

10. Look at the photo marked number 10 in your test book.
    (A) There is a big truck on the road.
    (B) The bridge crosses a river.
    (C) There isn't any traffic on the highway.
    (D) The cars are passing under the bridge.

    [5 second pause]

Part 2: Question-Response

Directions: You will hear a question and three possible responses. Choose the response that most closely answers the question and fill in the corresponding oval on your answer sheet.

Example

Now listen to the sample question.

You will hear:

How is the weather?

You will also hear:

(A) It's raining.
(B) He's fine, thanks.
(C) He's my boss.

The best response to the question *How is the weather?* is choice (A), *It's raining.* Therefore, you should choose answer (A).

11. What time did the program begin?
    (A) Just after 10:00.
    (B) Yes, he can program computers.
    (C) Please begin again.

    [5 second pause]

12. Is this your coat?
    (A) Yes, this wall needs a new coat of paint.
    (B) Yes, it's mine.
    (C) Yes, I saw the note.

    [5 second pause]

13. It looks like it's starting to rain.
    (A) I hope we'll meet again.
    (B) The train already left.
    (C) Here, please take my umbrella.

    [5 second pause]

14. Where did you leave the newspaper?
    (A) Yes, it's brand new.
    (B) I put it on your desk.
    (C) I usually read it before breakfast.

    [5 second pause]

15. How many people showed up for the meeting?
    (A) It was nice meeting you, too.
    (B) I showed them to everybody.
    (C) More than 20.

    [5 second pause]

16. Who gave you this assignment?
    (A) My boss told me to do it.
    (B) I haven't signed it yet.
    (C) He gave it to me yesterday.

    [5 second pause]

17. How long did the plane ride last?
    (A) About five hours.
    (B) No, it wasn't long.
    (C) The plane went very fast.

    [5 second pause]

18. It's very warm in here.
    (A) I think it's in here.
    (B) I warned you about it.
    (C) I'll open a window.

    [5 second pause]

19. That's your desk by the door, isn't it?
    (A) I plan to buy a new desk.
    (B) No, mine's over there.
    (C) Let's sit by the door.

    [5 second pause]

20. When will they arrive?
    (A) I expect them in an hour.
    (B) They plan to drive.
    (C) They'll arrive by train.

    [5 second pause]

21. Who was that on the phone?
    (A) Please call later.
    (B) I'll give you my phone number.
    (C) It was Mr. Kim.

    [5 second pause]

22. What color is your car?
    (A) It's black and silver.
    (B) No, that's not my car.
    (C) I don't drive it often.

    [5 second pause]

23. Where can I find the copy machine?
    (A) I agree. We need a new copy machine.
    (B) It's just down the hall to the left.
    (C) You'll find that it works very well.

    [5 second pause]

24. I'm really hungry.
    (A) There's no need to hurry.
    (B) Please don't be angry.
    (C) Me, too. Let's take a lunch break.

    [5 second pause]

25. Why did they get here so late?
    (A) We're going to need eight.
    (B) Their train was delayed.
    (C) Put it on that plate.

    [5 second pause]

26. Where do you want to eat?
    (A) I don't care for that kind of food.
    (B) Let's try the restaurant across the street.
    (C) It's not a comfortable seat.

    [5 second pause]

27. It takes about an hour to get to the airport.
    (A) Then we should leave here by 3:00.
    (B) It's a very modern airport.
    (C) I don't really like to fly.

    [5 second pause]

28. How much did the new computer cost?
    (A) Not much. I bought it on sale.
    (B) No, we're not lost.
    (C) I rarely use a computer.

    [5 second pause]

29. What day is the meeting?
    (A) We'll be meeting many new people.
    (B) There isn't enough seating.
    (C) It's scheduled for Friday.

    [5 second pause]

30. Who did you have dinner with?
    (A) She's looking much thinner.
    (B) Just a few business colleagues.
    (C) We ate in a hurry.

    [5 second pause]

31. Do you work in this building?
    (A) Yes, on the third floor.
    (B) It's quite an old building.
    (C) I often work weekends.

    [5 second pause]

32. Whose briefcase is this?
    (A) I think it's mine.
    (B) Please be brief.
    (C) Take it, just in case.

    [5 second pause]

33. Did you mail those letters?
    (A) We can talk about it later.
    (B) There are some envelopes in my desk.
    (C) Yes, I took them to the post office
        at noon.

    [5 second pause]

34. Why weren't you at the office yesterday?
    (A) I was feeling sick.
    (B) This is our office.
    (C) Yes, today is the day.

    [5 second pause]

35. This is a very nice hotel.
    (A) Don't worry. I won't tell.
    (B) Yes, it is. I always stay here.
    (C) You'll need to make a reservation.

    [5 second pause]

36. How can I get downtown?
    (A) Just put it down here.
    (B) The subway is the fastest way.
    (C) He works downtown.

    [5 second pause]

37. When can I call you?
    (A) There's a phone on my desk.
    (B) Just call me Kim.
    (C) Call me at my office tomorrow.

    [5 second pause]

38. What's the matter with Tom?
    (A) He just lost his job.
    (B) Please stop that chatter.
    (C) It needs to be flatter.

    [5 second pause]

39. What would you like to drink?
    (A) Here's a clean glass.
    (B) I don't know what to think.
    (C) Just some hot tea, please.

    [5 second pause]

40. Where did you leave your car?
    (A) He gave me his card.
    (B) I parked it across the street.
    (C) I drive almost every day.

    [5 second pause]

Part 3: Conversations

Directions: You will hear a conversation between two people. You will see three questions on each conversation and four possible answers. Choose the best answer to each question and fill in the corresponding oval on your answer sheet.

Questions 41–43 refer to the following conversation.

Woman: His plane is due to arrive at 4:30. I think we should go pick him up at the airport.

Man: Good idea. But we'll need to leave at 3 if we're going to be on time. It's a bit far to get there.

Woman: You're right. And I don't think we should take a taxi. The subway's much faster.

Man: Okay. That sounds like a good plan. I'll meet you at your office and we can walk to the station together.

41. What time will they leave for the airport?

[8 second pause]

42. How will they get to the airport?

[8 second pause]

43. Where will the speakers meet?

[8 second pause]

Questions 44–46 refer to the following conversation.

Man: Excuse me. Can you tell me where I can find manila envelopes?

Woman: They're on Aisle 6, on the shelf below the printer paper. And you're in luck. They're on sale this week for 20% off.

Man: Great. I always love to save money.

Woman: If you don't see the style you want, I'd be happy to order some for you, and you'd still get the 20% discount if you order today.

44. Where does this conversation take place?

[8 second pause]

45. What is the man looking for?

[8 second pause]

46. What does the woman offer to do?

[8 second pause]

Questions 47–49 refer to the following conversation.

Woman: Mr. Lee called. He'd like to set up an appointment with you at 11:00 tomorrow morning to go over the marketing plan.

Man: Can't do it. I'll be in a meeting with the accountants then. Do you think he can do it later in the day?

Woman: I'll call and find out. What time would be best for you?

Man: See if he can meet with me at 2:00. That'll give me time to get some lunch after I'm finished with the accountants.

47. What will the man be doing at 11:00 tomorrow morning?

   [8 second pause]

48. What does Mr. Lee want to discuss?

   [8 second pause]

49. What time does the man want to see Mr. Lee?

   [8 second pause]

Questions 50–52 refer to the following conversation.

Man: Do you think you can have those copies ready this afternoon? They need to be mailed out as soon as possible.

Woman: I'm sorry. I didn't get the originals until just before lunch, and you need them all collated and stapled, right? I'll have them for you tomorrow morning.

Man: All right. That'll have to do. I asked for 75 copies, didn't I?

Woman: Yes, but I'm going to make 85. We'll need those 10 extra for the office staff and the file. By the way, could you give me the addresses so I can get the labels ready?

50. When will the copies be ready?

   [8 second pause]

51. How many copies will the woman make?

   [8 second pause]

52. What does the woman ask the man for?

   [8 second pause]

Questions 53–55 refer to the following conversation.

Man: I called the Grand Hotel this morning and booked you a room for Wednesday and Thursday nights.

Woman: Would you mind calling back and asking them to add a night? I'd like to stay over Friday and get some sightseeing in.

Man: I'll do it after lunch, if you don't mind. Right now I have to finish typing these reports.

Woman: Fine. That's not a problem. Just please don't forget to do it.

53. How many nights does the woman want to stay at the hotel?

[8 second pause]

54. What does the woman ask the man to do?

[8 second pause]

55. When will the man do what the woman asks?

[8 second pause]

Questions 56–58 refer to the following conversation.

Woman: What terrible weather. Have you ever seen such thick fog? I've heard it's caused a lot of problems on the highway.
Man: I know. As a matter of fact, Jack just called and said he'll be at least an hour late because the traffic is so heavy.
Woman: He should have taken the train. I did, and I wasn't delayed even one minute.
Man: Lucky you. I hope it clears up soon because I have to get to a 2:00 meeting.

56. What's the weather like?

[8 second pause]

57. Why will Jack be late?

[8 second pause]

58. How late will he be?

[8 second pause]

Questions 59–61 refer to the following conversation.

Man: Can you tell me how to get to the post office, please?
Woman: Certainly. Just go straight ahead for five blocks, turn left, go down two blocks and you'll see it on the corner, next to the bank.
Man: Thank you. Do you know if there's any parking near there?
Woman: Oh, yes. The library parking lot is just across the street. You can usually find a space there, and it's free.

59. Where does the man want to go?

[8 second pause]

60. Where is it?

[8 second pause]

61. How many blocks away is it?

[8 second pause]

Questions 62–64 refer to the following conversation.

Man: Listen. You won't believe this. I just found out I've been chosen employee of the year.

Woman: How exciting! You deserve it. I suppose you'll have to give a speech at the annual banquet.

Man: Yes, I'm a little nervous about that part of it. I guess I'll have to do some preparation for it.

Woman: You'd better get started soon. It's already September and the banquet is next month. I could help you write your speech if you'd like.

62. Why is the man excited?

[8 second pause]

63. When is the banquet?

[8 second pause]

64. What does the woman offer to do?

[8 second pause]

Questions 65–67 refer to the following conversation.

Woman: It looks like this restaurant is closed. What'll we do? I am so hungry!

Man: I know a café that stays open late. I can call and check if they're still open. If you don't mind ordering sandwiches, that is. That's all they serve.

Woman: I don't mind sandwiches. I guess we shouldn't have waited till so late to eat. Oh, and I forgot my wallet, too. Did you bring a credit card?

Man: No, but don't worry. I'll pay. I have plenty of cash on me. It's only 10:00. We should be able to find some place that's open.

65. What does the woman want to do?

[8 second pause]

66. How will the man pay?

[8 second pause]

67. What time is it now?

[8 second pause]

Questions 68–70 refer to the following conversation.

Woman: I'm looking for a business suit, but not for myself. I want it for a birthday present for my husband.

Man: These summer suits just arrived. The material is very fine, and look at these colors—white, beige . . .

Woman: This light blue is very nice, but I need another color, something more serious. It's for a conference with his boss. This black suit is just what I want.

Man: Yes, it's a very fine suit and a real bargain, too, at only five hundred dollars. You couldn't get a suit like this for less than that.

68. Who is the woman shopping for?

[8 second pause]

69. What color suit does the woman want?

[8 second pause]

70. How much does the suit cost?

[8 second pause]

Part 4: Talks

Directions: You will hear a talk given by a single speaker. You will see three questions on each talk, each with four possible answers. Choose the best answer to each question and fill in the corresponding oval on your answer sheet.

Questions 71–73 refer to the following announcement.

May I have your attention, please? Train number 16 scheduled to depart for New York City at 7:30 will begin boarding in five minutes. All passengers for New York, please approach Gate 11 now. Have your ticket ready to show the gate agent. This is an all-reserved train. Please check your ticket to make sure you have a reservation on this train before approaching the gate. Carry-on luggage is permitted on this train and must be stored on the overhead racks. Let the gate agent know if you will need assistance with this.

71. What will happen in five minutes?

[8 second pause]

72. What gate will the train leave from?

[8 second pause]

73. What should passengers do with their luggage?

[8 second pause]

Questions 74–76 refer to the following recording.

Thank you for calling the Prescott downtown office. If you know your party's extension, you may dial it at any time. To open a new account, press 1. To transfer funds between accounts, press 2. For questions about an existing account or to report a lost or stolen credit card, press 3. To order checks, press 4. To apply for a loan, press 5. To speak with a customer service representative, press 6. To hear this menu again, press zero at any time.

74. What kind of a business is Prescott?

[8 second pause]

75. What should a caller press to speak to a customer service representative?

[8 second pause]

76. What can a caller do by pressing 0?

[8 second pause]

Questions 77–79 refer to the following talk.

Are there times when you find your energy lagging at work? Many people do. Most people do their best work in the morning. After lunch, however, people often find that it is hard to feel energetic enough to tackle the afternoon's work. How can you keep working productively until the workday ends? First, don't make the mistake of drinking coffee. After the caffeine has worn off, you will just feel more tired than ever. Sugary snacks have the same effect. Instead, stand up and take a brisk walk around the office. Do this for five minutes every hour to stay refreshed and energized.

77. When do people often lack energy?

[8 second pause]

78. What does the speaker recommend to maintain energy?

[8 second pause]

79. How often should this be done?

[8 second pause]

Questions 80–82 refer to the following advertisement.

Magruder's is closing its uptown branch, and everything in the store must go. Come on in to find the bargains of a lifetime. Desks, chairs, computer stands, bookshelves, filing cabinets, you name it, we've got it on sale. You won't have to look far to find bargains here. Everything is marked down 65% off its usual price. The sale begins next week and continues until the end of the month. Don't miss this sale. We promise you won't go home empty-handed.

80. What is sold at Magruders?

[8 second pause]

81. How big a discount is offered?

[8 second pause]

82. When does the sale begin?

[8 second pause]

Questions 83–85 refer to the following advertisement.

Are you feeling bored at your job? Do you want to be earning more money? At the Computer Training Institute, we will train you to become a sought-after, high-earning computer technician. You will learn how to repair computers and related equipment. After you finish our six-month course, our employment office will prepare you for job interviews and help you find a position as a computer technician or technical assistant. Take advantage of our special low tuition. You pay only $2,000 for six months of training. That's all! New courses start soon. Visit our website today to sign up.

83. What is being offered?

   [8 second pause]

84. How much does it cost?

   [8 second pause]

85. How can one take advantage of the offer?

   [8 second pause]

Questions 86–88 refer to the following weather report.

Welcome to the midday weather update. It's time to put away those shorts and sandals. Winter has arrived. Snow is falling over much of our region and will continue to fall throughout the afternoon and evening. The weather has caused dangerous road conditions, and several accidents have been reported. Commuter trains are also experiencing numerous delays. If you don't have urgent business away from home, then don't go out. Snowfall will continue overnight and will end by early tomorrow morning. Tomorrow promises to be clear, but cold and windy.

86. How is the weather today?

   [8 second pause]

87. What does the speaker suggest listeners do?

   [8 second pause]

88. When will the weather change?

   [8 second pause]

Questions 89–91 refer to the following announcement.

Good morning, and welcome to the third annual conference of the Business Owners Association. All conference workshops will take place in the conference rooms on the first floor of the hotel. At noon, lunch will be served in the Garden Restaurant on the ground floor. Following lunch, we will enjoy hearing our guest speaker, Dr. Lucille Snow of the Ambient Company. Afternoon workshops begin at 1:30. At 2:00 there will be a computer software demonstration in the auditorium for anyone interested. Because the weather is so nice, we will enjoy our afternoon refreshments outside on the patio between 5:00 and 6:00.

89. What will happen on the first floor?

[8 second pause]

90. What time will the demonstration be held?

[8 second pause]

91. Where will refreshments be served?

[8 second pause]

Questions 92–94 refer to the following announcement.

May I have your attention, please? Because of construction work, Park Street Station is closed. All passengers for Park Street Station will have to exit the train at Center Station. Bus service is available at Center Station to carry passengers to Park Street. After exiting the station, please line up at the curb for a bus. Please avoid crowding. Buses will leave frequently, but there may be some delays because of street traffic. We are very sorry for the inconvenience. The station is scheduled to reopen in three weeks. Thank you for your cooperation.

92. What is the problem?

[8 second pause]

93. What is the cause of the problem?

[8 second pause]

94. How long will the problem last?

[8 second pause]

Questions 95–97 refer to the following news report.

The president left early Tuesday for a five-nation tour of South America. During his 10-day tour, he will meet with national leaders to discuss the current economic situation. He will also attend a banquet given by the International Science Association, where he will present awards to leading international scientists. On his return, the president plans to take a few days of rest, which he will spend with his family at their beach house.

95. How many countries will the president visit on his tour?

[8 second pause]

96. What will the president talk about with national leaders?

[8 second pause]

97. What will the president do when his trip is over?

[8 second pause]

Questions 98–100 refer to the following talk.

Before we end the meeting, I'd like to let you all know of an opportunity. A management training workshop is being offered next month, on Tuesday, December 13. If any of you would like to attend, let me know and I will make the arrangements. The workshop will last all day and should be quite interesting. They will provide lunch, so all you will need to bring is a laptop computer, which we can provide from the office. I understand that they will be filming this session, so be prepared to appear on camera! Please let me know before the end of this week if you would like to attend, and I will put your name on the list.

98. What opportunity is offered?

[8 second pause]

99. When will it happen?

[8 second pause]

100. What should people bring?

[8 second pause]

TOEIC PRACTICE TEST 2

Listening Comprehension

Part 1: Photographs

Directions: You will see a photograph. You will hear four statements about the photograph. Choose the statement that most closely matches the photograph and fill in the corresponding oval on your answer sheet.

Example

Now listen to the four statements.

(A) She's getting on a plane.
(B) She's reading a magazine.
(C) She's taking a nap.
(D) She's holding a glass.

Statement (B), "She's reading a magazine," best describes what you see in the picture. Therefore, you should choose answer (B).

1. Look at the photo marked number 1 in your test book.
   (A) The car is parked in the garage.
   (B) The street is covered with snow.
   (C) The man is driving slowly.
   (D) The white flowers are in bloom.

   [5 second pause]

2. Look at the photo marked number 2 in your test book.
   (A) The janitor is fixing the lights.
   (B) The author is writing a book.
   (C) The professor is giving a lecture.
   (D) The student is cleaning the blackboard.

   [5 second pause]

3. Look at the photo marked number 3 in your test book.
   (A) The ship is loaded with cargo.
   (B) The passenger is standing on the deck.
   (C) The boat is in the middle of the ocean.
   (D) The captain is giving orders.

   [5 second pause]

4. Look at the photo marked number 4 in your test book.
   (A) She's drinking the liquid.
   (B) She's removing her mask.
   (C) She's washing her gloves.
   (D) She's looking at a test tube.

   [5 second pause]

5. Look at the photo marked number 5 in your test book.
   (A) The computers are on the table.
   (B) The curtains are closed.
   (C) The man has a magazine.
   (D) The woman is looking at the man.

   [5 second pause]

6. Look at the photo marked number 6 in your test book.
   (A) She's looking for a suit.
   (B) She's picking apples from the tree.
   (C) She's going to buy some fruit.
   (D) She's cleaning pears to make a pie.

   [5 second pause]

7. Look at the photo marked number 7 in your test book.
   (A) The waiters are drinking from glasses.
   (B) The two men are shaking hands.
   (C) The workers are filing the documents.
   (D) The women are climbing the stairs.

   [5 second pause]

8. Look at the photo marked number 8 in your test book.
   (A) They're waiting to enter the museum.
   (B) They're taking pictures of the room.
   (C) They're looking at paintings on the wall.
   (D) They're sitting on a bench.

   [5 second pause]

9. Look at the photo marked number 9 in your test book.
   (A) The station is empty.
   (B) The plane is ready to take off.
   (C) The passengers are buying tickets.
   (D) The train is underground.

   [5 second pause]

10. Look at the photo marked number 10 in your test book.
    (A) He's putting on his jacket.
    (B) He's opening his briefcase.
    (C) He's trying on the trousers.
    (D) He's lying on the bed.

    [5 second pause]

Part 2: Question-Response

Directions: You will hear a question and three possible responses. Choose the response that most closely answers the question and fill in the corresponding oval on your answer sheet.

Example

Now listen to the sample question.

You will hear:

How is the weather?

You will also hear:

(A) It's raining.
(B) He's fine, thanks.
(C) He's my boss.

The best response to the question *How is the weather?* is choice (A), *It's raining.* Therefore, you should choose answer (A).

11. It was nice meeting you.
    (A) Yes, it was nice meeting you, too.
    (B) No, it was a boring meeting.
    (C) The seating wasn't bad.

    [5 second pause]

12. Does Mr. Kim work here?
    (A) Yes, he left it here.
    (B) He's a hard worker.
    (C) No, his office is down the hall.

    [5 second pause]

13. Why can't you open the door?
    (A) We don't need more.
    (B) I don't have a key.
    (C) There's a pen on the floor.

    [5 second pause]

14. Whose car is that?
    (A) He has a brand new car.
    (B) It belongs to my boss.
    (C) Let's take a drive.

    [5 second pause]

15. What time did they arrive?
    (A) They never drive.
    (B) There were five of them.
    (C) They got here at 6:00.

    [5 second pause]

16. Did you forget something?
    (A) Yes, I left my coat at the office.
    (B) No, don't get anything.
    (C) I can get you something.

    [5 second pause]

17. Where is the bus stop?
    (A) It makes frequent stops.
    (B) It was a long ride.
    (C) It's right across the street.

    [5 second pause]

18. How often are there staff meetings?
    (A) About twice a month.
    (B) They're in the conference room.
    (C) He's reading very well.

    [5 second pause]

19. May I have your address?
    (A) That's my address book.
    (B) Thank you. It's a new dress.
    (C) I live at 16 Maple Avenue.

    [5 second pause]

20. Did anyone call while I was out?
    (A) Yes, there's a phone message on your desk.
    (B) No, it isn't cold outside.
    (C) He's quite a tall man.

    [5 second pause]

21. What do you want for dinner?
    (A) I almost never cook.
    (B) How about a steak and some salad?
    (C) He used to be thinner.

    [5 second pause]

22. How many books did you sell?
    (A) I read as often as I can.
    (B) I sold only ten.
    (C) I don't think he looks well.

    [5 second pause]

23. When is your vacation?
    (A) To the beach.
    (B) At the station.
    (C) Next August.

    [5 second pause]

24. Why didn't they come to lunch with us?
    (A) I don't usually drink punch.
    (B) They were too busy with work.
    (C) It was at a nice little restaurant.

    [5 second pause]

25. Do you need anything from the store?
    (A) Yes, I could use some paper and envelopes.
    (B) No, there were fewer than four.
    (C) I go shopping about once a week.

    [5 second pause]

26. Where do you keep pens?
    (A) They're in my desk drawer.
    (B) I prefer to use black ink.
    (C) That's my pen, I believe.

    [5 second pause]

27. It looks like it might rain soon.
    (A) Night will come soon.
    (B) The train arrives at noon.
    (C) Then don't forget to take your umbrella.

    [5 second pause]

28. Which coat is yours?
    (A) That's a very nice coat.
    (B) It's that black one in the closet.
    (C) I'm planning to buy a new coat soon.

    [5 second pause]

29. This room is very warm.
    (A) I warned you about them.
    (B) Let's open all the windows.
    (C) There's not enough room.

    [5 second pause]

30. How close is the subway station?
    (A) It's just down the street.
    (B) You can wear those clothes.
    (C) They just remodeled the station.

    [5 second pause]

31. Where can I buy a newspaper?
    (A) We could use some new paper.
    (B) I read it every day.
    (C) At the store on the corner.

    [5 second pause]

32. What's your favorite sport?
    (A) It's a very busy port.
    (B) I enjoy playing tennis.
    (C) He did me a favor.

    [5 second pause]

33. I thought the movie was very interesting.
    (A) No, he's not interested in movies.
    (B) Yes, I liked it, too.
    (C) We're moving tomorrow.

    [5 second pause]

34. Where did you put the package?
    (A) I left it on your desk.
    (B) I'll mail it tomorrow.
    (C) I packed all the suitcases.

    [5 second pause]

35. Weren't you at the workshop last Friday?
    (A) No, I was sick that day.
    (B) Yes, I work in that shop.
    (C) It's closed on Fridays.

    [5 second pause]

36. Who was at the meeting this morning?
    (A) He's always greeting everyone.
    (B) We're meeting in the morning.
    (C) Almost the whole staff was there.

    [5 second pause]

37. I'm really hungry.
    (A) Let's have lunch now.
    (B) Please don't be angry.
    (C) You don't need to hurry.

    [5 second pause]

38. Where do you live?
    (A) You can leave it on my desk.
    (B) In a small apartment downtown.
    (C) You don't need to give anything.

    [5 second pause]

39. When will the copies be ready?
    (A) I need 50 copies.
    (B) I'll have them for you this afternoon.
    (C) This machine makes very clear copies.

    [5 second pause]

40. Will you need more paper?
    (A) This paper is thicker.
    (B) No, I think this is enough.
    (C) I write quite a lot.

    [5 second pause]

Part 3: Conversations

Directions: You will hear a conversation between two people. You will see three questions on each conversation and four possible answers. Choose the best answer to each question and fill in the corresponding oval on your answer sheet.

Questions 41–43 refer to the following conversation.

Woman: I'm calling an emergency meeting for tomorrow morning at 10:00. Do you think you can be there?

Man: I can be there, but not on time. I'll probably be about 15 minutes late. Why are you calling the meeting, anyhow?

Woman: The accounting department has been having some difficulties, and paychecks will be delayed until next week. I want to explain the situation to everyone.

Man: You know this has happened before. It's really getting to be a bad problem. I can't pretend not to be annoyed about it.

41. What time will the man probably get to the meeting?

[8 second pause]

42. Why is the woman calling a meeting?

[8 second pause]

43. How does the man feel about the situation?

[8 second pause]

Questions 44–46 refer to the following conversation.

Man: May I see your ticket, please? Thank you. You're in Row 10, Seat A, right next to the window.

Woman: Great. Thanks. Can you tell me how long the flight will be?

Man: There shouldn't be any delays on a nice cloudless day like today, so I expect we'll be arriving right on schedule at 2:00. We'll begin food service in about half an hour.

Woman: I didn't know there would be food. That's wonderful. I'm starving. Will there be a movie, too?

44. Where does this conversation take place?

[8 second pause]

45. What's the weather like?

[8 second pause]

46. When will food be served?

[8 second pause]

Questions 47–49 refer to the following conversation.

Woman: Do you think you could help me move this desk to the other side of the room? I want to put it near the window so I can work in the daylight.

Man: I'm sorry. I hurt my back. I'm not supposed to lift heavy things. Why don't you get Samantha to help you?

Woman: She's not here. She'll be at a meeting downtown all afternoon. I guess I'll just have to wait until tomorrow and have her help me then.

Man: Yes, she'll be here tomorrow. She should be able to help you out.

47. What does the woman want to do?

[8 second pause]

48. Why can't the man help her do it?

[8 second pause]

49. When will she do it?

[8 second pause]

Questions 50–52 refer to the following conversation.

Man: I'm looking for some warm winter gloves. My wife said you had them on sale.

Woman: Yes, these gloves are on sale. They come with matching hats. We also have these scarves that would look just right with them.

Man: Yes, that's all very nice, but I really just want the gloves. That's what I came down here for. I'll take this black pair.

Woman: Very good. That comes to $15.50 with tax. Would you like me to put them in a bag for you?

50. What will the man buy?

   [8 second pause]

51. What color will he take?

   [8 second pause]

52. How much will he pay?

   [8 second pause]

Questions 53–55 refer to the following conversation.

Man: Could you make some copies of this report for me please? I need 225. I hope that's not too many.

Woman: It's not, but I hope you don't need them soon. Things are really busy now and there are three jobs ahead of you.

Man: That's okay. I actually don't need them today at all, but can you have them ready before the conference tomorrow morning?

Woman: That shouldn't be a problem. I'll have them all copied, collated, and stapled before the conference begins.

53. How many copies of the report does the man need?

   [8 second pause]

54. When does he need them?

   [8 second pause]

55. Why can't the woman make the copies now?

   [8 second pause]

Questions 56–58 refer to the following conversation.

Woman: Good morning. I'd like to see Mr. Lee, please.
Man: I'm sorry. He's not here. He's out of town on a business trip. Do you have an appointment?
Woman: Well, actually, no. I thought I could just come by. I didn't realize he was away. When do you expect him back?
Man: Not until next week. If you leave your name and phone number, I can have him call you when he returns to the office.

56. What does the woman want to do?

[8 second pause]

57. Where is Mr. Lee?

[8 second pause]

58. When will he return?

[8 second pause]

Questions 59–61 refer to the following conversation.

Man: Oh, no! Look at the time! There's no way I can make it downtown on time for my doctor's appointment.
Woman: Sure you can. Take my car. Just bring it back in time for me to get to my computer class tonight. Here's the key.
Man: Great. Thanks. Is it parked in the garage?
Woman: No, it's that old blue van across the street. Drive carefully. It looks like it might rain.

59. Where does the man have to go?

[8 second pause]

60. Where is the woman's car?

[8 second pause]

61. What color is the car?

[8 second pause]

Questions 62–64 refer to the following conversation.

Man: I'm sorry, Ms. Jones has already left the office and gone home.
Woman: She left already? That's not possible. She knew we had a meeting this afternoon.
Man: Well, she left right around 3:00. She wanted to avoid the traffic. You know how bad it gets when there's a heavy rain like this.
Woman: I'll have to call her at home, then. This report can't wait. We have to talk about it before tomorrow.

62. Why did Ms. Jones leave the office early?

[8 second pause]

63. What time did Ms. Jones leave the office?

[8 second pause]

64. What is the weather like?

[8 second pause]

Questions 65–67 refer to the following conversation.

Woman: I mailed you those photographs the other day. Did you get them?
Man: No. I've been looking out for them, but they haven't arrived yet. When did you mail them?
Woman: Three days ago. I think I should report them as lost.
Man: Relax. You mailed them Monday and today's only Thursday. Let's just wait another day before we panic. Then if they aren't here by tomorrow, you can resend them. You have copies, don't you?

65. What did the woman send the man?

[8 second pause]

66. When did she send them?

[8 second pause]

67. What does the woman want to do now?

[8 second pause]

Questions 68–70 refer to the following conversation.

Woman: We're playing tennis at the park this afternoon. Would you like to join us?
Man: Thanks, but I was at the club all morning playing golf, and I'm really wiped out.
Woman: Then you'd better rest. You're planning on going to the banquet at the hotel tonight, aren't you? There will be dinner and dancing.
Man: Yes, I wouldn't miss it for anything. I've been looking forward to it. I bought my tickets weeks ago.

68. What does the woman invite the man to do?

[8 second pause]

69. Why doesn't the man want to do it?

[8 second pause]

70. Where will the man be tonight?

[8 second pause]

Part 4: Talks

Directions: You will hear a talk given by a single speaker. You will see three questions on each talk, each with four possible answers. Choose the best answer to each question and fill in the corresponding oval on your answer sheet.

Questions 71–73 refer to the following recording.

Thank you for calling Jiffy Computer Services, your neighborhood computer sales and repair service. Is your computer giving you problems? No problem! We'll have it up and running in no time. Our technicians are available to help you 24 hours a day, seven days a week. To speak with Tech Support, please stay on the line. If you would like to purchase a new computer, press 1 to speak with the next available sales consultant. To make an appointment for a consultation in your home or office, press 2. For billing questions, press 3. To hear this menu again, press zero.

71. When can a customer speak with a technician?

    [8 second pause]

72. How can a caller make an appointment?

    [8 second pause]

73. What can a caller do by pressing 3?

    [8 second pause]

Questions 74–76 refer to the following talk.

Welcome to the first lecture in our series. We are fortunate to have as our speaker tonight Dr. Clothilde Swanson, who is visiting us as part of her book promotion tour. Dr. Swanson will talk with us tonight about her newest book, *Small Business Success*. She will explain the innovative business system that she has outlined in her book, a system that will result in success for any small-business man or woman. After the talk, Dr. Swanson's book will be available for sale at the back of the room near the exit sign. Books are $25 each. Unfortunately, because of unforeseen circumstances, refreshments will not be served this evening. Don't miss next month's lecture on Thursday, March 1, when Arnold Jones will speak about customer relations in the twenty-first century.

74. What will Dr. Swanson talk about?

    [8 second pause]

75. What will happen after the talk?

    [8 second pause]

76. When will the next lecture take place?

[8 second pause]

Questions 77–79 refer to the following advertisement.

Your comfort is important. That's why we developed the EZ Sit desk chair. Its special ergonomic construction supports your posture while you sit at your desk. Its high-class design looks great in any office. Go ahead and work at your computer all day. With the EZ Sit chair you'll feel so comfortable, you'll never want to leave your desk! But don't take our word for it. Visit your local EZ Furniture Showroom and try out our chairs in person. Or phone our customer service line at (800) 387-9876 for a free catalog and order form. Mention this ad and receive a 15% discount off your first in-store or catalog purchase of an EZ Sit chair. Offer ends May 20.

77. What product is being advertised?

[8 second pause]

78. Where would this product be used?

[8 second pause]

79. How much is the discount?

[8 second pause]

Questions 80–82 refer to the following weather report.

Good morning and welcome to the weather update. The drought continues today with clear skies and plenty of sunshine. Temperatures will reach a high of around 85 degrees this afternoon, with overnight lows in the high sixties. Expect more of the same tomorrow and for the rest of the week. But don't despair. Change is in the air! Over the weekend a cold front will be moving in, bringing with it cloudy skies, so we should be getting that long-awaited rain by Sunday.

80. What is the weather like today?

[8 second pause]

81. What will the high temperature be?

[8 second pause]

82. When will the weather change?

[8 second pause]

Questions 83–85 refer to the following talk.

If you travel frequently for business, you may find it difficult to maintain a healthful diet. When you're worn out from travel or work, you might just settle for the most convenient or cheapest meal—fast food, a salty snack, or a sweet dessert. Don't give up so easily. There is a simple way to make sure you get your basic nutrition even while on the road. The solution is to make sure to eat a big breakfast every morning. Most restaurants offer healthful breakfast choices such as cereal and eggs. By eating a big breakfast you guarantee that you get at least one nutritious meal a day. In addition, you will have the energy to work all morning.

83. Who is the talk for?

[8 second pause]

84. What does the speaker recommend eating?

[8 second pause]

85. Why is this recommended?

[8 second pause]

Questions 86–88 refer to the following recording.

Thank you for calling the dental office of Dr. Elizabeth Pekar. If this is an emergency, hang up immediately and contact the on-call dentist, Dr. Rogers, at 324-9014. Our normal office hours are Monday through Friday from 7:30 until 4:00, and Saturday from 9:00 until noon. To make an appointment for an office visit, please call back when the office is open. If you would like to speak with the doctor or any of the office staff, please leave a message after the beep and we will get back to you as soon as possible.

86. What should a caller do in an emergency?

[8 second pause]

87. What day is the office closed?

[8 second pause]

88. How can a caller make an appointment?

[8 second pause]

Questions 89–91 refer to the following announcement.

The fifth annual Center City Job Fair will take place this coming Saturday at the Royal Hotel from 11:30 until 4:00. Representatives from more than 100 companies will be on hand to talk with you about career opportunities in their fields. Preliminary job application forms will be available, and attendees are advised to bring up to 25 copies of their resume. Throughout the day special seminars will be offered on topics such as The Successful Job Interview, Write a Winning Resume, and Dressing for Business Success. Admission is just $10, and tickets will be available at the door. Don't miss the event that the Center City Daily newspaper has called "the best job fair in the country."

89. Who would be most interested in the advertised event?

[8 second pause]

90. What time will the event begin?

[8 second pause]

91. What should people bring to the event?

[8 second pause]

Questions 92–94 refer to the following announcement.

Welcome aboard flight 305 to Mexico City. Our travel time today will be just under six hours, putting us in Mexico City at 4:15. The rain clouds that were threatening us earlier have cleared up and we should have smooth sailing all the way to our destination, with bright, sunny skies. If you'll look out the windows on the left side, you should be able to see Lake Pine in the distance, with a view of the mountains behind it. Enjoy your trip and thank you for flying with us.

92. Where would this announcement be heard?

[8 second pause]

93. How many hours will the trip last?

[8 second pause]

94. What's the weather like?

[8 second pause]

Questions 95–97 refer to the following news report.

The heavy rains this month have caused flooding throughout the region. In Woodsville last night, the Green River overflowed its banks, sending water rushing through the main streets of the town. Streets are still under water this morning, and most of the downtown area has been closed off by the police. Citizens are asked to stay away from downtown until the streets have been reopened. Local flooding and mudslides have caused hazardous driving conditions throughout the area, so drive with caution. Clear skies are predicted for the next few days, and the floods should recede by the weekend.

95. What is the problem?

   [8 second pause]

96. What are citizens asked to do?

   [8 second pause]

97. When will the situation improve?

   [8 second pause]

Questions 98–100 refer to the following advertisement.

Spend your next vacation with us. The Lakeside Hotel and Resort offers a relaxing location with spectacular views and luxuriously comfortable rooms, April through January. Relax by the lake or enjoy the many activities available—lake and pool swimming, tennis, hiking, and boating. In the evenings enjoy a four-course meal at our top-rated restaurant. Our early season weekend package, including room, breakfast buffet, one dinner, and access to all resort activities costs just $700 per couple. This special low rate is available from April 15 through May 31. If you enjoy winter sports, call to find out about our winter vacation specials available December through January.

98. What can guests do at the Lakeside Resort?

   [8 second pause]

99. How much does the special weekend package cost?

   [8 second pause]

100. When is the resort closed?

   [8 second pause]

TOEIC PRACTICE TEST 3

Listening Comprehension

Part 1: Photographs

Directions: You will see a photograph. You will hear four statements about the photograph. Choose the statement that most closely matches the photograph and fill in the corresponding oval on your answer sheet.

Example

Now listen to the four statements.

(A) She's getting on a plane.
(B) She's reading a magazine.
(C) She's taking a nap.
(D) She's holding a glass.

Statement (B), "She's reading a magazine," best describes what you see in the picture. Therefore, you should choose answer (B).

1. Look at the photo marked number 1 in your test book.
   (A) The scientists are using a microscope.
   (B) The teachers are using a telescope.
   (C) The doctors are examining the patient.
   (D) The professors are hanging up their coats.

[5 second pause]

2. Look at the photo marked number 2 in your test book.
   (A) She's talking to a commuter.
   (B) She's making a cup of coffee.
   (C) She's writing on the computer.
   (D) She's cleaning off the table.

[5 second pause]

3. Look at the photo marked number 3 in your test book.
   (A) The drivers are having an argument.
   (B) The cars are parked in the lot.
   (C) The taxman is going to his office.
   (D) The cab is moving down the street.

[5 second pause]

4. Look at the photo marked number 4 in your test book.
   (A) They're arranging the seating.
   (B) They're having a meeting.
   (C) They're fixing the heating.
   (D) They're enjoying what they're eating.

[5 second pause]

5. Look at the photo marked number 5 in your test book.
   (A) It's starting to rain.
   (B) They're on a plane.
   (C) The aisle is crowded.
   (D) The bookstore is open.

[5 second pause]

6. Look at the photo marked number 6 in your test book.
   (A) They're standing on the steps.
   (B) They're waving good-bye to each other.
   (C) They're walking up the stairs.
   (D) They're holding on to the railing.

[5 second pause]

7. Look at the photo marked number 7 in your test book.
   (A) The customer is ordering drinks.
   (B) He's pouring the tea.
   (C) The man is drinking water.
   (D) The waiter is carrying a tray.

[5 second pause]

8. Look at the photo marked number 8 in your test book.
   (A) The attendant is parking the van.
   (B) The passenger is sitting in front.
   (C) The mechanic is repairing the car.
   (D) The driver is ready to leave.

   [5 second pause]

9. Look at the photo marked number 9 in your test book.
   (A) The cooks are finished working.
   (B) The shelves are filled with books.
   (C) The library is closed now.
   (D) The woman is writing a book.

   [5 second pause]

10. Look at the photo marked number 10 in your test book.
    (A) He's fixing the shelf.
    (B) He's opening the boxes.
    (C) He's lifting a heavy load.
    (D) He's driving through the city.

    [5 second pause]

Part 2: Question-Response

Directions: You will hear a question and three possible responses. Choose the response that most closely answers the question and fill in the corresponding oval on your answer sheet.

Example

Now listen to the sample question.

You will hear:

How is the weather?

You will also hear:

(A) It's raining.
(B) He's fine, thanks.
(C) He's my boss.

The best response to the question *How is the weather?* is choice (A), *It's raining.* Therefore, you should choose answer (A).

11. What time did they arrive?
    (A) At half past eleven.
    (B) I don't know how to drive.
    (C) I had a good time, too.

    [5 second pause]

12. Is Mr. Kim away on vacation?
    (A) Yes, the train is at the station.
    (B) Yes, he'll be back next week.
    (C) Yes, it's a very nice day.

    [5 second pause]

13. I don't have a pen with me.
    (A) Write your name on the line.
    (B) It will be open tomorrow.
    (C) Here, please use mine.

    [5 second pause]

14. Where can I put my coat?
   (A) It was a long trip by boat.
   (B) Hang it in this closet.
   (C) It's very cold outside.

[5 second pause]

15. How many books did you buy?
   (A) The time went by so fast.
   (B) She looks very well.
   (C) I bought only two.

[5 second pause]

16. Who did you have lunch with?
   (A) An old school friend.
   (B) At the restaurant on the corner.
   (C) I'm not very hungry.

[5 second pause]

17. How long did the meeting last?
   (A) He's always reading something.
   (B) It was the last one.
   (C) Only about 30 minutes.

[5 second pause]

18. This store looks very crowded.
   (A) Then let's shop someplace else.
   (B) I think I'd like some more.
   (C) It's a very cloudy day.

[5 second pause]

19. How long have you worked here?
   (A) Yes, I work here.
   (B) For close to five years.
   (C) No, I'm sorry, he's not here.

[5 second pause]

20. The carpet looks very dirty.
   (A) The books are in the car.
   (B) My car is outside.
   (C) It's time to get it cleaned.

[5 second pause]

21. How much did your train ticket cost?
   (A) They got lost in the rain.
   (B) About four hours or so.
   (C) More than $200.

[5 second pause]

22. The bank is open today, isn't it?
   (A) Yes, it's open every day except Sunday.
   (B) No, it's not a very fine day.
   (C) I opened an account there yesterday.

[5 second pause]

23. Why isn't Ms. Lee here today?
   (A) She's away on a business trip.
   (B) I'm sorry, I didn't hear.
   (C) I'll tell her when I see her.

[5 second pause]

24. How far is the restaurant from here?
   (A) The food is really delicious.
   (B) It's about a five-minute walk.
   (C) I ate there last week.

[5 second pause]

25. What did they talk about at the meeting?
   (A) The seating was not very comfortable.
   (B) Almost everyone talked at the meeting.
   (C) They discussed the budget for next year.

[5 second pause]

26. Who made these photocopies?
   (A) Use the copy machine downstairs.
   (B) Mr. Brown made them.
   (C) I made 10 photocopies.

[5 second pause]

27. Where can I park my car?
   (A) There's a garage across the street.
   (B) The park is two blocks from here.
   (C) My car is a dark color, too.

[5 second pause]

28. Which seat would you prefer?
    (A) I don't usually eat meat.
    (B) Their appointment was deferred.
    (C) I'd like to sit by the window.

    [5 second pause]

29. This office is very small.
    (A) No, she's not that tall.
    (B) Yes, I'm looking for a bigger one.
    (C) You can call me at the office.

    [5 second pause]

30. When will they arrive?
    (A) On the 10:00 train.
    (B) They almost never drive.
    (C) Look for them at the train station.

    [5 second pause]

31. How was the weather during your vacation?
    (A) We went to the beach.
    (B) It was sunny every day.
    (C) We were there for two weeks.

    [5 second pause]

32. Where did you put the newspaper?
    (A) Because I like to keep up with the news.
    (B) I read it before breakfast.
    (C) I left it in your office.

    [5 second pause]

33. Who did you see at the party?
    (A) Divide it into three parts.
    (B) Just a few old friends.
    (C) There was food and dancing.

    [5 second pause]

34. When will the report be ready?
    (A) I usually listen to the news report.
    (B) I'll finish it this afternoon.
    (C) I like reading.

    [5 second pause]

35. What did they serve for lunch?
    (A) A really delicious chicken dish.
    (B) They served it in the cafeteria.
    (C) It was just a small bunch.

    [5 second pause]

36. It's very dark in here.
    (A) He always wears dark colors.
    (B) I'm sorry. You can't park here.
    (C) I'll turn on some lights.

    [5 second pause]

37. Where will you be this afternoon?
    (A) We'll be there very soon.
    (B) In my office, as usual.
    (C) It's a lovely afternoon.

    [5 second pause]

38. Is that a new sweater?
    (A) Yes. Do you like it?
    (B) No, he isn't any better.
    (C) It's made of pure wool.

    [5 second pause]

39. What time did you get home last night?
    (A) You can use the phone on my desk.
    (B) It was after midnight by the time I
        got there.
    (C) Their home is quite modern.

    [5 second pause]

40. Excuse me. Do you have the time?
    (A) That's a good-looking watch.
    (B) No, I think this one's mine.
    (C) Yes, it's half past eight.

    [5 second pause]

Part 3: Conversations

Directions: You will hear a conversation between two people. You will see three questions on each conversation and four possible answers. Choose the best answer to each question and fill in the corresponding oval on your answer sheet.

Questions 41–43 refer to the following conversation.

Woman: They're showing a great movie at the theater tonight. Do you want to go with me?

Man: I wish I could, but I have to work late. Why don't you go ahead without me?

Woman: You're always working late. The movie doesn't start till after 9:00. Why don't you just work a few hours and then meet me at the theater?

Man: That's a good plan. You go early and get the tickets. I'll look for you by the front entrance at around nine.

41. What does the woman want to do?

   [8 second pause]

42. Why does the man say he can't do this?

   [8 second pause]

43. What time will the man and woman meet?

   [8 second pause]

Questions 44–46 refer to the following conversation.

Man: We really need to go over this report together. Why don't we meet in my office tomorrow at noon and look at it then. I could order some lunch to eat while we work.

Woman: That might be a problem. I have a doctor's appointment in the early afternoon and it's all the way downtown.

Man: Could we meet in the morning, then? I have a conference early, but I'd be free by 10:30.

Woman: That should be all right. I'll see you tomorrow.

44. Why does the man want to meet with the woman?

   [8 second pause]

45. Where will they meet?

   [8 second pause]

46. When will they meet?

   [8 second pause]

Questions 47–49 refer to the following conversation.

Woman: Are you going up? Great. Could you push the button for the tenth floor, please?
Man: Of course. Do you live in this building?
Woman: No, I'm just visiting a colleague from work. She recently moved here from another city. She has an apartment on the tenth floor. Do you live here?
Man: Yes, I do. It's not a bad building to live in, really. It's close to all the stores, the rooms are spacious, and there are nice views from the top floors.

47. Where does this conversation take place?

[8 second pause]

48. Who is the woman visiting?

[8 second pause]

49. What is the man's opinion of the building?

[8 second pause]

Questions 50–52 refer to the following conversation.

Man: Could I book Conference Room 3 for a meeting next Friday morning?
Woman: That depends. Will you be done before 11:00? The room's already booked from 11:00 to 1:00 for a luncheon.
Man: I don't think that'll be a problem. We're scheduled to start at 8:00 and should be finished by 10:00.
Woman: That should work out, then. You can use the chairs that will be set up for the luncheon. Just be sure to put them back in place before you leave.

50. What does the man want to do?

[8 second pause]

51. What time will he finish?

[8 second pause]

52. What does the woman ask him to do?

[8 second pause]

Questions 53–55 refer to the following conversation.

Man: After hours of conference, they've finally agreed on a cleaning schedule. They're starting on the hallways today.

Woman: It's about time. They're filthy! What about the front office? And the cafeteria?

Man: The front office is scheduled for cleaning on Wednesday. I don't know about the cafeteria, but I suppose they'll get to it someday soon.

Woman: Well, I hope they get to it before the end of next week. I'm giving a workshop that Friday, and I need to use the cafeteria space.

53. What will be cleaned today?

[8 second pause]

54. When will the front office be cleaned?

[8 second pause]

55. What will the woman do next week?

[8 second pause]

Questions 56–58 refer to the following conversation.

Woman: I'm visiting relatives in Chicago next week. How long do you think it would take me to get there by train?

Man: Oh, it's a long trip—16 hours at least. Why don't you take the plane? It would get you there in two hours.

Woman: I've done that too many times before, I'm afraid. I thought it would be more interesting to try the train this time.

Man: I think it sounds like a waste of time. I always fly, myself. If I'm going on a business trip or on vacation, I always take a plane, even if it is expensive.

56. Why is the woman going to Chicago?

[8 second pause]

57. How long does the trip take by train?

[8 second pause]

58. Why does the woman prefer the train to the plane?

[8 second pause]

Questions 59–61 refer to the following conversation.

Man: This package can't wait. I have to mail it today. Where's the local post office?

Woman: It's just two blocks from here, but it's closed for the holiday. You could try the main post office, but it's more than a mile from here.

Man: Maybe that's a bit far to walk. I suppose I could take the bus.

Woman: The buses are so slow on holidays, and the weather is getting bad. Take a taxi. I'll go find one for you.

59. Why is the local post office closed?

    [8 second pause]

60. How far away is the main post office?

    [8 second pause]

61. How will the man get to the post office?

    [8 second pause]

Questions 62–64 refer to the following conversation.

Man: I really enjoy my lunch break. It's the only time I have in the day to be alone.

Woman: Don't you eat in the cafeteria with everyone else from your department?

Man: No. My assistant eats there, and most of the rest of my officemates go to a restaurant together, but I prefer to eat at my desk and have 45 minutes to myself.

Woman: I usually meet some friends for a half-hour lunch at a café. Then I walk in the park for 15 minutes before going back to the office.

62. Who does the man eat lunch with?

    [8 second pause]

63. Where does the man eat lunch?

    [8 second pause]

64. How long is the lunch break?

    [8 second pause]

Questions 65–67 refer to the following conversation.

Woman: I reserved a room for three nights, but it turns out I'm going to have to stay four.

Man: That shouldn't be a problem. Here's your key—Room 107. Do you have any luggage?

Woman: Just this one suitcase. You know, it's so nice and warm out, I thought I'd go for a walk now before dinner. Is there a park near here?

Man: Yes, very near. Just go down to the corner, where you'll see a bank. Take a left onto Main Street, and you'll see the park right in front of you.

65. How many nights will the woman stay at the hotel?

[8 second pause]

66. What does the woman want to do now?

[8 second pause]

67. What is the weather like?

[8 second pause]

Questions 68–70 refer to the following conversation.

Woman: I've booked a seat on the 10:30 train to Vancouver, and, look, it's 10:15 now. I have to find the gate quickly.

Man: It's boarding now at Gate 9, right over there. May I see your ticket?

Woman: Here it is. Is there someone who can carry my suitcase for me? It's quite heavy.

Man: You can give it to the agent at the gate, and she'll check it for you.

68. Where does this conversation take place?

[8 second pause]

69. What time is it now?

[8 second pause]

70. What does the woman need help with?

[8 second pause]

Part 4: Talks

Directions: You will hear a talk given by a single speaker. You will see three questions on each talk, each with four possible answers. Choose the best answer to each question and fill in the corresponding oval on your answer sheet.

Questions 71–73 refer to the following recording.

Thank you for calling West Regional Electrical Utilities Company. Your call is important to us. Our regular office hours are 7:00 AM until 9:00 PM, Monday through Friday. If you are calling outside of office hours, please press zero to leave a message. To report a power outage or other emergency, press 1. For billing questions, press 2. To open a new account, press 3. To hear this message in Spanish, press 4. To repeat this message, press 5. If you wish to speak directly with a customer service representative, please stay on the line, and your call will be answered in turn.

71. What time does the office open?

[8 second pause]

72. How can a caller open an account?

[8 second pause]

73. What can a caller do by pressing 2?

[8 second pause]

Questions 74–76 refer to the following report.

This is your early-morning traffic update. Traffic is moving smoothly throughout the region with the exception of Highway 10 near the approach to the White River Bridge. Because of repairs, the bridge is closed and all traffic is being rerouted down Park Avenue to the City Tunnel. Expect delays in this area of up to 20 minutes during the morning rush hour. Unfortunately, this situation may continue for several more months, as repairs aren't due to be completed until early September. Tune in for the next traffic update at 9:00.

74. What is being repaired?

[8 second pause]

75. When will the repairs be finished?

[8 second pause]

76. When is the next traffic update?

[8 second pause]

Questions 77–79 refer to the following advertisement.

Are you looking for a better career? Why not try the exciting field of law? In just six short months, you can become a legal assistant. That's right! At the Legal Training Institute, we prepare you to work in any law office, assisting with document preparation, research, computer data entry, and customer service. Our evening and weekend class schedule is designed for busy people like you who work all day, and our low, low prices, starting at just $500 for introductory-level classes, will fit any budget. Call now to find out if a career as a legal assistant is right for you. Already convinced? Visit our website to download an application and start studying as soon as next week.

77. What kind of job does this school train for?

[8 second pause]

78. How many months does the course last?

[8 second pause]

79. How can someone get an application?

[8 second pause]

Questions 80–82 refer to the following announcement.

Good afternoon. Flight 546 to Honolulu is about to begin boarding at Gate 11. All passengers for Honolulu, please approach gate eleven now. We will board passengers with small children first, and then we will begin boarding from the back of the plane, starting with Rows 30 to 35. Please remember, only one piece of carry-on luggage, excluding purses and coats, is allowed. Passengers are asked to check extra luggage with the gate attendant. Have a pleasant trip and thank you for flying with us.

80. Where would this announcement be heard?

[8 second pause]

81. Which gate should passengers go to?

[8 second pause]

82. Who will get on first?

[8 second pause]

Questions 83–85 refer to the following announcement.

Don't miss the annual Summer Fun Festival coming up next month. Games, food, dancing, and crafts will be available to all at the City Fairgrounds from Thursday, July 15 through Sunday, July 18, all for the low, low admission price of twenty dollars. Thursday night's opening ceremonies are free and open to the public and will feature a special concert performed by local musicians. Remember, this event is free, but tickets must be reserved in advance. Call the Public Events Office to reserve your tickets now.

83. When was this announcement being made?

   [8 second pause]

84. When will the festival begin?

   [8 second pause]

85. What will happen on Thursday night?

   [8 second pause]

Questions 86–88 refer to the following report.

The National Airport Workers Union threatened a strike today following the announcement by Blue Sky Airlines that there will be a salary freeze for all airport workers effective immediately. This is because of the financial difficulties and the decrease in the number of passengers the airline has been suffering over the past few months. Airport workers had been expecting a salary increase next month. Blue Sky claims that they are acting within the terms of their contract with the airport workers. Union leaders disagree and plan to strike next week. Blue Sky officials and representatives from the mayor's office and the National Transportation Board will meet with union leaders at the Royal Hotel tomorrow afternoon to discuss ways to avert the strike.

86. Why will airport workers go on strike?

   [8 second pause]

87. When will the strike begin?

   [8 second pause]

88. Where will union leaders and airline officials meet?

   [8 second pause]

Questions 89–91 refer to the following announcement.

Welcome aboard train number 6 to New York City. We should be arriving at our destination in just under three hours. Please remember, smoking is prohibited on all parts of the train. The fourth car from the rear is the designated quiet car. Cell phone use is not permitted in that car and laptops may be used only with the sound turned off. The food service car will open in 15 minutes. Hot and cold drinks, sandwiches, and snacks will be available for sale. Enjoy your trip!

89. How long is the trip to New York?

   [8 second pause]

90. What is not allowed anywhere on the train?

   [8 second pause]

91. What will happen in 15 minutes?

   [8 second pause]

Questions 92–94 refer to the following recording.

Thank you for calling the Deluxe Downtown Theater. Tickets are now available for our new musical show, *Cats and Dogs!*, opening next week. Show times are Saturday and Sunday at 2:00 PM for the matinee, and Thursday through Saturday at 8:00 PM for the evening show. Matinee tickets are $24 each, and evening tickets are $30. Children under age 12 can see the show for half the price of a regular adult ticket. To reserve your tickets, wait for the beep, then leave a message. Be sure to speak slowly and clearly. Or, send your request by mail to the Deluxe Downtown Theater, 56 State Street, Springfield.

92. At which one of the following times will the musical be performed?

   [8 second pause]

93. What is the cost of a child's ticket to the 8:00 PM Friday show?

   [8 second pause]

94. How can tickets be reserved?

   [8 second pause]

Questions 95–97 refer to the following weather report.

Gardeners will be happy over the next few days as heavy rains arrive in our area, putting an end to the long dry spell. The sun and humidity we are enjoying this morning will give way to increasingly cloudy skies this afternoon. Expect heavy rains overnight with partial clearing toward morning. Today's highs will reach 80 around noon, then fall steadily throughout the afternoon. Expect lows of around 50 overnight. Rain is expected to continue on and off throughout the week, so put aside those beach plans, folks, and stay home with a good book. This is not the week to be outdoors.

95. What is the weather like now?

[8 second pause]

96. What will the low temperature be tonight?

[8 second pause]

97. What does the announcer recommend doing this week?

[8 second pause]

Questions 98–100 refer to the following announcement.

Welcome to the Adventure Vacations lecture series. Our guest speaker this evening is Jonas Jones, who will talk to us about the exciting adventures of mountain climbing. Mr. Jones was featured in a recent documentary film about climbing Mount Everest, a climb he has attempted several times. Tonight he will share with us the basics of extreme mountain climbing and talk about how to prepare and what equipment to buy. He has available for sale copies of his book *How to Climb Mountains,* for a special price of $32. As a reminder, next month's program has been canceled because of unforeseen circumstances. The following month we will enjoy a talk on scuba diving.

98. Who is the guest speaker?

[8 second pause]

99. How much does the book cost?

[8 second pause]

100. What will happen next month?

[8 second pause]

TOEIC PRACTICE TEST 4
Listening Comprehension

Part 1: Photographs

Directions: You will see a photograph. You will hear four statements about the photograph. Choose the statement that most closely matches the photograph and fill in the corresponding oval on your answer sheet.

Example

Now listen to the four statements.

(A) She's getting on a plane.
(B) She's reading a magazine.
(C) She's taking a nap.
(D) She's holding a glass.

Statement (B), "She's reading a magazine," best describes what you see in the picture. Therefore, you should choose answer (B).

1. Look at the photo marked number 1 in your test book.
   (A) They're delivering newspapers.
   (B) They're riding in an elevator.
   (C) They're signing the documents.
   (D) They're going down the escalator.

   [5 second pause]

2. Look at the photo marked number 2 in your test book.
   (A) The bridge crosses to the other shore.
   (B) The ferry is carrying cars over the water.
   (C) The boat is ready to tie up at the dock.
   (D) The cars are driving down a wide highway.

   [5 second pause]

3. Look at the photo marked number 3 in your test book.
   (A) They're in the pedestrian crosswalk.
   (B) They're talking with their friends.
   (C) They're driving their cars through the city.
   (D) They're strolling down the sidewalk.

   [5 second pause]

4. Look at the photo marked number 4 in your test book.
   (A) The customers are in the restaurant.
   (B) The man is feeding the chickens.
   (C) The chefs are in the kitchen.
   (D) The waiter is serving the meal.

   [5 second pause]

5. Look at the photo marked number 5 in your test book.
   (A) He's cleaning the window with rags.
   (B) He's walking through the door.
   (C) He's holding several bags.
   (D) He's shopping inside the store.

   [5 second pause]

6. Look at the photo marked number 6 in your test book.
   (A) The girl is laughing.
   (B) She can't stop coughing.
   (C) They're filing their papers.
   (D) Their cups are broken.

   [5 second pause]

7. Look at the photo marked number 7 in your test book.
   (A) He's buying a round-trip ticket.
   (B) He's on his way to court.
   (C) He's going to pack his bags.
   (D) He's walking through the airport.

   [5 second pause]

8. Look at the photo marked number 8 in your test book.
   (A) Their hats are in their hands.
   (B) One man is pointing at something.
   (C) The phone is on the desk.
   (D) They're painting one of the buildings.

   [5 second pause]

9. Look at the photo marked number 9 in your test book.
   (A) He's walking home.
   (B) He's dialing a number.
   (C) He's talking on the phone.
   (D) He's cooking a meal.

   [5 second pause]

10. Look at the photo marked number 10 in your test book.
    (A) They're having a conference.
    (B) They're all wearing glasses.
    (C) They're eating dinner.
    (D) They're reading the papers.

    [5 second pause]

Part 2: Question-Response

Directions: You will hear a question and three possible responses. Choose the response that most closely answers the question and fill in the corresponding oval on your answer sheet.

Example

Now listen to the sample question.

You will hear:

How is the weather?

You will also hear:

(A) It's raining.
(B) He's fine, thanks.
(C) He's my boss.

The best response to the question *How is the weather?* is choice (A), *It's raining.* Therefore, you should choose answer (A).

11. Who was that on the phone?
    (A) It's mine.
    (B) It was my boss.
    (C) It was on the desk.

    [5 second pause]

12. Let's take our lunch hour now.
    (A) Great idea. I'm starving.
    (B) I take an hour for lunch.
    (C) I usually have it at a restaurant.

    [5 second pause]

13. When is this report due?
    (A) We import our supplies.
    (B) Yes, there are two.
    (C) At the end of the week.

    [5 second pause]

14. Where's the bank?
    (A) I'll give it back.
    (B) Thank you very much.
    (C) It's right across the street.

[5 second pause]

15. Which car is yours?
    (A) It's the small blue one over there.
    (B) It isn't very far away.
    (C) It was an interesting tour.

[5 second pause]

16. Why did John leave early?
    (A) Nobody leave the room.
    (B) He had an urgent appointment.
    (C) It's still early.

[5 second pause]

17. How was the movie?
    (A) It was really boring.
    (B) We got the tickets online.
    (C) Just move everything over there.

[5 second pause]

18. Could you help me copy these documents?
    (A) I don't enjoy shopping.
    (B) I signed the documents.
    (C) I'm sorry. I'm too busy right now.

[5 second pause]

19. Whose coat is this?
    (A) It's in the closet.
    (B) It belongs to Mary.
    (C) It's a nice coat.

[5 second pause]

20. Will you have some coffee?
    (A) I can't stop coughing.
    (B) No, thank you. I'd prefer tea.
    (C) The cups are in the kitchen.

[5 second pause]

21. Which seat would you prefer?
    (A) I rarely eat meat.
    (B) It's not a comfortable chair.
    (C) I'll take this one by the window.

[5 second pause]

22. How long does it take to get there?
    (A) Only about an hour or so.
    (B) I long to see them.
    (C) They make delicious cake there.

[5 second pause]

23. What did you do with the package?
    (A) I put it on your desk.
    (B) It wasn't a heavy package.
    (C) They were packing all night.

[5 second pause]

24. Will you be at the meeting?
    (A) We enjoyed eating there.
    (B) It wasn't a long meeting.
    (C) Yes, but I'll probably arrive late.

[5 second pause]

25. Where can I find printer ink?
    (A) I think about it, too.
    (B) It's on the top shelf of that closet.
    (C) The printer is very efficient.

[5 second pause]

26. I'm really tired of this rainy weather.
    (A) It's supposed to be sunny tomorrow.
    (B) Yes, train rides can be tiring.
    (C) This jacket is genuine leather.

[5 second pause]

27. Who signed these papers?
    (A) I signed them.
    (B) You can buy the newspaper downstairs.
    (C) That sign says "Stop."

[5 second pause]

28. Is the photocopy machine still broken?
    (A) I'll make the copies later.
    (B) Yes, he's already spoken.
    (C) No, it was repaired this morning.

    [5 second pause]

29. I need a ride to the airport.
    (A) I can drive you.
    (B) The plane arrives at noon.
    (C) It's beside the airport.

    [5 second pause]

30. What time is it now?
    (A) We had a good time.
    (B) I'm fine, thank you.
    (C) It's just after ten.

    [5 second pause]

31. Which suit should I wear?
    (A) I don't care for fruit.
    (B) Wear this one.
    (C) I don't know where it is.

    [5 second pause]

32. Whose car is that parked by the front door?
    (A) I believe it's John's.
    (B) It's a really old car.
    (C) The park isn't far.

    [5 second pause]

33. When is the conference?
    (A) It's not my preference.
    (B) It's at a hotel.
    (C) It's next September.

    [5 second pause]

34. Why did you go to the office on Saturday?
    (A) I go to the office by bus.
    (B) Yes, I'll see you on Saturday.
    (C) I had a lot of work to do.

    [5 second pause]

35. This is your desk, isn't it?
    (A) Yes, it's a desk.
    (B) No, mine's the one by the door.
    (C) We each have our own desk.

    [5 second pause]

36. What can you see from that window?
    (A) A great view of the city.
    (B) It's very windy.
    (C) The window cleaner comes tomorrow.

    [5 second pause]

37. Where can I get a quick lunch?
    (A) There's a cafeteria on the first floor.
    (B) Pick one of these.
    (C) It has a nice crunch.

    [5 second pause]

38. How long are they planning to stay?
    (A) It was a short plane ride.
    (B) They're staying at a hotel.
    (C) Three or four days at the most.

    [5 second pause]

39. Have you finished the budget report yet?
    (A) No, I'll finish it tomorrow.
    (B) It's too heavy to budge.
    (C) I heard the news report this morning.

    [5 second pause]

40. It's quite chilly outside.
    (A) I think it's right outside.
    (B) It's a hilly area.
    (C) Then I'll put on an extra sweater.

    [5 second pause]

Part 3: Conversations

Directions: You will hear a conversation between two people. You will see three questions on each conversation and four possible answers. Choose the best answer to each question and fill in the corresponding oval on your answer sheet.

Questions 41–43 refer to the following conversation.

Woman: Was there a call for me? I thought I heard the phone ringing a few minutes ago, and I'm expecting my assistant to call with figures for the budget.

Man: You did hear the phone ring, but the call was for me. My boss wants me to go in to work early tomorrow.

Woman: Again? He's always asking you to do that. When's he going to call to offer you a bonus? Or a raise?

Man: He needs me to help finish the report for the accountant and wants it done before noon. If I go in early as he asks, maybe one day I will get that raise.

41. When was the phone call made?

   [8 second pause]

42. Who called?

   [8 second pause]

43. Why did this person call?

   [8 second pause]

Questions 44–46 refer to the following conversation.

Man: Room 220 is smaller than our other rooms, but the price is just $165 for the night.

Woman: Does that include use of the pool and the exercise room?

Man: Of course. It includes the use of all facilities except the tennis courts, which are closed for the winter.

Woman: Okay, I'll take it. I'll just carry my suitcase up and have a quick look at the room, and then I'm going out for a bite to eat. I'm starving.

44. Where does this conversation take place?

   [8 second pause]

45. How much will the woman pay?

   [8 second pause]

46. What will the woman do now?

   [8 second pause]

Questions 47–49 refer to the following conversation.

Woman: I was surprised to see that Mr. Wing wasn't at the meeting this morning.
Man: No, he'll be out of the office until next week. He's on vacation.
Woman: Oh, I didn't realize he was away on a trip. That's unfortunate, because I wanted his help with my project. My boss wants it done by Friday.
Man: Why don't you ask Mr. Wing's assistant? She'll be in tomorrow. She'll help you with it.

47. Where is Mr. Wing now?

[8 second pause]

48. When will he return to the office?

[8 second pause]

49. Who will help the woman with her project?

[8 second pause]

Questions 50–52 refer to the following conversation.

Man: I can't believe how much those museum tickets cost. I've never paid so much before to see art.
Woman: Yes, but don't you think it was worth it? The paintings we saw were fantastic.
Man: I guess you're right. There was some very fine work there. So, do you want to go back to the hotel now?
Woman: No, it's only 3:00. Let's get a snack, then we can take a walk in the park. It's not far from here.

50. What is the man's complaint?

[8 second pause]

51. What time is it now?

[8 second pause]

52. What will they do now?

[8 second pause]

Questions 53–55 refer to the following conversation.

Man: What a nice, sunny day. I'm really enjoying this walk.
Woman: Me, too. There's not a cloud in the sky. What a treat this is after all that rain last week.
Man: We should walk more often. We should do it every day.
Woman: Well, not every day. The weather is nice today, but that'll end. Tomorrow it's supposed to rain again.

53. How is the weather today?

   [8 second pause]

54. What are the speakers doing?

   [8 second pause]

55. When will the weather change?

   [8 second pause]

Questions 56–58 refer to the following conversation.

Woman: I'm so sorry I'm late. The bus was delayed by the bad weather.
Man: You should take the subway to work like I do. It's faster and the weather doesn't affect it.
Woman: That wouldn't work for me. The subway station is too far from my house, but the bus stop is just a two-minute walk.
Man: The bus fare is cheaper, too, isn't it? You pay just $2.50 a ride and I pay $1.50 more than that for the subway.

56. Why is the woman late?

   [8 second pause]

57. How does the man get to work?

   [8 second pause]

58. How much is the bus fare?

   [8 second pause]

Questions 59–61 refer to the following conversation.

Man: I'm starving. Is there a good place to eat around here?
Woman: Yes, there's a restaurant just two blocks away. Go to the corner, turn right, go one more block, and you'll see it just before the post office.
Man: Turn right at the corner. Do you mean by the bank?
Woman: No, the other corner, by the grocery store. But hurry. They stop serving lunch at 2:00 and it's almost 1:30.

59. Where does the man want to go?

   [8 second pause]

60. How many blocks away is it?

   [8 second pause]

61. What time is it now?

   [8 second pause]

Questions 62–64 refer to the following conversation.

Man: I'm so glad I left my old job. It was closer to home than my new job,
          but the pay was so low, I had to leave.

Woman: So you're happy with the new job.

Man: I am. The only thing I don't like is the vacation time. I get only three
          weeks a year.

Woman: That's too bad. I get six weeks a year, and you can be sure I need every
          one of them.

  62. Why did the man leave his old job?

       [8 second pause]

  63. How does he feel about his new job?

       [8 second pause]

  64. How many weeks of vacation does he get?

       [8 second pause]

Questions 65–67 refer to the following conversation.

Woman: If we leave the office by 6:15, we should get to the theater in plenty of
          time.

Man: Oh, no. We should leave here by 5:45 at the latest. It'll be rush hour,
          and then it'll take time to find a place to park. The parking garage is
          closed, don't forget.

Woman: That's right. I forgot about that part. Say, I hope the play isn't over too
          late. I'm feeling a bit tired.

Man: Don't worry. As soon as it's over, we'll go straight home and you can get
          your rest.

  65. Where are the speakers going?

       [8 second pause]

  66. What time does the man want to leave?

       [8 second pause]

  67. Where will they go later?

       [8 second pause]

Questions 68–70 refer to the following conversation.

Woman: Would you like a nice cup of hot tea, or would you prefer coffee?
Man: Actually, I'd like to have a glass of water, if you don't mind. With ice. I'm really quite thirsty.
Woman: Of course. You haven't tried this cake, have you? I got the recipe out of a magazine. Let me serve you a slice.
Man: Oh, no thank you. It looks very good, but I'm not at all hungry.

68. What does the man want to drink?

    [8 second pause]

69. How does the man feel?

    [8 second pause]

70. What does the woman offer the man?

    [8 second pause]

Part 4: Talks

Directions: You will hear a talk given by a single speaker. You will see three questions on each talk, each with four possible answers. Choose the best answer to each question and fill in the corresponding oval on your answer sheet.

Questions 71–73 refer to the following announcement.

May I have your attention, please. Flight 43 for Caracas, scheduled for departure at 5:00, has been delayed. It is now scheduled to depart two hours later than the originally scheduled time. In the meantime, all ticketed passengers for flight 43 to Caracas are invited to enjoy a complimentary meal at the Sky View Restaurant. To receive your meal ticket, please show your boarding pass to the gate agent. Any passengers wishing to be rebooked on a different flight are asked to approach the ticket office on the other side of the main lounge. You will be asked to pick up your suitcases from the baggage claim area and recheck them when receiving your new boarding pass.

71. What time will the flight to Caracas leave?

    [8 second pause]

72. What is offered to the passengers?

    [8 second pause]

73. How can passengers take advantage of the offer?

    [8 second pause]

Questions 74–76 refer to the following advertisement.

Mayflower and Company, the area's newest and largest department store, will be celebrating its grand opening next Saturday. Don't miss this once-in-a-lifetime event. Free food and entertainment for the whole family will be provided. Take advantage of deep discounts on items in all store departments—home furnishings, office supplies, garden supplies, clothing, and more! Discounts will be in effect for one day only. This event will be held rain or shine, from 8:00 in the morning until 8:00 in the evening. Free parking will be available all day. So come on down! Mayflower and Company is just 10 minutes from downtown across the road from City Mall.

74. What place is opening?

   [8 second pause]

75. When will the opening take place?

   [8 second pause]

76. Where is this place?

   [8 second pause]

Questions 77–79 refer to the following report.

Road conditions are dangerous out there folks, so stay home and don't drive anywhere unless absolutely necessary. This morning's snowfall has already led to a seven-car accident near the train station. Schools are closed and many businesses are as well. Snow is expected to continue falling throughout the afternoon and evening, and temperatures will remain chilly. The skies should start clearing toward morning, and tomorrow should be sunny and a good bit warmer.

77. What is the weather like?

   [8 second pause]

78. How many cars were in the accident?

   [8 second pause]

79. When will the weather change?

   [8 second pause]

Questions 80–82 refer to the following announcement.

The City Center Theater announces that the Smith Brothers Circus is coming to town next month. The circus will be performing at the theater during the first week of August with two shows daily at 3:00 PM and 7:00 PM. Tickets are just $15 each and are available by calling (800) 964-8434. Smith Brothers Circus will also be giving away a limited number of free tickets. To request your free ticket, simply send a postcard to the Smith Brothers in care of the theater. Include your name and address and a brief statement explaining why you love the circus. You could be one of the 25 lucky winners!

80. What are the tickers for?

[8 second pause]

81. How much do the tickets cost?

[8 second pause]

82. How can you get a free ticket?

[8 second pause]

Questions 83–85 refer to the following report.

The Riverside Park Elementary School was destroyed by fire last night. The fire was first reported by Ethel Rogers, owner of the Corner Bookstore, located on the same block. As Ms. Rogers was leaving the store around 9:00, she noticed smoke rising out of the school building and immediately notified authorities. Firefighters arrived on the scene within minutes and worked for five hours to put out the blaze. Fortunately, there were no injuries. All the schoolchildren and school staff had left the building several hours before the fire was noticed. The cause of the fire is under investigation.

83. What was destroyed by a fire?

[8 second pause]

84. What time was the fire reported?

[8 second pause]

85. Who was hurt in the fire?

[8 second pause]

Questions 86–88 refer to the following announcement.

Attention, passengers. Train 56 to Toronto will begin boarding in three minutes at Gate 10. All passengers for Train 56 to Toronto, please approach Gate 10 now. First-class passengers are asked to line up to the right of the gate and all other passengers to the left. This is an all-reserved train. Only passengers with reserved seats will be permitted to board. Please have a form of photo identification, such as a passport or driver's license, ready to show to the gate agent when you board. Also, please be aware that each passenger is allowed just one item of carry-on luggage, exclusive of coats and purses.

86. When can passengers get on the train?

   [8 second pause]

87. What must passengers have to get on the train?

   [8 second pause]

88. What are passengers not allowed to take on the train?

   [8 second pause]

Questions 89–91 refer to the following talk.

Good afternoon, and welcome to today's edition of *Business Talks*, the radio program that brings listeners information and ideas for the modern businessperson every afternoon from 1:15 until 2:00. Our guest today is Dr. Jose Silva, author of the best-selling book *Keeping Fit in the Office*. Dr. Silva will talk with us about health and fitness issues facing office workers. After his talk, Dr. Silva will answer calls from you, our listeners. Call 756-9887 if you have a question for Dr. Silva. Following our program will be the *Up-to-the-Minute News* at 2:00. And don't forget to tune in to tomorrow's *Business Talks* program, when we will discuss banks and banking.

89. How long does the radio program last?

   [8 second pause]

90. What will Dr. Silva talk about?

   [8 second pause]

91. What will Dr. Silva do after his talk?

   [8 second pause]

Questions 92–94 refer to the following news report.

The president met with world leaders in the capital city this afternoon to discuss the current economic situation. He will speak about the issues discussed at the meeting when he addresses the nation on TV tonight. Tomorrow he flies to Tokyo, where he will begin his three-week tour of Asia and Australia to promote his international economic program. After his return home, he will prepare for the International Conference on the Environment, to take place next month.

92. What did the president do this afternoon?

[8 second pause]

93. Where will the president go tomorrow?

[8 second pause]

94. How long will his trip last?

[8 second pause]

Questions 95–97 refer to the following recording.

Thank you for calling the State Street Bank. We're here to serve you. Our hours are Monday through Friday from 9:00 AM until 4:30 PM, and Saturday from 8:30 AM until 2:00 PM. For information on an existing checking or savings account, press 1. To open a new checking or savings account, press 2. To apply for a credit card, press 3. To get information about loans, press 4. For all other issues, press 5. To repeat this menu, press zero.

95. At which one of the following times is the bank open?

[8 second pause]

96. How can a customer find out the balance of his savings account?

[8 second pause]

97. What happens when a customer presses 0?

[8 second pause]

Questions 98–100 refer to the following talk.

All job seekers need a good strategy. The first thing to consider is where to look for jobs. In the past, people relied on newspaper ads, university career counseling offices, and employment agencies for job leads. These things still exist, but the best place to look for jobs is on the Internet. It provides the most current and the widest range of job opportunities, of all sorts. Online you can find job listings in all fields, from education to medicine to engineering. There is something for everyone. When applying for a job, you need to have a good resume prepared. It is your most important tool, more important even than interview skills, university degrees, or work experience. It is the image you present.

98. According to the speaker, what is the best place to look for a job?

   [8 second pause]

99. What kinds of jobs can be found in this place?

   [8 second pause]

100. According to the speaker, what is a job seeker's most important tool?

   [8 second pause]

TOEIC PRACTICE TEST 5

Listening Comprehension

1. Look at the photo marked number 1 in your test book.
   (A) He's loading boxes onto the plane.
   (B) He's getting ready to board the train.
   (C) He's walking up the ramp with a cane.
   (D) He's getting out of the rain.

   [5 second pause]

2. Look at the photo marked number 2 in your test book.
   (A) The computer is closed.
   (B) The chair is occupied.
   (C) The books are under the desk.
   (D) The lamp is behind the chair.

   [5 second pause]

3. Look at the photo marked number 3 in your test book.
   (A) The tailor is measuring the cloth.
   (B) The carpenter is building a house.
   (C) The cyclist is wearing a helmet.
   (D) The painter is painting the walls.

   [5 second pause]

4. Look at the photo marked number 4 in your test book.
   (A) They're walking to the office.
   (B) They're cooking a big meal.
   (C) They're working on computers.
   (D) They're looking out the window.

   [5 second pause]

5. Look at the photo marked number 5 in your test book.
   (A) They're wearing raincoats.
   (B) They're getting on the train.
   (C) They're holding their umbrellas.
   (D) They're walking down the sidewalk.

   [5 second pause]

6. Look at the photo marked number 6 in your test book.
   (A) The man is checking the wires.
   (B) The door to the box is closed.
   (C) The factory is on fire.
   (D) The gloves are on the table.

   [5 second pause]

7. Look at the photo marked number 7 in your test book.
   (A) He's working at his desk.
   (B) He's sitting in the airport.
   (C) He's opening his briefcase.
   (D) He's buying a computer.

   [5 second pause]

8. Look at the photo marked number 8 in your test book.
   - (A) The food is on the stove.
   - (B) The coffee is in the pot.
   - (C) The dishes are in the sink.
   - (D) The fruit is on a plate.

   [5 second pause]

9. Look at the photo marked number 9 in your test book.
   - (A) He's taking a nap.
   - (B) He's reading a map.
   - (C) He's wearing a cap.
   - (D) He's opening the tap.

   [5 second pause]

10. Look at the photo marked number 10 in your test book.
    - (A) They all have jackets on.
    - (B) One man is reading a sign.
    - (C) They're all wearing glasses.
    - (D) One man is signing the document.

    [5 second pause]

Part 2: Question-Response

Directions: You will hear a question and three possible responses. Choose the response that most closely answers the question and fill in the corresponding oval on your answer sheet.

Example

Now listen to the sample question.

You will hear:

How is the weather?

You will also hear:

- (A) It's raining.
- (B) He's fine, thanks.
- (C) He's my boss.

The best response to the question *How is the weather?* is choice (A), *It's raining.* Therefore, you should choose answer (A).

11. Where were you waiting?
    - (A) I was waiting on the corner.
    - (B) I weigh the same as you.
    - (C) Because it was raining.

    [5 second pause]

12. Which shop sells children's books?
    - (A) The library has lots of books.
    - (B) There's a children's bookstore in the shopping center.
    - (C) I read books to my children.

    [5 second pause]

13. Why don't you join us for dinner?
    - (A) I didn't join the club until December.
    - (B) Thank you. I'd love to.
    - (C) These coins are thinner.

    [5 second pause]

14. This coffee is cold.
    (A) He's had a cold all week.
    (B) Those are old copies.
    (C) I'll heat it up for you.

[5 second pause]

15. What are your plans for this afternoon?
    (A) The plane leaves at noon.
    (B) I think I'll play golf.
    (C) The planning meeting was yesterday.

[5 second pause]

16. Excuse me. Is this the express train?
    (A) Express mail is a one-day service.
    (B) You may leave the room.
    (C) No, it's across the platform.

[5 second pause]

17. Who delivered the package?
    (A) The housekeeper packed the bags.
    (B) A messenger brought it this morning.
    (C) She won't tell her age.

[5 second pause]

18. How will we get to the airport?
    (A) The plane is late.
    (B) They met us at the port.
    (C) We'll take a taxi.

[5 second pause]

19. There's a phone call for you from Mr. Kim.
    (A) It's out in the hall.
    (B) Tell him I'll call him back later.
    (C) This is his phone number.

[5 second pause]

20. When will you return?
    (A) I'll be back after lunch.
    (B) She returned the book.
    (C) Take the first right turn.

[5 second pause]

21. Do you often stay at this hotel?
    (A) No, usually I play at my club.
    (B) Yes, I always stay here.
    (C) I added this telephone bill.

[5 second pause]

22. What type of movies do you like?
    (A) I'm moving to a quiet neighborhood.
    (B) I like my meat rare.
    (C) I prefer comedies.

[5 second pause]

23. Why was the flight canceled?
    (A) There was some mechanical problem.
    (B) The flight lasted only five minutes.
    (C) She can sell anything.

[5 second pause]

24. Which suitcase is yours?
    (A) Mine is the black one on the left.
    (B) This suit is Italian.
    (C) I spoke to her about this case.

[5 second pause]

25. Where are the supplies kept?
    (A) The floor was swept this morning.
    (B) In the room at the end of the hall.
    (C) We had supper after work.

[5 second pause]

26. How was your vacation?
    (A) The room was vacant.
    (B) There are flags from all nations.
    (C) Very relaxing, thank you.

[5 second pause]

27. Did you turn your computer off?
    (A) No, I always leave it on.
    (B) The lights are turned off at midnight.
    (C) This is my first computer.

[5 second pause]

28. Who attended the seminar?
    (A) The doctor attended to the patients.
    (B) All senior management went.
    (C) They came at 10:00.

    [5 second pause]

29. What's for lunch?
    (A) I think it's chicken salad.
    (B) It's at noon.
    (C) We're having two guests.

    [5 second pause]

30. These shoes are too tight.
    (A) You need a larger size.
    (B) We had a good night, too.
    (C) Yes, I heard the news.

    [5 second pause]

31. Where is the software manual?
    (A) This shirt I'm wearing is soft.
    (B) It's on the bookshelf.
    (C) He's a man you know well.

    [5 second pause]

32. When did you last put gas in the car?
    (A) The oil refinery opened in December.
    (B) The elastic stretches far.
    (C) I filled the tank two days ago.

    [5 second pause]

33. What caused the forest fire?
    (A) We fired the receptionist last week.
    (B) Lightning struck a tree.
    (C) Because he went away for a rest.

    [5 second pause]

34. The bus should be here soon.
    (A) They left this afternoon.
    (B) Good. I'm tired of waiting.
    (C) I need another spoon.

    [5 second pause]

35. Why haven't you written me?
    (A) The letters are on the desk.
    (B) You will write me soon.
    (C) I haven't had time to write.

    [5 second pause]

36. Shouldn't we leave before it starts to rain?
    (A) The rain caused the leaves to fall.
    (B) Yes, let's take an umbrella with us.
    (C) It didn't rain the night we left.

    [5 second pause]

37. How often do you make international calls?
    (A) I telephone my international clients
        almost every day.
    (B) I'll call information for the number.
    (C) We have about 10 phones.

    [5 second pause]

38. They say it'll snow next week.
    (A) Good, we can go skiing.
    (B) He's feeling very weak.
    (C) I don't know the way.

    [5 second pause]

39. When would you be able to come?
    (A) I can come any day next week.
    (B) The table is made of wood.
    (C) We came as soon as we could.

    [5 second pause]

40. May I sit down?
    (A) Yes, I went in May.
    (B) Please do. This seat isn't occupied.
    (C) The cushion is filled with down.

    [5 second pause]

Part 3: Conversations

Directions: You will hear a conversation between two people. You will see three questions on each conversation and four possible answers. Choose the best answer to each question and fill in the corresponding oval on your answer sheet.

Questions 41–43 refer to the following conversation.

Man: Front desk. How may I help you?
Woman: I'm in Room 624. I'm afraid the television set doesn't work.
Man: I'll send someone up right away.
Woman: Okay, but I'm about to take a shower. I'll be going out in half an hour, so could you send someone then?

41. What is the woman's room number?

    [8 second pause]

42. What will the desk clerk do?

    [8 second pause]

43. When will the woman go out?

    [8 second pause]

Questions 44–46 refer to the following conversation.

Woman: This coffeepot is really dirty.
Man: There's a small kitchen on the sixth floor.
Woman: Great. I'll wash it there. While I'm at it, would you like me to make you a cup of coffee?
Man: Actually, I'd prefer cocoa, if you don't mind. I think there's some milk down there you can make it with.

44. What does the woman want to do?

    [8 second pause]

45. Where is the kitchen?

    [8 second pause]

46. What does the man want to drink?

    [8 second pause]

Questions 47–49 refer to the following conversation.

Man: I'm glad to be off that plane. Shall we catch a cab or take the subway?
Woman: Well, before we decide that, I have to get my suitcase at baggage claim.
Man: That means we'll be stuck here for a while.
Woman: Relax. It won't take too long. I have only one bag.

47. Where does this conversation take place?

    [8 second pause]

48. Why is the man annoyed?

    [8 second pause]

49. How many suitcases does the woman have?

    [8 second pause]

Questions 50–52 refer to the following conversation.

Woman: It's a beautiful day. Let's have lunch at the sidewalk café. They have wonderful salads there.
Man: I brought a sandwich from home, and I was planning to eat it in the park.
Woman: That sounds like a nice idea. I'll buy a sandwich and meet you there.
Man: Okay. I'll wait for you by the fountain. Don't take too long.

50. Where are they going to eat?

    [8 second pause]

51. What are they going to eat?

    [8 second pause]

52. Where will the man wait for the woman?

    [8 second pause]

Questions 53–55 refer to the following conversation.

Woman: I'm lucky to have an office overlooking the park with such a great view.
Man: My office faces the parking lot!
Woman: Don't feel too bad. You've been at that company for only seven months. You could get a better office after a while.
Man: You're right. I shouldn't worry, especially since I like everything else about my job.

53. How does the woman feel about her office?

    [8 second pause]

54. What is true of the man's office?

   [8 second pause]

55. How long has the man been at his company?

   [8 second pause]

Questions 56–58 refer to the following conversation.

Man: We'll meet at the bus at 9:00 tomorrow for a drive through the river valley. Don't be late.

Woman: Do we need to bring anything with us?

Man: Just remember to dress warmly. It'll be a cold day, and we'll be getting out of the bus often to look at the landscapes.

Woman: Too bad I forgot my camera.

56. What is the man's job?

   [8 second pause]

57. What time will they meet tomorrow?

   [8 second pause]

58. What should people bring?

   [8 second pause]

Questions 59–61 refer to the following conversation.

Woman: There's a problem with my hotel bill. I was charged $200 for three nights, but I stayed only one.

Man: Let's see. My poor addition could account for the problem. Oh, I'm terribly sorry. I've given you the wrong bill. Here's yours.

Woman: Thank you. Yes, this looks right. Will you take a personal check?

Man: I'm sorry, we don't take checks or cash. You'll need to give me a credit card.

59. How many nights did the woman stay at the hotel?

   [8 second pause]

60. Why was there a problem with her bill?

   [8 second pause]

61. How will the woman pay the bill?

   [8 second pause]

Questions 62–64 refer to the following conversation.

Man: You can still order breakfast. We don't stop serving it until 11:30.
Woman: Wonderful. Then I'll have the breakfast special with whole-wheat toast and coffee.
Man: Certainly, ma'am. Cream and sugar in your coffee?
Woman: No, thank you. I drink it black.

62. Where does this conversation take place?

    [8 second pause]

63. When is breakfast over?

    [8 second pause]

64. What does the woman order?

    [8 second pause]

Questions 65–67 refer to the following conversation.

Man: What do I like to do in my spare time? Well, I like to cook, and I play golf every Saturday.
Woman: I never thought golf was much fun, but I love to eat!
Man: Why don't you come over sometime soon, and I'll cook a meal for you. What about tomorrow?
Woman: I can't tomorrow. Let's do it on Friday.

65. What does the man do in his spare time?

    [8 second pause]

66. What does the woman like to do?

    [8 second pause]

67. When does the woman want to have a meal with the man?

    [8 second pause]

Questions 68–70 refer to the following conversation.

Man: You can borrow books and videos for three weeks, and you can renew once for three more weeks. Magazines and newspapers can't be renewed.
Woman: I just want this one book for now. What if I bring it back late?
Man: There's a fine of 25 cents for each day it's overdue.
Woman: I'll be sure to return it on time, then!

68. What is the woman borrowing?

    [8 second pause]

69. What is the maximum time she could have it without paying a fine?

   [8 second pause]

70. What is the charge for overdue books?

   [8 second pause]

Part 4: Talks

Directions: You will hear a talk given by a single speaker. You will see three questions on each talk, each with four possible answers. Choose the best answer to each question and fill in the corresponding oval on your answer sheet.

Questions 71–73 refer to the following recording.

Thank you for calling Financial Information Service. We take care of all your financial needs. Our regular business hours are Monday through Friday from 8:30 AM until 6:30 PM. For directions to our main office, press 1. To hear a description of the services we offer, press 2. To leave a message for a specific person, please dial that person's extension number. To speak with one of our trained financial advisers, please stay on the line. To hear this message again, press zero.

71. What time does this business open in the morning?

   [8 second pause]

72. What happens if a caller presses 1?

   [8 second pause]

73. How can a caller speak to an advisor?

   [8 second pause]

Questions 74–76 refer to the following announcement.

This station is Downtown Central, transfer point for the East–West subway line. Take the elevator or the stairs to the transfer platform on the lower level. Please be advised that trains on the East–West line are running about 15 minutes behind schedule because of repair work on the track. Thank you for your patience.

74. What kind of subway station in Downtown Central?

   [8 second pause]

75. Where do passengers catch the East–West line?

   [8 second pause]

76. Why are East–West line subways behind schedule?

   [8 second pause]

Questions 77–79 refer to the following weather report.

We are expecting partly sunny weather for the area with a high of 72 degrees. The wind will be getting stronger this afternoon with gusts of up to 25 miles per hour, calming down again by early evening. Overnight temperatures will be cool, with lows in the forties. Expect cool and cloudy weather tomorrow. Tune in again at 11 AM for the next weather update.

77. What will the weather be like today?

    [8 second pause]

78. What will increase during the afternoon?

    [8 second pause]

79. When can you hear the next weather report?

    [8 second pause]

Questions 80–82 refer to the following advertisement.

Our catalog now offers even faster service. For an additional $9 handling charge, we guarantee delivery anywhere in the continental United States within two business days. The same two-day service is offered to our customers in Alaska and Hawaii for just $19. Just tell your customer service representative that you want guaranteed two-day service. This offer is available only on orders of $150 or more.

80. What new service is being offered?

    [8 second pause]

81. What is different about the service for customers in Alaska?

    [8 second pause]

82. What is the minimum order size to qualify for this service?

    [8 second pause]

Questions 83–85 refer to the following announcement.

For the latest information on upcoming events in and around the city, call the City Events Hotline. We can provide you with the times and places of special events as well as the most convenient public transportation routes to get you there. Free movie tickets are given away to the first 10 callers every day, so call now.

83. What is the purpose of this hotline?

    [8 second pause]

84. What additional information does the hotline provide?

    [8 second pause]

85. Who gets free movie tickets?

[8 second pause]

Questions 86–88 refer to the following instructions.

It's very easy to greet a visitor at the reception desk. First, say hello. Then ask his name and the name of the person he is here to see. Have him sign the guest book and take a seat in the lobby. Then call the person he is visiting. Make sure this person comes to escort the visitor to his or her office. Or, you can take the visitor there yourself. Visitors should never be allowed to walk around the building alone.

86. What is the first thing the receptionist should do for a visitor?

[8 second pause]

87. Where should the visitor wait?

[8 second pause]

88. What should visitors never do?

[8 second pause]

Questions 89–91 refer to the following recording.

Please note the following change in local bus service. Buses on Route 21A will continue to start their route at the current time but will arrive at the final stop four minutes later. There will be no change in the number of scheduled trips. June 5 is the effective date for this service change. At this time there are no plans to raise bus fares. They will stay the same at least until the end of the year.

89. What changes are planned for buses on this route?

[8 second pause]

90. When will this change take place?

[8 second pause]

91. What is true about bus fares?

[8 second pause]

Questions 92–94 refer to the following advertisement.

Greenway Conference Center can take the problems out of planning your next conference. We can accommodate groups from 10 to 200. Our meeting rooms can be set up with your choice of state-of-the-art audiovisual equipment. A cafeteria and catering services on-site provide meals and snacks at your request. Our comfortable guest rooms overlook beautiful countryside. Both indoor and outdoor recreation facilities are available.

92. What is the largest group that the conference center can handle?

    [8 second pause]

93. Where do participants stay while attending the conference?

    [8 second pause]

94. Where is the conference center probably located?

    [8 second pause]

Questions 95–97 refer to the following announcement.

We interrupt this program for a special news bulletin. Because of the violent thunderstorm, neighborhoods throughout the city have lost electrical power. Service crews are already working to restore power in some of these areas, and additional crews are on their way to other sites. Residents are asked to turn off all electrical appliances to prevent potential hazards until power has been restored.

95. What problem is occurring?

    [8 second pause]

96. What has caused the problem?

    [8 second pause]

97. What are residents asked to do?

    [8 second pause]

Questions 98–100 refer to the following talk.

Welcome to the city's new central library. With 10 floors, it's twice the size of our old library. Here's what you'll find on each of the floors. On the first floor are the meeting rooms and the restrooms. The children's room is on the second floor, and books for teens are on the third floor. The adult collection is on floors four through six, with fiction on the fourth floor, and nonfiction on the fifth and sixth. The music collection, including tapes, CDs, and DVDs, is on the seventh floor. Magazines and periodicals are on the eighth floor. The reference section is on the ninth floor, and the tenth floor houses our administrative offices.

98. How many floors did the old library have?

    [8 second pause]

99. On which floor can you find novels for adults?

    [8 second pause]

100. What is on the tenth floor?

    [8 second pause]

TOEIC PRACTICE TEST 6

Listening Comprehension

Part 1: Photographs

Directions: You will see a photograph. You will hear four statements about the photograph. Choose the statement that most closely matches the photograph and fill in the corresponding oval on your answer sheet.

Example

Now listen to the four statements.

(A) She's getting on a plane.
(B) She's reading a magazine.
(C) She's taking a nap.
(D) She's holding a glass.

Statement (B), "She's reading a magazine," best describes what you see in the picture. Therefore, you should choose answer (B).

1. Look at the photo marked number 1 in your test book.
   (A) They're putting the chairs inside.
   (B) They're enjoying their food outdoors.
   (C) They're moving the tables around.
   (D) They're walking through the doors.

[5 second pause]

2. Look at the photo marked number 2 in your test book.
   (A) The ship is at sea.
   (B) The coat got wet.
   (C) The captain is on deck.
   (D) The ocean is rough.

[5 second pause]

3. Look at the photo marked number 3 in your test book.
   (A) She's learning to cook.
   (B) She's meeting her friends.
   (C) She's reading a book.
   (D) She's cleaning the cages.

[5 second pause]

4. Look at the photo marked number 4 in your test book.
   (A) They're entering the building.
   (B) They're working very hard.
   (C) They're talking about business.
   (D) They're all carrying bags.

[5 second pause]

5. Look at the photo marked number 5 in your test book.
   (A) The barber is using a brush.
   (B) The photographer is taking a picture.
   (C) The artist is painting the scene.
   (D) The painter is preparing the walls.

[5 second pause]

6. Look at the photo marked number 6 in your test book.
   (A) They're listening to a presentation.
   (B) They're setting up the screen.
   (C) They're sleeping at the hotel.
   (D) They're watching television.

[5 second pause]

7. Look at the photo marked number 7 in your test book.
   (A) The medical records are on the wall.
   (B) The doctor is holding a file.
   (C) The patient is getting out of bed.
   (D) The hospital is closed for renovation.

[5 second pause]

8. Look at the photo marked number 8 in your test book.
   (A) He's working on a project at his desk.
   (B) He's taking a nap on the bed.
   (C) He's checking into the hotel.
   (D) He's looking at something on the computer.

   [5 second pause]

9. Look at the photo marked number 9 in your test book.
   (A) The receptionist is at her desk.
   (B) The plant is on the counter.
   (C) The chairs are against the wall.
   (D) The pictures are on the wall.

   [5 second pause]

10. Look at the photo marked number 10 in your test book.
    (A) The duck is flying over the river.
    (B) The highway is filled with traffic.
    (C) The truck is crossing the bridge.
    (D) The driver is taking a rest.

    [5 second pause]

Part 2: Question-Response

Directions: You will hear a question and three possible responses. Choose the response that most closely answers the question and fill in the corresponding oval on your answer sheet.

Example

Now listen to the sample question.

You will hear:

How is the weather?

You will also hear:

(A) It's raining.
(B) He's fine, thanks.
(C) He's my boss.

The best response to the question *How is the weather?* is choice (A), *It's raining.* Therefore, you should choose answer (A).

11. Dinner will be ready soon.
    (A) Great. I'm starving.
    (B) Yes, I read it this afternoon.
    (C) I think she's much thinner.

    [5 second pause]

12. What is your address?
    (A) The woman's dress is blue.
    (B) The adding machine is mine.
    (C) I live on Wilson Boulevard.

    [5 second pause]

13. Who cleans the offices?
    (A) A cleaning company comes in at night.
    (B) The office is closed.
    (C) His voice is awful.

    [5 second pause]

14. Where did you leave your umbrella?
   (A) It's raining now.
   (B) Probably on the bus.
   (C) My leisure time is spent at home.

[5 second pause]

15. The printer's out of paper.
   (A) We just bought a new printer.
   (B) I read the newspaper this morning.
   (C) There's more in the supply closet.

[5 second pause]

16. Why didn't you put an ad in the newspaper?
   (A) They wrapped the food in newspaper.
   (B) That would have been a good idea.
   (C) I'll put the newspaper on the table.

[5 second pause]

17. How many times have you been to China?
   (A) Only once.
   (B) We bought several sets of dishes.
   (C) It's time to go.

[5 second pause]

18. Has the fax been sent?
   (A) Yes, it was sent this morning.
   (B) No, the facts weren't checked.
   (C) The rent was paid on time.

[5 second pause]

19. Who developed the marketing plan?
   (A) The market sells vegetables.
   (B) Our sales staff.
   (C) The film was developed overnight.

[5 second pause]

20. When will you purchase a new computer?
   (A) The purpose is for education.
   (B) The commuter train leaves at 6:00 AM.
   (C) When the prices go down.

[5 second pause]

21. What is the best season to visit?
   (A) There's only one reason.
   (B) I think summer is best.
   (C) The stock prices may fall.

[5 second pause]

22. Why were you late?
   (A) Yes, I already ate.
   (B) The date has not been set.
   (C) My watch was slow.

[5 second pause]

23. Which chair is more comfortable?
   (A) There are more coming.
   (B) The table by the window is wider.
   (C) I like this big, soft one.

[5 second pause]

24. I'd like to make an appointment with Ms. Park.
   (A) She pointed it out to us.
   (B) She's free tomorrow at 2:00.
   (C) She thinks it's too dark.

[5 second pause]

25. Where is the post office?
   (A) It's across from the bank.
   (B) The letter was delivered to the office.
   (C) The postal workers are on duty.

[5 second pause]

26. Would you pass the salt, please?
   (A) Cars must not pass on hills.
   (B) Certainly. Here you are.
   (C) The woman was insulted.

[5 second pause]

27. What is the purpose of your visit?
   (A) The visitors are in the next room.
   (B) Porpoises are sea mammals.
   (C) I'm here on business.

[5 second pause]

28. Who would like to take a break?
    (A) All of the rules were broken.
    (B) Let's all rest for a while.
    (C) We take a walk every week.

    [5 second pause]

29. Why was the meeting postponed?
    (A) Use the mail or the phone.
    (B) The meat market is across from the post office.
    (C) Because the participants were ill.

    [5 second pause]

30. When was this memo written?
    (A) The menu was in French.
    (B) On the computer.
    (C) The same day it was sent.

    [5 second pause]

31. Where are our suitcases?
    (A) In the hall closet.
    (B) I came in case you needed me.
    (C) They're very nice suits.

    [5 second pause]

32. Susan's train gets in at 4:30.
    (A) I'll meet her at the station.
    (B) I'll get the tickets next week.
    (C) I don't think it'll stain.

    [5 second pause]

33. Doesn't your receptionist speak other languages?
    (A) No, only English.
    (B) The linguist's lecture was well received.
    (C) She speaks very softly.

    [5 second pause]

34. What will you do when you retire?
    (A) I'll read this book before going to bed.
    (B) There are new tires on the car.
    (C) I plan to play a lot of golf.

    [5 second pause]

35. When will the exhibition close?
    (A) The models are on exhibit.
    (B) It will be open for another two weeks.
    (C) I put my clothes in the closet.

    [5 second pause]

36. Why are airfares so expensive?
    (A) Because there is no competition.
    (B) A haircut doesn't cost very much.
    (C) The airport isn't far from town.

    [5 second pause]

37. Where can I buy a newspaper?
    (A) I knew where the paper was.
    (B) The radio has the news every hour.
    (C) At the newsstand in the lobby.

    [5 second pause]

38. It was after midnight by the time we got home last night.
    (A) He was on the phone all night.
    (B) There's a clock in my office.
    (C) You must be very tired now.

    [5 second pause]

39. Let's take a walk.
    (A) He let them make it up.
    (B) Yes, let's. I could use the exercise.
    (C) I took it away already.

    [5 second pause]

40. When is the concert over?
    (A) It's over the river.
    (B) We're very concerned about it.
    (C) It will be over by 10:00.

    [5 second pause]

Part 3: Conversations

Directions: You will hear a conversation between two people. You will see three questions on each conversation and four possible answers. Choose the best answer to each question and fill in the corresponding oval on your answer sheet.

Questions 41–43 refer to the following conversation.

Man: I'd like to order room service for Room 574.

Woman: Of course, sir. What would you like?

Man: The steak with mushrooms, please, and a dish of ice cream. Can I pay with a check?

Woman: I'm sorry, sir, we don't take checks or cash. We charge all orders to your room account.

41. What is the man's room number?

   [8 second pause]

42. What does the man want to eat?

   [8 second pause]

43. How will he pay for his meal?

   [8 second pause]

Questions 44–46 refer to the following conversation.

Woman: Here's your ticket. Your flight departs from Gate 24 in just 30 minutes.

Man: Thank you. Which way do I go to get there?

Woman: Turn left at the café and follow the signs. It's just across from the main newsstand.

Man: Follow the signs. That sounds easy enough. I hope it's not far.

44. How is the man traveling?

   [8 second pause]

45. Which gate will he leave from?

   [8 second pause]

46. Where is the gate?

   [8 second pause]

Questions 47–49 refer to the following conversation.

Man: It looks like we have a flat tire.

Woman: Oh, no. We'll certainly be late for the dinner now. It's already 5:30.

Man: Don't worry. It won't take long to fix, and we don't have to be there until after 7:00.

Woman: Well, I'm going to call and tell them we might be late. Just in case. I would hate to disappoint them.

47. What is the problem?

   [8 second pause]

48. What time is it now?

   [8 second pause]

49. What is the woman going to do right now?

   [8 second pause]

Questions 50–52 refer to the following conversation.

Woman: I'm getting this folder ready for my sales appointment at 3:00 this afternoon.

Man: It's starting to rain. You should take your umbrella when you walk over.

Woman: You know, I think I'll take the bus. It's no fun getting wet.

Man: I know what you mean. That's probably a good idea.

50. What time is the woman's appointment?

   [8 second pause]

51. How will she get to her appointment?

   [8 second pause]

52. How is the weather now?

   [8 second pause]

Questions 53–55 refer to the following conversation.

Man: Didn't you order office supplies last week?

Woman: Yes, I put in a big order for computer paper and printer ink on Wednesday, but it hasn't arrived yet.

Man: Call the supplier again and find out why the order is delayed.

Woman: They're closed for the day, but I'll call as soon as I arrive at the office tomorrow morning.

53. What is the problem?

   [8 second pause]

54. What supplies were ordered?

   [8 second pause]

55. When will the woman call the supplier again?

   [8 second pause]

Questions 56–58 refer to the following conversation.

Woman: I've got a lot of work I have to get done by 5:00.
Man: Do you want me to bring you some lunch from the cafeteria?
Woman: No, thanks. I brought a sandwich from home. I'll eat it at my desk.
Man: You know, you really should stop for a break. You'll drive yourself crazy working like that. You'll make yourself sick.

56. What will the woman do by 5:00?

   [8 second pause]

57. Where will the woman eat lunch?

   [8 second pause]

58. What does the man offer to do for the woman?

   [8 second pause]

Questions 59–61 refer to the following conversation.

Man: I finally moved into my new office last Wednesday. I really like it. It has a lot more room than my old one.
Woman: And it's right across from the company health club.
Man: Yes, but unfortunately I never use it. Maybe someday I'll have time.
Woman: Well, at least the location is better than your old basement office with the view of the parking lot.

59. When did the man move into his new office?

   [8 second pause]

60. Why is it better than his old office?

   [8 second pause]

61. Where is the new office?

   [8 second pause]

Questions 62–64 refer to the following conversation.

Man: Do you have guided tours of the galleries?
Woman: No, but here is a brochure that contains a map of the entire museum and a description of each art exhibit.
Man: Thank you. What do I owe you for it?
Woman: There's no charge. It's free.

62. Where does this conversation take place?

[8 second pause]

63. What does the woman give the man?

[8 second pause]

64. How much does the man have to pay for it?

[8 second pause]

Questions 65–67 refer to the following conversation.

Man: I have to work Saturday, but I have a free day Sunday, so we can go to that concert in the park.
Woman: No, I don't like to be outdoors so long. I'd rather go to the movies. Then we can eat at that new restaurant.
Man: I can't eat there. You know I'm on a diet.
Woman: All right then. We'll just stay home.

65. What day does the man have off work?

[8 second pause]

66. What does the man want to do on his day off?

[8 second pause]

67. Why doesn't the man want to eat at the restaurant?

[8 second pause]

Questions 68–70 refer to the following conversation.

Woman: We'll begin our tour here at the art museum in 15 minutes. Then we'll see the plaza. If there's time, we'll visit the park.
Man: Will we get to go inside the houses along the plaza?
Woman: No, I'm sorry. They're closed to the public. We'll have to limit ourselves to admiring the front gardens.
Man: That's too bad. I was looking forward to seeing the interior architecture.

68. When does the tour start?

[8 second pause]

69. What will the tour members do first?

[8 second pause]

70. What does the man want to look at in the houses?

[8 second pause]

Part 4: Talks

Directions: You will hear a talk given by a single speaker. You will see three questions on each talk, each with four possible answers. Choose the best answer to each question and fill in the corresponding oval on your answer sheet.

Questions 71–73 refer to the following recording.

Thank you for calling Union Savings. To access information about your personal savings or checking account, press 1. Please have your account number and PIN ready. To learn about the services Union Savings has to offer, press 2. To leave a message for a specific bank staff member, dial that person's extension number. Press 3 to hear a list of extension numbers. To speak with a customer service representative, please stay on the line.

71. Where would you hear this message?

[8 second pause]

72. How can you hear information about your account?

[8 second pause]

73. What happens if you press 2?

[8 second pause]

Questions 74–76 refer to the following news report.

A new study suggests that secretaries may be more efficient than their managers. Evidence comes from the fact that secretaries have to keep track of the schedules of several managers, control the department record keeping, type letters, and coordinate events such as meetings and conferences. Even managers admit that work is easier with their secretaries' help. This study was carried out over a period of six months at 75 different businesses around the country, with the cooperation of 250 secretaries and 100 managers.

74. What has this study found?

    [8 second pause]

75. What do managers say?

    [8 second pause]

76. How many people participated in the study?

    [8 second pause]

Questions 77–79 refer to the following announcement.

We will be happy to take your catalog order by phone. For faster ordering, complete the order form in the catalog, including size, color, and item number. Please have your credit card number handy. If you are ready to place your order now, please stay on the line and the next available customer service representative will take your order. The current wait time is 16 minutes. You may continue to hold or try again later.

77. What is the fastest way to order over the phone?

    [8 second pause]

78. What else is needed to complete the order?

    [8 second pause]

79. How long will the caller have to wait to place an order?

    [8 second pause]

Questions 80–82 refer to the following advertisement.

Joe's Restaurant has openings for waiters, cooks, and hostesses. If you have experience in the food service industry, one of these jobs is right for you. Good pay and benefits for full-time employees. To apply, call Marina at 843-2000, Monday through Friday between noon and 5:00 PM, or weekends between 8:00 and 11:00 AM.

80. Which of the following jobs is NOT advertised?

    [8 second pause]

81. What sort of experience should applicants have?

    [8 second pause]

82. When is a good time to call to apply for a job?

    [8 second pause]

Questions 83–85 refer to the following weather report.

We can expect rain and sleet this morning, with snow developing by noon and continuing throughout the afternoon. Strong winds tonight with falling snow will create a visibility hazard for drivers. The skies should clear up by late tomorrow morning, and then we can expect sunny skies but cold temperatures for the next few days. More stormy conditions are expected to move in by early Sunday.

83. What weather conditions will develop by noon?

[8 second pause]

84. What problem can drivers expect tonight?

[8 second pause]

85. When will there be another storm?

[8 second pause]

Questions 86–88 refer to the following announcement.

We have been cleared for landing at Gate 29 in 15 minutes. We ask that you prepare by putting your luggage under the seat in front of you and returning your seat to its upright position. Cabin attendants will collect any trash you may wish to throw away.

86. Where would you hear this announcement?

[8 second pause]

87. Where will the passengers get off?

[8 second pause]

88. What should passengers do to prepare?

[8 second pause]

Questions 89–91 refer to the following advertisement.

Visit us for all your printing needs. We offer the lowest prices available for business cards, stationery, and brochures. If you don't know what you want, consult one of our design specialists, who can help you pick the right look for your business from our samples. We have thousands of designs to choose from. Place your order today and pick it up within one week guaranteed, or it's free!

89. Why should you go to this store?

[8 second pause]

90. What can you do if you need help?

[8 second pause]

91. How long does it take for an order to be ready?

    [8 second pause]

Questions 92–94 refer to the following announcement.

Please be advised that the elevator from the subway platform to the street level is not in service at this station. Passengers with disabilities who are unable to use the escalators or stairs should stay on the train, exit at the next station, and use the elevators there. Buses are available to take these passengers to their destinations. Any concerns should be directed to the station manager. We regret any inconvenience this may cause our passengers.

92. What is wrong at the station?

    [8 second pause]

93. How has the problem been solved for passengers in need?

    [8 second pause]

94. What does the announcer do at the end of the statement?

    [8 second pause]

Questions 95–97 refer to the following announcement.

Because of the high demand for electrical power due to the extremely cold weather, the city is facing a serious power shortage and the possibility of blackouts. We are asking residents to help us avoid this situation. Please reduce your power consumption as much as possible. Lower household heat to 60 degrees. Turn off all unnecessary appliances. Postpone energy-consuming tasks such as doing the laundry. Stay tuned to this station for further updates throughout the day.

95. Why is there a high demand for electric power?

    [8 second pause]

96. What is the public asked to do?

    [8 second pause]

97. What temperature should residents keep their houses at?

    [8 second pause]

Questions 98–100 refer to the following talk.

Little Italy Italian restaurant is opening in a new location in the Brookridge Shopping Mall. Join us for our grand opening next Friday. That's just two days away! Free drinks and prizes will be offered to all our lunchtime customers on our opening day. Little Italy has something for everybody, including a special menu for children, and a senior citizen discount for adults ages 65 and over. We will also be serving weekend brunch on Saturdays and Sundays. We still serve all of your favorite meals, too. Come and join us for the city's best pizza and pasta.

98. When will the new restaurant have its grand opening?

[8 second pause]

99. What kind of food is served at the restaurant?

[8 second pause]

100. Who gets a discount?

[8 second pause]

CD1

Track
1 Introduction
2 TOEIC Practice Test 1—Part 1: Photographs
3 TOEIC Practice Test 1—Part 2: Question-Response
4 TOEIC Practice Test 1—Part 3: Conversations
5 TOEIC Practice Test 1—Part 4: Talks
6 TOEIC Practice Test 2—Part 1: Photographs
7 TOEIC Practice Test 2—Part 2: Question-Response

CD2

Track
1 TOEIC Practice Test 2—Part 3: Conversations
2 TOEIC Practice Test 2—Part 4: Talks
3 TOEIC Practice Test 3—Part 1: Photographs
4 TOEIC Practice Test 3—Part 2: Question-Response
5 TOEIC Practice Test 3—Part 3: Conversations
6 TOEIC Practice Test 3—Part 4: Talks

CD3

Track
1 TOEIC Practice Test 4—Part 1: Photographs
2 TOEIC Practice Test 4—Part 2: Question-Response
3 TOEIC Practice Test 4—Part 3: Conversations
4 TOEIC Practice Test 4—Part 4: Talks
5 TOEIC Practice Test 5—Part 1: Photographs
6 TOEIC Practice Test 5—Part 2: Question-Response

CD4

Track
1 TOEIC Practice Test 5—Part 3: Conversations
2 TOEIC Practice Test 5—Part 4: Talks
3 TOEIC Practice Test 6—Part 1: Photographs
4 TOEIC Practice Test 6—Part 2: Question-Response
5 TOEIC Practice Test 6—Part 3: Conversations
6 TOEIC Practice Test 6—Part 4: Talks